Introduction to Speech Communication

INTRODUCTION TO SPEECH COMMUNICATION

SARAH E. HOLLINGSWORTH; MEGAN LINSENMEYER; TERRISA ELWOOD; SASHA HANRAHAN; AND MARY WALKER

Oklahoma State University Libraries
Stillwater, OK

Introduction to Speech Communication Copyright © 2025 by Individual authors retain copyright of their work. is licensed under a Creative Commons Attribution-NonCommercial-ShareAlike 4.0 International License, except where otherwise noted.

The print edition of *Introduction to Speech Communication* by Sarah E. Hollingsworth, Terrisa Elwood, Sasha Hanrahan, Megan Linsenmeyer, Mary Walker, and Kathryn Weinland is licensed CC BY-NC-SA. In addition to original material, it has been adapted and remixed from *Exploring Public Speaking: 4th Edition* licensed CC BY-NC-SA, *Stand Up, Speak Out* licensed CC BY-NC-SA and *Fundamentals of Public Speaking* licensed CC BY.

The digital edition of *Introduction to Speech Communication* is available at no cost at https://open.library.okstate.edu/speech2713/

Library of Congress Control Number: 2025935492

ISBN 9781957983073

CONTENTS

Acknowledgements   xi
                                                                xiii

1 Why Public Speaking Matters Today

1.1 Public Speaking in the Twenty-First Century   3
1.2 Why is Public Speaking Important?   8
1.3 The Process of Public Speaking   16
1.4 Enrichment   28

2 Building Confidence

2.1 What is Communication Apprehension?   31
2.2 Classifying Communication Apprehension   35
2.3 Learning Confidence   40
2.4 Enrichment   49

3 Delivery

3.1 The Importance of Delivery   53
3.2 Methods of Speech Delivery   57
3.3 Preparing for Your Delivery   63

3.4 Practicing Your Delivery — 70
3.5 What to do When Delivering Your Speech — 78
3.6 Public Speaking Online — 90
3.7 Enrichment — 101

4 Ethics

4.1 The Ethics Pyramid — 105
4.2 Ethics in Public Speaking — 112
4.3 Free Speech — 130
4.5 Enrichment — 133

5 Audience Analysis

5.1 What is Audience Analysis? — 139
5.2 Why Conduct an Audience Analysis? — 142
5.3 Three Types of Audience Analysis — 151
5.4 Conducting Audience Analysis — 162
5.5 Using Your Audience Analysis — 166
5.6 Enrichment — 170

6 Culture

6.1 Culture and Communication — 175
6.2 Foundations of Culture and Identity — 178
6.3 Exploring Specific Cultural Identities — 189
6.4 Intercultural Communication — 207

6.5 Intercultural Communication Competence   218
6.6 Enrichment   226

7 Organizing and Outlining

7.1 Why is Organizing and Outlining Important?   229
7.2 The Topic, General Purpose, Specific Purpose, and Thesis   233
7.3 Organizational Patterns of Arrangement   237
7.4 Outlining Your Speech   242
7.5 Enrichment   248

8 Researching Your Speech

8.1 Library Resources   251
8.2 What Is Research?   256
8.3 Developing a Research Strategy   262
8.4 Citing Sources   281
8.5 Enrichment   291

9 Supporting Ideas and Building Arguments

9.1 Crafting Supporting Ideas   297
9.2 Using Research as Support   300
9.3 Exploring Types of Support   307
9.4 Using Support and Creating Arguments   321
9.5 Enrichment   333

10 Introductions and Conclusions

10.1 Introductions	337
10.2 Conclusions	345
10.3 Enrichment	350

11 The Importance of Listening

11.1 Importance of Listening	353
11.2 Listening vs. Hearing	356
11.3 Listening Styles	363
11.4 Why Listening Is Difficult	369
11.5 Stages of Listening	378
11.6 Listening Critically	387
11.7 Enrichment	396

12 Language

12.1 What Language Is and Does	401
12.2 Standards for Language in Public	407
12.3 Using Effective Language in Public Speaking	420
12.4 Enrichment	422

13 Presentation Aids

13.1 What are Presentation Aids?	425
13.2 Functions of Presentation Aids	429

13.3 Types of Presentation Aids	436
13.4 Using Presentation Slides	451
13.5 Low-Tech Presentation Aids	464
13.6 Enrichment	468

14 Informative Speaking

14.1 What is an Informative Speech?	471
14.2 Types of Informative Speeches	476
14.3 Guidelines for Selecting an Informative Speech Topic	481
14.4 Guidelines for Preparing an Informative Speech	484
14.5 Giving Informative Speeches in Groups	487
14.6 Sample Informative Speech Outline	490
14.7 Enrichment	500

15 Understanding Small Group Communication

15.1 Communicating in Small Groups	503
15.2 Understanding Small Groups	506
15.3 Small Group Development	519
15.4 Small Group Dynamics	525
15.5 Enrichment	538

16 Small Groups & Decision Making

16.1 Leadership, Roles, and Problem Solving in Groups	543
16.2 Leadership and Small Group Communication	546

16.3 Group Member Roles   559
16.4 Problem Solving and Decision Making in Groups   575
16.5 Enrichment   595

17 Persuasive Speaking

17.1 Why Persuade?   601
17.2 A Definition of Persuasion   605
17.3 Why is Persuasion Hard?   610
17.4 Traditional Views of Persuasion   614
17.5 Theories of Persuasive Communication   618
17.6 Constructing a Persuasive Speech   625
17.8 Enrichment   637

18 Special Occasion Speaking

18.1 Understanding Special Occasion Speaking   641
18.2 Types of Special Occasion Speeches   647
18.3 Special Occasion Language   660
18.4 Special Occasion Delivery   662
18.6 Enrichment   664

ACKNOWLEDGEMENTS

This book, *Introduction to Speech Communication,* is used to support teaching, learning and research for SPCH 2713 at Oklahoma State University (OSU). This resource has been customized for use at OSU by faculty members Sarah E. Hollingsworth, Kathryn Weinland, Sasha Hanrahan, Mary Walker, Terrisa Elwood and Megan Linsenmeyer. In addition to inclusion of original work authored by the editors to meet the needs of their course at OSU, the editors adapted and mixed together portions of *Exploring Public Speaking: 4th Edition, Stand Up, Speak Out,* and *Fundamentals of Public Speaking.* The Online Delivery section comes from a combination of multiple sources from Maricopa Community College, Lousiana Library Network, Lumen Learning, University of Arkansas, and Douglas College. Please see below for full citations of each of these works. We at Oklahoma State University Libraries acknowledge our gratitude for the expertise and generosity of the scholars at Affordable Learning Georgia, College of the Canyons, the Open Education Network and elsewhere for creating and sharing customizable versions of their work.

Pistol Pete scenarios are all based on hypothetical events and were written with the use of Chatgpt and careful editing by Speech Communication faculty.

Attribution statement:

The print edition of *Introduction to Speech Communication* by Sarah E. Hollingsworth, Kathryn Weinland, Sasha Hanrahan, Mary Walker, Terrisa Elwood and Megan Linsenmeyer is licensed CC BY-NC-SA. In addition to original material, it has been adapted and remixed from *Exploring Public Speaking: 4th Edition* licensed CC BY-NC-SA, *Stand Up, Speak Out* licensed CC BY-NC-SA and *Fundamentals of Public Speaking* licensed CC BY.

Recommended APA citation for the print edition of this work:

Hollingsworth, S., Weinland, K., Hanrahan, S., Walker, M. Elwood, T. & Linsenmeyer, M. (Eds.). (2025). *Introduction to speech communication*. Oklahoma State University Libraries. https://open.library.okstate.edu/speech2713/

Citations for works acknowledged above:

Goodman, & Green, (n.d.) Online delivery considerations. *Public Speaking*. Maricopa Community Colleges. https://open.maricopa.edu/com225/chapter/online-delivery/

Lousiana Library Network. (2022). *It's about them: Public speaking in the 21st century.* https://louis.pressbooks.pub/publicspeaking/chapter/online-public-speaking/

Lumen Learning. (n.d.). Introduction to speaking online. *Public Speaking*. https://courses.lumenlearning.com/wm-publicspeaking/chapter/introduction-to-speaking-online/

Mead, L. (2021). Chapter 34: Speaking to a Camera: Making eye contact is key. *Advanced Public Speaking*. https://uark.pressbooks.pub/speaking/chapter/speaking-to-a-camera/

Schechter, S. (2023). Chapter 16: Public speaking online. *Public Speaking For Today's Audiences*. https://pressbooks.bccampus.ca/speaking/chapter/chapter-16/

Stand up, Speak Out. Okay, this is Kathy, that work has such an interesting history I cannot pretend to provide an authoritative, accurate citation. Feel free to contact me at kathy.essmiller@okstate.edu if you have one, and I will add it here.

Stokes-Rice, T., Leonard, V., & Rome, L. *Fundamentals of public speaking.* (T. Radtke, Ed.). College of the Canyons. https://www.oercommons.org/courses/fundamentals-of-public-speaking

Tucker, B., Barton, K., Burger, A., Drye, J., Hunsicker, C., Mendes, A., & LeHew, M. *Exploring public speaking: 4th edition.* Communication Open Textbooks. https://oer.galileo.usg.edu/communication-textbooks/1

Introduction to Speech Communication

Copyright 2025 by Sarah E. Hollingsworth, Megan Linsenmeyer, Terrisa Elwood, Sasha Hanrahan and Mary Walker.
Introduction to Speech Communication by Hollingsworth, Linsenmeyer, Elwood, Hanrahan and Walker is licensed CC BY-NC-SA. Logos, trademarks, and linked material retains the original copyright.

Print ISBN: 9781957983073
Library of Congress Number: 2025935492
Published by Oklahoma State University Libraries, Stillwater, Oklahoma.

1 WHY PUBLIC SPEAKING MATTERS TODAY

Learning Objectives

- Describe the three types of public speaking in everyday life: informative, persuasive, and entertaining.
- Explain the benefits of taking a course in and engaging in public speaking.
- Identify the three components of getting your message across to others.
- Distinguish between the interactional models of communication and the transactional model of communication.
- Explain the three principles discussed in the dialogical theory of public speaking.

Key Terms

- **Channel**
- **Cultural Dimension**
- **Decoding**
- **Dialogic Theory of Public Speaking**
- **Dialogue**
- **Encoding**
- **Entertaining Speaking**

- Feedback
- Informative Speaking
- Interactional Model of Public Speaking
- Linear Model of Public Speaking
- Mediated
- Message
- Monologue
- Noise
- Nonverbal Communication
- Persuasive Speaking
- Physical Dimension
- Receiver
- Social-Psychological Dimension
- Source
- Temporal Dimension
- Thought Leader
- Transactional Model of Public Speaking
- Verbal Communication

1.1 PUBLIC SPEAKING IN THE TWENTY-FIRST CENTURY

"Good communication is the bridge between clarity and confusion."
-Nat Turner

Humans' ability to communicate using formalized systems of language sets us apart from other living creatures on the Earth. Whether these language conventions make us superior to other creatures is debatable, but there is no question that overall, the most successful and most powerful people over the centuries have mastered the ability to communicate effectively. In fact, the skill of speaking is so important that it has been formally taught for thousands of years.

Public speaking is the process of designing and delivering a **message** to an audience. Effective public speaking involves understanding your audience and speaking goals, choosing elements for the speech that will engage your audience with your topic, and delivering your message skillfully. The ironic feature of public speaking is that while we recognize that it is an important skill to have, many of us do not like or want to give speeches. You may be reading this book because it was assigned to you in a class, or you may be reading it because you have to give a speech in your personal or professional life. If you are reading this book because you like public speaking or you have a burning desire to learn more about it, you are in the minority. However, people continue to spend millions of dollars every year to listen to professional speakers. For example, attendees of the 2010 TED (Technology, Entertainment, Design) conference, which invites speakers from around the world to share their ideas in short, eighteen-minute presentations, paid six thousand dollars per person to listen to fifty speeches over a four-day period! We realize that you may not be invited to TED to give the speech of your life or create a speech so inspirational that it touches the lives of millions via YouTube; however, all of us will find ourselves in situations where we will be asked to give a speech, make a presentation, or just deliver a few words. Even the ability to speak effectively on a personal camera at home or in your office has now become a needed skill as many corporations, nonprofit organizations, and others have turned to virtual meeting spaces as an alternative to face to face interactions.

The good news about public speaking is that although it may not be on the top of the list of our favorite activities, anyone can learn to give effective presentations. You do not have to look like a celebrity and you do not have to use fancy words to be a successful speaker. What is important is that the audience understands you and remembers what you have to say. By learning and using the techniques provided in this book, you will discover how to create engaging speeches and present them using your own delivery style.

Impactful public speakers understand that they should plan, organize, and revise their material in order to develop an effective speech. This book will help you understand the basics of effective public speaking and guide you through the process of creating your own presentations. In this chapter, we will first introduce Pistol Pete, our very own Oklahoma State mascot, who will travel with you through this course, the principles of communication, why public speaking is important, and then we will discuss models that illustrate the process of public speaking itself.

Pete Takes Introduction to Speech Communication

Howdy! Y'all ready to saddle up and ride alongside me? I'm Pistol Pete, the livewire mascot of Oklahoma State University, and I'm here to bring the thunder and fire up the Cowboy and Cowgirl spirit like no other! Since the roaring '20s, I've been the epitome of grit and determination for the Oklahoma State faithful. With my trusty cowboy hat, chiseled jawline, and sharp wit, I'm hard to miss and even harder to forget. I'm the embodiment of the Orange Pride that courses through our veins. My roots run deep, partner. Drawing inspiration from the remarkable life of Frank Eaton, known as Pistol Pete, I earned my nickname for my lightning-fast aim and fiery passion. But my story doesn't end there. I've channeled that unwavering determination into becoming a legendary cowboy and lawman. From thunderous football games to nail-biting basketball showdowns, I electrify the atmosphere and ignite that Cowboy spirit in each of you. But it's not just about the games, my friends. You may ask, why is ole Pete taking a public speaking course? There are lots of good reasons I need to develop strong communication skills like representing our beloved university, enhancing fan interaction, improving alumni and donor engagements, and handling interviews and media appearances. I'm out there making a difference in the community too, spreading love and inspiring the next generation with the indomitable spirit that encompasses this great university. Let's celebrate the traditions, history, and unmatched pride that define Oklahoma State

University. So, saddle up, my friends, and let's ride this trail together! Join me, Pistol Pete, and let's show the world what it means to be a true Orange Cowboy by becoming an effective communicator!

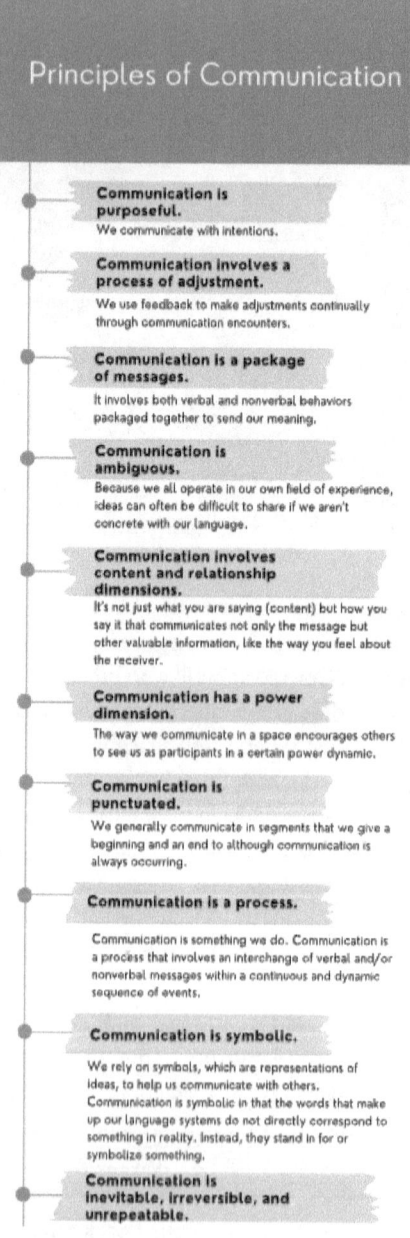

Principles of Communication

Communication is purposeful.
We communicate with intentions.

Communication involves a process of adjustment.
We use feedback to make adjustments continually through communication encounters.

Communication is a package of messages.
It involves both verbal and nonverbal behaviors packaged together to send our meaning.

Communication is ambiguous.
Because we all operate in our own field of experience, ideas can often be difficult to share if we aren't concrete with our language.

Communication involves content and relationship dimensions.
It's not just what you are saying (content) but how you say it that communicates not only the message but other valuable information, like the way you feel about the receiver.

Communication has a power dimension.
The way we communicate in a space encourages others to see us as participants in a certain power dynamic.

Communication is punctuated.
We generally communicate in segments that we give a beginning and an end to although communication is always occurring.

Communication is a process.
Communication is something we do. Communication is a process that involves an interchange of verbal and/or nonverbal messages within a continuous and dynamic sequence of events.

Communication is symbolic.
We rely on symbols, which are representations of ideas, to help us communicate with others. Communication is symbolic in that the words that make up our language systems do not directly correspond to something in reality. Instead, they stand in for or symbolize something.

Communication is inevitable, irreversible, and unrepeatable.

References

Berkun, S. (2009, March 4). *Does public speaking matter in 2009?* [Web log message]. Retrieved from http://www.scottberkun.com/blog.

Survey of Human Communication (OER text). Retrieved from https://creativecommons.org/licenses/by-nc-nd/3.0/. LibreTexts content is licensed by CC BY-NC-SA 3.0.

1.2 WHY IS PUBLIC SPEAKING IMPORTANT?

In today's world, we are constantly bombarded with all kinds of messages. No matter where you live, where you work or go to school, or what kinds of media you use, you are probably exposed to hundreds, if not thousands, of advertising messages every day. Because we live in a world where we are overwhelmed with content, communicating information in a way that is accessible to others is more important today than ever before. To help us further understand why public speaking is important, we will first examine public speaking in everyday life. We will then discuss how public speaking can benefit you personally.

EVERYDAY PUBLIC SPEAKING

Every single day people across the United States and around the world stand up in front of some kind of audience and speak. In a typical day, you may find yourself speaking in front of a group of college students for an organization you belong to, giving a presentation in your psychology class, addressing the Student Government

Association about a pressing concern, or even speaking to a crowd at a religious function. Each and everyday you go out and interact with your community, you will find a variety of opportunities to make a difference in the world through public speaking. Although public speeches are of various types, they can generally be grouped into three categories based on their intended purpose: informative, persuasive, and special occasion.

Informative Speaking

One of the most common types of public speaking is **informative speaking**. The primary purpose of informative presentations is to share one's knowledge of a subject with an audience. Reasons for making an informative speech vary widely. For example, you might be asked to instruct a group of coworkers on how to use new computer software or to report to a group of managers how your latest project is coming along. A local community group might wish to hear about your volunteer activities in Tulsa during spring break, or your classmates may want you to share your expertise on new agricultural practices. What all these examples have in common is the goal of imparting information to an audience.

TV announcers, teachers, lawyers, and entertainers should be able to speak well, but most other professions require or at the very least can benefit from the skills found in public speaking. Informative speaking is integrated into many different occupations. Physicians often lecture about their areas of expertise to medical students, other physicians, and patients. Teachers find themselves presenting to parents as well as to their students. Firefighters give demonstrations about how to effectively control a fire in the house.

Financial planners might address a group at the public library for an information session on retirement planning. Being able to effectively transmit your ideas to other individuals is an important personal and professional skill. It is believed 70% of jobs today involve some form of public speaking (Aras, 2012). Informative speaking is a common part of numerous jobs and other everyday activities. As a result, learning how to speak effectively has become an essential skill in today's world.

Persuasive Speaking

A second common reason for speaking to an audience is to **persuade** others. In our everyday lives, we are often called on to convince, motivate, or otherwise persuade others to change their beliefs, take an action, or reconsider a decision. Advocating for music education in your local school district, convincing clients to purchase your company's products, or inspiring high school students to attend college all involve influencing other people through public speaking.

With the recent economic shift from manufacturing to service careers, the ability to communicate with others has become crucial. Top CEOs advise that great leaders should be able to communicate ideas effectively, they should be able to persuade, build support, negotiate and speak effectively in public (Farrell, 2011). Professional and motivational speakers can make millions of dollars each year from people who want to be motivated to do better in their lives. Whether public speaking is something you do every day or just a few times a year, persuading others is a challenging task. If you develop the skill to persuade effectively, it can be personally and professionally rewarding.

Special Occasion Speaking

Special occasion speaking involves an array of speaking occasions ranging from introductions to wedding toasts, to presenting and accepting awards, to delivering eulogies at funerals and memorial services in addition to after-dinner speeches and motivational speeches. This form of speaking has been important since the time of the ancient Greeks, when Aristotle identified epideictic speaking (speaking in a ceremonial context) as an important type of address.

As with persuasive and informative speaking, there are professionals, from religious leaders to comedians, who make a living simply from delivering entertaining, special occasion speeches. As anyone who has watched an awards show on television or has seen an incoherent best man deliver a wedding toast can attest, special occasion speaking is a task that requires preparation and practice for most speakers to be effective.

Personal Benefits of Public Speaking

Oral communication skills were the number one skill that college graduates found useful in a business setting, according to a study by sociologist Andrew Zekeri (2004). That fact alone makes learning about public speaking worthwhile. However, there are many other benefits of communicating effectively for the hundreds of thousands of college students every year who take public speaking courses. Let's take a look at some specific personal benefits you will get both from taking a course in public speaking and from actually giving public speeches.

Benefits of Public Speaking Courses

In addition to learning the process of creating and delivering an effective speech, students of public speaking leave the class with a number of other benefits as well. Some of these benefits include developing critical thinking skills, strengtheningverbal and nonverbal skills, and building public speaking confidence.

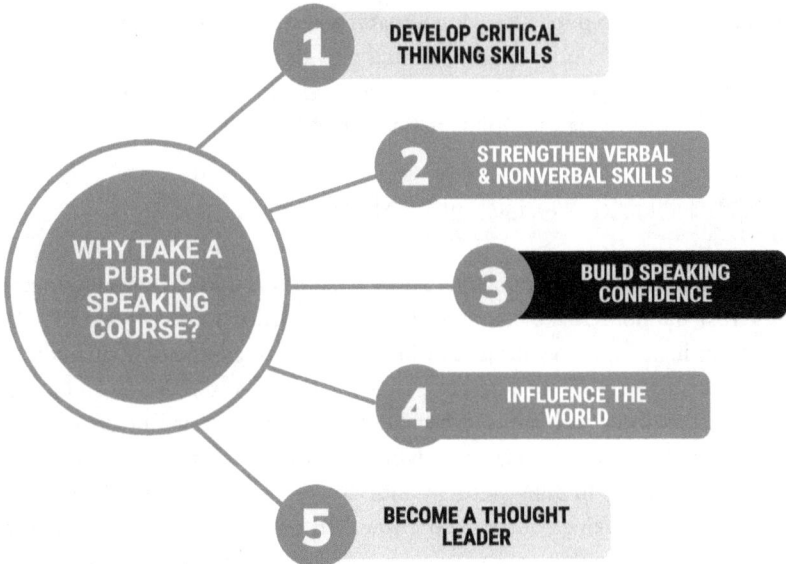

Developing Critical Thinking Skills

One of the very first benefits you will gain from your public speaking course is an increased ability to think critically. Problem solving is one of many critical thinking skills you will engage in during this course. For example, when preparing a persuasive speech, you will have to think through real problems affecting your campus, community, or the world and provide possible solutions to those problems. You will also have to think about the positive and negative consequences of your solutions and then communicate your ideas to others. At first, it may seem easy to come up with solutions for a campus problem such as a shortage of parking spaces: just build more spaces. But after thinking and researching further you may find out that building costs, environmental impact from loss of green space, maintenance needs, or limited locations for additional spaces make this solution impractical. Being able to think through problems and analyze the potential costs and benefits of solutions is an essential part of critical thinking and of public speaking aimed at persuading others. These skills will help you not only in public speaking contexts but throughout your life as well. As we stated earlier, college graduates in Zekeri's study rated oral communication skills as the most useful for success in the business sector. The second most valuable skill they reported was problem-solving ability, so your public speaking course is doubly valuable!

Another benefit to public speaking is that it will enhance your ability to conduct and analyze research. Public speakers should provide credible evidence within their speeches if they are going to persuade various audiences. So your public speaking course will further refine your ability to find and utilize a range of sources.

Strengthening Verbal and Nonverbal Skills

A second benefit of taking a public speaking course is that it will help you strengthen your verbal and nonverbal communication skills. Whether you competed in public speaking in high school or this is your first time speaking in front of an audience, having the opportunity to actively practice communication skills and receive professional feedback will help you become a better overall communicator. Often, people do not even realize that they twirl their hair or repeatedly mispronounce words while speaking in public settings until they receive feedback from a professor during a public speaking course. Before you even start a career, you have to get a job. Effective speaking skills make you more attractive to employers, enhancing your chances of securing employment and later advancing within your career. Employers, career counselors, and the National Association of Colleges and Employers (NACE) all list good communication skills at the top of the list of qualities sought in potential employees. According to NACE's executive director, Marilyn Mackes, the Job Outlook 2013 Report found that employers are looking for people who can communicate effectively (Koncz & Allen, 2012). Monster.com advises, "articulating thoughts clearly and concisely will make a difference in both a job interview and subsequent job performance" (McKay, 2005). Additionally, many folks around the United States will often pay speech coaches, seek out workshops, or read self help books to help them enhance their nonverbal speaking skills. People around the United States will often pay speech coaches over one hundred dollars per hour to help them enhance their speaking skills. You have a built-in speech coach right in your classroom, so it is to your advantage to use the opportunity to improve your verbal and nonverbal communication skills with the help of your professor.

Building Confidence in Public Speaking

An additional benefit of taking a public speaking class is that it will help improve your confidence with public speaking. Whether they have spoken in public a lot or are just getting started, most people experience some anxiety when engaging in public speaking. Heidi Rose and Andrew Rancer evaluated students' levels of public speaking anxiety during both the first and last weeks of their public speaking class and found that those levels decreased over the course of the semester (Rose & Rancer, 1993). One explanation is that people often have little exposure to public speaking. By taking a course in public speaking, students become better acquainted with the public speaking process, making them more confident and less apprehensive. In addition, you will learn specific strategies for overcoming the challenges of speech anxiety. We will discuss this topic in greater detail throughout this book.

Benefits of Engaging in Public Speaking

Once you have learned the basic skills associated with public speaking, you will find that being able to effectively speak in public has profound benefits, including influencing the world around you, developing leadership skills, and becoming a thought leader.

Influencing the World around You

If you do not like something about your local government, then speak out about your issue! One of the best ways to get our society to change is through the power of speech. Common citizens in the United States and around the world, like you, are influencing the world in real ways through the power of speech. Just type the words "citizens speak out" in a search engine and you will find numerous examples of how common citizens use the power of speech to make real changes in the world—for example, by speaking out against "fracking" for natural gas (a process in which chemicals are injected into rocks in an attempt to open them up for fast flow of natural gas or oil) or in favor of retaining a popular local sheriff. One of the amazing parts of being a citizen in a democracy is the right to stand up and speak out, which is a luxury many people in the world do not have. So if you do not like something, be the force of change you are looking for through the power of speech.

Developing Leadership Skills

Have you ever thought about climbing the corporate ladder and eventually finding yourself in a management or other leadership position? If so, then public speaking skills are very important. Hackman and Johnson assert that effective public speaking skills are a necessity for all leaders (Hackman & Johnson, 2004). If you want people to follow you, you have to communicate effectively and clearly what people should do. According to Bender, "Powerful leadership comes from knowing what matters to you. Powerful presentations come from expressing this effectively. It is important to develop both" (Bender, 1998). One of the most important skills for leaders to develop is their public speaking skills, which is why executives spend millions of dollars every year going to public speaking workshops; hiring public speaking coaches; and buying public speaking books or listening to online tutorials.

Becoming a Thought Leader

Even if you are not in an official leadership position, effective public speaking can help you become a "**thought leader**." Joel Kurtzman, editor of Strategy & Business, coined this term to call attention to individuals who contribute new ideas to the world of business. According to business consultant Ken Lizotte, "when your colleagues, prospects, and customers view you as one very smart guy or gal to know, then you are a thought leader" (Lizotte, 2008). Typically, thought leaders engage in a range of behaviors, including enacting and conducting research on business practices. To achieve thought leader status, individuals should communicate their ideas to others through both writing and public speaking. Lizotte demonstrates how becoming a thought leader can be personally and financially rewarding at the same time: when others look to you as a thought leader, you will be more desired and make more money as a result. Business gurus often refer to "intellectual capital," or the combination of your knowledge and ability to communicate that knowledge to others (Lizotte, 2008). Whether standing before a group of executives discussing the next great trend in business or delivering a webinar (a seminar over the web), thought leaders use public speaking every day to create the future that the rest of us live in.

References

Bender, P. U. (1998). Stand, deliver and lead. *Ivey Business Journal, 62*(3), 46–47.

Edmund, N. W. (2005). *End the biggest educational and intellectual blunder in history: A $100,000 challenge to our top educational leaders.* Ft. Lauderdale, FL: Scientific Method Publishing Co.

Hackman, M. Z., & Johnson, C. E. (2004). *Leadership: A communication perspective* (4th ed.). Long Grove, IL: Waveland.

Lizotte, K. (2008). *The expert's edge: Become the go-to authority people turn to every time* [Kindle 2 version]. New York, NY: McGraw-Hill. Retrieved from Amazon.com (locations 72–78).

Rose, H. M., & Rancer, A. S. (1993). The impact of basic courses in oral interpretation and public speaking on communication apprehension. *Communication Reports, 6,* 54–60.

Zekeri, A. A. (2004). College curriculum competencies and skills former students found essential to their careers. *College Student Journal, 38,* 412–422.

1.3 THE PROCESS OF PUBLIC SPEAKING

As noted earlier, all of us encounter thousands of messages in our everyday environments, so getting your idea heard above all the other ones is a constant battle. Some speakers will try gimmicks, but we strongly believe that getting your message heard depends on three fundamental components: message, skill, and passion. The first part of getting your message across is the message itself. When what you are saying is clear and coherent, people are more likely to pay attention to it. On the other hand, when a message is ambiguous, people will often stop paying attention. Our discussions in the first part of this book involve how to have clear and coherent content. The second part of getting your message heard is having effective communication skills. You may have the best ideas in the world, but if you do not possess basic public speaking skills, you are going to have a problem getting anyone to listen. In this book, we will address the skills you should possess to effectively communicate your ideas to others.

Lastly, if you want your message to be heard, you should communicate passion for your message. One mistake that novice public speakers make is picking topics in which they have no emotional investment. If an audience can tell that you do not really care about your topic, they will just tune you out. Passion is the extra spark that draws people's attention and makes them want to listen to your message.

In this section, we will examine the process of public speaking by first introducing you to some basic components of public speaking, a few basic models of public speaking and then discussing how public speaking functions as dialogue. To start at the beginning, let us look a little more in depth at some basic terms. Next the models will give you a basic understanding of the communication process and some challenges that you may face as a speaker.

Basic Components of Public Speaking

Source/Encoder

When we communicate, it all starts with an origin. Generally speaking, the source refers to the person sending the message. This role can be called speaker, sender, encoder, or source. Because encoding is the act of sending a message, many communication scholars refer to the sender as the encoder. Because we can send messages while speaking and listening, sometimes using the term "speaker" does not fit the circumstances. We can operate as sources both verbally and nonverbally while speaking and listening during public speaking.

Receiver/Decoder

Usually there is a primary intended audience when we are speaking. In conversation it may just be one or two people, but with public speaking it can be anywhere from a handful of people to thousands of people packed in an arena. These people are thought of as the receivers of the message. This role can be called listener, receiver or decoder. Because decoding is the act of receiving and making sense of a message, communication scholars often refer to the receiver as the decoder. Receivers can receive all sorts of messages whether they are intended or not.

Channel

The channel is usually the primary method or medium for communicating and can occur through face to face communication, telephone conversations, texting, letters, mass media, etc. It is important to recognize that the channel you select may have implications for your message. Some messages are best delivered face to face, while some can be handled in a simple email or text message. Which channel is your primary method for communicating? How does public speaking in a face to face setting differ from delivering a speech through a computer screen?

Message

The message is the basic idea or information you are hoping to convey. Messages can present themselves in a variety of ways, but we primarily identify them in two primary categories: verbal and nonverbal. Verbal messages are those that we use language to deliver. They communicate our ideas or information through the use of the words we select to use. The way we word messages can have a major impact on the way the message is received. Nonverbal messages are the ways we communicate without using words. This can involve our vocal characteristics, our gestures, body movements, facial expressions and more. As indicated above, you can tell when someone is excited to talk about a topic versus someone who lacks care and concern for the topic they are discussing. What kinds of nonverbal behavior indicate a lack of passion in a person's presentation? Feedback is a specific type of message that indicates the receiver's response to the information. Feedback can also be presented verbally or nonverbally. When we clap for a speaker or we ask challenging questions, these behaviors communicate feedback to the speaker.

Noise

Oftentimes when a source is trying to send a message to a receiver, there is a problem that prevents the message from being received as intended. This problem is generally considered to be noise. Noise is anything that interferes with the message in its transmission or reception of the message. The noise can be external to the participants engaged in communication or it can be internal. Common types of noise include physical noise, physiological noise, psychological noise, and semantic noise. You will learn more about these different types of noise in section 11.4 of this text.

Understanding the basic components of communication will help give you a foundational understanding that will benefit you as you move through this course. Additionally, it is useful to learn about the different views of communication and how they have changed through time as well as the differences of the models between different channels of communication.

Models of Public Speaking

A basic model of human communication is one of the first topics that most communication teachers start with in any class. For our focus on public speaking, we will introduce three widely discussed models in communication: linear, interactional, and transactional.

LINEAR MODEL OF COMMUNICATION

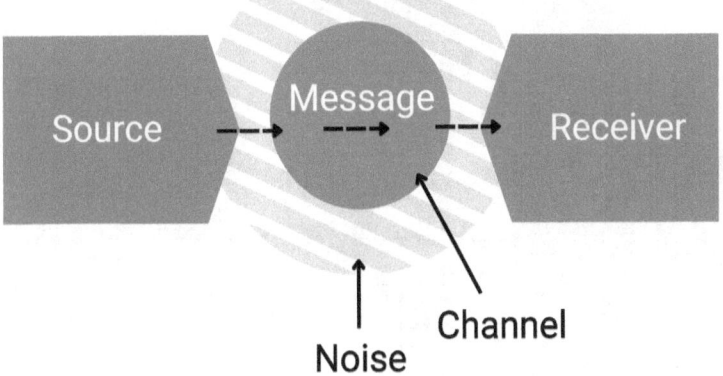

The linear model of public speaking comes from the work of Claude Shannon and Warren Weaver (1949). The original model mirrored how radio and telephone technologies functioned and consisted of three primary parts: source, channel, and receiver. The **source** was the part of a telephone a person spoke into, the **channel** was the telephone itself, and the **receiver** was the part of the phone where one could hear the other person. Shannon and Weaver also recognized that often there is static that interferes with listening to a telephone conversation, which they called noise.

Although there are a number of problems with applying this model to human communication, it does have some useful parallels to public speaking. In public speaking, the source is the person who is giving the speech, the channel is the speaker's use of **verbal** and **nonverbal communication**, and the receivers are the audience members listening to the speech. As with a telephone call, a wide range of distractions (**noise**) can inhibit an audience member from accurately attending to a speaker's speech. Avoiding or adapting to these types of noise is an important challenge for public speakers.

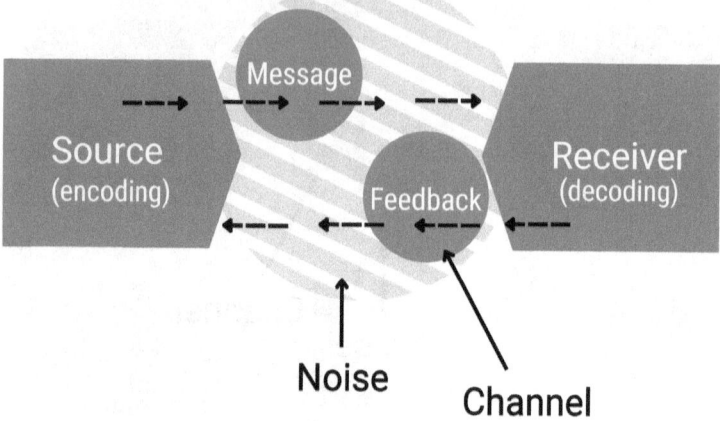

The interactional model of communication developed by Wilbur Schramm builds upon the linear model (Schramm, 1954). Schramm added three major components to the Shannon and Weaver model. First, Schramm identified two basic processes of communication: encoding and decoding. **Encoding** is what a source does when "creating a message, adapting it to the receiver, and transmitting it across some source-selected channel" (Wrench, McCroskey & Richmond, 2008). When you are at home preparing your speech or standing in front of your classroom talking to your peers, you are participating in the encoding process.

The second major process is the **decoding** process, or "sensing (for example, hearing or seeing) a source's message, interpreting the source's message, evaluating the source's message, and responding to the source's message" (Wrench, McCroskey & Richmond, 2008). Decoding is relevant in the public speaking context when, as an audience member, you listen to the words of the speech, pay attention to nonverbal behaviors of the speaker, and attend to any presentation aids that the speaker uses. You should then interpret what the speaker is saying.

Although interpreting a speaker's message may sound easy in theory, in practice many problems can arise. A speaker's verbal message, nonverbal communication, and **mediated** presentation aids can all make a **message** either clearer or harder to understand. For example, unfamiliar vocabulary, speaking too fast or too softly, or small print on presentation aids may make it difficult for you to figure out what the speaker means. Conversely, by providing definitions of complex terms, using well-timed gestures, or displaying graphs of quantitative information, the speaker can help you interpret his or her meaning.

Once you have interpreted what the speaker is communicating, you then evaluate the message. Was it good? Do you agree or disagree with the speaker? Is a speaker's argument logical? These are all questions that you may ask yourself when evaluating a speech.

The last part of decoding is "responding to a source's message," when the receiver encodes a message to send to the source. When a receiver sends a message back to a source, we call this process **feedback**. Schramm talks about three types of feedback: direct, moderately direct, and indirect (Schramm, 1954). The first type, direct feedback, occurs when the receiver directly talks to the source. For example, if a speech ends with a question-and-answer period, listeners will openly agree or disagree with the speaker. The second type of feedback, moderately direct, focuses on nonverbal messages sent while a source is speaking, such as audience members smiling and nodding their heads in agreement or looking at their watches or surreptitiously sending text messages during the speech. The final type of feedback, indirect, often involves a greater time gap between the actual message and the receiver's feedback. For example, suppose you run for student body president and give speeches to a variety of groups all over campus, only to lose on student election day. Your audiences (the different groups you spoke to) have offered you indirect feedback on your message through their votes. One of the challenges you may face as a public speaker is how to respond effectively to audience feedback, particularly the direct and moderately direct forms of feedback you receive during your presentation.

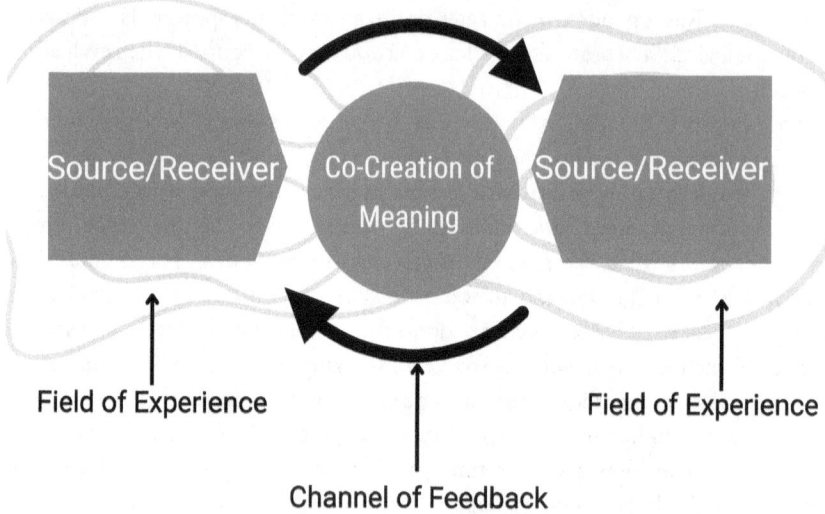

One of the biggest concerns that some people have with the interactional model of communication is that it tends to place people into the category of either source or receiver with no overlap. Even with Schramm's model, encoding and decoding are perceived as distinct for sources and receivers. Furthermore, the interactional model cannot handle situations where multiple sources are interacting at the same time (Mortenson, 1972). To address these weaknesses, Dean Barnlund (2008) proposed a **transactional model** of communication. The basic premise of the transactional model is that individuals are sending and receiving messages at the same time. Whereas the interactional model has individuals engaging in the role of either source or receiver and the meaning of a message is sent from the source to the receiver, the transactional model assumes that meaning is co-created by both people interacting together.

The idea that meanings are co-created between people is based on a concept called the "field of experience." According to West and Turner, a field of experience involves "how a person's culture, experiences, and heredity influence his or her ability to communicate with another" (West & Turner, 2010). Our education, race, gender, ethnicity, religion, personality, beliefs, actions, attitudes, languages, social status, past experiences, and customs are all aspects of our field of experience, which we bring to every interaction. For meaning to occur, we should have some shared experiences with our audience; this makes it challenging to speak effectively to audiences with very different experiences from our own. Our goal as public speakers is to build upon shared fields of experience so that we can help audience members interpret our message.

Dialogic Theory of Public Speaking

Most people think of public speaking as engaging in a monologue where the speaker stands and delivers information and the audience passively listens. Based on the work of numerous philosophers, however, Ronald Arnett and Pat Arneson proposed that all communication, even public speaking, could be viewed as a dialogue (Arnett & Arneson, 1999). The **dialogic theory** is based on three overarching principles:

1. Dialogue is more natural than monologue.
2. Meanings are in people not words.
3. Contexts and social situations impact perceived meanings (Bakhtin, 2001a; Bakhtin, 2001b).

Let's look at each of these in turn.

Dialogue vs. Monologue

The first tenet of the dialogic perspective is that communication should be a dialogue and not a monologue. Lev Yakubinsky argued that even public speaking situations often turn into dialogues when audience members actively engage speakers by asking questions. He even claimed that nonverbal behavior (e.g., nodding one's head in agreement or scowling) functions as feedback for speakers and contributes to a dialogue (Yakubinsky, 1997). Overall, if you approach your public speaking experience as a dialogue, you will be more actively engaged as a speaker and more attentive to how your audience is responding, which will, in turn, lead to more actively engaged audience members.

Meanings Are in People, Not Words

Part of the dialogic process in public speaking is realizing that you and your audience may differ in how you see your speech. Hellmut Geissner and Edith Slembeck (1986) discussed Geissner's idea of responsibility, or the notion that the meanings of words should be mutually agreed upon by people interacting with each other (Geissner & Slembek, 1986). If you say the word "dog" and think of a soft, furry pet and your audience member thinks of the animal that attacked him as a child, the two of you perceive the word from very different vantage points. As speakers, we should do our best to craft messages that take our audience into account and use audience feedback to determine whether the meaning we intend is the one that is received. To be successful at conveying our desired meaning, we should know quite a bit about our audience so we can make language choices that will be the most appropriate for the context. Although we cannot predict how all our audience members will interpret specific words, we do know that—for example—using teenage slang when speaking to the audience at a senior center would most likely hurt our ability to convey our meaning clearly.

Contexts and Social Situations

Russian scholar Mikhail Bahktin (2001a, 2001b) notes that human interactions take place according to cultural norms and rules. How we approach people, the words we choose, and how we deliver speeches are all dependent on different speaking contexts and social situations. On September 8, 2009, President Barack Obama addressed school children with a televised speech (https://obamawhitehouse.archives.gov/the-press-office/remarks-president-a-national-address-americas-schoolchildren). If you look at the speech he delivered to kids around the country and then at his speeches targeted toward adults, you will see lots of differences. These dissimilar speeches are necessary because the audiences (speaking to kids vs. speaking to adults) have different experiences and levels of knowledge. Ultimately, good public speaking is a matter of taking into account the cultural background of your audience and attempting to engage your audience in a dialogue from their own vantage point.

Considering the **context** of a public speech involves thinking about four dimensions: physical, temporal, social-psychological, and cultural (DeVito, 2009).

Physical Dimension

The **physical dimension** of communication involves the real or touchable environment where communication occurs. For example, you may find yourself speaking in a classroom, a corporate board room, or a large amphitheater. Each of these real environments will influence your ability to interact with your audience. Larger physical spaces may require you to use a microphone and speaker system to make yourself heard or to use projected presentation aids to convey visual material.

How the room is physically decorated or designed can also impact your interaction with your audience. If the room is dimly lit or is decorated with interesting posters, audience members' minds may start wandering. If the room is too hot, you will find people becoming sleepy. As speakers, we often have little or no control over our physical environment, but we always need to take it into account when planning and delivering our messages.

Temporal Dimension

According to Joseph DeVito, the **temporal dimension** "has to do not only with the time of day and moment in history but also with where a particular message fits into the sequence of communication events" (DeVito, 2009). The time of day can have a dramatic effect on how alert one's audience is. Don't believe us? Try giving a speech in front of a class around 12:30 p.m. when no one's had lunch. It is amazing how impatient audience members get once hunger sets in.

In addition to the time of day, we often face temporal dimensions related to how our speech will be viewed in light of societal events. Imagine how a speech on the importance of campus security would be interpreted on the day after a shooting occurred. Compare this with the interpretation of the same speech given at a time when the campus had not had any shootings for years, if ever.

Another element of the temporal dimension is how a message fits with what happens immediately before it. For example, if another speaker has just given an intense speech on death and dying and you stand up to speak about something more trivial, people may downplay your message because it does not fit with the serious tone established by the earlier speech. You never want to be the funny speaker who has to follow an emotional speech where people cried. Most of the time in a speech class, you will have no advance notice as to what the speaker before you will be talking about. Therefore, it is wise to plan on being sensitive to previous topics and be prepared to ease your way subtly into your message if the situation so dictates.

Social-Psychological Dimension

The **social-psychological** dimension of context refers to "status relationships among participants, roles and games that people play, norms of the society or group, and the friendliness, formality, or gravity of the situation" (DeVito, 2009). You have to know the types of people in your audience and how they react to a wide range of messages.

Cultural Dimension

The final context dimension Joseph DeVito mentions is the **cultural dimension** (DeVito, 2009). When we interact with others from different cultures, misunderstandings can result from differing cultural beliefs, norms, and practices. As public speakers engaging in a dialogue with our audience members, we should attempt to understand the cultural makeup of our audience so that we can avoid these misunderstandings as much as possible.

Each of these elements of context is a challenge for you as a speaker. Throughout the rest of the book, we will discuss how you can meet the challenges presented by the audience and context and become a more effective public speaker in the process.

References

Arnett, R. C., & Arneson, P. (1999). *Dialogic civility in a cynical age: Community, hope, and interpersonal relationships.* Albany, NY: SUNY Press.

Bakhtin, M. (2001a). The problem of speech genres. (V. W. McGee, Trans., 1986). In P. Bizzell & B. Herzberg (Eds.), *The rhetorical tradition* (pp. 1227–1245). Boston, MA: Bedford/St. Martin's. (Original work published in 1953.).

Bakhtin, M. (2001b). Marxism and the philosophy of language. (L. Matejka & I. R. Titunik, Trans., 1973). In P. Bizzell & B. Herzberg (Eds.), *The rhetorical tradition* (pp. 1210–1226). Boston, MA: Medford/St. Martin's. (Original work published in 1953).

Barnlund, D. C. (2008). A transactional model of communication. In C. D. Mortensen (Ed.), *Communication theory* (2nd ed., pp. 47–57). New Brunswick, NJ: Transaction.

DeVito, J. A. (2009). *The interpersonal communication book* (12th ed.). Boston, MA: Allyn & Bacon.

Geissner, H., & Slembek, E. (1986). *Miteinander sprechen und handeln* [Speak and act: Living and working together]. Frankfurt, Germany: Scriptor.

Mortenson, C. D. (1972). *Communication: The study of human communication.* New York, NY: McGraw-Hill.

Schramm, W. (1954). How communication works. In W. Schramm (Ed.), *The process and effects of communication* (pp. 3–26). Urbana, IL: University of Illinois Press.

Shannon, C. E., & Weaver, W. (1949). *The mathematical theory of communication.* Urbana, IL: University of Illinois Press.

West, R., & Turner, L. H. (2010). *Introducing communication theory: Analysis and application* (4th ed.). New York, NY: McGraw-Hill, p. 13.

Wrench, J. S., McCroskey, J. C., & Richmond, V. P. (2008). *Human communication in everyday life: Explanations and applications*. Boston, MA: Allyn & Bacon, p. 17.

Yakubinsky, L. P. (1997). On dialogic speech. (M. Eskin, Trans.). *PMLA, 112*(2), 249–256. (Original work published in 1923).

1.4 ENRICHMENT

Discussion Questions

1. What areas of public speaking do you think will be most challenging for you? Why? What are some plans to overcome these challenges?
2. How might becoming a more effective and confident public speaker affect your life? Consider the differences between personal and professional impacts.
3. What are your feelings and/or experiences with public speaking? How might this skill be used in your future?
4. Think about your own field of experience through positionality and perspectives. How has your gender, work history, religious affiliation, relationship status, educational experiences, major, socioeconomic status, age, ethnicity, race, hometown, political affiliation and life experiences influenced your attitudes, beliefs, and values? Give some concrete examples.
5. What are the three fundamental components of getting your message across according to your text? Do you feel any components are missing or should be added?
6. What are three ways that you will use public speaking in your future career (personal & professional)?

Activities

1. Reflect on your own desire for improved communication and public speaking skills in your life. Set three or four personal and/or professional goals you hope to achieve by taking this class.
2. Think of a career path that you are considering. Using that occupation do a quick internet search of that position with the term, "public speaking". Discuss your findings with a classmate or friend.(e.g. "nurse and public speaking").
3. Form six groups. Each group will be given a blank piece of paper, crayons/markers/colored pencils, and a different process of public speaking from Section 1:3: The Public Speaking Process (linear model of public speaking, interactional model of public speaking, transactional model of public speaking, dialogic theory of public speaking, contexts and social situations of public speaking). Groups should draw a model or picture that represents their selected process of public speaking. Groups will display and explain their drawings to the class.

2 BUILDING CONFIDENCE

Learning Objectives

- Employ methods to build public speaking confidence.
- Describe the nature of communication apprehension (CA), and be in a better position to deal with your particular "brand" of CA.
- Apply cognitive restructuring (CR) techniques to create a more positive frame of reference.
- Recognize the importance of customized practice to become conversant in your topic.
- Create a personal preparation routine to minimize your apprehension.

Key Terms

- **"Breathe and Release"**
- **Cognitive Restructuring (CR)**
- **Communication Apprehension**
- **Conversant**
- **Scrutiny Fear**
- **State-Anxiety**
- **Systematic De-sensitization**
- **Trait-Anxiety**

2.1 WHAT IS COMMUNICATION APPREHENSION?

"The brave man is not he who does not feel afraid, but he who conquers that fear." -Nelson Mandela

"I have to do what?"

You receive your syllabus on the first day of history class, and you see that a significant percentage of your overall grade for the semester depends upon one, ten-minute oral presentation in front of the class. The presentation is to be based on an original research project and is due in eight weeks.

You are excited to get an email after a very positive job interview. They ask you to come to a second interview prepared to answer a number of questions from a panel made up of senior management. The questions are contained in an attachment. "Please be ready to stand in the front of the room to answer," the email reads; ending with "See you next week!"

The plans are finalized: You will have dinner to meet your new fiancé's family on Saturday night – just days away. But, then you are told that your fiancé's father, a former Marine and retired police officer, will want to talk about politics and current *events – and that he will likely judge what sort of person you are based on how well you can defend your ideas.*

In this chapter, you will learn about dealing with one of the most common fears in our society: the fear of public speaking. Fear of public speaking is associated with **communication apprehension** (CA), which is an individuals level of fear or anxiety associated with either real or anticipated communication with another person or persons (McCrosky, 1977). If you are one of those folks – take comfort in the fact that you are not alone! Research indicates that 20% or more of the U.S. population has a high degree of communicative apprehension (McCroskey, 1976).

CA is a real phenomenon that represents a well-documented obstacle not only to academic, but also to professional success. CA can impact many diverse areas; from one's level of self-esteem (Adler, 1980) and how you are perceived by others (Dwyer & Cruz, 1998), to success in school, achieving high grade-point averages, and even landing job interview opportunities (Daly & Leth, 1976).

People with higher levels of CA have demonstrated that they will avoid communicative interaction in personal and professional relationships, social situations, and importantly, classrooms. Such avoidance can result in miscommunication and misunderstanding, which only becomes compounded by further avoidance.

CA left unaddressed can even lead to a negative disposition toward public interaction, which leads to a lesser degree of engagement, thus perpetuating the fear and further compounding the situation (Menzel & Carrell, 1994). The anxiety creates a vicious cycle and becomes a self-fulfilling prophecy. But it is a cycle that need not continue.

By reading this chapter, you will learn about CA; not necessarily how it develops, as that can be different in every individual, but rather about how people can deal with it effectively. CA is not something that can easily be eliminated – turned "off" as if controlled by an internal toggle switch. But it doesn't have to remain an obstacle to success either.

Effective public speaking is not simply about learning what to say, but about developing the confidence to say it. For many, it all comes down to overcoming those nerves and convincing yourself that you can actually get up there and speak! Each individual deals with CA most effectively through increased self-awareness and a willingness to work on reducing its impact. To conquer the nervousness associated with public speaking, one must identify the factors that lead to this anxiety, and then take specific steps to overcome this apprehension.

Pete's Panic

The morning sun rose high in the sky, casting a warm glow over the campus of Oklahoma State University. Inside the classroom, a hushed anticipation filled the air as the students settled into their seats, awaiting the start of their public speaking class. Among them sat Pistol Pete, the spirited mascot known for his exuberance and energy. But today, a different energy emanated from him—a nervousness that churned in his stomach and made his hands tremble.

As the professor called his name to deliver his speech, Pete's heart skipped a beat. Doubt and fear clouded his mind, causing his usually boisterous spirit to waver. A thousand thoughts raced through his head—what if he stumbled over his words? What if his enthusiasm didn't translate into his voice? The weight of expectations felt heavy upon his shoulders.

As he rose from his seat, Pete could feel the gaze of his classmates upon him. The room suddenly felt suffocating, the walls closing in. His throat tightened, and words seemed to escape him. A wave of self-doubt washed over him, threatening to extinguish the fire within.

Taking a deep breath, Pete reminded himself of his purpose. He knew that his role as Pistol Pete went beyond the confines of the field or the court. He represented the resilience, spirit, and wholesome pride of Oklahoma State University. It was this realization that fueled his determination to push through his fears and share his story.

With shaky steps, Pete made his way to the front of the class. His palms were sweaty, and his voice trembled as he began to speak. But as he looked into the eyes of his classmates, he saw understanding and support. Their encouraging smiles gave him the strength he needed to carry on.

As he delved into his speech, Pete's nervousness slowly transformed into a passionate fervor. He spoke of the unifying force he embodied as Pistol Pete, the impact he had on the community, and the legacy he carried on from Frank Eaton. His voice grew stronger, filled with conviction, and his words resonated with the hearts of his classmates.

By the end of his speech, the nervousness that had plagued Pete had dissipated, replaced by a newfound sense of accomplishment. Despite his initial fear, he had conquered the challenge of speaking in front of the class. The room erupted in applause, a testament to the courage he had displayed.

In that moment, Pistol Pete realized that even heroes have their moments of doubt. But it is in facing those fears head-on, embracing vulnerability, and summoning the strength within that true growth and triumph are achieved. From that day forward, Pete carried the memory of that experience, using it as a reminder that even in the face of nerves and fear, he could rise above and inspire others with his voice. How does your body show anxiety prior to presentations? What can you do to calm your nerves?

2.2 CLASSIFYING COMMUNICATION APPREHENSION

Forms of Communication Apprehension (CA)

CA is not the result of a single cause, and so the phenomenon itself comes in many forms. It is important for each person to recognize that their particular sort of CA (we'll call it a "personal brand") is a phenomenon that has developed uniquely through each of their lives and experiences.

Trait-anxiety

Some researchers (McCroskey, et al. 1976) describe CA as **trait-anxiety**, meaning that it is a type of anxiety that is aligned with an individual's personality. People who would call themselves "shy" often seek to avoid interaction with others because they are uncertain of how they will be perceived. Avoiding such judgment is generally not difficult, and so becomes a pattern of behavior. These folks, according to researchers, are likely to view any chance to express themselves publicly with skepticism and hesitation. This personal tendency is what is known as trait-anxiety.

State-anxiety

Other researchers (Beatty, 1988) describe CA as **state-anxiety**, meaning that it is a type of anxiety that is derived from the external situation which individuals find themselves. While some may fear public speaking due to some personal trait or broader social anxiety, researchers have found that CA more often stems from the fear associated with scrutiny and negative evaluation. Some people may have had a negative experience in public at an early age – they forgot a line in a play, they lost a spelling bee, they did poorly when called on in front of their class – something that resulted in a bit of public embarrassment. Others may have never actually experienced that stress themselves, but may have watched friends struggle and thus empathized with them. These sorts of experiences can often lead to the formation of a state-anxiety in an individual.

Scrutiny Fear

Still other researchers (Mattick et al., 1989) discuss CA as what is called a **scrutiny fear**; which stems from an activity that does not necessarily involve interacting with other people, but is simply the fear of being in a situation where one is being watched or observed, or one perceives him or herself as being watched, while undertaking an activity. When asked to categorize their own type of CA, many people will identify with this phenomenon.

In order for anybody to effectively deal with CA, the first step is to consider what may be its primary cause. CA is what is known as a resultant condition; and those who are dealing with the challenge will recognize different intensities associated with different situations or triggers. This means that overcoming the condition requires first that you recognize, and then minimize, the cause. Each person is different, and so each case of CA is personal and unique.

Trait-anxiety can be one contributing factor to CA, but is often part of a much larger condition. It is important to understand that, while the techniques discussed here would help in improving an individual's approach to public speaking opportunities, we do not claim that these techniques would work with more significant personality disorders. However, both the presence of state anxiety, and the appearance of scrutiny fear, can be effectively addressed through the application of cognitive restructuring (CR) and careful, deliberate experience.

FORMS OF COMMUNICATION APPREHENSION

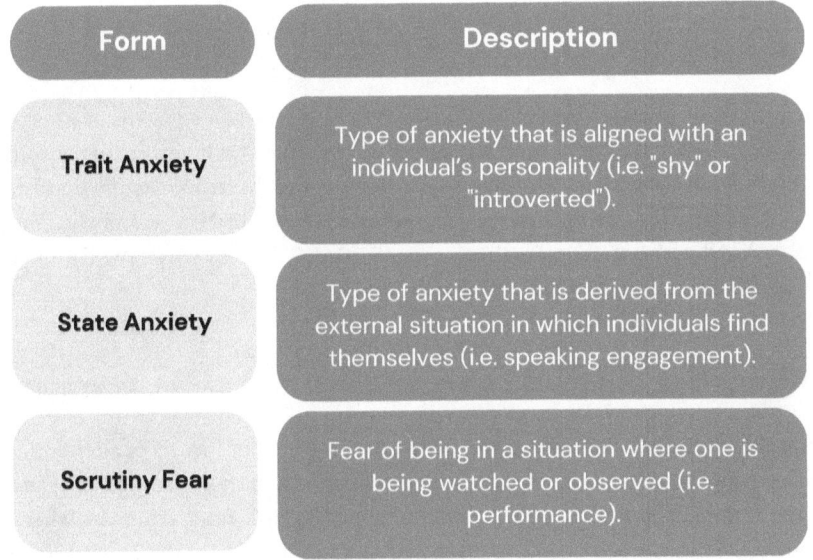

Form	Description
Trait Anxiety	Type of anxiety that is aligned with an individual's personality (i.e. "shy" or "introverted").
State Anxiety	Type of anxiety that is derived from the external situation in which individuals find themselves (i.e. speaking engagement).
Scrutiny Fear	Fear of being in a situation where one is being watched or observed (i.e. performance).

Cognitive Restructuring

Since the major difference between "presenting" to a public audience versus "presenting" to a small group of close friends involves one's attitude about the situation. Overcoming CA is as much a matter of changing one's attitude as it is developing one's skills as a speaker. A change in attitude can be fostered through a self- reflective regimen called **cognitive restructuring** (CR), which is an internal process through which individuals can deliberately adjust how they perceive an action or experience (Mattick et al., 1989). Cognitive Restructuring is a three-step, internal process:

1. Identify objectively what you think
2. Identify any inconsistencies between perception and reality
3. Replace destructive thinking with supportive thinking

These steps are easy to understand, but perhaps may be a bit difficult to execute! The first step is to identify objectively what you are thinking as you approach a public speaking opportunity. Recall your habitual frame of reference. The first step in CR is to shine a bright light directly on it. This will be different for each student as this is an internal process.

Sources of Apprehension

After years of interviewing students from my classes, the two concerns most often described are the feeling of being the center of attention – as if you are under some collective microscope with everybody's eyes on you; and the feeling that the audience is just waiting for you to make a mistake or slip up somehow – and that their disapproval will be swift, immediate, and embarrassing. Let's discuss how CR might be applied to each of these widely held perceptions.

Center of Attention

Probably the most common concern people have is being the "center of attention." When people describe this specific scrutiny fear, they use phrases like "everyone just stares at me," or "I don't like having all eyes on me." Consider for a moment what your experiences have been like when you have been a member of the audience for another speaker. Where did you look while the person spoke? Did you look at the speaker?

Direct eye contact can mean different things in different cultures, but in U.S. culture, eye contact is the primary means for an audience to demonstrate that they are listening to a speaker. Nobody likes to be ignored, and most members of an audience would not want to be perceived as ignoring the speaker – that would be rude!

Compare: before CR, the frame of reference reflects the idea that "everyone is staring at me"; after CR, the perception is altered to "the audience is looking at me to be supportive and polite– after all, I'm the one doing the talking."

Fear of Judgment

Another common concern is the fear of being judged harshly or making an embarrassing mistake. Go back to that memory of you as a member of the audience, but this time reflect on what sort of expectations you had at the time. Did you expect the speaker to be flawless and riveting? Did you have in mind some super-high level of performance – below which the speaker would have disappointed you? You probably did not (unless you had the chance to watch some prominent speaker).

Think back to any experiences you may have had watching another speaker struggle – perhaps a classmate during one of their presentations. Witnessing something like that can be uncomfortable. Did you feel empathy for the person struggling? Isn't it a much more pleasant experience when the speaker does well? Again, the vast majority of people empathize with the speaker when it comes to the quality of the presentation. They are willing to give the speaker a
chance to say what they want to say.

Thus: before CR, the frame of reference reflects the idea that "everyone is judging me harshly"; and after CR, the perception is altered to "the audience is willing to listen to what I have to say because it's a more pleasant experience for them if the speaker is successful."

2.3 LEARNING CONFIDENCE

"Believe you can, and you're halfway there." -Theodore Roosevelt

Consider what comes into your mind if you are to deliver a public presentation. Are your thoughts consumed with many uncertainties? What if I make a mistake? What if they don't like what I'm talking about? What if? Try your own version of CR. Put yourself in the role of audience member and ask yourself whether your fears as a speaker are consistent with your expectations as an audience member. Remember that, just like you, the audience wants the speaker to succeed.

Of course CR, unfortunately, is always easier said than done. It is a process that takes time, patience, and practice. The most important thing to remember is that you are trying CR as a means of breaking a habit, and habits are formed over periods of time, never instantaneously. The breaking of a habit, similarly, cannot be done instantaneously, but gradually, over time and with deliberate effort.

Changing your attitude is only one element in overcoming CA. The other involves improving your skills as a speaker. The presence of CA in any student brings with it the need to prepare more deliberately and more diligently. The other chapters in this book deal with the importance of preparation in all areas of public presentation. Readers should consider how the challenges involved with overcoming CA can impact the preparation process.

Techniques for Building Confidence

Prepare Well

The correlation between preparation and nervousness is consistent. More practice results in less nervousness. The best, most consistent and direct way to minimize the level of nervousness you feel is through effective preparation. This is always true.

Michael Jordan was once asked the best way to learn how to shoot free throws. To everyone's surprise, the first step he described did not entail actually shooting the ball. He described how the first step in learning to shoot free throws is to run sprints. Most importantly, his advice was to run until your body was under the same stress as it would be in a game when you needed to make those free throws – because only under those conditions would your practice become truly productive. Only then do you pick up the ball and shoot.

All types of preparation and practice yield some benefits, but there is a significant difference between practice that is merely helpful and practice that is sufficient. There is a difference between "knowing what you are talking about," and "knowing what you are going to say."

Thinking about your presentation can be helpful, but that sort of preparation will not give you a sense of what you are actually going to say. Athletes know that the best practices will re-create game conditions and test their abilities to perform in real-life scenarios.

Many students do not practice effectively, and this can result in the wrong idea that practice isn't helpful. Unfortunately, these same students usually have had little, if any, training in how one might prepare for a presentation, and so they employ the scholastic training they are most familiar with – how to write a paper. This is not the same activity as presenting, and so the lack of proper preparation only contributes to the lack of confidence. Let's look at a few elements of effective practice.

Visualize Success

Athletes and performers are often coached to visualize what they are trying to do as a way to perform correctly. Football and basketball players must envision how each member of the team will move during a particular play because team success depends on speedy and flawless coordination between individuals. Dancers and divers are trained to visualize the form and positioning of their bodies as they execute their moves. Engaging the imagination in this way can be beneficial to performance.

Speakers too, should visualize success. As you practice, visualize yourself presenting with confidence to a receptive audience. "See" your relaxed facial expressions and "hear" your confident tone of voice. Imagine yourself moving gracefully, complementing what you say with expressive gestures.

Imagine the audience reacting appropriately – nodding appreciatively and giving thoughtful consideration to your points. Imagine the gratification of watching the audience really "get it." When you can honestly envision yourself performing at this level, you are taking an important step toward achieving that goal.

Avoid Gimmicks

Some acting coaches (and speech teachers) encourage their students to practice in front of mirrors, so that they can watch themselves perform and evaluate how they move. In acting, this can be very useful; but in speaking, it is less so.

When you practice your presentation, the most important element is expressiveness. You want to become more familiar with the volume of material, the order in which you plan to present it, and the phrasing you think would be most effective to express it.

Watching yourself perform in a mirror will focus your attention on your appearance first – and on what you express second. This makes using a mirror during practice a distraction from what the practice ought to achieve.

For some reason, the myth persists that imagining your audience in their pajamas – or something similarly silly – is an effective way to make standing in front of them seem less scary. These sorts of gimmicks don't work! In fact, concentrating on anything other than what you are doing is distracting and not beneficial at all. Do your best to avoid such advice. Visualize success!

Breathe and Release

One type of pre-presentation exercise that might be helpful is based on a therapeutic idea called **systematic de-sensitization**. A multi-stage regimen to help patients deal with phobias through coping mechanisms, which involves gradual exposure to what produces the anxiety, long-term self-reflection, and mental discipline.

Here, we will discuss a shortened version called "**breathe and release**." This relaxation technique could be useful for nervous speakers – especially those who are concerned with the physical manifestations of nervousness, such as shaky hands or knees.

The key to "breathe and release" is to understand that when nervous tension results in minor trembling, the effort of trying to keep one's hands from shaking can contribute to the whole situation – that is, trying to stop literally can make it worse! Therefore, the best approach is through relaxation.

How to Breathe and Release

1. Imagine the nervousness within your body. Imagine the energy bubbling inside you, like boiling water.
2. Draw that energy to a high point within your body through a deep, cleansing breath. Imagine this cleansing breath like a vacuum, inhaling all of the bubbling liquid.
3. Release the energy by deliberately relaxing your upper body, all the way from your fingertips to your shoulder blades. Imagine how keeping any part of your upper extremities tense would result in a "kink" in the release valve, and so complete relaxation is the key to success.

Minimize What You Memorize

One important hint for speech preparation involves avoiding the writing of an entirely scripted version of the presentation. A speech outline is not a monologue or manuscript; it is a guideline and should be used as a roadmap for your speech.

Remember that lunch with your friends? When you were describing the movie plot, you were being conversant in a prepared way. This means that you knew what you were describing, but you were not concerned with the specific words you were using. Being conversant is the condition of being prepared to discuss an issue intelligently.

A well-prepared speaker is with regard to her topic. Consider how being conversant in this manner allows freer, more fluid communication, with no stress associated with your ability to remember what words you wanted to use. Being conversant also gives the speaker the best chance to recognize and react to audience feedback.

If you are completely focused on the integrity of scripted comments, then you will be unable to read and react to your audience in any meaningful way. Imagine how frustrating it would be for your friends at that lunch if you would not respond to any of their questions until you were finished reading a few descriptive paragraphs about the movie. They would probably just wait until you were done reading and then try to engage you in a conversation!

Practice Out Loud

Remember the very first time you tried to do anything – a game, a sport, an activity, anything at all. How good were you out of the gate? Perhaps you had talent or were gifted with a "feel" for what you were doing. But even then, didn't you get better with more experience? Nobody does anything the very best they can on their very first attempt, and everyone – even the most talented among us – benefit from effective practice.

Speaking in public is no different from any other activity in this way. To maximize the chance that your presentation will come out smooth and polished, you will need to hear it all the way through. By practicing out loud, from the beginning to the ending, you will be able to listen to your whole speech and properly gauge the flow of your entire presentation.

Additionally, without at least one complete out-loud practice, there will be no way to accurately estimate the length of your speech and your preparation will remain insufficient.

When dealing with CA, the last thing you want is to leave some questions unanswered in your own mind! The out-loud "dress rehearsal" is the single, most important element to your preparation. Without it, you will be delivering your presentation in full for the first time when it counts the most. Putting yourself at that sort of disadvantage isn't wise, and is easily avoided.

You might even consider trying that initial practice without the benefit of any notes. Stand up; start speaking; see what comes out! During your initial practice consider these questions:

1. Where, during your presentation, are you most – and least – conversant?
2. Where, during your presentation, are you most in need of supportive notes?
3. What do your notes need to contain?

Prepare for your public presentation by speaking and listening to yourself, rather than by writing, editing, and rewriting. Remember that when you are having a conversation, you never use the same sort of language and syntax as you do when you are writing a formal paper. Practice with the goal of becoming conversant in your topic, not fluent with a script.

Customize Your Practice

Depending on your personal level of CA, you may choose to implement techniques previously mentioned in different ways. Take a moment to reflect on what causes your CA. Do you dislike the feeling of being the center of attention? Are you more concerned with who is in the audience and what they might think of you? Or are you worried about "freezing" in front of the audience and forgetting what you wanted to say?

Write some of these concerns down and put them into a priority order. If you are worried about a particular issue or problem, how might you prepare to minimize the chance of that issue arising?

Now, consider your current method of preparation. Do you prepare more for a written paper than for an oral presentation? Do you have the goal of presenting a scripted message? Do you practice out loud? When, during your process, do you practice aloud? Do you practice at all before you begin to compose your speaking notes; or do you only practice after? Remember that dealing with CA often involves the breaking of a mental habit. It is a good idea to change what you have done previously. Be deliberate. Observe what works for your situation.

As stated earlier in the chapter: Each individual deals with CA most effectively through increased self-awareness and a willingness to take each of the steps in the entire process. After you acknowledge your reality, then you take the steps necessary to overcome apprehension.

When you've read about the ways to overcome the debilitating impact of CA, the next steps in your process involve seeing what works best for you. Do not continue to prepare in exactly the same way as before. Speak more; write and revise less. Be sure to practice out-loud at least once during your preparation, in order to prepare yourself sufficiently. Reflect on your personal concerns and try Cognitive Restructuring on those concerns. Take your time. Do the work. Have confidence that your preparation will yield positive results.

Conclusion

In this chapter, we've discussed Communication Apprehension or CA. This difficult condition can be the result of many, varied causes. Even professional researchers don't always agree on whether CA is inherent in the person, or the result of what the person experiences or perceives– with some calling it "trait-anxiety;" others "state-anxiety;" and still others classifying it as "scrutiny fear." The first step for any person to address this condition is self-reflection.

Try to identify what has caused you to feel the way you do about public speaking. Careful introspection can result in a more productive level of self-awareness. Whatever the root cause of CA might be for any particular individual, the first step in addressing CA is to objectively view the habitual frame of reference that has emerged in your mind regarding public speaking. Consider all those "what-if's" that keep cropping up in your mind and how you might begin to address them productively, rather than simply to ignore them and hope they go away. Go through the steps of Cognitive Restructuring or CR. Consider how many of those "what-if's" are nothing more than invented pressure that you place upon yourself.

Relaxation techniques, such as "Breathe and Release," have proven to be effective for many speakers, especially those concerned with the physical manifestations of nervousness like trembling hands or shaky knees. Remember that those sorts of tremors can often be exacerbated by efforts to hold still. Don't force yourself to hold still! Relax instead.

Lastly, we discussed the most effective means to prepare – which is toward the goal of becoming conversant in your topic, rather than being able to recite a memorized script. By familiarizing yourself with your topic, you become better able to consider the best way to talk to your audience, rather than becoming "married to your script" and ultimately consumed with saying the words in the right order. Practicing out-loud, without a mirror to distract you, is the best way to prepare yourself.

CA is a real issue, but it need not be an obstacle to success. Take the time to become more aware of your personal brand of CA. Take positive steps to minimize its impact. Your willingness to work and your positive attitude are the keys to your success.

The author of this chapter says that one of the keys to overcoming nervousness is preparation. Make a list of the barriers to your own preparation process (e.g. "I don't know how to use the library," or "I have young children at home who make demands on my time"). Having identified some of the things that make it difficult for you to prepare, now think of at least one way to overcome each obstacle you have listed. If you need to, speak with other people to get their ideas too.

References

Adler, R. B., (1980). Integrating reticence management into the basic communication curriculum. *Communication Education, 29*, 215-221.

Beatty, M.J. (1988). Public speaking apprehension, decision-making errors in the selection of speech introduction strategies and adherence to strategy. *Communication Education, 37*, 297 – 311.

Daly, J. A. & Leth, S. A., (1976), Communication Apprehension and the Personnel Selection Decision, Paper presented at the *International Communication Association Convention*, Portland, OR.

Dwyer, K. & Cruz, A (1998), Communication Apprehension, Personality, and Grades in the Basic Course: Are There Correlations? *Communication Research Reports, 15*(4), 436- 444.

Mattick, R. P., Peters, L., & Clarke, J. C., (1989) Exposure and cognitive restructuring for social phobia: A controlled study. *Behavior Therapy, 20*, 3-23.

McCroskey, J. C., & Anderson, J. (1976). The relationship between communication apprehension and academic achievement among college students, *Human Communication Research, 3*, 73-81.

McCroskey, J. C. (1977). Oral Communication Apprehension: A summary of recent theory and research. *Human Communication Research, 4*, 78-96

McCroskey, J. C. (1984). The communication apprehensive perspective. In J. A.

Daly & J. C. McCroskey (Eds.), *Avoiding communication: Shyness, reticence, and communication apprehension.* Beverly Hills, CA: Sage Publications, Inc.

McCroskey, J. C. (1976) The Problem of Communication Apprehension in the Classroom, Paper prepared for the special edition of Communication, *Journal of the Communication Association of the Pacific compiled for the C.A.P. Convention* (Kobe, Japan, June 1976).

Menzel, K. E., &Carrell, L. J., (1994). The relationship between preparation and performance in public speaking, *Communication Education, 43,* 17-26.

Pelias, M. H. (1989). Communication apprehension in basic public speaking texts: An examination of contemporary textbooks. *Communication Education, 38*(1), 41- 53.

2.4 ENRICHMENT

Discussion Questions

1. What are some suggestions from the lecture and/or textbook regarding speaking with confidence that you plan to utilize?
2. When you see a speaker who is obviously feeling nervous, how can you as an audience member help put the speaker at ease? How can thinking about your experiences as an audience member help you feel less nervous as a speaker?
3. Which form of communication apprehension discussed in Section 2:2: Classifying Communication Apprehension affects you most? How so?

Activities

1. Complete the Personal Report of Public Speaking Anxiety (PRPSA, McCroskey, 1970) and determine your score. Consider whether that score seems accurate. Visit with a friend or classmate about your results. Document your score so you can fill out the PRPSA again at the end of the class and compare your beginning and ending scores.
2. Go to the following website and follow along with Dr. Ellisha Goldstein's 3-Minute Body Scan. Pay particular attention to your own body and decide whether a body scan or a meditation practice may help with your communication apprehension.

3 DELIVERY

Learning Objectives

- List the different methods of speech delivery.
- Identify key elements in preparing to deliver a speech.
- Describe the benefits of delivery-related behaviors.
- Utilize specific techniques to enhance speech delivery.

Key Terms

- **Extemporaneous Speaking**
- **Impromptu Speaking**
- **Lectern**
- **Manuscript Speaking**
- **Memorized Speaking**
- **Monotone**
- **Pitch**
- **Rate**
- **Tone**
- **Vocal Cue**
- **Vocalized Pauses**
- **Volume**

3.1 THE IMPORTANCE OF DELIVERY

"We are what we repeatedly do. Excellence, then, is not an act, but a habit." -Will Durant

Some surveys indicate that many people claim to fear public speaking more than death, but this finding is somewhat misleading. No one is afraid of writing their speech or conducting the research. Instead, people generally only fear the delivery aspect of the speech, which, compared to the amount of time you will put into writing the speech (days, hopefully), will be the shortest part of the speech giving process (5-8 minutes, generally, for classroom speeches). The irony, of course, is that delivery, being the thing people fear the most, is simultaneously the aspect of public speaking that will require the least amount of time.

Consider this scenario about two students, Bob and Chris. Bob spends weeks doing research and crafting a beautifully designed speech that, on the day he gets in front of the class, he messes up a little because of nerves. While he may view it as a complete failure, his audience will have gotten a lot of good information and most likely written off his mistakes due to nerves, since they would be nervous in the same situation!

Chris, on the other hand, does almost no preparation for his speech, but, being charming and comfortable in front of a crowd, smiles a lot while providing virtually nothing of substance. The audience takeaway from Chris's speech is, "I have no idea what he was talking about" and other feelings ranging from "He's good in front of an audience" to "I don't trust him." So the moral here is that a well-prepared speech that is delivered poorly is still a well-prepared speech, whereas a poorly written speech delivered superbly is still a poorly written speech.

Despite this irony, we realize that delivery is what you are probably most concerned about when it comes to giving speeches, so this chapter is designed to help you achieve the best delivery possible and eliminate some of the nervousness you might be feeling. To do that, ***we should first dismiss the myth that public speaking is just reading and talking at the same time.*** You already know how to read, and you already know how to talk, which is why you're taking a class called "public speaking" and not one called "public talking" or "public reading."

Speaking in public has more formality than talking. During a speech, you should present yourself professionally. This doesn't necessarily mean you must wear a suit or "dress up" unless your instructor asks you to. However, it does mean making yourself presentable by being well-groomed and wearing clean, appropriate clothes. It also means being prepared to use language correctly and appropriately for the audience and the topic, to make eye contact with your audience, and to look like you know your topic very well.

While speaking has more formality than talking, it has less formality than reading. Speaking allows for flexibility, meaningful pauses, eye contact, small changes in word order, and vocal emphasis. Reading is a more or less exact replication of words on paper without the use of any nonverbal interpretation. Speaking, as you will realize if you think about excellent speakers you have seen and heard, provides a more animated message.

Pete's Practice

As the day of his public speaking engagement drew near, Pistol Pete found himself grappling with a common concern that many speakers face – what to do with his hands during his speech. As the spirited mascot of Oklahoma State University, Pete was well-versed in captivating audiences with his energetic presence on the field, but standing behind a podium in a formal setting felt entirely different.

With each passing day, his anxiety grew. During his practice sessions, Pete would awkwardly fidget with his hands, unsure of where to place them or how to use them effectively. He worried that his usual animated gestures might be too distracting or inappropriate for a formal speech.

Late one evening, Pete confided in a close friend, expressing his nervousness and concern about his upcoming speech. His friend, a seasoned public speaker, offered some reassuring advice. They encouraged Pete to focus on being natural and genuine, advising him to use his hands to emphasize important points and to express his passion for the topic.

Taking the advice to heart, Pete decided to rehearse his speech once more. This time, he consciously let go of his worries about his hand movements and embraced a more relaxed approach. He discovered that by using his hands to complement his words, he felt more connected to the audience and his message.

On the day of his speech, as Pete stood before the audience, he took a deep breath and reminded himself of the advice he had received. As he began to speak, he felt a newfound confidence in his gestures. He allowed his hands to express his enthusiasm, creating a natural flow that resonated with the crowd.

As the speech progressed, Pete's worries about his hands faded away. Instead, he focused on sharing the captivating story of Frank Eaton and his legacy, letting his gestures amplify the emotions and importance of his words. In that moment, Pistol Pete realized that sometimes, the best thing to do with his hands was to let them be an extension of his authentic self, creating a genuine connection with the audience and leaving a lasting impression. How comfortable are you with using your hands effectively during a presentation?

3.2 METHODS OF SPEECH DELIVERY

What follows are four methods of delivery that can help you balance between too much and too little formality when giving a speech. Each has its own strengths and weaknesses, but you will most likely want to focus on the extemporaneous approach, since that is probably what your instructor will want from you.

Impromptu Speaking

Impromptu speaking is the presentation of a short message without advance preparation. You have probably done impromptu speaking many times in informal, conversational settings. Self-introductions in group settings are examples of impromptu speaking: "Hi, my name is Steve, and I'm a volunteer with the Homes for the Brave program." Another example of impromptu speaking occurs when you answer a question such as, "What did you think of the movie?" Your response has not been preplanned, and you are constructing your arguments and points as you speak. Even worse, you might find yourself going into a meeting and your boss says, "I want you to talk about the last stage of the project. . . " and you have no warning.

The advantage of this kind of speaking is that it's spontaneous and responsive in an animated group context. The disadvantage is that the speaker is given little or no time to contemplate the central theme of his or her message. As a result, the message may be disorganized and difficult for listeners to follow.

Here is a step-by-step guide that may be useful if you are called upon to give an impromptu speech in public:

1. Take a moment to collect your thoughts and plan the main point or points you want to make.
2. Thank the person for inviting you to speak. Do not make comments about being unprepared, called upon at the last moment, on the spot, or uneasy. No one wants to hear that and it will embarrass others and yourself.
3. Deliver your message, making your main point as briefly as you can while still covering it adequately and at a pace your listeners can follow.
4. Stay on track. Answer the question or prompt as given; resist the temptation to go elsewhere.
5. If you can, use a structure, using numbers if possible: "Two main reasons..." or "Three parts of our plan..." or "Two side effects of this drug..." Past, present, and future or East Coast, Midwest, and West Coast are common structures.
6. Thank the person again for the opportunity to speak.
7. Stop talking (it is easy to "ramble on" when you don't have something prepared). If in front of an audience, don't keep talking as you move back to your seat.

Impromptu speeches are generally most successful when they are brief and focus on a single point.

Manuscript Speaking

Manuscript speaking is the word-for-word iteration of a written message. In a manuscript speech, the speaker maintains his or her attention on the printed page except when using visual aids. The advantage to reading from a manuscript is the exact repetition of original words. In some circumstances this can be extremely important. For example, reading a statement about your organization's legal responsibilities to customers may require that the original words be exact.

In reading one word at a time, in order, the only errors would typically be mispronunciation of a word or stumbling over complex sentence structure. A manuscript speech may also be appropriate at a more formal affair (like a funeral), when your speech must be said exactly as written in order to convey the proper emotion or decorum the situation deserves.However, there are costs involved in manuscript speaking. First, it's typically an uninteresting way to present. Unless the speaker has rehearsed the reading as a complete performance animated with vocal expression and gestures (well-known authors often do this for book readings), the presentation tends to be dull. Keeping one's eyes glued to the script prevents eye contact with the audience. For this kind of "straight" manuscript speech to hold audience attention, the audience must be already interested in the message and speaker before the delivery begins.It is worth noting that professional speakers, actors, news reporters, and politicians often read from an autocue device, such as a TelePrompTer, especially when appearing on television, where eye contact with the camera is crucial. With practice, a speaker can achieve a conversational tone and give the impression of speaking extemporaneously and maintaining eye contact while using an autocue device. However, success in this medium depends on two factors: (1) the speaker is already an accomplished public speaker who has learned to use a conversational tone while delivering a prepared script, and (2) the speech is written in a style that sounds conversational and in spoken rather than written, edited English, for example, with shorter sentences and clearer transitions.For the purposes of your public speaking class, you will not be encouraged to read your speech. Instead, you will be asked to give an extemporaneous presentation.

Extemporaneous Speaking

Extemporaneous speaking is the presentation of a carefully planned and rehearsed speech, spoken in a conversational manner using brief notes. By using notes rather than a full manuscript, the extemporaneous speaker can establish and maintain eye contact with the audience and assess how well they are understanding the speech as it progresses. And since you will be graded (to some degree) on establishing and maintaining eye contact with your audience, extemporaneous speaking can be extremely beneficial in that regard. Without all the words on the page to read, you have little choice but to look up and make eye contact with your audience. In some cases, your instructor will require you to prepare strong preparation and speaking (notes) outlines as a foundation for your speech; this topic is addressed in Chapter 6.

Speaking extemporaneously has some advantages. It promotes the likelihood that you, the speaker, will be perceived as knowledgeable and credible since you know the speech well enough that you don't need to read it. In addition, your audience is likely to pay better attention to the message because it is engaging both verbally and nonverbally. It also allows flexibility; you are working from the strong foundation of an outline, but if you need to delete, add, or rephrase something at the last minute or to adapt to your audience, you can do so. The outline also helps you be aware of main ideas vs. subordinate ones.

The disadvantage of extemporaneous speaking is that it in some cases it does not allow for the verbal and the nonverbal preparation that are almost always required for a good speech. Adequate preparation cannot be achieved the day before you're scheduled to speak, so be aware that if you want to present a credibly delivered speech, you will need to practice many times. Because extemporaneous speaking is the style used in the great majority of public speaking situations, most of the information in the subsequent sections of this chapter is targeted toward this kind of speaking.

Memorized Speaking

Memorized speaking is the rote recitation of a written message that the speaker has committed to memory. Actors, of course, recite from memory whenever they perform from a script. When it comes to speeches, memorization can be useful when the message needs to be exact and the speaker doesn't want to be confined by notes.

The advantage to memorization is that it enables the speaker to maintain eye contact with the audience throughout the speech. Being free of notes means that you can move freely around the stage and use your hands to make gestures. If your speech uses visual aids, this freedom is even more of an advantage.

However, there are some real and potential costs. First, unless you also plan and

3.2 METHODS OF SPEECH DELIVERY

memorize every **vocal cue** (the subtle but meaningful variations in speech delivery, which can include the use of pitch, tone, volume, and pace), gesture, and facial expression, your presentation will be flat and uninteresting, and even the most fascinating topic will suffer. You might end up speaking in a monotone or a sing-song repetitive delivery pattern. You might also present your speech in a rapid "machine-gun" style that fails to emphasize the most important points.

Second, if you lose your place and start trying to ad lib, the contrast in your style of delivery will alert your audience that something is wrong. If you go completely blank during the presentation, it will be extremely difficult to find your place and keep going. Obviously, memorizing a typical seven-minute classroom speech takes a great deal of time and effort, and if you aren't used to memorizing, it is very difficult to pull off. Realistically, you probably will not have the time necessary to give a completely memorized speech. However, if you practice adequately, you will approach the feeling of memorized while still being extemporaneous.

As we said earlier, for the purposes of this class you will use extemporaneous speaking. Many professional speakers who are paid to make speeches use this approach because, while they may largely know what they want to say, they usually make changes and adjustments based on the audience or event. This approach also incorporates most of the benefits of memorized speaking (knowing what you want to say; being very thoroughly rehearsed) and manuscript speaking (having some words in front of you to refer to) without the inherent pitfalls those approaches bring with them.

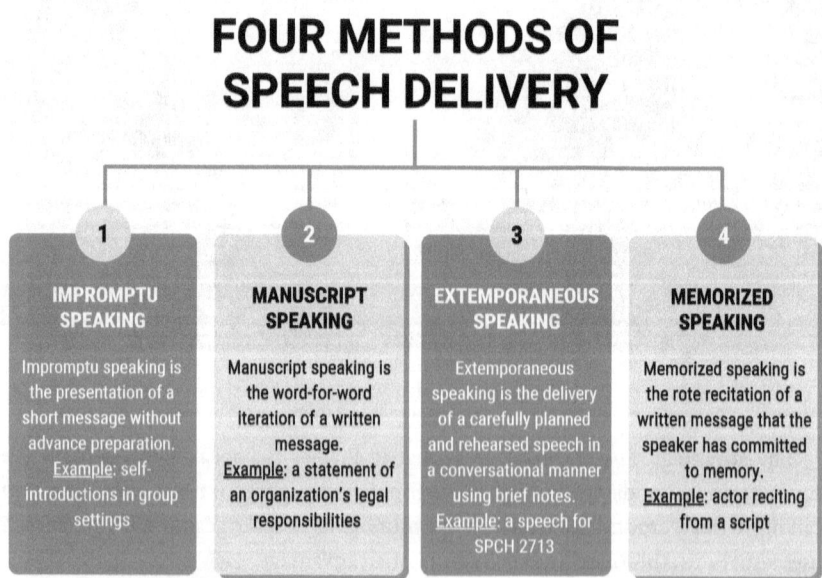

3.3 PREPARING FOR YOUR DELIVERY

In the 1970s, before he was an author, playwright, and film actor, Steve Martin was an up-and-coming stand-up comedian whose popularity soared as a result of his early appearances on *The Tonight Show with Johnny Carson* and *Saturday Night Live*. As Martin notes in his autobiography, *Born Standing Up* (2008), as the audiences for his act got bigger and bigger, he needed to adapt his delivery to accommodate:

> Some promoters got on board and booked me into a theater in Dallas. Before the show I asked one of them, How many people are out there?" "Two thousand," he said. Two thousand? How could there be two thousand? That night I did my usual bit of taking people outside, but it was starting to get dangerous and difficult. First, people were standing in the streets, where they could be hit by a car. Second, only a small number of the audience could hear or see me (could Charlton Heston really have been audible when he was addressing a thousand extras?). Third, it didn't seem as funny or direct with so many people; I reluctantly dropped it from my repertoire. (p. 168)

Martin's audiences would grow to be around 50,000 at the height of his popularity as a stand-up comedian, again requiring him to make adjustments to his delivery (he began wearing his iconic all-white suit so that people in the nosebleed seats at his shows could still see his frenetic movements from afar). Most of us will never speak to so many people at once, but even though you don't expect an audience of such size, you should still be prepared to adapt to the setting in which you will speak.

Your audiences, circumstances, and physical contexts for public speaking will vary. At some point in your life you may run for public office or rise to a leadership role in a business or volunteer organization. Or you may be responsible for informing coworkers about a new policy, regulation, or opportunity. You may be asked to deliver remarks in the context of a worship service, wedding, or funeral. You may be asked to introduce a keynote speaker or simply to make an important announcement in some context. Sometimes you will speak in a familiar environment, while at other times you may be faced with an unfamiliar location and have very little time to get used to speaking with a microphone. Being prepared to deal with different speaking situations will help reduce anxiety you may have about giving a speech, so let's look at factors you need to keep in mind as you prepare for your speech in this class, as well as future speeches you may need to give.

Using Lecterns

A **lectern** is a small raised surface, usually with a slanted top, where a speaker can place notes during a speech. While a lectern adds a measure of formality to the speaking situation, it also allows speakers the freedom to do two things: to come out from behind the lectern to establish more immediate contact with the audience and to use both hands for gestures. By the way, this piece of furniture is often mistakenly called a podium, which is a raised platform or stage.

However, for inexperienced speakers who feel anxious, it is all too tempting to grip the edges of the lectern with both hands for security. You might even wish you could hide behind it. Be aware of these temptations so you can manage them effectively and present yourself to your audience in a manner they will perceive as confident. One way to achieve this is by limiting your use of the lectern to a place to rest your notes only. Try stepping to the side or front of the lectern when speaking with free hands, only occasionally standing at the lectern to consult your notes. This will enhance your eye contact as well as free up your hands for gesturing.

Speaking in a Small or Large Physical Space

If you are accustomed to being in a classroom of a certain size, you will need to make adjustments when speaking in a smaller or larger space than what you are used to. A large auditorium can be intimidating, especially for speakers who feel shy and "exposed" when facing an audience. However, the maxim that "proper preparation prevents poor performance" is just as true here as anywhere. If you have prepared and practiced well, you can approach a large-venue speaking engagement with confidence.

In terms of practical adjustments, be aware that your voice is likely to echo, especially if far fewer people are in the space than it can hold, so you will want to speak more slowly as well as more loudly than usual and make use of pauses to mark the ends of phrases and sentences. Similarly, your facial expressions and gestures should be larger so that they are visible from farther away. If you are using visual aids, they need to be large enough to be visible from the back of the auditorium. Of course, if the speaker can get the audience to move to the front, that is the best situation, but it tends not to happen.

Limited space is not as disconcerting for most speakers as enormous space, and it has the advantage of minimizing the tendency to pace back and forth while you speak. A small space also calls for more careful management of note cards and visual aids, as your audience will be able to see up close what you are doing with your hands. Do your best to minimize fumbling, including setting up in advance or arriving early to decide how to organize your materials in the physical space. Of course, if you have any control over the location of the presentation, you should choose one that fits the size of your audience.

Speaking Outdoors

Outdoor settings can be charming, but they are prone to distractions. If you're giving a speech in a setting that is picturesquely beautiful or prone to noise such as from cars, it may be difficult to maintain the audience's attention. If you know this ahead of time, you might plan your speech to focus more on mood than information and perhaps to make reference to the lovely view.

More typically, outdoor speech venues can pose challenges with weather, sun glare, and uninvited guests, such as insects and pigeons. If the venue is located near a busy highway, it might be difficult to make yourself heard over the ambient noise. You might lack the usual accommodations, such as a lectern or table. Whatever the situation, you will need to use your best efforts to project your voice clearly without sounding like you're yelling or straining your voice. In the best outdoor situation, you will have access to a microphone.

Using A Microphone

Most people today are familiar with microphones that are built into video recorders, phones, and other electronic devices, but they may be new at using a microphone to deliver a speech. One overall principle to remember is that a microphone only amplifies, it does not clarify. If you are not enunciating clearly, the microphone will merely enable your audience to hear amplified mumbling. Microphones come in a wide range of styles and sizes. Generally, the easiest microphone to use is the clip-on style worn on the front of your shirt or blouse. (These are commonly referred to as a Lavalier mic, which is a brand name.) If you look closely at many television personalities and news anchors, you will notice these tiny microphones clipped to their clothing. They require very little adaptation. You simply have to avoid looking down—at your notes, for instance—because your voice will be amplified when you do so. If you have to use a hand-held microphone, making gestures and using notes becomes very difficult. Lectern and handheld microphones require more adaptation.

If they're too close to your mouth, they can screech. If they're too far away, they might not pick up your voice. Some microphones are directional, meaning that they are only effective when you speak directly into them. If there is any opportunity to do so, ask for tips about how to use a particular microphone. Also practice with it for a few minutes while you have someone listen from a middle row in the audience and signal whether you can be heard well. The best plan, of course, would be to have access to the microphone for practice ahead of the speaking date. Often a microphone is provided when it isn't necessary. If the room is small or the audience is close to you, do not feel obligated to use the microphone. Sometimes an amplified voice can feel less natural and less compelling than a direct voice. However, if you forgo the microphone, make sure to speak loudly enough for all audience members to hear you—not just those in front.

Audience Size

A small audience is an opportunity for a more intimate, informal tone. If your audience has only eight to twelve people, you can generate greater audience contact. Make use of all the preparation you have done. You do not have to revamp your speech just because the audience is small. When the presentation is over, there will most likely be opportunities to answer questions and have individual contact with your listeners.

One problem with a small audience is that some people will feel it is their right, or they have permission, to interrupt you or raise their hands to ask questions in the middle of your speech. This makes for a difficult situation, because the question may be irrelevant to your topic or cause you to go on a side track if answered. The best you can do is say you'll try to deal with that question at the end of the speech if you have time and hope they take the hint. Better, good rules should be established at the beginning that state there is limited time but discussion may be possible at the end.

Your classroom audience may be as many as twenty to thirty students. The format for an audience of this size is formal but conversational. Depending on how your instructor structures the class, you may or may not be asked to leave time after your speech for questions and answers. Some audiences are much larger. If you have an audience that fills an auditorium, or if you have an auditorium with only a few people in it, you still have a clearly formal task, and you should be guided as much as possible by your preparation.

3.4 PRACTICING YOUR DELIVERY

There is no foolproof recipe for good delivery. Each of us is unique, and we each embody different experiences and interests. This means each person has an approach, or a style, that is effective for her or him. This further means that anxiety can accompany even the most carefully researched and interesting message. But there are some techniques you can use to minimize that anxious feeling and put yourself in the best possible position to succeed on speech day. If you've ever watched your favorite college football team practice, you may have noticed that sometimes obnoxiously loud crowd noise is blaring over the speaker system in the stadium. The coaches know that the crowd, whether home or away, will be raucous and noisy on game day. So to prepare, they practice in as realistic an environment as possible. You need to prepare for your speech in a similar way. What follows are some general tips you should keep in mind, but they all essentially derive from one very straight-forward premise:

Practice your speech beforehand, at home or elsewhere, the way you will give it in class.

Practice Your Speech Out Loud

We sometimes think that the purpose of practicing a speech is to learn the words and be prepared for what we will need to say. Certainly that is part of it, but practice also lets you know where potential problems lie. For example, if you only read your speech in your head, or whisper the words quietly, you're not really practicing what you will be doing in front of the class. Since you will be speaking with a normal volume for your assignment, you need to practice that way, even at home. Not only will this help you learn the speech, but it will help identify any places where you tend to mispronounce or stumble over words. Also, sentences on paper do not always translate well to the spoken medium. Practicing out loud allows you to actually hear where your sentences and phrases are awkward, unnatural, or too long, and allows you to correct them before getting up in front of the audience.

Practice Your Speech Standing Up

In all the time that the authors of this book have been teaching speech, not once have either of us come into a classroom and seen a bed behind the lectern for students to speak from. This is to say that when you practice at home, lying on your bed reading your speech really only prepares you for one thing: lying on a bed reading a speech. Since you will be standing in front of your class, you need to practice that way. As we mention in more detail below, the default position for delivering a speech is with your feet shoulder-width apart and your knees slightly bent. Practicing this way will help develop muscle memory and will make it feel more natural when you are doing it for real. We also suggest you wear the same shoes you will be wearing on the day of your speech.

Practice Your Speech with a Lectern

One of the biggest challenges with practicing a speech as you're going to give it is usually the fact that most of us don't own a lectern. This is problematic, since you don't want to practice giving your speech while holding your notes in front of you because that is what will feel comfortable when you give your speech for real. So the solution is to practice your speech while standing behind something that approximates the lectern you will have in your classroom. Sometime this may be a kitchen counter or maybe even a dresser you pull away from the wall. One particularly creative idea that has been used in the past is to pull out an ironing board and stand behind that. The point is that you want to get experience standing behind something and resting your speech on it.

Of course, if you really want to practice with an actual lectern, it might be worth the time to see if your classroom is empty later in the day or find out if another classroom has the same type of lectern in it. Practicing with the "real thing" is always ideal.

Practice Your Speech with an Audience

Obviously on the day you give your speech you will have an audience of your fellow students and your professor watching you. The best way to prepare for the feeling of having someone watch you while giving a speech is to have someone watch you while you practice giving a speech. We don't mean a collection of stuffed animals arranged on your bed or locking your pets in the room with you, but actual human beings. Ask your parents, siblings, friends, or significant other to listen to you while running through what you will say. Not only will you get practice in front of an audience, but they may be able to tell you about any parts that were unclear or problems you might encounter when you give it for a grade.

Not to overcomplicate the issue, but remember that when you speak to your class, you will have an entire room full of people watching. Therefore, if you only have one person watching you practice, be sure to simulate an entire audience by looking around the room and not focusing on just that one person. When you give your speech for real, you will want to make eye contact with the people on the left side of the room as well as the right; with the people in the front as well as in the back. You also want the eye contact to be around five seconds long, not just a glance; the idea is that you are talking to individuals, not just a glob of people. During practice, it may help to pick out some strategically placed objects around the room to occasionally focus on just to get into the habit of looking around more often.

Practice Your Speech for Time

You will undoubtedly be given a time limit for each of your speeches, and points will probably be deducted from your grade if you go over or under that time. Therefore, you want to make sure you are well within time. As a general rule, if your speech window is 5-7 minutes, your ideal speech time is going to be 6 minutes; this gives you an extra 60 seconds at the beginning in case you talk very fast and race through it, and 60 seconds on the back end in case you get lost or want to add something at the last minute. If you practice at home and your 5-7 minute speech lasts 5:06, you are probably going to be in trouble on speech day. Most likely your nerves will cause you to speak slightly faster and put you under the 5:00 mark. If your times are vastly different, you may have to practice four or more times.

When practicing your speech at home for time, it is a good idea to time yourself at least three times. This way you can see if you are generally coming in around the same time and feel pretty good that it is an accurate reflection of how long you will speak. Conversely, if during your three rehearsals your times are 5:45, 5:12, and 6:37, then that is a clear indicator that you need to be more consistent in what you are saying and doing.

Although we are using examples of practicing for classroom speeches, the principle is even more important for non-classroom speeches. One of the authors had to give a very important presentation about the college to an accreditation board. She practiced about 15 times, to make sure the time was right, that her transitions made sense, that she was fluid, and that the presentational slides and her speech matched. Each time something improved.

Practice Your Speech by Recording Yourself

There is nothing that gets us to change what we're doing or correct a problem more quickly than seeing ourselves doing something we don't like on video. Your instructor may record your speech in class and have you critique it afterwards, but it may be more helpful to do that in advance of giving your speech. By watching yourself, you will notice all the small things you do that might prove to be distracting and affect your grade during the actual speech. Many times students aren't aware that they have low energy or a monotone/monorate voice, or that they bounce, sway, pull at their clothes, play with hair or jewelry, or make other unusual and distracting movements. At least, they don't know this until they see themselves doing it. Since we are generally our own harshest critics, you will be quick to notice any flaws in your speech and correct them.

It is important enough that it deserves reiterating:

Practice your speech beforehand, at home or elsewhere, the way you will give it in class.

Following these steps will not only prepare you better for delivering the speech, but they may also help reduce anxiety since you will feel more familiar with the situation you find yourself in when faced with a speaking engagement. Additionally, the more you speak publicly, whether for practice or in front of a live audience, the more fluid you will become for later speeches.

3.5 WHAT TO DO WHEN DELIVERING YOUR SPEECH

The interplay between the verbal and nonverbal components of your speech can either bring the message vividly to life or confuse or bore the audience. Therefore, it is best that you neither overdramatize your speech delivery behaviors nor downplay them. This is a balance achieved through rehearsal, trial and error, and experience. One way to think of this is in terms of the Goldilocks paradigm: you don't want to overdo the delivery because you might distract your audience by looking hyper or overly animated. Conversely, someone whose delivery is too understated (meaning they don't move their hands or feet at all) looks unnatural and uncomfortable, which can also distract. Just like Goldilocks, you want a delivery that is "just right." This middle ground between too much and too little is a much more natural approach to public speaking delivery. This natural approach will be covered in more detail in the following sections where we discuss specific aspects of your delivery and what you need to think about while actually giving your speech.

Hands

Almost everyone who gives a speech in public gets scared or nervous to some extent. Even professionals who do this for a living feel that way, but they have learned how to combat those nerves through experience and practice. When we get scared or nervous, our bodies emit adrenaline into our systems so we can deal with whatever problem is causing us to feel that way. Unfortunately, you will need to be standing relatively still for the next 5-7 minutes, so that burst of adrenaline is going to try to work its way out of your body and manifest itself somehow. One of the main ways is through your hands.

It may sound funny, but we have seen more than one student unknowingly incorporate "jazz hands" (shaking your hands at your sides with fingers opened wide) at various points in their speech. While certainly an extreme example, this and behaviors like it can easily becoming distracting. At the other end of the scale, people who don't know what to do with their hands or use them "too little" sometimes hold their arms stiffly at their sides, behind their backs, or in their pockets, all of which can also look unnatural and distracting.

The key for knowing what to do with your hands is to use them naturally as you would in normal conversation. If you were standing around talking to your friends and wanted to list three reasons why you should all take a road trip this weekend, you would probably hold up your fingers as you counted off the reasons ("First, we hardly ever get this opportunity. Second, we can..."). Try to pay attention to what you do with your hands in regular conversations and incorporate that into your delivery.

However, with all that said, if you have nothing else to do with your hands, such as meaningful gestures, the default position for them is to be resting gently on the sides of the lectern. You don't want to grip the lectern tightly, but resting them on the edges keeps them in position to move your notes on if you need to or use them to gesture. As stated above, you want to practice this way beforehand so you are used to speaking this way when you come to class.

Feet

Just like your hands, a lot of nervous energy is going to try to work its way out of your body through your feet. On the "too much" end, this is most common when people start "dancing" behind the lectern Another variation is twisting feet around each other or the lower leg. On the other end are those who put their feet together, lock their knees, and never move from that position. Both of these options look unnatural, and therefore will prove to be distracting to your audience. Locking your knees can also lead to loss of oxygen in your brain, not a good state to be in, because it can cause you to faint.

The default position for your feet, then, is to have them shoulder-width apart with your knees slightly bent. Again, you want to look and feel natural, so it is fine to adjust your weight or move out from behind the lectern, but constant motion (or perpetual stillness) will not lead to good overall delivery.

These two sections on hands and feet mention "energy." Public speakers need to look energetic—not hyperactive, but engaged and upbeat about communicating their message. Slumping, low and unvarying pitch and rate, and lack of gestures telegraph "I don't care" to an audience.

Objects

There is a very simple rule when it comes to what you should bring with you to the lectern when you give your speech: **Only bring to the lectern what you absolutely need to give the speech.** Anything else you have with you will only serve as a distraction for both you and the audience. For the purposes of this class, the only objects you should need to give your speech are whatever materials you are speaking from, and possibly a visual aid if you are using one. Beyond that, don't bring pens, laptops, phones, lucky charms, or notebooks with you to the lectern. These extra items can ultimately become a distraction themselves when they fall off the lectern or get in your way. Some students like to bring their electronic tablet, laptop computer, or cell phone with them, but there are some obvious disadvantages to these items, especially if you don't turn the ringer on your cell phone off. Cell phones are not usually large enough to serve as presentation notes; we've seen students squint and hold the phone up to their faces.

Not only do you need to be aware of what you bring with you, but you should also be aware of what you have on your person as well. Sometimes, in the course of dressing for a speech, we can overlook simple issues that can cause problems while speaking. Some of these can include:

- Jewelry that 'jingles' when you move, such as heavy bracelets;
- Uncomfortable shoes or shoes that you are not used to;
- Anything with fringe, zippers, or things hanging off it. They might become irresistible to play with while speaking;
- For those with longer hair, remember that you will be looking down at your notes and then looking back up. Don't be forced to "fix" your hair or tuck it behind your ear every time you look up. Use a hairband, clip, or some other method to keep your hair totally out of your face so that the audience can see your eyes and you won't have to adjust your hair constantly. It can be very distracting to an audience to watch a speaker pull hair from his face after every sentence.

The Lectern and Posture

We have already discussed the lectern, but it is worth mentioning again briefly here. The lectern is a tool for you to use that should ultimately make your speech easier to give, and you need to use it that way. On the "too much" end, some people want to trick their audience into thinking they are not nervous by leaning on the podium in a relaxed manner, sometime going so far as to actually begin tipping the podium forward. Your lectern is NOT part of your skeletal system, to prop you up, so don't do this. On the "too little" end are those who are afraid to touch it, worried that they will use it incorrectly or somehow knock it over (you won't!).

As always, you want the "Goldilocks" middle ground. As stated above, rest your notes and hands on it, but don't lean on the lectern or "hug" it. Practicing with a lectern (or something similar to a lectern) will eliminate most of your fears about using it.

The lectern use is related to posture. Most of us let gravity pull us down. One of the muscle memory tricks of public speaking is to roll your shoulders back. Along with making your shoulder muscles feel better, doing so with feet apart and knees bent, rolling your shoulders back will lead to a more credible physical presence—you'll look taller and more energetic. You'll also feel better, and you'll have larger lung capacity for breathing to support your tone and volume.

Eye Contact

As we've said consistently throughout this book, your audience is the single biggest factor that influences every aspect of your speech. And since eye contact is how you establish and maintain a rapport with your audience during your speech, it is an extremely important element of your delivery. Your professor may or may not indicate a standard for how much eye contact you need during the speech, such as 50%, but he or she will absolutely want to see you making an effort to engage your audience through looking directly at them.

What is important to note here is that you want to establish genuine eye contact with your audience, and not "fake" eye contact. There have been a lot of techniques generated for "faking" eye contact, and none of them look natural. For example, these are not good ideas:

- Three points on the back wall – You may have heard that instead of making eye contact, you can just pick three points on the back wall and look at those. What ends up happening, though, is you look like you are staring off into space and your audience will spend the majority of your speech trying to figure out what you are looking at. To avoid this, look around the entire room, including the front, back, left, and right sides of the space.
- The swimming method – This happens when someone is reading his or her speech and looks up quickly and briefly to try to make it seem like they are making eye contact, not unlike a swimmer who pops his head out of the water for a breath before going back under. Eye contact is more than just physically moving your head; it is about looking at your audience and establishing a connection. In general, your eye contact should last at least five seconds at a time and should be with individuals throughout the room.
- The stare down – Since you will, to some degree, be graded on your eye contact, some students think (either consciously or not), that the best way to ensure they get credit for establishing eye contact is to always and exclusively look directly at their professor. While we certainly appreciate the attention, we

want to see that you are establishing eye contact with your entire audience, not just one person. Also, this behavior is uncomfortable for the instructor.

Vocal Considerations

Volume

Volume refers to the relative softness or loudness of your voice. Like most of the other issues we've discussed in this section, the proper volume for a given speaking engagement usually falls on a scale like the one above. If you speak too softly ("too little" volume), your audience will struggle to hear and understand you and may give up trying to listen. If you speak with "too much" volume, your audience may feel that you are yelling at them, or at least feel uncomfortable with you shouting. The volume you use should fit the size of the audience and the room.

Fortunately, for the purposes of this class, your normal speaking voice will probably work just fine since you are in a relatively small space with around twenty people. However, if you know that you are naturally a soft-spoken person, you will need to work on breathing to get more air into your lungs, and on projecting your voice to the people in the last row, not just those in t he front. Of course, if you are naturally a very loud talker, you may want to make other adjustments when giving your speech. Obviously this will all change if you are asked to speak in a larger venue or given a microphone to use.

Public speaking relies on the voice for interest, credibility, audibility, and clarity. The British Prime Minister of the 19th century was quoted saying, "There is no greater index of character so sure as the voice." While that seems exaggerated today, a public speaker at any level cannot ignore the energy, loudness, and clarity in their voice. There are four steps to voice production: *breathing (produced by the lungs, which are largely responsible for the vocal characteristic of volume)*; phonation (the production of the sound in the vocal folds, which close and vibrate to produce sound for speaking as the air is exhaled over them; phonation creates pitch); *resonation (a type of amplification of the sound in the larynx, oral cavity, and nasal cavity, which creates the characteristic of quality); and* articulation, which produces the sounds of language others can understand and is responsible for rate and for being understood.

Your instructor may give you more directions on maximizing the power of your voice to achieve more variety and power. We have all listened to a low-energy, monotone, monorate speaker and know how hard it is, so you should pay attention to your recording, perhaps by closing your eyes and just listening, to see if your voice is flat and lifeless.

Pitch

Pitch is the relative highness or lowness of your voice, and like everything, you can have too much or too little (with regard to variation of it). Too much pitch variation occurs when people "sing" their speeches, and their voices oscillate between very high pitched and very low pitched. While uncommon, this is sometimes attributed to nerves. More common is too little variation in pitch, which is known as being **monotone**.

Delivering a speech in a monotone manner is usually caused by reading too much; generally the speaker's focus is on saying the words correctly (because they have not practiced). They forget to speak normally to show their interest in the topic, as we would in everyday conversation. For most people, pitch isn't a major issue, but if you think it might be for you, ask the people in your practice audience what they think. Generally, if we are interested in and passionate about communicating our thoughts, we are not likely to be monotone. We are rarely monotone when talking to friends and family about matters of importance to us, so pick topics you care about.

Rate

How quickly or slowly you say the words of your speech is the **rate**. Too little rate (i.e. speaking too slowly) will make it sound like you may not fully know your speech or what you are talking about, and will ultimately cost you some credibility with your audience. It may also result in the audience being bored and lose focus on what you are saying. Rate is one reason you should try to record yourself, even if just audio on your phone, beforehand and be mindful of time when you practice. Your voice's rate will affect the time it takes to give the speech.

By contrast, too much rate (i.e. speaking too fast) can be overly taxing on an audience's ability to keep up with and digest what you are saying. It sometimes helps to imagine that your speech is a jog or run that you and your friends (the audience) are taking together. You (as the speaker) are setting the pace based on how quickly you speak. If you start sprinting, it may be too difficult for your audience to keep up and they may give up halfway through. If you know you speak quickly, especially when nervous, be sure to practice slowing down and writing yourself delivery cues in your notes to maintain a more comfortable rate. As always, recording and timing your speech during practice helps.

You especially will want to maintain a good, deliberate rate at the beginning of your speech because your audience will be getting used to your voice. We have all called a business where the person answering the phone mumbles the name of the business in a rushed way. We aren't sure if we called the right number. Since the introduction is designed to get the audience's attention and interest in your speech, you will want to focus on clear delivery there. Regulating rate is another reason why video-recording yourself can be so helpful because we often to not realize how fast we speak.

Pauses

The common misconception for public speaking students is that pausing during your speech is bad, but that isn't necessarily true. You pause in normal conversations, so you shouldn't be afraid of pausing while speaking. This is especially true if you are making a particularly important point or want for a statement to have a more powerful impact: you will want to give the audience a moment to digest what you have said.

For example, consider the following statement: "Because of issues like pollution and overpopulation, in 50 years the earth's natural resources will be so depleted that it will become difficult for most people to obtain enough food to survive." Following a statement like this, you want to give your audience just a brief moment to fully consider what you are saying. Hopefully they will think something along the lines of *What if I'm still alive then?* or *What will my children do?* and become more interested in hearing what you have to say.

Of course, there is such a thing as pausing too much, both in terms of frequency and length. Someone who pauses too often (after each sentence) may come off seeming like they don't know their speech very well. Someone who pauses too long (more than a few seconds), runs the risk of the audience feeling uncomfortable or, even worse becoming distracted or letting their attention wander. We are capable of processing words more quickly than anyone can speak clearly, which is one of the reasons listening is difficult. Pauses should be controlled to maintain attention of the audience.

Vocalized pauses

At various points during your speech, you may find yourself in need of a brief moment to collect your thoughts or prepare for the next section of your speech. At those moments, you will be pausing, but we don't always like to let people know that we're pausing. So what many of us do in an attempt to "trick" the audience is fill in those pauses with sounds so that it appears that we haven't actually paused. These are known as **vocalized pauses**, or sometimes "fillers." Another term for them is "nonfluencies."

Everyone uses vocalized pauses to some degree, but not everyone's are problematic. This obviously becomes an issue when the vocalized pauses become distracting due to their overuse. We have little doubt that you can remember a time when you were speaking to someone who said the word "like" after every three words and you became focused on it. One of your authors remembers attending a wedding and (inadvertently) began counting the number of times the best man said "like" during his toast (22 was the final count). The most common vocalized pause is "uh," but then there are others. Can you think of any?

The bad news here is that there is no quick fix for getting rid of your vocalized pauses. They are so ingrained into all of our speech patterns that getting rid of them is a challenge. However, there is a two-step process you can employ to begin eliminating them. First, you need to identify what your particular vocalized pause is. Do you say "um," "well," or "now" before each sentence? Do you finish each thought with, "you know?" Do you use "like" before every adjective (as in "he was like so unhappy")?

After figuring out what your vocalized pause is, the second step is to carefully and meticulously try to catch yourself when you say it. If you hear yourself saying "uh," remind yourself, *I need to try to not say that*. Catching yourself and being aware of how often you use vocalized pauses will help you begin the process of reducing your dependence on them and hopefully get rid of them completely.

One of the authors uses a game in her class that she adopted from a couple of disc jockeys she used to hear. It is called the "uh game." The callers had to name six things in a named category (items in a refrigerator, pro-football teams, makes of cars, etc.) in twenty seconds without saying a vocalized pause word or phrase. It sounds easy, but it isn't, especially on the spot with a radio audience. It is a good way to practice focusing on the content and not saying a vocalized pause.

The ten items listed above represent the major delivery issues you will want to be aware of when giving a speech, but it is by no means an exhaustive list. There is however, one final piece of delivery advice we would like to offer. We know that no matter how hard you practice and how diligent you are in preparing for your speech, you are most likely going to mess up some aspect of your speech when you give it in class, at least a little. That's normal. Everyone does it. The key is to not make a big deal about it or let the audience know you messed up. Odds are that they will never even realize your mistake if you don't tell them there was a mistake. Saying something like "I can't believe I messed that up" or "Can I start over?" just telegraphs to the audience your mistake. In fact, you have most likely never heard a perfect speech delivered in your life. It is likely that you just didn't realize that the speaker missed a line or briefly forgot what they wanted to say.

Practice your speech beforehand, at home or elsewhere, the way you will give it in class.

Since you know you are likely going to make some sort of mistake in class, use your practice time at home to work on how you will deal with those mistakes. If you say a word incorrectly or start reading the wrong sentence, don't go back and begin that section anew. That's not what you would do in class, so just correct yourself and move on. If you practice dealing with your mistakes at home, you will be better prepared for the inevitable errors that will find their way into your speech in class.

A final thought on practice. We have all heard, "Practice makes perfect." That is not always true. Practice makes permanent; the actions become habitual. If you practice incorrectly, your performance will be incorrect. Be sure your practice is correct.

3.6 PUBLIC SPEAKING ONLINE

Traditionally, public speaking has been understood as a face-to-face exchange between a designated speaker and an audience. In fact, when you imagine a public speaker, you likely picture a person standing on a stage with a podium and speaking in front of a live audience.

However, new media and digital technologies have begun expanding both our access to public speakers and our platforms to speak and reach new audiences. YouTube—a global video sharing service—has more than 2.7 billion monthly users (Global Media Insight, 2024), and these are just people who log in! If you're like us, you've likely watched hours of content published on YouTube, from instructional videos to political commentary. You have probably also accessed hundreds of videos on Instagram, Facebook, or other media sites. With access to these platforms, speakers are now able to broadcast their insights and advocacies to a global audience.

Businesses, too, have begun using online public speaking. Webinars, video conferences, and digital speakers have permeated professional industries, and it's becoming increasingly important to consider best practices for creating speeches and being in the audience for online public speeches.

With this growth in popularity, we have a growth in the number of problems and common behaviors (or misbehaviors) in web conferencing and, thus, online public speaking. Much of the advice on web conference public speaking comes as antidotes to the worst practices that have developed in them:

1. the audience's multitasking (and thus not fully attending to the webinar)
2. the audience's being bored to death and tuning out (or even falling asleep)

Both of these conditions come from the fact that the communication is mediated and that, in many cases, the speaker and audience don't see each other. Even when the participants use their web cameras (which doesn't always happen), the screen is often covered with a slide and the speaker is invisible. Therefore, the speaker has to depend on something else to address the temptation to multitask or nod off.

Like any approach toward public speaking, online public speaking offers a variety of opportunities and constraints. Below, we outline what digital public speaking is and how to prepare to speak online.

Online Public Speaking

Online public speaking—also known as digital oratory—is a "thesis-driven, vocal, embodied public address that is housed within (online) new media platforms" (Lind, 2012, p. 164). Like all public speeches, an online speech should be well-prepared, organized, well-reasoned, and well-rehearsed. Purpose, synchronicity, and the audience all play key roles in online public speaking.

Purpose

Online speaking opportunities are not created equally, and each speech will have a different general purpose—informing, persuading, or entertaining. Remember that just like other forms of public speaking, digital oratory requires a thesis statement, and the purpose of your speech will dictate how you craft the information that you're going to present. With ready access to video technology that can be transmitted through our phones, it can be tempting to log in and let our followers into our lives through a stream-of-consciousness vlog, but that's not the type of digital oratory that constitutes prepared public speaking. Instead, prepare by considering your purpose for speaking and your thesis, then organize your speech around the answer.

For example, you might be participating in—or leading—a live webinar via Zoom or recording an instructional video that explains how to use a new piece of technology and which you might upload to YouTube. Each speech will have a different purpose and, in turn, different expectations on what you should include.

Once you've identified the goal, use later chapters in this text to begin crafting content.

Pro-tip: Know your purpose for speaking.

Synchronicity

Synchronicity describes whether your digital oratory will be delivered live or recorded for people to use later; if you're presenting a speech live, you're speaking synchronously, meaning your audience is experiencing it in real-time. Some online public speeches occur synchronously. For example, if you're speaking to a non-profit organization about a local food pantry project through Zoom and the members of the organization are tuning in live to watch and hear your presentation, the speech is synchronous. In synchronous online speaking, many of the same face-to-face speaking principles apply. Live presentations are ephemeral, meaning they happen once. In synchronous online speaking—unless it's being recorded—you have one chance to create a clear message, so it's imperative that your content and information are crafted for clear understanding.

Alternatively, you may speak asynchronously, meaning that the speech may be recorded and watched at a different time. YouTube, for example, houses many asynchronous videos, allowing audiences to tune in and watch when their schedule allows it. With an asynchronous video, speakers may have additional time to record, watch, and re-do if necessary. Similarly, audiences also have the ability to re-watch your presentation or pause the speech, if needed.

Each option provides different opportunities and constraints.

In synchronous speaking, you may be more comfortable adopting and applying face-to-face public speaking strategies, including integrating live audience feedback. It's common in synchronous online speaking for audiences to post questions or provide live feedback, allowing you to adjust your content and fill in gaps. If there is a technological mishap, however, you can't correct it later. The mishap also happens in real time, and those barriers can influence your credibility as a speaker.

In asynchronous speaking, you can control the content more easily because you can re-record the material to fix any technological errors. However, in asynchronous speaking, you cannot get live feedback from your audience, so you may be unaware if there's a key question or issue they need answered.

The Audience

New media has expanded the audience pool for public speaking. In traditional public speaking, the audience is often limited to those individuals who show up for the event—the audience is explicit (the people who are physically present in the audience) or discrete (or targeted audience). In online speaking, you may have a discrete or dispersed audience (an audience whose members hear the speech in different times and locations). These different audience types, along with synchronicity, alter how audience engagement can occur.

Consider our earlier example about presenting to a non-profit organization through Zoom. In this example, it's likely that you're aware of who the audience is, so you're able to link your content to the discrete (or defined) audience. However, in other instances, your audience may be dispersed and more difficult to determine. If you become passionate about a local policy, for example, and decide to post a speech on YouTube, the audience is dispersed because it's unclear who will click the link. With a dispersed audience, it can be difficult to make specific references or calls to action because geographic locations may alter what individuals are able to do.

With a dispersed audience, there's also an increased risk that audience members won't view your digital speech. Digital communication has led to information overload – we've all experienced it. If you're like us, you might scan through Instagram stories, clicking past images or videos that don't catch your attention. If you're posting a digital speech with a less-defined audience, the first few lines—the attention-getter—become crucial to hook them into watching. Spend a little extra time crafting and rehearsing your attention-getter.

Being a Member of the Audience: You'll likely be an audience member for many online public speeches—synchronous and asynchronous. Remember to take your position as an audience member seriously and avoid negative comments or trolling behavior. Even if you don't know the speaker, how you contribute to the dialogue online (or how you communicate) still functions constitutively, so make sure the world-making that you're participating in is ethical.

As you can see, there are quite a few variations that define the context of a digital speech: an informative, asynchronous speech with a discrete audience; a persuasive synchronous speech with a dispersed audience. The more information you have about these variations, the more you can be prepared to digitally speak with confidence and clarity.

Rehearsing to Speak Online

Rehearsing to speak online can feel a bit odd, especially when video software enters the mix. You'll be more effective in rehearsal if you're aware of the speaking context, including the categories mentioned in the previous section: purpose, synchronicity, and audience. Knowing the context will and should inform how you rehearse for a digital speech because you should always rehearse under the conditions that you'll speak.

Pro-Tip: Rehearse under the conditions that you'll speak.

Integrate the presentation strategies for an online speech as you would for other speeches—including the purposeful development of verbal, nonverbal delivery, and presentation aids. There are a few additional variables for delivering a speech digitally that we'll track below.

Verbal Delivery

Verbal delivery is key in a digital speech—particularly webinars or web conferencing where your vocals overlay a slideshow and your body isn't visible to an audience. Verbal enunciation, punctuation, rate, and pauses become key to maintaining your audiences' attention. If monotone and monorate speaking is horrible for face-to-face speaking, it is truly the "kiss of death" for web speaking. The key word is "energy"; an energetic voice has tonal variation and emphasis, variation in pace and meter, planned pauses, and sometimes word play (which can be subtle or overt, but shouldn't be overdone—this isn't Dr. Seuss).

Audio-recording yourself during rehearsal on your smartphone or other device is a good first step, followed by thinking critically and honestly about whether your voice is listless, flat, or lacks energy. Since we tend to have a lower energy level when we sit, some experts suggest that web conference speakers stand to approximate the real speaking experience. As we have mentioned repeatedly throughout this book, preparing means practicing your speech orally and physically, many times.

Sound and projection are two variables that can affect your verbal delivery in digital contexts. It's important to rehearse with any technology—including a microphone—that will be present and in the physical context that you'll record the formal speech. If you have a microphone, you will need to alter your projection level. If you don't have a microphone, be aware of how the recording device will pick up sound—including your voice and other noise around you.

Be sensitive about what can be heard on camera if you aren't careful like interruptions by barking dogs, passing traffic outside, the voices of others who are not on camera, papers near the speakers, or the sounds of toilets flushing or lawn crews working next door.

Remember that extra noise is distracting: it can influence your credibility and the likelihood that an audience will continue listening.

Pro-tip: Many rounds of rehearsal are necessary for improving your online presentation.

Nonverbal Delivery

When rehearsing your nonverbal delivery, ask, "What's visible in the video?"

If your body is visible, you should rehearse with Chapter 3 in mind. As you rehearse, be conscious of where the camera will be. Will there be just one? Will there be multiple cameras? How far away is the camera? In some instances, audiences may have the ability to view your speech from multiple vantage points. Being aware of where those cameras are—one or multiple—is key to rehearsing your eye contact and facial expressions. Eye contact is still a key part of a digital speech. While you can avoid staring directly into the camera for an extended period of time, audiences still want some form of engagement, and eye contact allows you to make that connection. If you are recording the speech with or without a live audience, view the camera as your "audience substitute."

Background and Lighting

Your background is also part of your video's nonverbal aesthetics. Make sure that you consider how the background might translate to your audience. Is it messy? Distracting? Is it a white background? If so, you should avoid wearing white and disappearing into the walls. Are there windows behind you with bright light streaming through, making you almost invisible? If so, can you close the blinds or curtains or move? Can you set up a ring light to offset the light coming through outside sources and enhance your appearance? Do you have a ceiling fan whirring above your head? If so, turn it off while you record. Does your video conferencing software have filters that blur out imperfections that might otherwise be heightened by visual photography?

Pro-tip: Make sure you have adequate lighting.

1. Never be in front of a window where you are backlit.
2. Always have adequate lighting on your face.
3. Use a lamp or lighting system to light your face and adjust it properly.
4. If you use a ring light, try bouncing it off the ceiling so you do not get light rings in your pupils.
5. Avoid using an overhead light because it casts shadows under your eyes.

Camera Positioning

Because your facial expressions and body language are also visible in a digital speech, you will want to pay some attention to how the camera(s) is positioned. Don't position the camera so closely that your head fills the frame, or so far away that you are a tiny object in the frame. To look your best, position the camera so that you are viewed from above from between 15° to 30° from eye level. Filming yourself at eye-level might make your facial features appear flat, while filming yourself from below eye level gives the impression that you are towering over your audience. If your camera is in your laptop computer, try balancing it on a small stack of books to achieve an optimal level.

https://www.youtube.com/watch?v=7ppTAA-1tm0

Pro-tip: Frame the shot. Depending on the type of speech, you want to frame your head or do a 3/4 shot. It is best to frame the shot so the audience can see your gestures.

https://www.youtube.com/watch?v=KYNO7cAzuYQ

Pro-tip: Talk directly into the camera to connect with your audience.

https://www.youtube.com/watch?v=sTFWC1PiLVE&t=3s

Wardrobe, Hair, and Makeup

Wear appropriate clothing on all parts of your body. By now, everyone has heard at least one story of someone in a Zoom meeting who stood up to reveal that he was wearing pajamas or sweatpants below more formal clothing on top, or worse. Dress as if the audience might see your entire body to avoid such embarrassment. Also, make sure that your clothing looks good on camera in terms of color and lighting in your setting. Avoid noisy jewelry such as earrings or bangles that jingle if you move. Style your hair the way you would if you were meeting with this audience in person. Also, if you normally wear cosmetics when you meet with this type of audience in person, wear them on camera as well. Your goal is to look just as you would in the same setting if you were meeting face to face.

For more detailed information, check out "Six Tips for Looking Great in a Zoom Meeting," Jefferson Graham (2020).

Dress Rehearsal

Rehearse under these conditions and record your facial expressions to see how they are translating to others. Is your body language clear? Do some gestures or facial expressions look exaggerated? Can you adjust the camera position or lighting? Are your clothing and accessories distracting or do they make you fade into the background? Do you look professional? A videoed rehearsal will provide you with answers to these questions.

Remember that effective rehearsal occurs under the conditions that you'll speak. Your goal is to create an aesthetic experience that honors the purpose of your speech, so being accountable to all nonverbal factors will increase your ethos.

Additional Pro-Preparation Tips:

- Stand up (if possible) so that you have more breath support during your presentation.

- Make sure you will not be interrupted during the web conference.

- Have notes and anything else you need at hand. While you can use a computer to display them, be conscious of your audience's ability to see you reading.

- If you can be seen, be seen—use the technology to your advantage so that you are not an entirely disembodied voice talking over slides.

- Watch your practice video to make sure there are no issues for the listeners. Make sure the ending isn't cut off.

- Edit the video if necessary.

Presentation Aids

In some cases, an online speech will include presentation aids. It's important to determine a) if the presentation aid is necessary and b) if you're able to provide that presentation aid in a different form.

First, are you certain you need a presentation aid? It can be tempting to use a presentation aid for a digital speech to avoid being visible to the audience. After all, it's common for digital presentation software to display either a visual aid or your body. Don't use a visual aid to avoid being seen because the audience will be much more interested in your embodied presentation. Second, do you know how to share your visual aid via the digital platform you will be speaking through? As with all other aspects of online public speaking, you need to practice beforehand so that you know what your audience will see as well as how to quickly switch from your screen to the visual aid and back again. Demonstrating technical competence

If you deem that a presentation aid is absolutely necessary (or required) also, ask: do I need to provide it live or in the recording? If you're presenting to a discrete audience and want to provide a graph or some data, send the information in a report ahead of time. This will allow your audience to feel acquainted with the information and can spare you from having an additional technological component. You want to avoid information overload as you speak and presentation aids can often cause more of a distraction than serve as an aid. Therefore, keep your visuals simple. One rule business speakers like to use is the "10-20-30: rule: No more than 10 slides, no more than 20 words on the slides, and no font smaller than 30 point." Using 30 point font will definitely minimize the amount of text. Inserting short videos and planning interactivity (such as polls, which the software supports) are also helpful.

Like any public speech, when speaking online, you are responsible for crafting an effective advocacy that is composed of well-reasoned arguments that are delivered with purposeful aesthetic choices. Rehearse under the conditions that you'll speak. Be confident that you're aware of

- the technology you will need,
- where it will be placed,
- which technology that you are responsible for running, and
- how your embodiment of information translates.

Pro-tip: If you can be seen, be seen; use the technology to your advantage so that you are not an entirely disembodied voice talking over slides.

Sharing Audiovisual Recordings

If you are recording an asynchronous presentation to share with others, post it to a cloud first (such as Canvas's Studio, SoundCloud or YouTube) and post a link and/or embed it on the corresponding project discussion board on Canvas. Audiovisual recording files are too large to be emailed easily. Other participants will not want to download a large file to view your presentation, so embedding or providing a link will make it easier on everyone. Remember to change the privacy settings so that your link is viewable to everyone.

Conclusion

Mastering online delivery in public speaking is a critical skill in today's digital age. Speaking in a virtual environment may present new and unique challenges, such as managing technology, engaging with a remote and, often diverse, audience, and adapting traditional speaking techniques to an online setting. Whether you are addressing a live audience via Zoom or recording a video for YouTube, understanding the nuances of purpose, synchronicity, and audience engagement is crucial. By paying careful attention to verbal and nonverbal delivery, background aesthetics, camera positioning, and the use of presentation aids, you can create compelling and professional digital speeches. With preparation, practice, and an understanding of the online speaking techniques presented in this chapter, speakers can successfully convey their message and leave a lasting impact on their audience.

References

Global Media Insight. (2024, August 1). YOUTUBE STATISTICS 2024 (DEMOGRAPHICS, USERS BY COUNTRY, and MORE). https://www.globalmediainsight.com/blog/youtube-users-statistics/

Goodman, & Green, (n.d.) Online delivery considerations. *Public Speaking.* Maricopa Community Colleges. https://open.maricopa.edu/com225/chapter/online-delivery/

Graham, J. (2020). Six tips for looking great in a Zoom meeting. *USA Today.* https://www.usatoday.com/story/tech/2020/04/11/zoom-meetings-go-better-these-6-tips-look-your-best/5125980002/

Lind, S. (2012). Teaching digital oratory: Public speaking 2.0. *Communication Teacher, 26*(3), 163-169.

Lousiana Library Network. (2022). *It's about them: Public speaking in the 21st century.* https://louis.pressbooks.pub/publicspeaking/chapter/online-public-speaking/

Lumen Learning. (n.d.). Introduction to speaking online. *Public Speaking.* https://courses.lumenlearning.com/wm-publicspeaking/chapter/introduction-to-speaking-online/

Mead, L. (2021). Chapter 34: Speaking to a Camera: Making eye contact is key. *Advanced Public Speaking.* https://uark.pressbooks.pub/speaking/chapter/speaking-to-a-camera/

Schechter, S. (2023). Chapter 16: Public speaking online. *Public Speaking For Today's Audiences.* https://pressbooks.bccampus.ca/speaking/chapter/chapter-16/

3.7 ENRICHMENT

Discussion Questions

1. As a class or with a group of friends, discuss what makes an effective speaker. Write the traits or characteristics on the board.
2. Why do many people think that Memorized Speaking is the best method of delivery? What do you think? Which method do you feel best suits most occasions?
3. How does delivery of a presentation differ between in-person and online settings?
4. Which aspects of delivery discussed in Section 3:5: What to do When Delivering Your Speech are you most concerned about for your speech delivery? Discuss with a classmate or group. Do you have any tips for improving those aspects of speech delivery?

Activities

1. Volunteer to take turns delivering a sample speech using the ABCs or your favorite poem or song in conversational form in front of the class. Be sure to incorporate facial expressions, gestures, movement, vocal characteristics, and eye contact. Discuss your feelings and thoughts as you presented. Provide feedback to others after they present.
2. Set a timer on your phone for one to two minutes and record yourself presenting an impromptu speech. Choose a topic you are able to speak about like, "What is the best vacation you have ever taken?" or "What is your favorite book or movie?" or "Why did you come to OSU?" Speaking off the cuff can help mitigate anxiety and give you priceless practice and mental confidence when a presentation counts.
3. List three areas of delivery that you would like to improve this semester. Based on tips in Section 3:5: What to do When Delivering Your Speech, how will you improve these aspects of delivery in your next speech?
4. The entire class forms a circle (sitting or standing). Each class member thinks of their favorite childhood cartoon or film and a couple of reasons why it is the best. Each class member will deliver an impromptu speech about their favorite cartoon or film while making eye contact with everyone in the circle and without using a vocalized pause. If the speaker uses a vocalized pause, other class members let them know and they will begin their impromptu speech

again until everyone can make eye contact with the circle without using a vocalized pause.

4 ETHICS

Learning Objectives

- Explain the three levels of the ethics pyramid and how they might be used in evaluating the ethical choices of a public speaker or listener.
- Apply the National Communication Association (NCA) Credo for Ethical Communication to the context of public speaking.
- Apply ethics to your public speaking preparation process.
- Describe free speech as outlined in the First Amendment to the US Constitution and how free speech relates to other guaranteed freedoms.
- Discuss patterns of media ownership, the relationship of media and globalization, and the effects of diversity (or lack thereof) or media representations.
- Employ media-literacy skills to evaluate media messages.

Key Terms

- **Distortion**
- **Ends**
- **Ethical Pyramid**

- **Free Speech**
- **Globalization**
- **Intent**
- **Means**
- **Media Convergence**
- **Media Imperialism**
- **Media Literacy**
- **Plagiarism**
- **Social Learning Theory**

4.1 THE ETHICS PYRAMID

Passionate Pete

"Our lives begin to end the day we become silent about things that matter." -Martin Luther King, Jr.

The sun shone brightly on the library lawn as students went about their day, engrossed in their studies or leisurely conversations. Among them, Pistol Pete strolled, his presence exuding the vibrant spirit of Oklahoma State University. Suddenly, a commotion drew his attention to a figure standing on a soapbox, fervently preaching his beliefs to a gathering crowd of students.

It was Preacher Bob, known for his fiery speeches and confrontational style. Pete observed as Preacher Bob's words turned from passionate to hostile, his voice rising in volume and his demeanor becoming aggressive. Pete's heart sank as he witnessed his fellow students being subjected to a barrage of insults and derogatory remarks.

With a sense of duty and a desire to stand up for his peers, Pete approached the scene. His footsteps were purposeful, his eyes focused, and his voice filled with conviction. Taking a deep breath, he stepped forward, drawing the attention of the crowd and Preacher Bob.

In a calm and composed manner, Pete addressed Preacher Bob, acknowledging his right to freedom of speech while emphasizing the importance of respect and understanding within a diverse community. He encouraged open dialogue and the exchange of ideas without resorting to demeaning or offensive language.

Pete's words resonated with the students gathered around, who had felt disheartened and attacked by Preacher Bob's inflammatory rhetoric. They listened intently as Pete reminded them of the values they held as a university community – inclusivity, empathy, and mutual respect.

As the crowd absorbed Pete's message, a wave of understanding and unity washed over them. They began to engage in a peaceful and constructive dialogue, countering prejudice with thoughtful questions and rational arguments. Pete's presence had diffused the tension, providing a platform for open-mindedness and fostering an environment of tolerance and acceptance.

In that moment, Pistol Pete demonstrated the power of his role as a unifying figure. By respectfully addressing Preacher Bob's actions while defending the rights and dignity of his fellow students, he created an atmosphere where diverse perspectives could be heard and respected.

As Pete walked away from the library lawn, he knew that the impact of his actions extended far beyond that moment. He had empowered his fellow students to stand up against prejudice, to engage in meaningful conversations, and to foster an inclusive community that celebrated the richness of different backgrounds and beliefs.

With a renewed sense of pride, Pistol Pete continued his journey, knowing that his presence would always be a beacon of unity, respect, and unwavering support for his fellow students at Oklahoma State University. How do ethics play a role in your daily communication?

Ethics Today

Every day, people around the world make ethical decisions regarding public speech. Is it ever appropriate to lie to a group of people if it's in the group's best interest? As a speaker, should you use evidence within a speech that you are not sure is correct if it supports the speech's core argument? As a listener, should you refuse to listen to a speaker with whom you fundamentally disagree? These three examples represent ethical choices speakers and listeners face in the public speaking context. In this chapter, we will explore what it means to be both an ethical speaker and an ethical listener. To help you understand the issues involved with thinking about ethics, this chapter begins by presenting a model for ethical communication known as the ethics pyramid. We will then show how the National Communication Association (NCA) Credo for Ethical Communication can be applied to public speaking. The chapter will conclude with a general discussion of free speech.

The word "ethics" can mean different things to different people. Whether it is an ethical lapse in business or politics or a disagreement about medical treatments and end-of-life choices, people come into contact with ethical dilemmas regularly. Speakers and listeners of public speech face numerous ethical dilemmas as well. What kinds of support material and sources are ethical to use? How much should a speaker adapt to an audience without sacrificing his or her own views? What makes a speech ethical?

ETHICS PYRAMID

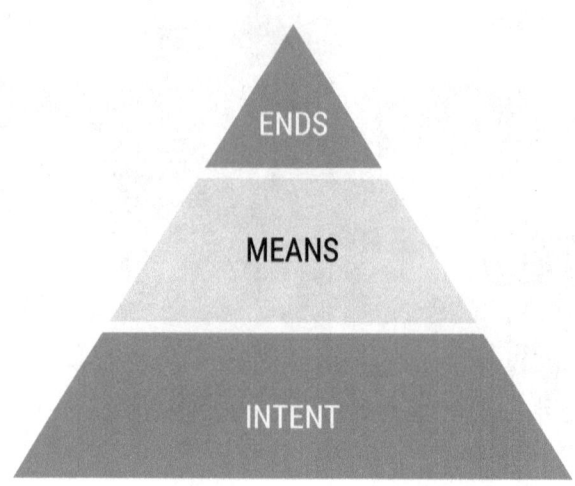

Elspeth Tilley, a public communication ethics expert from Massey University, proposes a structured approach to thinking about ethics (Tilley, 2005). Her **ethics pyramid** involves three basic concepts: intent, means, and ends. The graphic above illustrates the Tilley pyramid.

Intent

According to Tilley, the first major consideration to be aware of when examining the ethicality of something is the issue of **intent**. To be an ethical speaker or listener, it is important to begin with ethical intentions. For example, if we agree that honesty is ethical, it follows that ethical speakers will prepare their remarks with the intention of telling the truth to their audiences. Similarly, if we agree that it is ethical to listen with an open mind, it follows that ethical listeners will be intentional about letting a speaker make his or her case before forming judgments.

One option for assessing intent is to talk with others about how ethical they think a behavior is; if you get a variety of answers, it might be a sign that the behavior is not ethical and should be avoided. A second option is to check out existing codes of ethics. Many professional organizations, including the Independent Computer Consultants Association, American Counseling Association, and American Society of Home Inspectors, have codes of conduct or ethical guidelines for their members.

Individual corporations such as Monsanto, Coca-Cola, Intel, and ConocoPhillips also have ethical guidelines for how their employees should interact with suppliers or clients. Even when specific ethical codes are not present, you can apply general ethical principles, such as whether a behavior is beneficial for the majority or whether you would approve of the same behavior if you were listening to a speech instead of giving it.

In addition, it is important to be aware that people can engage in unethical behavior unintentionally. For example, suppose we agree that it is unethical to take someone else's words and pass them off as your own—a behavior known as plagiarism. What happens if a speaker makes a statement that he believes he thought of on his own, but the statement is actually quoted from a radio commentator whom he heard without clearly remembering doing so? The plagiarism was unintentional, but does that make it ethical?

Means

Tilley describes the **means** you use to communicate with others as the second level of the ethics pyramid. According to McCroskey, Wrench, and Richmond (McCroskey, Wrench, & Richmond, 2003), "means" are the tools or behaviors we employ to achieve a desired outcome. We must realize that there are a range of possible behavioral choices for any situation and that some choices are good, some are bad, and some fall in between.

For example, suppose you want your friend Marty to spend an hour reviewing a draft of your speech according to criteria, such as audience appropriateness, adequate research, strong support of assertions, and dynamic introduction and conclusion. What means might you use to persuade Marty to do you this favor? You might explain that you value Marty's opinion and will gladly return the favor the next time Marty is preparing a speech (good means), or you might threaten to tell a professor that Marty cheated on a test (bad means). While both of these means may lead to the same end—having Marty agree to review your speech—one is clearly more ethical than the other.

Ends

The final part of the ethics pyramid is the ends. According to McCroskey, Wrench, and Richmond (McCroskey, Wrench, & Richmond, 2003), **ends** are those outcomes that you desire to achieve. Examples of ends might include persuading your audience to make a financial contribution for your participation in Relay for Life, persuading a group of homeowners that your real estate agency would best meet their needs, or informing your fellow students about newly required university fees. Whereas the means are the behavioral choices we make, the ends are the results of those choices.

Like intentions and means, ends can be good or bad, or they can fall into a gray area where it is unclear just how ethical or unethical they are. For example, suppose a city council wants to balance the city's annual budget. Balancing the budget may be a good end, assuming that the city has adequate tax revenues and areas of discretionary spending for nonessential services for the year in question. However, voters might argue that balancing the budget is a bad end if the city lacks these things for the year in question, because in that case balancing the budget would require raising taxes, curtailing essential city services, or both.

When examining ends, we need to think about both the source and the receiver of the message or behavior. Some end results could be good for the source but bad for the receiver, or vice versa. Suppose, for example, that Anita belongs to a club that is raffling off a course of dancing lessons. Anita sells Ben a ten-dollar raffle ticket. However, Ben later thinks it over and realizes that he has no desire to take dancing lessons and that if he should win the raffle, he will never take the lessons. Anita's club has gained ten dollars—a good end—but Ben has lost ten dollars—a bad end. Again, the ethical standards you and your audience expect to be met will help in deciding whether a particular combination of speaker and audience ends is ethical.

Thinking through the Pyramid

Ultimately, understanding ethics is a matter of balancing all three parts of the ethical pyramid: intent, means, and ends. When thinking about the ethics of a given behavior, Tilley recommends asking yourself three basic questions:

"Have I discussed the ethicality of the behavior with others and come to a general consensus that the behavior is ethical?"
"Does the behavior adhere to known codes of ethics?"
"Would I be happy if the outcomes of the behavior were reversed and applied to me?"
(Tilley, 2005)

While you do not need to ask yourself these three questions before enacting every behavior as you go through a day, they do provide a useful framework for thinking through a behavior when you are not sure whether a given action, or statement, may be unethical. Ultimately, understanding ethics is a matter of balancing all three parts of the ethical pyramid: intent, means, and ends.

References

McCroskey, J. C., Wrench, J. S., & Richmond, V. P. (2003). *Principles of public speaking*. Indianapolis, IN: The College Network.

Tilley, E. (2005). The ethics pyramid: Making ethics unavoidable in the public relations process. *Journal of Mass Media Ethics, 20*, 305–320.

4.2 ETHICS IN PUBLIC SPEAKING

The study of ethics in human communication is hardly a recent endeavor. One of the earliest discussions of ethics in communication (and particularly in public speaking) was conducted by the ancient Greek philosopher Plato in his dialogue *Phaedrus*. In the centuries since Plato's time, an entire subfield within the discipline of human communication has developed to explain and understand communication ethics.

Communication Code of Ethics

In 1999, the National Communication Association officially adopted the Credo for

Ethical Communication (see the text box). Ultimately, the NCA Credo for Ethical Communication is a set of beliefs communication scholars have about the ethics of human communication.

National Communication Association Credo for Ethical Communication

Questions of right and wrong arise whenever people communicate. Ethical communication is fundamental to responsible thinking, decision making, and the development of relationships and communities within and across contexts, cultures, channels, and media. Moreover, ethical communication enhances human worth and dignity by fostering truthfulness, fairness, responsibility, personal integrity, and respect for self and others. We believe that unethical communication threatens the quality of all communication and consequently the well-being of individuals and the society in which we live. Therefore we, the members of the National Communication Association, endorse and are committed to practicing the following principles of ethical communication:

- We advocate truthfulness, accuracy, honesty, and reason as essential to the integrity of communication.
- We endorse freedom of expression, diversity of perspective, and tolerance of dissent to achieve the informed and responsible decision making fundamental to a civil society.
- We strive to understand and respect other communicators before evaluating and responding to their messages.
- We promote access to communication resources and opportunities as necessary to fulfill human potential and contribute to the well-being of families, communities, and society.
- We promote communication climates of caring and mutual understanding that respect the unique needs and characteristics of individual communicators.

4.2 ETHICS IN PUBLIC SPEAKING

- We condemn communication that degrades individuals and humanity through distortion, intimidation, coercion, and violence, and through the expression of intolerance and hatred.
- We are committed to the courageous expression of personal convictions in pursuit of fairness and justice.
- We advocate sharing information, opinions, and feelings when facing significant choices while also respecting privacy and confidentiality.
- We accept responsibility for the short- and long-term consequences of our own communication and expect the same of others.

Source: http://www.natcom.org/Default.aspx?id=134&terms=Credo

The NCA Credo for Ethical Communication is designed to inspire discussions of ethics related to all aspects of human communication. For our purposes, we want to think about each of these principles in terms of how they affect public speaking.

We Advocate Truthfulness, Accuracy, Honesty, and Reason as Essential to the Integrity of Communication

As public speakers, one of the first ethical areas we should be concerned with is information honesty. While there are cases where speakers have blatantly lied to an audience, it is more common for speakers to prove a point by exaggerating, omitting facts that weigh against their message, or distorting information. We believe that speakers build a relationship with their audiences, and that lying, exaggerating, or distorting information violates this relationship. Ultimately, a speaker will be more persuasive by using reason and logical arguments supported by facts rather than relying on emotional appeals designed to manipulate the audience.

It is also important to be honest about where all your information comes from in a speech. As speakers, examine your information sources and determine whether they are biased or have hidden agendas. For example, you are not likely to get accurate information about nonwhite individuals from a neo-Nazi website. While you may not know all your sources of information firsthand, you should attempt to find objective sources that do not have an overt or covert agenda that skews the argument you are making.

The second part of information honesty is to fully disclose where we obtain the information in our speeches. As ethical speakers, it is important to always cite your sources of information within the body of a speech. Whether you conducted an interview or read a newspaper article, you must tell your listeners where the information came from. Using someone else's words or ideas without giving credit is called **plagiarism**. The word "plagiarism" stems from the Latin word *plagiaries*, or kidnapper. The American Psychological Association states in its publication manual that ethical speakers do not claim "words and ideas of another as their own; they give credit where credit is due" (American Psychological Association, 2001).

In the previous sentence, we placed quotation marks around the sentence to indicate that the words came from the American Psychological Association and not from us. When speaking informally, people sometimes use "air quotes" to signal direct quotations—but this is not a recommended technique in public speaking. Instead, speakers need to verbally tell an audience when they are using someone else's information. The consequences for failing to cite sources during public speeches can be substantial. When Senator Joseph Biden was running for president of the United States in 1988, reporters found that he had plagiarized portions of his stump speech from British politician Neil Kinnock. Biden was forced to drop out of the race as a result. More recently, the student newspaper at Malone University in Ohio alleged that the university president, Gary W. Streit, had plagiarized material in a public speech. Streit retired abruptly as a result.

Even if you are not running for president of the United States or serving as a college president, citing sources is important to you as a student. Many universities have policies that include dismissal from the institution for student plagiarism of academic work, including public speeches. Our university's policies regarding Academic Integrity can be found here. Failing to cite your sources might result, at best, in lower credibility with your audience and, at worst, in a failing grade on your assignment or expulsion from your school. We cannot emphasize enough the importance of giving credit to the speakers and authors whose ideas we pass on within our own speeches and writing.

Speakers tend to fall into one of three major traps with plagiarism. The first trap is failing to tell the audience the source of a direct quotation. In the previous paragraph, we used a direct quotation from the American Psychological Association; if we had not used the quotation marks and clearly listed where the cited material came from, you, as a reader, wouldn't have known the source of that information. To avoid plagiarism, you always need to tell your audience when you are directly quoting information within a speech.

The second plagiarism trap public speakers fall into is paraphrasing what someone else said or wrote without giving credit to the speaker or author. For example, you may have read a book and learned that there are three types of schoolyard bullying. In the middle of your speech you talk about those three types of schoolyard bullying. If you do not tell your audience where you found that information, you are plagiarizing. Typically, the only information you do not need to cite is information that is general knowledge. General knowledge is information that is publicly available and widely known by a large segment of society. For example, you would not need to provide a citation within a speech for the name of Delaware's capital. Although many people do not know the capital of Delaware without looking it up, this information is publicly available and easily accessible, so assigning credit to one specific source is not useful or necessary.

The third plagiarism trap that speakers fall into is re-citing someone else's sources within a speech. To explain this problem, let's look at a brief segment from a research paper written by Wrench, DiMartino, Ramirez, Oviedio, and Tesfamariam:

> The main character on the hit Fox television show *House*, Dr. Gregory House, has one basic mantra, "It's a basic truth of the human condition that everybody lies. The only variable is about what" (Shore & Barclay, 2005). This notion that "everybody lies" is so persistent in the series that t-shirts have been printed with the slogan. Surprisingly, research has shown that most people do lie during interpersonal interactions to some degree. In a study conducted by Turner, Edgley, and Olmstead (1975), the researchers had 130 participants record their own conversations with others. After recording these conversations, the participants then examined the truthfulness of the statements within the interactions. Only 38.5% of the statements made during these interactions were labeled as "completely honest."

In this example, we see that the authors of this paragraph cited information from two external sources: Shore and Barclay and Tummer, Edgley, and Olmstead. These two groups of authors are given credit for their ideas. The authors make it clear that they did not produce the television show *House* or conduct the study that found that only 38.5 percent of statements were completely honest. Instead, these authors cited information found in two other locations. This type of citation is appropriate.

However, if a speaker read the paragraph and said the following during a speech, it would be plagiarism: "According to Wrench DiMartino, Ramirez, Oviedio, and Tesfamariam, in a study of 130 participants, only 38.5 percent of the responses were completely honest." In this case, the speaker is attributing the information cited to the authors of the paragraph, which is not accurate. If you want to cite the information within your speech, you need to read the original article by Turner, Edgley, and Olmstead and cite that information yourself.

There are two main reasons we do this. First, Wrench, DiMartino, Ramirez, Oviedio, and Tesfamariam may have mistyped the information. Suppose the study by Turner, Edgley, and Olstead really actually found that 58.5 percent of the responses were completely honest. If you cited the revised number (38.5 percent) from the paragraph, you would be further spreading incorrect information.

The second reason we do not re-cite someone else's sources within our speeches is because it's intellectually dishonest. You owe your listeners an honest description of where the facts you are relating came from, not just the name of an author who cited those facts. It is more work to trace the original source of a fact or statistic, but by doing that extra work you can avoid this plagiarism trap.

118 | 4.2 ETHICS IN PUBLIC SPEAKING

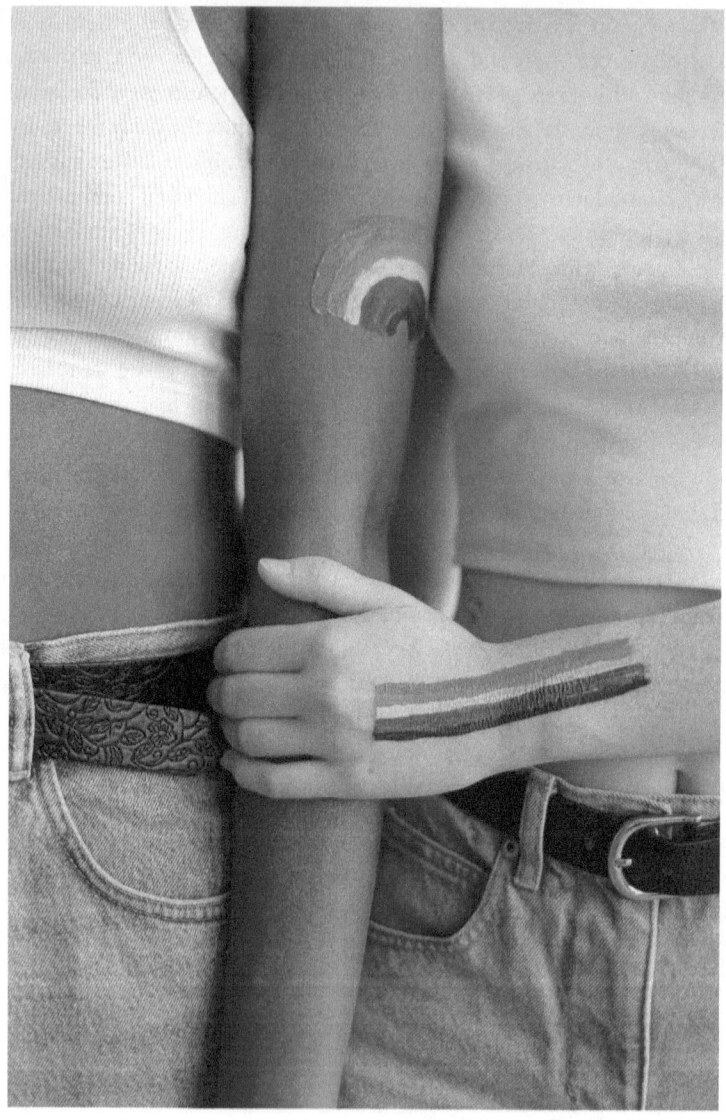

We Endorse Freedom of Expression, Diversity of Perspective, and Tolerance of Dissent to Achieve the Informed and Responsible Decision Making Fundamental to a Civil Society

This ethical principle affirms that a civil society depends on freedom of expression, diversity of perspective, and tolerance of dissent and that informed and responsible decisions can only be made if all members of society are free to express their thoughts and opinions. Further, it holds that diverse viewpoints, including those that disagree with accepted authority, are important for the functioning of a democratic society.

If everyone only listened to one source of information, then we would be easily manipulated and controlled. For this reason, we believe that individuals should be willing to listen to a range of speakers on a given subject. As listeners or consumers of communication, we should realize that this diversity of perspectives enables us to be more fully informed on a subject. Imagine voting in an election after listening only to the campaign speeches of one candidate. The perspective of that candidate would be so narrow that you would have no way to accurately understand and assess the issues at hand or the strengths and weaknesses of the opposing candidates. Unfortunately, some voters do limit themselves to listening only to their candidate of choice and, as a result, base their voting decisions on incomplete—and, not infrequently, inaccurate—information.

Listening to diverse perspectives includes being willing to hear dissenting voices. Dissent is by nature uncomfortable, as it entails expressing opposition to authority, often in very unflattering terms. Legal scholar Steven H. Shiffrin has argued in favor of some symbolic speech (e.g., flag burning) because we as a society value the ability of anyone to express their dissent against the will and ideas of the majority (Shiffrin, 1999). Ethical communicators will be receptive to dissent, no matter how strongly they may disagree with the speaker's message because they realize that a society that forbids dissent cannot function democratically.

Ultimately, honoring **free speech** and seeking out a variety of perspectives is very important for all listeners.

We Strive to Understand and Respect Other Communicators before Evaluating and Responding to Their Messages

This is another ethical characteristic that is specifically directed at receivers of a message. As listeners, we often let our perceptions of a speaker's nonverbal behavior—his or her appearance, posture, mannerisms, eye contact, and so on—determine our opinions about a message before the speaker has said a word. We may also find ourselves judging a speaker based on information we have heard about him or her from other people. Perhaps you have heard from other students that a particular teacher is a really boring lecturer or is really entertaining in class. Even though you do not have personal knowledge, you may prejudge the teacher and his or her message based on information you have been given from others. The NCA credo reminds us that to be ethical listeners, we need to avoid such judgments and instead make an effort to listen respectfully; only when we have understood a speaker's viewpoint are we ready to begin forming our opinions of the message.

Listeners should try to objectively analyze the content and arguments within a speech before deciding how to respond. Especially when we disagree with a speaker, we might find it difficult to listen to the content of the speech and, instead, work on creating a rebuttal the entire time the speaker is talking. When this happens, we do not strive to understand the speaker and do not respect the speaker.

Of course, this does not just affect the listener in the public speaking situation. As speakers, we are often called upon to evaluate and refute potential arguments against our positions. While we always want our speeches to be as persuasive as possible, we do ourselves and our audiences a disservice when we downplay, distort, or refuse to mention important arguments from the opposing side. Fairly researching and evaluating counterarguments is an important ethical obligation for the public speaker.

We Promote Access to Communication Resources and Opportunities as Necessary to Fulfill Human Potential and Contribute to the Well-Being of Families, Communities, and Society

Human communication is a skill that can and should be taught. We strongly believe that you can become a better, more ethical speaker. One of the reasons the authors of this book teach courses in public speaking and wrote this college textbook on public speaking is that we, as communication professionals, have an ethical obligation to provide others, including students like you, with resources and opportunities to become better speakers.

We Promote Communication Climates of Caring and Mutual Understanding That Respect the Unique Needs and Characteristics of Individual Communicators

Speakers need to take a two-pronged approach when addressing any audience: caring about the audience and understanding the audience. When you as a speaker truly care about your audience's needs and desires, you avoid setting up a manipulative climate. This is not to say that your audience will always perceive their own needs and desires in the same way you do, but if you make an honest effort to speak to your audience in a way that has their best interests at heart, you are more likely to create persuasive arguments that are not just manipulative appeals.

Second, it is important for a speaker to create an atmosphere of mutual understanding. To do this, you should first learn as much as possible about your audience, a process called audience analysis.

To create a climate of caring and mutual respect, it is important for us as speakers to be open with our audiences so that our intentions and perceptions are clear. Nothing alienates an audience faster than a speaker with a hidden agenda unrelated to the stated purpose of the speech. One of our coauthors once listened to a speaker give a two-hour talk, allegedly about workplace wellness, which actually turned out to be an infomercial for the speaker's weight-loss program. In this case, the speaker clearly had a hidden (or not-so-hidden) agenda, which made the audience feel disrespected.

We Condemn Communication That Degrades Individuals and Humanity through Distortion, Intimidation, Coercion, and Violence and through the Expression of Intolerance and Hatred

This ethical principle is very important for all speakers. Hopefully, intimidation, coercion, and violence will not be part of your public speaking experiences, but some public speakers have been known to call for violence and incite mobs of people to commit atrocities. Thus distortion and expressions of intolerance and hatred are of special concern when it comes to public speaking.

Distortion occurs when someone purposefully twists information in a way that detracts from its original meaning. Unfortunately, some speakers take information and use it in a manner that is not in the spirit of the original information. One place we see distortion frequently is in the political context, where politicians cite a statistic or the results of a study and either completely alter the information or use it in a deceptive manner. FactCheck.org, a project of the Annenberg Public Policy Center (http://www.factcheck.org), and the St. Petersburg Times's Politifact (http://www.politifact.com) are nonpartisan organizations devoted to analyzing political messages and demonstrating how information has been distorted.

Expressions of intolerance and hatred that are to be avoided include using **ageist**, **heterosexist**, **racist**, **sexist**, and any other form of speech that demeans or belittles a group of people. Hate speech from all sides of the political spectrum in our society is detrimental to ethical communication. As such, we as speakers should be acutely aware of how an audience may perceive words that could be considered bigoted. For example, suppose a school board official involved in budget negotiations used the word "shekels" to refer to money, which he believes the teachers' union should be willing to give up (Associated Press, 2011). The remark would be likely to prompt accusations of anti-Semitism and to distract listeners from any constructive suggestions the official might have for resolving budget issues. Although the official might insist that he meant no offense, he damaged the ethical climate of the budget debate by using a word associated with bigotry.

At the same time, it is important for listeners to pay attention to expressions of intolerance or hatred. Extremist speakers sometimes attempt to disguise their true agendas by avoiding bigoted "buzzwords" and using mild-sounding terms instead. For example, a speaker advocating the overthrow of a government might use the term "regime change" instead of "revolution"; similarly, proponents of genocide in various parts of the world have used the term "ethnic cleansing" instead of "extermination." By listening critically to the gist of a speaker's message as well as the specific language he or she uses, we can see how that speaker views the world.

We Are Committed to the Courageous Expression of Personal Convictions in Pursuit of Fairness and Justice

We believe that finding and bringing to light situations of inequality and injustice within our society is important. Public speaking has been used throughout history to point out inequality and injustice, from Patrick Henry arguing against the way the English government treated the American colonists and Sojourner Truth describing the evils of slavery to Martin Luther King Jr.'s "I Have a Dream" speech and Army Lt. Dan Choi's speeches arguing that the military's "don't ask, don't tell policy" is unjust. Many social justice movements have started because young public speakers have decided to stand up for what they believe is fair and just.

We Advocate Sharing Information, Opinions, and Feelings When Facing Significant Choices While Also Respecting Privacy and Confidentiality

This ethical principle involves balancing personal disclosure with discretion. It is perfectly normal for speakers to want to share their own personal opinions and feelings about a topic; however, it is also important to highlight information within a speech that represents your own thoughts and feelings. Your listeners have a right to know the difference between facts and personal opinions.

Similarly, we have an obligation to respect others' privacy and confidentiality when speaking. If information is obtained from printed or publicly distributed material, it's perfectly appropriate to use that information without getting permission, as long as you cite it. However, when you have a great anecdote one of your friends told you in confidence, or access to information that is not available to the general public, it is best to seek permission before using the information in a speech.

This ethical obligation even has legal implications in many government and corporate contexts. For example, individuals who work for the Central Intelligence Agency are legally precluded from discussing their work in public without prior review by the agency. And companies such as Google also have policies requiring employees to seek permission before engaging in public speaking in which sensitive information might be leaked.

We Accept Responsibility for Short- and Long-Term Consequences of Our Communication and Expect the Same of Others

The last statement of NCA's ethical credo may be the most important one. We live in a society where a speaker's message can literally be heard around the world in a matter of minutes, thanks to our global communication networks. Extreme remarks made by politicians, media commentators, and celebrities, as well as ordinary people, can unexpectedly "go viral" with regrettable consequences. It is not unusual to see situations where a speaker talks hatefully about a specific group, but when one of the speaker's listeners violently attacks a member of the group, the speaker insists that he or she had no way of knowing that this could possibly have happened. Washing one's hands of responsibility is unacceptable: all speakers should accept responsibility for the short-term and long-term consequences of their speeches. Although it is certainly not always the speaker's fault if someone commits an act of violence, the speaker should take responsibility for her or his role in the situation. This process involves being truly reflective and willing to examine how one's speech could have tragic consequences.

Furthermore, attempting to persuade a group of people to take any action means you should make sure that you understand the consequences of that action. Whether you are persuading people to vote for a political candidate or just encouraging them to lose weight, you should know what the short-term and long-term consequences of that decision could be. While our predictions of short-term and long-term consequences may not always be right, we have an ethical duty to at least think through the possible consequences of our speeches and the actions we encourage.

Practicing Ethical Public Speaking

Thus far in this section we've introduced you to the basics of thinking through the ethics of public speaking. Knowing about ethics is essential, but even more important to being an ethical public speaker is putting that knowledge into practice by thinking through possible ethical pitfalls prior to standing up and speaking out. Below is a list of some examples of unethical public speaking behaviors based on our discussion in this chapter.

Examples of Unethical Public Speaking

- Knowingly adding false information to a speech
- Attempting to persuade by unnecessarily emotional rather than logical appeals
- Not clearly citing all of the information used in the speech
- Using unknown or incredible sources
- Not considering the audience while developing the speech
- Altering facts to make the speech more persuasive
- Using bigoted or intolerant language in the speech
- Manipulating the audience to take the speaker's position
- Blending personal opinion with actual fact during the speech
- Not distinguishing between personal opinion and fact during the speech
- Using information from a friend, colleague or source that should not be repeated or was "off the record"
- Failing to consider the short- or long-term consequences of the speech

References

American Psychological Association. (2001). *Publication manual of the American Psychological Association* (5th ed.). Washington, DC: Author, p. 349.

Associated Press. (2011, May 5). Conn. shekel shellacking. *New York Post*.

Shiffrin, S. H. (1999). *Dissent, injustice and the meanings of America*. Princeton, NJ: Princeton University Press.

4.3 FREE SPEECH

Free speech has been a constitutional right since the founding of our nation, and according to *Merriam Webster's Dictionary of Law*, **free speech** entails "the right to express information, ideas, and opinions free of government restrictions based on content and subject only to reasonable limitations (as the power of the government to avoid a clear and present danger) esp. as guaranteed by the First and Fourteenth Amendments to the U.S. Constitution" (Freedom of speech). Free speech is especially important to us as public speakers because expressing information and ideas is the purpose of public speaking. It is also important to audiences of public speeches because free speech allows us to hear and consider multiple points of view so that we can make more informed decisions.

The First Amendment to the Constitution

Free speech was so important to the founders of the United States that it is included in the first of the ten amendments to the US Constitution that are known as the Bill of Rights. This is not surprising, considering that many American colonists had crossed the Atlantic to escape religious persecution and that England had imposed many restrictions on personal freedoms during the colonial era. The text of the First Amendment reads, "Congress shall make no law respecting an establishment of religion, or prohibiting the free exercise thereof; or abridging the freedom of speech, or of the press; or the right of the people peaceably to assemble, and to petition the Government for a redress of grievances" (National Archives and Records Administration, 2011).

The freedoms protected by the First Amendment may seem perfectly natural today, but they were controversial in 1791 when the Bill of Rights was enacted. Proponents argued that individuals needed protection from overreaching powers of government, while opponents believed these protections were unnecessary and that amending them to the Constitution could weaken the union.

Freedom of speech, of the press, of religion, of association, of assembly and petition are all guaranteed in amendments to the US Constitution. Free speech allows us to exercise our other First Amendment rights. Freedom of assembly means that people can gather to discuss and protest issues of importance to them. If free speech were not protected, citizens would not be able to exercise their right to protest about activities such as war or policies such as health care reform.

Free speech does not mean, however, that every US citizen has the legal right to say anything at any time. If your speech is likely to lead to violence or other illegal acts, it is not protected. One recent example is a 2007 Supreme Court decision in the *Morse et al. v. Frederick* case. In this case, a high school student held up a sign reading "Bong Hits 4 Jesus" across from the school during the 2002 Olympic Torch Relay. The principal suspended the teenager, and the teen sued the principal for violating his First Amendment rights. Ultimately, the court decided that the principal had the right to suspend the student because he was advocating illegal behavior (Supreme Court of the United States, 2007).

The meaning of "free speech" is constantly being debated by politicians, judges, and the public, even within the United States, where this right has been discussed for over two hundred years. As US citizens, it is important to be aware of both the protections afforded by free speech and its limits so that we can be both articulate speakers and critical listeners when issues such as antiwar protests at military funerals or speech advocating violence against members of specific groups come up within our communities.

References

Freedom of speech. (n.d.). In *Merriam-Webster's dictionary of law*. Retrieved from Dictionary.com website: http://dictionary.reference.com/browse/freedom%20of%20speech

National Archives and Records Administration. (2011). Bill of rights transcription. Retrieved from http://www.archives.gov/exhibits/charters/bill_of_rights_transcript.html

Supreme Court of the United States. (2007). Syllabus: Morse et al. v. Frederick. No. 06–278. Argued March 19, 2007–Decided June 25, 2007. Retrieved from http://www.supremecourt.gov/opinions/06pdf/06-278.pdf

4.5 ENRICHMENT

Discussion Questions

1. Robert is preparing a speech about legalizing marijuana use in the United States. He knows that his roommate wrote a paper on the topic last semester and asks his roommate about the paper in an attempt to gather information. During his speech, Robert orally cites his roommate by name as a source of his information but does not report that the source is his roommate, whose experience is based on writing a paper. In what ways does Robert's behavior violate the guidelines set out in the NCA Credo for Ethical Communication?
2. Do you feel we have freedom of speech in our country? How has free speech been challenged and defended in our country?
3. Why do you think the U.S. Supreme Court has historically considered flag burning and pornography to be "free speech acts"?
4. Why do you think the authors of the NCA Credo for Ethical Communication included a statement about the importance of listening before responding to speakers? Why do you think our culture often places more of an emphasis on speaking than listening? And, what impact does this have on our communication?
5. What do you think it means to accept responsibility for your own communication and expect the same of other communicators?
6. Think about the following scenarios involving an ethical dilemma. How would you react?

    - You attend a political debate on campus. The candidate's speech contains many ideas that you do not agree with. How can you demonstrate ethical listening during the speech?
    - You are preparing to give a persuasive speech and realize that you have lost the citation information for one of your primary sources. You cannot find the link to your source again. What would you do to ethically prepare for the speech?

Activities

In class, review the NCA Credo for Ethical Communication together out loud. After reading/discussing the Credo, students can discuss the following in small groups:

- What aspects of the Credo are most important to you?
- Is there anything missing from the Credo?
- Who is a speaker/celebrity/athlete/family member/friend who embodies these principles of ethical communication? Why do you think this person is especially ethical? How could we model their behavior in our own communication?
- Finally, create one to three statements that we can add to our own SPCH 2713 Credo for Ethical Communication. These can be as long or as brief as you like and do not need to use the same language as the Credo.
- As a class, create our SPCH 2713 Credo for Ethical Communication – the instructor should record each group's statements and then discuss as a class.

Case Study

In class, form four or five groups. Each group will be given a different scenario to discuss the ethical implications of the conversations/language. As a group, can you reach a consensus on how ethical behavior is or is not illustrated? Trigger Warning: Some of these scenarios are sensitive and may cause you to experience a variety of emotional responses.

Case 1: In his speech about covid protocols, Jason referred to covid-19 as "the Chinese virus." Many in the audience were visibly offended by his language choice, while some audience members snickered at the label and/or the awkwardness of the expression. How did Jason's language align or misalign with ethical considerations of public speaking?

Case 2: After a group presentation, the professor referred to a transgendered classmate by their "dead name" (the name they no longer go by) multiple times and continually used the wrong pronouns. Knowing this is an important violation to acknowledge, how do you think you can address the professor's misgendering in an ethical manner? Would/should you say something? Would/should it be in public or private?

Case 3: One of your group members has a speaking impediment that impacts their fluency when speaking. Despite this, the group member enjoys speaking in public and asks to present the largest section of the presentation. You are concerned about their ability to complete their speaking portion in a timely manner so that the project meets the time criteria. Should you ask them to take a smaller section of the presentation? How do you handle this scenario in an ethical manner?

Case 4: In a persuasive speech in class, Rebecca advocates working out and eating healthy. During her speech, she body shamed audience members when she said, "Besides, no one wants to date a fat person!" Knowing the issues that impact self esteem, mental health, and body image, how do you as an audience member address this offense ethically in the question and answer session?

Case 5: Aaron gave a presentation about the January 6th capitol riot and analogized former President Trump's supporters to being members of a cult. Knowing that in Oklahoma, there are probably more conservative leaning folks (possibly Trump supporters), do you think Aaron's language aligned or misaligned with ethical considerations of public speaking? How do you think his language impacts the audience?

4.5 ENRICHMENT

5 AUDIENCE ANALYSIS

Learning Objectives

- Recognize the value of acknowledging your audience.
- Explain how to adapt your speech to your audience's needs including choosing a worthwhile topic.
- Explain the value of speaking with credibility.
- Demonstrate how to gather and use demographic, psychographic, and situational information.
- Create effective tools for gathering audience information.
- Use your audience analysis to prepare a speech and to alter your speech while speaking.

Key Terms

- **Audience Analysis**
- **Captive Audience**
- **Chronocentrism**
- **Demographic Analysis**
- **Demographic Information**
- **Diversity**
- **Elitism**

- **Ethnocentrism**
- **Ethos**
- **Focus Group**
- **Frame of Reference**
- **Idiom**
- **Interview**
- **Psychographic Analysis**
- **Psychographic Information**
- **Racism**
- **Sexism**
- **Situational Analysis**
- **Socioeconomic Status**
- **Stereotyping**
- **Survey**
- **Voluntary Audience**

5.1 WHAT IS AUDIENCE ANALYSIS?

"When you know your audience, your audience knows." -Unknown

One of the consequences of the First Amendment to the Constitution, which protects our right to speak freely, is that we focus so much on what we want to say that we often overlook the question of who our audience is. Does your audience care what you as a speaker think? Can they see how your speech applies to their lives and interests? The act of public speaking is a shared activity that involves interaction between speaker and audience. In order for your speech to get a fair hearing, you need to create a relationship with your listeners. Scholars Sprague, Stuart, and Bodary explain, "Speakers do not give speeches *to* audiences; they jointly create meaning *with* audiences" (Sprague, et al., 2010). The success of your speech rests in large part on how your audience receives and understands it.

Think of a time when you heard a speech that sounded "canned" or that fell flat because the audience didn't "get it." Chances are that this happened because the speaker neglected to consider that public speaking is an audience-centered activity. Worse, lack of consideration for one's audience can result in the embarrassment of alienating listeners by telling a joke they don't appreciate, or using language they find offensive. The best way to reduce the risk of such situations is to conduct an audience analysis as you prepare your speech.

Audience analysis is the process of gathering information about the people in your audience so that you can understand their needs, expectations, beliefs, values, attitudes, and likely opinions. In this chapter, we will first examine some reasons why audience analysis is important. We will then describe three different types of audience analysis and some techniques to use in conducting audience analysis. Finally, we will explain how you can use your audience analysis not only during the creation of your speech but also while you are delivering it.

Pete's People

As Pistol Pete, the spirited mascot of Oklahoma State University, I understand the vital importance of connecting with my audience and tailoring my message to resonate with them. To effectively analyze my audience, I utilize various strategies that allow me to understand their needs, values, and interests.

First and foremost, I observe the diverse composition of the Oklahoma State University community. From students to faculty, alumni to visitors, each group brings unique perspectives and experiences to the table. By recognizing this diversity, I can adapt my communication style to ensure inclusivity and relevance for all.

Additionally, I pay close attention to the context and setting in which I engage with my audience. Whether it's a sporting event, a pep rally, or a community outreach program, each environment offers distinct opportunities to connect. By considering the expectations and atmosphere of the specific event, I can tailor my message and delivery accordingly, ensuring maximum impact and resonance.

Furthermore, I engage in active listening and dialogue with the Oklahoma State community. I seek feedback, whether through formal channels or informal conversations, to gain insights into their needs, concerns, and aspirations. This two-way communication allows me to understand their perspectives, build trust, and ensure that my messages align with their values and aspirations.

Lastly, I remain attuned to current events, cultural shifts, and emerging trends that shape the collective mindset of the Oklahoma State community. By staying informed, I can address relevant topics, spark conversations, and adapt my message to reflect the ever-evolving interests and sensitivities of my audience.

By employing these strategies, I can effectively analyze my audience at Oklahoma State University, understanding their diversity, needs, and aspirations. Armed with this knowledge, I can engage with authenticity, relevance, and the unwavering spirit that defines the Orange Cowboy community. Together, we can forge meaningful connections, foster unity, and inspire each other to reach greater heights. Go Pokes! How can you go about learning who will be in your audience?

References

Sprague, J., Stuart, D., & Bodary, D. (2010). *The speaker's handbook* (9th ed.). Boston, MA: Wadsworth Cengage.

5.2 WHY CONDUCT AN AUDIENCE ANALYSIS?

Acknowledge the Audience

Picture yourself in front of the audience, about to deliver your speech. This is the moment when your relationship with your audience begins, and the quality of this relationship will influence how receptive they will be to your ideas, or at least how willing they'll be to listen to what you have to say. One of the best ways to initiate this relationship is by finding a way to acknowledge your audience. This can be as simple as establishing eye contact and thanking them for coming to hear your presentation. If they've braved bad weather, are missing a world-class sports event, or are putting up with an inconvenience such as a stuffy conference room, tell them how much you appreciate their presence in spite of the circumstances. This can go a long way toward getting them "on board" with your message.

For a political candidate who is traveling from town to town giving what may be perceived as the same campaign speech time and time again, a statement like "It's great to be here in Springfield, and I want to thank the West Valley League of Women Voters and our hosts, the Downtown Senior Center, for the opportunity to be with you today" lets the audience know that the candidate has at least taken the trouble to tailor the speech to the present audience. Stephanie Coopman and James Lull tell us that Microsoft chairman Bill Gates often adapts to his audiences by thanking them for their participation in the computer industry or for their preparation to participate in an electronic world. The authors say, "Even those brief acknowledgments let audience members know that Gates had prepared his speech with them in mind" (Coopman & Lull, 2009).

Choose a Worthwhile Topic

Your selection of a topic should reflect your regard for the audience. There is no universal list of good or bad topics, but you have an ethical responsibility to select a topic that will be worth listening to. As a student, you are probably sensitive to how unpleasant it would be to listen to a speech on a highly complex or technical topic that you found impossible to understand. However, have you considered that audiences do not want to waste their time or attention listening to a speech that is too simple? Many students find themselves tempted to choose an easy topic, or a topic they already know a great deal about. This is an understandable temptation; if you are like most students, you have many commitments and the demands on your time are considerable. Many experts encourage students to begin with something they already know. However, our experience tells us that students often do this simply to reduce their workload. For example, if the purpose of your speech is to inform or persuade students in your public speaking class, a topic such as fitness, drunk driving, the Greek system (campus fraternities and sororities), or credit card responsibility may be easy for you to address, but it is unlikely to go very far toward informing your audience, and in all likelihood, it will not be persuading them either. Instead, your audience members and your professor will quickly recognize that you were thinking of your own needs rather than those of your audience.

To avoid this trap, it behooves you to seek a topic that will be novel and interesting both for you and for your audience. It will also be important to do some credible research in order to ensure that even the most informed audience members will learn something from you. There are many topics that could provide a refreshing departure from your usual academic studies. Topics such as the Bermuda Triangle, biopiracy, the environmental niche of sharks, the green lifestyle, and the historic Oneida Community all provide interesting views of human and natural phenomena not usually provided in public education. Such topics might be more likely to hold the interest of your classroom audience than topics they've heard about time and time again.

You should be aware that your audience will not have the same set of knowledge that you do. For instance, if you are speaking about biopiracy, you should probably define it and give a clear example. If your speech is on the green lifestyle, it would be important to frame it as a realistic choice, not a goal so remote as to be hopeless.

In each case, you should use audience analysis to consider how your audience will respond to you, your topic, and your message.

Clarity

Nothing is more lamentable than a rhetorical actor who endeavors to make grandiose the impressions of others through the utilization of an elephantine albeit nonsensical argot—or nothing is worse than a speaker who tries to impress the audience with a giant vocabulary that no one understands. In the first portion of the preceding sentence, we pulled out as many polysyllabic words as we could find. Unfortunately, most people will just find the sentence wordy and the meaning will pass right over their heads. As such, we as public speakers must ensure that we are clear in what we say.

Make sure that you state your topic clearly at the outset, using words that your audience will understand. Letting them know what to expect from your speech shows consideration for them as listeners and lets them know that you value their time and attention.

Throughout your speech, define your terms clearly and carefully in order to avoid misleading or alarming people by mistake. Be careful not to use jargon or "insider" language that will exclude listeners who aren't "in the know." If you approach audience analysis in haste, you might find yourself presenting a speech with no clear message. You might avoid making any statements outright from fear of offending. It is much better to know to whom you're speaking and to present a clear, decisive message that lets listeners know what you think.

Controversial Topics Are Important and Risky

Some of the most interesting topics are controversial. They are controversial topics because people have deeply felt values and beliefs on different sides of those topics. For instance, before you choose nuclear energy as your topic, investigate the many voices speaking out both in favor and against increasing its use. Many people perceive nuclear energy as a clean, reliable, and much-needed source of energy. Others say that even the mining of uranium is harmful to the environment, that we lack satisfactory solutions for storing nuclear waste, and that nuclear power plants are vulnerable to errors and attacks. Another group might view the issue economically, believing that industry needs nuclear energy. Engineers might believe that if the national grid could be modernized, we would have enough energy, and that we should strive to use and waste less energy until modernization is feasible. Some might feel deep concern about our reliance on foreign oil. Others might view nuclear energy as more tried-and-true than other alternatives. The topic is extremely controversial, and yet it is interesting and very important.

You shouldn't avoid controversy altogether, but you should choose your topic carefully. Moreover, how you treat your audience is just as important as how you treat your topic. If your audience has widely diverse views, take the time to acknowledge the concerns they have. Treat them as intelligent people, even if you don't trust the completeness or the accuracy of their beliefs about your topic.

Adapt Your Speech to Audience Needs

When preparing a speech for a classroom audience consisting of other students and your professor, you may feel that you know their interests and expectations fairly well. However, we learn public speaking in order to be able to address other audiences where we can do some good. In some cases, your audience might consist of young children who are not ready to accept the fact that a whale is not a fish or that the moon is always round even though it sometimes appears to be a crescent or a half circle. In other cases, your audience might include retirees living on fixed incomes and who therefore might not agree that raising local taxes is a vital "investment in the future."

Even in an audience that appears to be homogeneous—composed of people who are very similar to one another—different listeners will understand the same ideas in different ways. Every member of every audience has his or her own **frame of**

reference—the unique set of perspectives, experience, knowledge, and values belonging to every individual. An audience member who has been in a car accident caused by a drunk driver might not appreciate a lighthearted joke about barhopping. Similarly, stressing the importance of graduate school might be discouraging to audience members who don't know whether they can even afford to stay in college to complete an undergraduate degree.

These examples illustrate why audience analysis—the process of learning all you reasonably can about your audience—is so centrally important. Audience analysis includes consideration of **demographic information**, such as the gender, age range, marital status, race, and ethnicity of the people in your audience. Another, perhaps less obvious, demographic factor is **socioeconomic status**, which refers to a combination of characteristics including income, wealth, level of education, and occupational prestige. Each of these dimensions gives you some information about which kinds of topics, and which aspects of various topics, will be well received.

Suppose you are preparing to give an informative speech about early childhood health care. If your audience is a group of couples who have each recently had a new baby and who live in an affluent suburb, you can expect that they will be young adults with high socioeconomic status; they will likely be eager to know about the very best available health care for their children, whether they are healthy or have various medical problems. In contrast, if your audience is a group of nurses, they may differ in age, but will be similar in education and occupational prestige. They will already know quite a lot about the topic, so you will want to find an aspect that may be new for them, such as community health care resources for families with limited financial resources or for referring children with special needs. As another example, if you are addressing a city council committee that is considering whether to fund a children's health care initiative, your audience is likely to have very mixed demographics.

Audience analysis also takes into account what market researchers call **psychographic information**, which is more personal and more difficult to predict than demographics. Psychographic information involves the beliefs, attitudes, and values that your audience members embrace. Respecting your audience means that you avoid offending, excluding, or trivializing the beliefs and values they hold. Returning to the topic of early childhood health care, you can expect new parents to be passionate about wanting the best for their child. The psychographics of a group of nurses would revolve around their professional competence and the need to provide "standard of care" for their patients. In a city council committee meeting, the topic of early childhood health care may be a highly personal and emotional issue for some of your listeners, while for others it may be strictly a matter of dollars and cents.

Consider Audience Diversity

Diversity is a key dimension of audience membership and, therefore, of audience analysis. While the term "diversity" is often used to refer to racial and ethnic minorities, it is important to realize that audiences can be diverse in many other ways as well. Being mindful of diversity means being respectful of all people and striving to avoid **racism, ethnocentrism, sexism, ageism, elitism**, and other assumptions. An interesting "ism" that is not often mentioned is **chronocentrism**, or the assumption that people today are superior to people who lived in earlier eras (Russell, 1991).

Sociologists John R. Logan and Wenquan Zhang analyzed racial and ethnic diversity in US cities and observed a pattern that rewrites the traditional "rules" of neighborhood change (Logan & Zhang, 2010). Whereas in our grandparents' day a racially mixed neighborhood was one with African American and white residents, in recent decades, many more people from a variety of Asian and Latin American countries have immigrated to the United States. As a result, many cities have neighborhoods that are richly diverse with Asian, Hispanic, and African American cultural influences as well as those of white European Americans. Each cultural group consists of people from many communities and occupations. Each cultural group came to the United States for different reasons and came from different communities and occupations within their original cultures. Even though it can be easy to assume that people from a culture are exactly like each other, we undermine our credibility when we create our message as though members of these cultures are carbon copies of each other.

One of the author's classes included two students from China. During a discussion of cultural similarity and difference, one remarked, "I thought we would have the same tastes in food because we are both from China, but she likes different spices and cooking techniques than I do."

While race, ethnicity, and culture may be relatively visible aspects of diversity, there are many other aspects that are less obvious, so your audience is often more diverse than you might initially think. Suppose you are going to give a talk on pool safety to residents of a very affluent suburban community—will all your audience members be wealthy? No. There might be some who are unemployed, some who are behind on their mortgage payments, some who live in rented rooms, not to mention some who work as babysitters or housekeepers. Furthermore, if your listeners have some characteristic in common, it doesn't mean that they all think alike. For instance, if your audience consists of people who are members of military families, don't assume that they all have identical beliefs about national security. If there are many business students in your audience, don't assume they all agree about the relative importance of ethics and profits. Instead, recognize that a range of opinion exists.

This is where the frame of reference becomes an important concept. People have a wide variety of reasons for making the choices they make and for doing the things they do. For instance, a business student, while knowing that profitability is important, might have a strong interest in green lifestyles, low energy use, and alternative energy sources, areas of economic development that might require a great deal of investment before profits are realized. In fact, some business students may want to be involved in a paradigm shift away from "business as usual."

These examples illustrate how important it is to use audience analysis to avoid **stereotyping**—taking for granted that people with a certain characteristic in common have the same likes, dislikes, values, and beliefs. All members of our audiences deserve to have the same sensitivity and the same respect extended to them as unique individuals. Respecting diversity is not merely a responsibility within public speaking; it should be a responsibility we strive to embrace in all our human interactions.

Avoid Offending Your Audience

It might seem obvious that speakers should use audience analysis to avoid making offensive remarks, but even very experienced speakers sometimes forget this basic rule. People are members of groups they didn't choose and can't change. We didn't choose our race, ethnicity, sex, age, sexual orientation, intellectual potential, or appearance. We already know that jokes aimed at people because of their membership in these groups are not just politically incorrect but also ethically wrong.

It is not only insensitive humor that can offend an audience. Speakers also need to be aware of language and nonverbal behaviors that state or imply a negative message about people based on their various membership groups. Examples include language that suggests that all scientists are men, that all relationships are heterosexual, or that all ethnic minorities are unpatriotic. By the same token, we should avoid embedding assumptions about people in our messages. Even the most subtle suggestion may not go unnoticed. For example, if, in your speech, you assume that elderly people are frail and expensively medicated, you may offend people whose elder loved ones do not conform in any way to your assumptions.

Scholars Samovar and McDaniel tell us that ethical language choices require four guidelines:

1. Be accurate; present the facts accurately.
2. Be aware of the emotional impact; make sure that you don't manipulate feelings.
3. Avoid hateful words; refrain from language that disparages or belittles people.
4. Be sensitive to the audience; know how audience members prefer to be identified (e.g., Native American instead of Indian, women instead of girls, African American instead of black, disabled instead of crippled) (Samovar & McDaniel, 2007).

If you alienate your audience, they will stop listening. They will refuse to accept your message, no matter how true or important it is. They might even become hostile. If you fail to recognize the complexity of your audience members and if you treat them as stereotypes, they will resent your assumptions and doubt your credibility.

Ethical Speaking Is Sincere Speaking

Ethos is the term Aristotle used to refer to what we now call **credibility**: the perception that the speaker is honest, knowledgeable, and rightly motivated. Your ethos, or credibility, must be established as you build rapport with your listeners. Have you put forth the effort to learn who they are and what you can offer to them in your speech? Do you respect them as individual human beings? Do you respect them enough to serve their needs and interests? Is your topic relevant and appropriate for them? Is your approach honest and sensitive to their preexisting beliefs? Your ability to answer these questions in a constructive way must be based on the best demographic and psychographic information you can use to learn about your listeners.

The audience needs to know they can trust the speaker's motivations, intentions, and knowledge. They must believe that the speaker has no hidden motives, will not manipulate or trick them, and has their best interests at heart.

In order to convey regard and respect for the audience, you must be sincere. You must examine the motives behind your topic choice, the true purpose of your speech, and your willingness to do the work of making sure the content of the speech is true and represents reality. This can be difficult for students who face time constraints and multiple demands on their efforts. However, the attitude you assume for this task represents, in part, the kind of professional, citizen, parent, and human being you want to be. Even if you've given this issue little thought up to now, you can examine your motives and the integrity of your research and message construction. Ethically, you should.

References

Coopman, S. J., & Lull, J. (2009). *Public speaking: The evolving art*. Boston, MA: Wadsworth Cengage.

Logan, J. R., and Zhang, C. (2010). Global neighborhoods: New pathways to diversity and separation. *American Journal of Sociology, 115*, 1069–1109.

Russell, J. (1991). Inventing the flat earth. *History Today, 41*(8), 13–19.

Samovar, L. A., & McDaniel, E. R. (2007). *Public speaking in a multicultural society*. Los Angeles, CA: Roxbury.

Shahid, A. (2011, June 24). Rick Perry's Jose Cuervo joke at Latino convention bombs in Texas, as governor mulls 2012 GOP bid. *New York Daily News*. http://www.nydailynews.com/news/politics/2011/06/24/2011-06-24_rick_perrys_jose_cuervo_joke_at_latino_convention_bombs_in_texas_as_governor_mul.html

5.3 THREE TYPES OF AUDIENCE ANALYSIS

While audience analysis does not guarantee against errors in judgment, it will help you make good choices in topic, language, style of presentation, and other aspects of your speech. The more you know about your audience, the better you can serve their interests and needs. There are certainly limits to what we can learn through information collection, and we need to acknowledge that before making assumptions, but knowing how to gather and use information through audience analysis is an essential skill for successful speakers.

Demographic Analysis

As indicated earlier, demographic information includes factors such as gender, age range, marital status, race and ethnicity, and socioeconomic status. In your public speaking class, you probably already know how many students are male and female, their approximate ages, and so forth. But how can you assess the demographics of an audience ahead of time if you have had no previous contact with them? In many cases, you can ask the person or organization that has invited you to speak; it's likely that they can tell you a lot about the demographics of the people who are expected to come to hear you.

Whatever method you use to form your **demographic analysis**, exercise respect from the outset. For instance, if you are collecting information about whether audience members have ever been divorced, be aware that not everyone will want to answer your questions. You can't require them to do so, and you may not make assumptions about their reluctance to discuss the topic. You must allow them their privacy.

Age

There are certain things you can learn about an audience based on age. For instance, if your audience members are first-year college students, you can assume that they have grown up in the post-9/11 era and have limited memory of what life was like before the "war on terror." If your audience includes people in their forties and fifties, it is likely they remember a time when people feared they would contract the AIDS virus from shaking hands or using a public restroom. People who are in their sixties today came of age during the 1960s, the era of the Vietnam War and a time of social confrontation and experimentation. They also have frames of reference that contribute to the way they think, but it may not be easy to predict which side of the issues they support.

Gender

Gender can define human experience. Clearly, most women have had a different cultural experience from that of men within the same culture. Some women have found themselves excluded from certain careers. Some men have found themselves blamed for the limitations imposed on women. In books such as You Just Don't Understand and Talking from 9 to 5, linguist Deborah Tannen has written extensively on differences between men's and women's communication styles. Tannen explains, "This is not to say that all women and all men, or all boys and girls, behave any one way. Many factors influence our styles, including regional and ethnic backgrounds, family experience and individual personality. But gender is a key factor, and understanding its influence can help clarify what happens when we talk" (Tannen, 1994).

Marriage tends to impose additional roles on both men and women and divorce even more so, especially if there are children. Even if your audience consists of young adults who have not yet made occupational or marital commitments, they are still aware that gender and the choices they make about issues such as careers and relationships will influence their experience as adults.

Culture

In past generations, Americans often used the metaphor of a "melting pot" to symbolize the assimilation of immigrants from various countries and cultures into a unified, harmonious "American people." Today, we are aware of the limitations in that metaphor, and have largely replaced it with a multiculturalist view that describes the American fabric as a "patchwork" or a "mosaic." We know that people who immigrate do not abandon their cultures of origin in order to conform to a standard American identity. In fact, cultural continuity is now viewed as a healthy source of identity.

We also know that subcultures and cocultures exist within and alongside larger cultural groups. For example, while we are aware that Native American people do not all embrace the same values, beliefs, and customs as mainstream white Americans, we also know that members of the Navajo nation have different values, beliefs, and customs from those of members of the Sioux or the Seneca. We know that African American people in urban centers like Detroit and Boston do not share the same cultural experiences as those living in rural Mississippi. Similarly, white Americans in San Francisco may be culturally rooted in the narrative of distant ancestors from Scotland, Italy, or Sweden or in the experience of having emigrated much more recently from Australia, Croatia, or Poland.

Not all cultural membership is visibly obvious. For example, people in German American and Italian American families have widely different sets of values and practices, yet others may not be able to differentiate members of these groups. Differences are what make each group interesting and are important sources of knowledge, perspectives, and creativity.

Religion

There is wide variability in religion as well. The Pew Forum on Religion and Public Life found in a nationwide survey that 84 percent of Americans identify with at least one of a dozen major religions, including Christianity, Judaism, Buddhism, Islam, Hinduism, and others. Within Christianity alone, there are half a dozen categories including Roman Catholic, Mormon, Jehovah's Witness, Orthodox (Greek and Russian), and a variety of Protestant denominations. Another 6 percent said they were unaffiliated but religious, meaning that only one American in ten is atheist, agnostic, or "nothing in particular" (Pew Forum on Religion & Public Life, 2008).

Even within a given denomination, a great deal of diversity can be found. For instance, among Roman Catholics alone, there are people who are devoutly religious, people who self-identify as Catholic but do not attend mass or engage in other religious practices, and others who faithfully make confession and attend mass but who openly question Papal doctrine on various issues. Catholicism among immigrants from the Caribbean and Brazil is often blended with indigenous religion or with religion imported from the west coast of Africa. It is very different from Catholicism in the Vatican.

The dimensions of diversity in the religion demographic are almost endless, and they are not limited by denomination. Imagine conducting an audience analysis of people belonging to an individual congregation rather than a denomination: even there, you will most likely find a multitude of variations that involve how one was brought up, adoption of a faith system as an adult, how strictly one observes religious practices, and so on.

Yet, even with these multiple facets, religion is still a meaningful demographic lens. It can be an indicator of probable patterns in family relationships, family size, and moral attitudes.

Group Membership

In your classroom audience alone, there will be students from a variety of academic majors. Every major has its own set of values, goals, principles, and codes of ethics. A political science student preparing for law school might seem to have little in common with a student of music therapy, for instance. In addition, there are other group memberships that influence how audience members understand the world. Fraternities and sororities, sports teams, campus organizations, political parties, volunteerism, and cultural communities all provide people with ways of understanding the world as it is and as we think it should be.

Because public speaking audiences are very often members of one group or another, group membership is a useful and often easy to access facet of audience analysis. The more you know about the associations of your audience members, the better prepared you will be to tailor your speech to their interests, expectations, and needs.

Education

Education is expensive, and people pursue education for many reasons. Some people seek to become educated, while others seek to earn professional credentials. Both are important motivations. If you know the education levels attained by members of your audience, you might not know their motivations, but you will know to what extent they could somehow afford the money for an education, afford the time to get an education, and survive educational demands successfully.

The kind of education is also important. For instance, an airplane mechanic undergoes a very different kind of education and training from that of an accountant or a software engineer. This means that not only the attained level of education but also the particular field is important in your understanding of your audience.

Occupation

People choose occupations for reasons of motivation and interest, but their occupations also influence their perceptions and their interests. There are many misconceptions about most occupations. For instance, many people believe that teachers work an eight-hour day and have summers off. When you ask teachers, however, you might be surprised to find out that they take work home with them for evenings and weekends, and during the summer, they may teach summer school as well as taking courses in order to keep up with new developments in their fields. But even if you don't know those things, you would still know that teachers have had rigorous generalized and specialized qualifying education, that they have a complex set of responsibilities in the classroom and the institution, and that, to some extent, they have chosen a relatively low-paying occupation over such fields as law, advertising, media, fine and performing arts, or medicine. If your audience includes doctors and nurses, you know that you are speaking to people with differing but important philosophies of health and illness. Learning about those occupational realities is important in avoiding wrong assumptions and stereotypes. We insist that you not assume that nurses are merely doctors "lite." Their skills, concerns, and responsibilities are almost entirely different, and both are crucially necessary to effective health care.

Penn State – MLK speaking to a crowd at Rec Hall – CC BY-NC-ND 2.0.

Psychographic Analysis

Earlier, we mentioned psychographic information, which includes such things as values, opinions, attitudes, and beliefs. Authors Grice and Skinner present a model in which values are the basis for beliefs, attitudes, and behaviors (Grice & Skinner, 2009). Values are the foundation of their pyramid model. They say, "A value expresses a judgment of what is desirable and undesirable, right and wrong, or good and evil. Values are usually stated in the form of a word or phrase. For example, most of us probably share the values of equality, freedom, honesty, fairness, justice, good health, and family. These values compose the principles or standards we use to judge and develop our beliefs, attitudes, and behaviors."

It is important to recognize that, while demographic information is fairly straightforward and verifiable, psychographic information is much less clear-cut. Two different people who both say they believe in equal educational opportunity may have very different interpretations of what "equal opportunity" means. People who say they don't buy junk food may have very different standards for what specific kinds of foods are considered "junk food."

We also acknowledge that people inherit some values from their family upbringing, cultural influences, and life experiences. The extent to which someone values family loyalty and obedience to parents, thrift, humility, and work may be determined by these influences more than by individual choice.

Psychographic analysis can reveal preexisting notions that limit your audience's frame of reference. By knowing about such notions ahead of time, you can address them in your speech. Audiences are likely to have two basic kinds of preexisting notions: those about the topic and those about the speaker.

Preexisting Notions about Your Topic

Many things are a great deal more complex than we realize. Media stereotypes often contribute to our oversimplifications. For instance, one of your authors, teaching public speaking in the past decade, was surprised to hear a student claim that "the hippies meant well, but they did it wrong." Aside from the question of the "it" that was done wrong, there was a question about how little the student actually knew about the diverse hippy cultures and their aspirations. The student seemed unaware that some of "the hippies" were the forebears of such things as organic bakeries, natural food co-ops, urban gardens, recycling, alternative energy, wellness, and other arguably positive developments.

It's important to know your audience in order to make a rational judgment about how their views of your topic might be shaped. In speaking to an audience that might have differing definitions, you should take care to define your terms in a clear, honest way.

At the opposite end from oversimplification is the level of sophistication your audience might embody. Your audience analysis should include factors that reveal it. Suppose you are speaking about trends in civil rights in the United States. You cannot pretend that advancement of civil rights is virtually complete nor can you claim that no progress has been made. It is likely that in a college classroom, the audience will know that although much progress has been made, there are still pockets of prejudice, discrimination, and violence. When you speak to an audience that is cognitively complex, your strategy must be different from one you would use for an audience that is less educated in the topic. With a cognitively complex audience, you must acknowledge the overall complexity while stating that your focus will be on only one dimension. With an audience that's uninformed about your topic, that strategy in a persuasive speech could confuse them; they might well prefer a black-and-white message with no gray areas. You must decide whether it is ethical to represent your topic this way.

When you prepare to do your audience analysis, include questions that reveal how much your audience already knows about your topic. Try to ascertain the existence of stereotyped, oversimplified, or prejudiced attitudes about it. This could make a difference in your choice of topic or in your approach to the audience and topic.

Preexisting Notions about You

People form opinions readily. For instance, we know that students form impressions of teachers the moment they walk into our classrooms on the first day. You get an immediate impression of our age, competence, and attitude simply from our appearance and nonverbal behavior. In addition, many have heard other students say what they think of us.

The same is almost certainly true of you. But it's not always easy to get others to be honest about their impressions of you. They're likely to tell you what they think you want to hear. Sometimes, however, you do know what others think. They might think of you as a jock, a suit-wearing conservative, a nature lover, and so on. Based on these impressions, your audience might expect a boring speech, a shallow speech, a sermon, and so on. However, your concern should still be serving your audience's needs and interests, not debunking their opinions of you or managing your image. In order to help them be receptive, you address their interests directly, and make sure they get an interesting, ethical speech.

Situational Analysis

The next type of analysis is called the **situational audience analysis** because it focuses on characteristics related to the specific speaking situation. The situational audience analysis can be divided into two main questions:

1. How many people came to hear my speech and why are they here? What events, concerns, and needs motivated them to come? What is their interest level, and what else might be competing for their attention?
2. What is the physical environment of the speaking situation? What is the size of the audience, layout of the room, existence of a podium or a microphone, and availability of digital media for visual aids? Are there any distractions, such as traffic noise?

Audience Size

In a typical class, your audience is likely to consist of twenty to thirty listeners. This audience size gives you the latitude to be relatively informal within the bounds of good judgment. It isn't too difficult to let each audience member feel as though you're speaking to him or her. However, you would not become so informal that you allow your carefully prepared speech to lapse into shallow entertainment. With larger audiences, it's more difficult to reach out to each listener, and your speech will tend to be more formal, staying more strictly within its careful outline. You will have to work harder to prepare visual and audio material that reaches the people sitting at the back of the room, including possibly using amplification.

Occasion

There are many occasions for speeches. Awards ceremonies, conventions and conferences, holidays, and other celebrations are some examples. However, there are also less joyful reasons for a speech, such as funerals, disasters, and the delivery of bad news. As always, there are likely to be mixed reactions. For instance, award ceremonies are good for community and institutional morale, but we wouldn't be surprised to find at least a little resentment from listeners who feel deserving but were overlooked. Likewise, for a speech announcing bad news, it is likely that at least a few listeners will be glad the bad news wasn't even worse. If your speech is to deliver bad news, it's important to be honest but also to avoid traumatizing your audience. For instance, if you are a condominium board member speaking to a residents' meeting after the building was damaged by a hurricane, you will need to provide accurate data about the extent of the damage and the anticipated cost and time required for repairs. At the same time, it would be needlessly upsetting to launch into a graphic description of injuries suffered by people, animals, and property in neighboring areas not connected to your condominium complex.

Some of the most successful speeches benefit from situational analysis to identify audience concerns related to the occasion. For example, when the president of the United States gives the annual State of the Union address, the occasion calls for commenting on the condition of the nation and outlining the legislative agenda for the coming year. The speech could be a formality that would interest only "policy wonks," or with the use of good situational audience analysis, it could be a popular event reinforcing the connection between the president and the American people. In January 2011, knowing that the United States' economy was slowly recovering and that jobless rates were still very high, President Barack Obama and his staff knew that the focus of the speech had to be on jobs. Similarly, in January 2003, President George W. Bush's State of the Union speech focused on the "war on terror" and his reasons for justifying the invasion of Iraq. If you look at the history of State of the Union Addresses, you'll often find that the speeches are tailored to the political, social, and economic situations facing the United States at those times.

Voluntariness of Audience

A **voluntary audience** gathers because they want to hear the speech, attend the event, or participate in an event. A classroom audience, in contrast, is likely to be a captive audience. **Captive audiences** are required to be present or feel obligated to do so. Given the limited choices perceived, a captive audience might give only grudging attention. Even when there's an element of choice, the likely consequences of nonattendance will keep audience members from leaving. The audience's relative perception of choice increases the importance of holding their interest.

Whether or not the audience members chose to be present, you want them to be interested in what you have to say. Almost any audience will be interested in a topic that pertains directly to them. However, your audience might also be receptive to topics that are indirectly or potentially pertinent to their lives. This means that if you choose a topic such as advances in the treatment of spinal cord injury or advances in green technology, you should do your best to show how these topics are potentially relevant to their lives or careers.

However, there are some topics that appeal to audience curiosity even when it seems there's little chance of direct pertinence. For instance, topics such as Blackbeard the pirate or ceremonial tattoos among the Maori might pique the interests of various audiences. Depending on the instructions you get from your instructor, you can consider building an interesting message about something outside the daily foci of our attention.

Physical Setting

The physical setting can make or break even the best speeches, so it is important to exercise as much control as you can over it. In your classroom, conditions might not be ideal, but at least the setting is familiar. Still, you know your classroom from the perspective of an audience member, not a speaker standing in the front—which is why you should seek out any opportunity to rehearse your speech during a minute when the room is empty. If you will be giving your presentation somewhere else, it is a good idea to visit the venue ahead of time if at all possible and make note of any factors that will affect how you present your speech. In any case, be sure to arrive well in advance of your speaking time so that you will have time to check that the microphone works, to test out any visual aids, and to request any needed adjustments in lighting, room ventilation, or other factors to eliminate distractions and make your audience more comfortable.

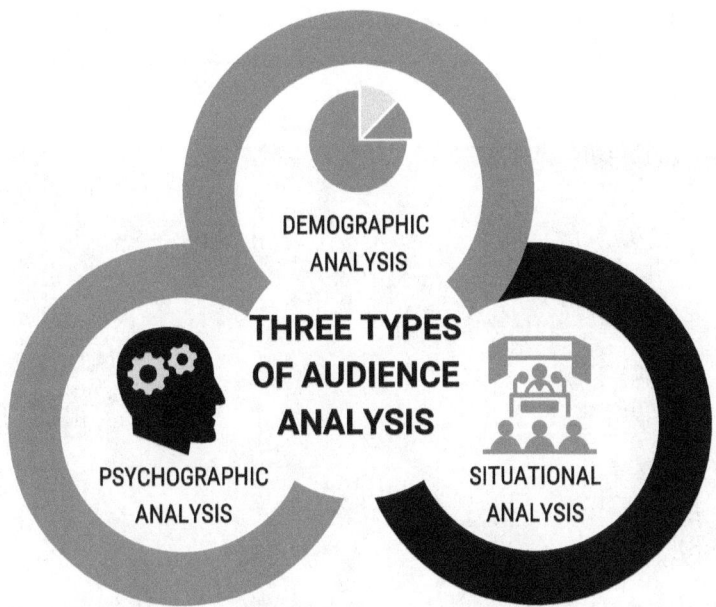

References

Grice, G. L., & Skinner, J. F. (2009). *Mastering public speaking: The handbook* (7th ed.). Boston, MA: Pearson.

Pew Forum on Religion & Public Life. (2008, February). Summary of key findings. In *U.S. religious landscape survey*. Retrieved from http://religions.pewforum.org/reports#

Tannen, D. (1994, December 11). The talk of the sandbox: How Johnny and Suzy's playground chatter prepares them for life at the office. *The Washington Post*. Retrieved from http://www9.georgetown.edu/faculty/tannend/sandbox.htm

5.4 CONDUCTING AUDIENCE ANALYSIS

Now that we have described what audience analysis is and why it is important, let's examine some details of how to conduct it. Exactly how can you learn about the people who will make up your audience?

Direct Observation

One way to learn about people is to observe them. By observing nonverbal patterns of behavior, you can learn a great deal as long as you are careful how you interpret the behaviors. For instance, do people greet each other with a handshake, a hug, a smile, or a nod? Do members of opposite sexes make physical contact? Does the setting suggest more conservative behavior? By listening in on conversations, you can find out the issues that concern people. Are people in the campus center talking about political unrest in the Middle East? About concerns over future Pell Grant funding? We suggest that you consider the ethical dimensions of eavesdropping, however. Are you simply overhearing an open conversation, or are you prying into a highly personal or private discussion?

Interviews and Surveys

Because your demographic analysis will be limited to your most likely audience, your most accurate way to learn about them is to seek personal information through interviews and surveys. An **interview** is a one-on-one exchange in which you ask questions of a respondent, whereas a **survey** is a set of questions administered to several—or, preferably, many—respondents. Interviews may be conducted face-to-face, by phone, or by written means, such as texting. They allow more in-depth discussion than surveys, and they are also more time consuming to conduct. Surveys are also sometimes conducted face-to-face or by phone, but online surveys are increasingly common. You may collect and tabulate survey results manually, or set up an automated online survey through the free or subscription portals of sites like Survey Monkey and Zoomerang. Using an online survey provides the advantage of keeping responses anonymous, which may increase your audience members' willingness to participate and to answer personal questions. Surveys are an efficient way to collect information quickly; however, in contrast to interviews, they don't allow for follow-up questions to help you understand why your respondent gave a certain answer.

When you use interviews and surveys, there are several important things to keep in mind:

- Make sure your interview and survey questions are directly related to your speech topic. Do not use interviews to delve into private areas of people's lives. For instance, if your speech is about the debate between creationism and evolution, limit your questions to their opinions about that topic; do not meander into their beliefs about sexual behavior or their personal religious practices.
- Create and use a standard set of questions. If you "ad lib" your questions so that they are phrased differently for different interviewees, you will be comparing "apples and oranges" when you compare the responses you've obtained.
- Keep interviews and surveys short, or you could alienate your audience long before your speech is even outlined. Tell them the purpose of the interview or survey and make sure they understand that their participation is voluntary.
- Don't rely on just a few respondents to inform you about your entire audience. In all likelihood, you have a cognitively diverse audience. In order to accurately identify trends, you will likely need to interview or survey at least ten to twenty people.

In addition, when you conduct interviews and surveys, keep in mind that people are sometimes less than honest in describing their beliefs, attitudes, and behavior. This widely recognized weakness of interviews and survey research is known as socially desirable responding: the tendency to give responses that are considered socially acceptable. Marketing professor Ashok Lalwani divides socially desirable responding into two types: (1) impression management, or intentionally portraying oneself in a favorable light and (2) self-deceptive enhancement, or exaggerating one's good qualities, often unconsciously (Lalwani, 2009).

You can reduce the effects of socially desirable responding by choosing your questions carefully. As marketing consultant Terry Vavra advises, "one should never ask what one can't logically expect respondents to honestly reveal" (Vavra, 2009). For example, if you want to know audience members' attitudes about body piercing, you are likely to get more honest answers by asking "Do you think body piercing is attractive?" rather than "How many piercings do you have and where on your body are they located?"

Focus Groups

A **focus group** is a small group of people who give you feedback about their perceptions. As with interviews and surveys, in a focus group you should use a limited list of carefully prepared questions designed to get at the information you need to understand their beliefs, attitudes, and values specifically related to your topic.

If you conduct a focus group, part of your task will be striking a balance between allowing the discussion to flow freely according to what group members have to say and keeping the group focused on the questions. It's also your job to guide the group in maintaining responsible and respectful behavior toward each other.

In evaluating focus group feedback, do your best to be receptive to what people had to say, whether or not it conforms to what you expected. Your purpose in conducting the group was to understand group members' beliefs, attitudes, and values about your topic, not to confirm your assumptions.

Using Existing Data about Your Audience

Occasionally, existing information will be available about your audience. For instance, if you have a student audience, it might not be difficult to find out what their academic majors are. You might also be able to find out their degree of investment in their educations; for instance, you could reasonably assume that the seniors in the audience have been successful students who have invested at least three years pursuing a higher education. Sophomores have at least survived their first year but may not have matched the seniors in demonstrating strong values toward education and the work ethic necessary to earn a degree.

In another kind of an audience, you might be able to learn other significant facts. For instance, are they veterans? Are they retired teachers? Are they members of a voluntary civic organization such as the Lions Club or Mothers Against Drunk Driving (MADD)? This kind of information should help you respond to their concerns and interests.

In other cases, you may be able to use demographics collected by public and private organizations. Demographic analysis is done by the US Census Bureau through the American Community Survey, which is conducted every year, and through other specialized demographic surveys (Bureau of the Census, 2011; Bureau of the Census, 2011). The Census Bureau analysis generally captures information about people in all the regions of the United States, but you can drill down in census data to see results by state, by age group, by gender, by race, and by other factors.

Demographic information about narrower segments of the United States, down to the level of individual zip codes, is available through private organizations such as The Nielsen Company (http://www.claritas.com/MyBestSegments/Default.jsp?ID=20&SubID=&pageName=ZIP%2BCode%2BLook-up) and Sperling's Best Places (http://www.bestplaces.net). Sales and marketing professionals use this data, and you may find it useful for your audience analysis as well.

References

Bureau of the Census. (2011). About the American community survey. Retrieved from http://www.census.gov/acs/www/about_the_survey/american_community_survey/.

Bureau of the Census. (2011). Demographic surveys. Retrieved from http://www.census.gov/aboutus/sur_demo.html

Lalwani, A. K. (2009, August). The distinct influence of cognitive busyness and need for closure on cultural differences in socially desirable responding. *Journal of Consumer Research*, *36*, 305–316. Retrieved from http://business.utsa.edu/marketing/files/phdpapers/lalwani2_2009-jcr.pdf

Vavra, T. G. (2009, June 14). The truth about truth in survey research. Retrieved from http://www.terryvavra.com/customer-research/the-truth-about-truth-in-survey-research

5.5 USING YOUR AUDIENCE ANALYSIS

A good audience analysis takes time, thought, preparation, implementation, and processing. If done well, it will yield information that will help you interact effectively with your audience. Professional speakers, corporate executives, sales associates, and entertainers all rely on audience analysis to connect with their listeners. So do political candidates, whose chances of gaining votes depend on crafting the message and mood to appeal to each specific audience. One audience might be preoccupied with jobs, another with property taxes, and another with crime. Similarly, your audience analysis should help you identify the interests of your audience. Ultimately, a successful audience analysis can guide you in preparing the basic content of your speech and help you adjust your speech "on the fly." Utilizing the communication accommodation theory is one effective way to prepare and adjust your speech based on your audience analysis.

Communication Accommodation Theory

Communication accommodation theory is a theory that explores why and how people modify their communication to fit situational, social, cultural, and relational contexts. (Giles et al., 1973). Within communication accommodation, conversational partners may use convergence, meaning a person makes his or her communication more like another person's. People who are accommodating in their communication style are seen as more competent, which illustrates the benefits of communicative flexibility. In order to be flexible, of course, people have to be aware of and monitor their own and others' communication patterns. Conversely, conversational partners may use divergence, meaning a person uses communication to emphasize the differences between his or her conversational partner and his or herself.

Convergence and divergence can take place within the same conversation and may be used by one or both conversational partners. Convergence functions to make others feel at ease, to increase understanding, and to enhance social bonds. Divergence may be used to intentionally make another person feel unwelcome or perhaps to highlight a personal, group, or cultural identity. For example, African American women use certain verbal communication patterns when communicating with other African American women as a way to highlight their racial identity and create group solidarity. In situations where multiple races interact, the women usually do not use those same patterns, instead accommodating the language patterns of the larger group.

Utilizing your audience analysis and the communication accommodation theory in advance will allow you to be prepared to adjust both the content and delivery of your speech as needed in order to best reach your audience.

Prepare Content with Your Audience in Mind

The first thing a good audience analysis can do is help you focus your content for your specific audience. If you are planning on a delivering a persuasive speech on why people should become vegans and you find out through analysis that half of your audience are daughters and sons of cattle ranchers, you need to carefully think through your approach to the content. Maybe you'll need to tweak your topic to focus on just the benefits of veganism without trying to persuade the audience explicitly. The last thing you want to do as a speaker is stand before an audience who is highly negative toward your topic before you ever open your mouth. While there will always be some naysayers in any audience, if you think through your topic with your audience in mind, you may be able to find a topic that will be both interesting to you as a speaker and beneficial to your audience as well.

In addition to adjusting the topic of your speech prior to the speaking event, you can also use your audience analysis to help ensure that the content of your speech will be as clear and understandable as humanly possible. We can use our audience analysis to help sure that we are clear.

One area of clarity to be careful of is the use of idioms your audience may not know. An **idiom** is a word or phrase where the meaning cannot be predicted from normal, dictionary definitions. Many idioms are culturally or temporally based. For example, the phrase "according to Hoyle" indicates that something is done "by the book" or "by the rules," as in "These measurements aren't according to Hoyle, but they're close enough to give a general idea." Most of us have no clue who Hoyle was or what this idiom means. It refers to Edmond Hoyle, who wrote some of the most popular card-playing rule books back in the 1700s in England. Today, card game enthusiasts may understand the intent of "according to Hoyle," but for most people it no longer carries specific meaning. When thinking about your speech, be careful not to accidentally use idioms that you find commonplace but your audience may not.

Adjusting Your Speech Based on Your Analysis

In addition to using audience analysis to help formulate speech content, we can also use our audience analysis to make adjustments during the actual speech. These adjustments can pertain to the audience and to the physical setting.

The feedback you receive from your audience during your speech is a valuable indication of ways to adjust your presentation. If you're speaking after lunch and notice audience members looking drowsy, you can make adjustments to liven up the tone of your speech. You could use humor. You could raise your voice slightly. You could pose some questions and ask for a show of hands to get your listeners actively involved. As another example, you may notice from frowns and headshaking that some listeners aren't convinced by the arguments you are presenting. In this case, you could spend more time on a specific area of your speech and provide more evidence than you originally intended. Good speakers can learn a lot by watching their audience while speaking and then make specific adjustments to both the content and delivery of the speech to enhance the speech's ultimate impact.

The second kind of adjustment has to do with the physical setting for your speech. For example, your situational analysis may reveal that you'll be speaking in a large auditorium when you had expected a nice, cozy conference room. If you've created visual aids for a small, intimate environment, you may have to omit it, or tell your listeners that they can view it after the presentation. You may also need to account for a microphone. If you're lucky enough to have a cordless microphone, then you won't have to make too many adjustments to your speaking style. If, on the other hand, the microphone is corded or is attached to an unmovable podium, you'll have to make adjustments to how you deliver the presentation.

In preparing a speech about wealth distribution in the United States, one of our students had the opposite problem. Anticipating a large room, she had planned to use a one-hundred-foot tape measure to illustrate the percentage of the nation's wealth owned by the top one-fifth of the population. However, when she arrived she found that the room was only twelve by twenty feet, so that she had to walk back and forth zigzagging the tape from end to end to stretch out one hundred feet. Had she thought more creatively about how to adapt to the physical setting, she could have changed her plans to use just ten feet of the tape measure to symbolize 100 percent of the wealth.

References

Giles, H., Taylor, D. M., & Bourhis, R. (1973). Toward a theory of interpersonal accommodation through language: Some Canadian data. *Language and Society, 2*(2), 177–92.

5.6 ENRICHMENT

Discussion Questions

1. What are some ways that you can establish common ground with your classmates as the audience?
2. Ceally wants to educate his college classmates about the increased use of profanity in contemporary music. He would like to play sound clips of some of the most offensive lyrics to illustrate his point. Would you advise Ceally to play these songs, even though doing so might offend or upset members of the audience? Why?
3. Tynisha wants to convince her audience that we need a ban on alcoholic drinks at sporting events. Her survey results suggest that nearly 85% of her audience wants to continue the current policy of allowing alcohol sales at athletic events. Should she change her purpose to fit the existing attitudes of her audience? Why or why not? How can she establish common ground with this audience?
4. What are some ways you can establish ethos with your audience before, during and after your presentation?
5. Why is it important to understand the demographics, psychographics, and interests of your audience? What are the pitfalls of not conducting any audience analysis before speaking?
6. Think of other areas of life in which audience analysis (or something like it) is essential (for example: needs assessments, strategic planning, individualized education planning). Why is it important to first understand the unique needs of a group before offering information or solutions to problems? How can we use our understanding of audience analysis to inform our communication in other areas of life?

Activities

1. Identify your values. On a sheet of paper, take a minute to write down how you would spend a million dollars on others. Next, take a minute to write down how you would spend a million dollars on yourself. Finally, review your two lists and identify common themes. What you choose to spend your money on reflects your values. Here are a few ideas of some of the value categories that may include things you would buy: items for your family, home, community, health, education, adventure, luxury, or nature/environment. These would be some of the values by which you live your life.

2. Form six groups. Each group will be given a different type of product (i.e. cereal box, pizza restaurant, big-box store, movie, TV show). Groups perform an audience analysis including demographics and psychographics on the target audience for that product. Finally, groups create and deliver an advertisement to their target audience. Discuss the following:

    - Who was the target audience intended by each group?
    - Was the class able to determine the type of audience (demographics and psychographics) each group was targeting? How?
    - In this activity, what do the cereal boxes, restaurants, stores, movies, etc. represent in the public speaking situation?
    - Why is it important for speakers to imagine/analyze their target audience before creating or delivering a speech?

6 CULTURE

Learning Objectives

- Define culture and describe personal, social, and cultural identities.
- Summarize non-dominant and dominant identity development.
- Define the social constructionist view of culture and identity.
- Discuss how each of the four cultural identities discussed affects and/or relates to communication.
- Define intercultural communication and list the six dialectics of intercultural communication.
- Discuss how intercultural communication affects interpersonal relationships.
- Define intercultural communication competence.
- Summarize the three ways to cultivate intercultural communication competence that are discussed.
- Apply the concept of "thinking under the influence" as a reflective skill for building intercultural communication competence.

Learning Objectives

- **Ableism**
- **Acculturated**
- **Ascribed Identity**

6 CULTURE

- Avowed Identity
- Code-switching
- Culture
- Cultural Identity
- Dialectic
- Dichotomies
- Digital Divide
- Dominant Identities
- Essentialize
- Ethnocentrism
- Feminism
- Gender
- Heterosexism
- Intercultural Communication
- Intercultural Communication Competence
- Intersectionality
- Non-Dominant Identities
- Personal Identity
- Race
- Salience
- Sex
- Sexual Orientation
- Social constructionism
- Social Identity
- Transgender

6.1 CULTURE AND COMMUNICATION

"Cultural differences should not separate us from each other, but rather cultural diversity brings a collective strength that can benefit all of humanity." -Robert Alan Aurthur

Humans have always been diverse in their cultural beliefs and practices. But as new technologies have led to the perception that our world has shrunk, and demographic and political changes have brought attention to cultural differences, people communicate across cultures more now than ever before. The oceans and continents that separate us can now be traversed instantly with an e-mail, phone call, tweet, or status update. Additionally, our workplaces, schools, and neighborhoods have become more integrated in terms of race and gender, increasing our interaction with domestic diversity. The Disability Rights Movement and Gay Rights Movement have increased the visibility of people with disabilities and sexual minorities. But just because we are exposed to more difference doesn't mean we understand it, can communicate across it, or appreciate it. This chapter will help you do all three.

Pete's Pal

Pistol Pete found himself grappling with a profound conflict. Known for his unwavering spirit and deep love for his country, Pete was a symbol of unity and school pride. But recent events of police brutality and systemic injustice had cast a shadow over the land he held dear, causing distress among the Black students at OSU, including one of his closest friends, James.

Pete and James had shared many moments on and off the field, their bond going beyond their shared love for their university. James had always been there for Pete, supporting him in every endeavor, just as Pete had stood by him. The recent unrest had affected James deeply, and Pete could see the pain and frustration in his friend's eyes. The usually vibrant and positive James now wore a look of weariness, his spirits dampened by the grim reality that he and many others faced.

This personal connection made the issue even more real and urgent for Pete. He felt a strong urge to support his friend and the other students who were feeling the same distress. But at the same time, his patriotism stirred within him, his deep-rooted respect for the country conflicting with the disheartening circumstances.

Pete decided to lean into the conflict rather than shy away from it. He reached out to James, engaging in heartfelt conversations about the experiences and fears James was dealing with. He attended open dialogues and town hall meetings to understand the broader experiences of the Black students at OSU. Through these interactions,

Pete was striving not only to comprehend the gravity of their concerns but also to explore how he, as Pistol Pete, could contribute to the solution.

As Pete listened to James and the other students, he began to understand that standing up against injustice and advocating for equality was, in itself, a deeply patriotic act. It was about aspiring for a better, fairer country — a place where everyone, including his dear friend James, could feel safe, valued, and respected.

Motivated by this newfound understanding, Pete used his platform to promote awareness, foster unity, and advocate for change. His actions sent a clear message of his commitment to the OSU community, reinforcing the idea that patriotism and support for the fight against systemic injustice were not mutually exclusive but could harmoniously coexist.

Navigating this delicate balance was challenging, but Pistol Pete, driven by his love for his friend and his community, was determined to play his part in fostering a more inclusive and equitable environment at Oklahoma State University. What qualities and actions demonstrate Pete's intercultural competence during this challenging situation?

6.2 FOUNDATIONS OF CULTURE AND IDENTITY

Culture is a complicated word to define, as there are at least six common ways that culture is used in the United States. For the purposes of exploring the communicative aspects of culture, we will define **culture** as the ongoing negotiation of learned and patterned beliefs, attitudes, values, and behaviors. Unpacking the definition, we can see that culture shouldn't be conceptualized as stable and unchanging. Culture is "negotiated," and as we will learn later in this chapter, culture is dynamic, and cultural changes can be traced and analyzed to better understand why our society is the way it is. The definition also points out that culture is learned, which accounts for the importance of socializing institutions like family, school, peers, and the media. Culture is patterned in that there are recognizable widespread similarities among people within a cultural group. There is also deviation from and resistance to those patterns by individuals and subgroups within a culture, which is why cultural patterns change over time. Last, the definition acknowledges that culture influences our beliefs about what is true and false, our attitudes including our likes and dislikes, our values regarding what is right and wrong, and our behaviors. It is from these cultural influences that our identities are formed.

Personal, Social, and Cultural Identities

Ask yourself the question "Who am I?" We develop a sense of who we are based on what is reflected back on us from other people. Our parents, friends, teachers, and the media help shape our identities. While this happens from birth, most people in Western societies reach a stage in adolescence where maturing cognitive abilities and increased social awareness lead them to begin to reflect on who they are. This begins a lifelong process of thinking about who we are now, who we were before, and who we will become (Tatum, B. D., 2000). Our identities make up an important part of our self-concept and can be broken down into three main categories: personal, social, and cultural identities (see examples in graphic below).

We must avoid the temptation to think of our identities as constant. Instead, our identities are formed through processes that started before we were born and will continue after we are gone; therefore our identities aren't something we achieve or complete. Two related but distinct components of our identities are our personal and social identities (Spreckels, J. & Kotthoff, H., 2009). **Personal identities** include the components of self that are primarily intrapersonal and connected to our life experiences. For example, I consider myself a puzzle lover, and you may identify as a fan of hip-hop music. Our **social identities** are the components of self that are derived from involvement in social groups with which we are interpersonally committed.

For example, we may derive aspects of our social identity from our family or from a community of fans for a sports team. Social identities differ from personal identities because they are externally organized through membership. Our membership may be voluntary (Greek organization on campus) or involuntary (family) and explicit (we pay dues to our labor union) or implicit (we purchase and listen to hip-hop music). There are numerous options for personal and social identities. While our personal identity choices express who we are, our social identities align us with particular groups. Through our social identities, we make statements about who we are and who we are not.

Personal identities may change often as people have new experiences and develop new interests and hobbies. A current interest in online video games may give way to an interest in graphic design. Social identities do not change as often because they take more time to develop, as you must become interpersonally invested. For example, if an interest in online video games leads someone to become a member of a MMORPG, or a massively multiplayer online role-playing game community, that personal identity has led to a social identity that is now interpersonal and more entrenched.

Cultural identities is based on socially constructed categories that teach us a way of being and include expectations for social behavior or ways of acting (Yep, G. A.,

2002). Since we are often a part of them since birth, cultural identities are the least changeable of the three. The ways of being and the social expectations for behavior within cultural identities do change over time, but what separates them from most social identities is their historical roots (Collier, M. J., 1996). For example, think of how ways of being and acting have changed for African Americans since the civil rights movement. Additionally, common ways of being and acting within a cultural identity group are expressed through communication. In order to be accepted as a member of a cultural group, members must be **acculturated**, essentially learning and using a code that other group members will be able to recognize. We are acculturated into our various cultural identities in obvious and less obvious ways. We may literally have a parent or friend tell us what it means to be a man or a woman. We may also unconsciously consume messages from popular culture that offer representations of gender.

Any of these identity types can be ascribed or avowed. **Ascribed identities** are personal, social, or cultural identities that are placed on us by others, while **avowed identities** are those that we claim for ourselves (Martin & Nakayama, 2010). Sometimes people ascribe an identity to someone else based on stereotypes. You may see a person who likes to read science-fiction books, watches documentaries, has glasses, and collects Star Trek memorabilia and label him or her a nerd. If the person doesn't avow that identity, it can create friction, and that label may even hurt the other person's feelings. But ascribed and avowed identities can match up. To extend the previous example, there has been a movement in recent years to reclaim the label nerd and turn it into a positive, and a nerd subculture has been growing in popularity. For example, MC Frontalot, a leader in the nerdcore hip-hop movement, says that being branded a nerd in school was terrible, but now he raps about "nerdy" things like blogs to sold-out crowds (Shipman, 2007). We can see from this example that our ascribed and avowed identities change over the course of our lives, and sometimes they match up and sometimes not.

PERSONAL, SOCIAL, AND CULTURAL IDENTITIES

PERSONAL	SOCIAL	CULTURAL
Antique Collector	Member of Historical Society	Irish American
Dog or Cat Lover	Member of an Humane Society	Man/Woman/Non-Binary
Cyclist	Fraternity/Sorority Member	American
Singer	High School Music Teacher	Multiracial
Shy	Book Club Member	LGBTQIA+

Although some identities are essentially permanent, the degree to which we are aware of them, also known as **salience**, changes. The intensity with which we avow an identity also changes based on context. For example, a person who identifies as African American may not have difficulty deciding which box to check on the demographic section of a survey. But if a person who identifies as African American becomes president of her college's Black Student Union, she may more intensely avow her African American identity, which has now become more salient. If she studies abroad in Africa her junior year, she may be ascribed an identity of American by her new African friends rather than African American. For the Africans, their visitor's identity as American is likely more salient than her identity as someone of African descent. If someone is biracial or multiracial, they may change their racial identification as they engage in an identity search. One intercultural communication scholar writes of his experiences as an "Asianlatinoamerican" (Yep, 2002). He notes repressing his Chinese identity as an adolescent living in Peru and then later embracing his Chinese identity and learning about his family history while in college in the United States. This example shows how even national identity fluctuates. Obviously one can change nationality by becoming a citizen of another country, although most people do not. My identity as a US American became very salient for me for the first time in my life when I studied abroad in Sweden.

Throughout modern history, cultural and social influences have established dominant and non-dominant groups (Allen, 2011). **Dominant identities** historically had and currently have more resources and influence, while **non-**

dominant identities historically had and currently have less resources and influence. It's important to remember that these distinctions are being made at the societal level, not the individual level. There are obviously exceptions, with people in groups considered non-dominant obtaining more resources and power than a person in a dominant group. However, the overall trend is that difference based on cultural groups has been institutionalized, and exceptions do not change this fact. Because of this uneven distribution of resources and power, members of dominant groups are granted privileges while non-dominant groups are at a disadvantage. The main non-dominant groups must face various forms of institutionalized discrimination, including **racism**, **sexism**, **heterosexism**, and **ableism**. As we will discuss later, privilege and disadvantage, like similarity and difference, are not "all or nothing." No two people are completely different or completely similar, and no one person is completely privileged or completely disadvantaged.

Identity Development

There are multiple models for examining identity development. Given our focus on how difference matters, we will examine similarities and differences in nondominant and dominant identity formation. While the stages in this model help us understand how many people experience their identities, identity development is complex, and there may be variations. We must also remember that people have multiple identities that intersect with each other. So, as you read, think about how circumstances may be different for an individual with multiple nondominant and/or dominant identities.

Nondominant Identity Development

There are four stages of nondominant identity development (Martin & Nakayama, 2010). The first stage is unexamined identity, which is characterized by a lack of awareness of or lack of interest in one's identity. For example, a young woman who will later identify as a lesbian may not yet realize that a nondominant sexual orientation is part of her identity. Also, a young African American man may question his teachers or parents about the value of what he's learning during Black History Month. When a person's lack of interest in their own identity is replaced by an investment in a dominant group's identity, they may move to the next stage, which is conformity.

In the conformity stage, an individual internalizes or adopts the values and norms of the dominant group, often in an effort not to be perceived as different. Individuals may attempt to assimilate into the dominant culture by changing their appearance, their mannerisms, the way they talk, or even their name. Moises, a Chicano man interviewed in a research project about identities, narrated how he changed his "Mexican sounding" name to Moses, which was easier for his middle-school classmates and teachers to say (Jones Jr., 2009). He also identified as white instead of Mexican American or Chicano because he saw how his teachers treated the other kids with "brown skin." Additionally, some gay or lesbian people in this stage of identity development may try to "act straight." In either case, some people move to the next stage, resistance and separation, when they realize that despite their efforts they are still perceived as different by and not included in the dominant group.

In the resistance and separation stage, an individual with a nondominant identity may shift away from the conformity of the previous stage to engage in actions that challenge the dominant identity group. Individuals in this stage may also actively try to separate themselves from the dominant group, interacting only with those who share their nondominant identity. For example, there has been a Deaf culture movement in the United States for decades. This movement includes people who are hearing impaired and believe that their use of a specific language, American Sign Language (ASL), and other cultural practices constitutes a unique culture, which they symbolize by capitalizing the D in Deaf (Allen, 2011).

While this is not a separatist movement, a person who is hearing impaired may find refuge in such a group after experiencing discrimination from hearing people. Staying in this stage may indicate a lack of critical thinking if a person endorses the values of the nondominant group without question.

The integration stage marks a period where individuals with a nondominant identity have achieved a balance between embracing their own identities and valuing other dominant and nondominant identities. Although there may still be residual anger from the discrimination and prejudice they have faced, they may direct this energy into positive outlets such as working to end discrimination for their own or other groups. Moises, the Chicano man I mentioned earlier, now works to support the Chicano community in his city and also has actively supported gay rights and women's rights.

Dominant Identity Development

Dominant identity development consists of five stages (Martin & Nakayama, 2010). The unexamined stage of dominant identity formation is similar to nondominant in that individuals in this stage do not think about their or others' identities. Although they may be aware of differences—for example, between races and genders—they either don't realize there is a hierarchy that treats some people differently than others or they don't think the hierarchy applies to them. For example, a white person may take notice that a person of color was elected to a prominent office. However, he or she may not see the underlying reason that it is noticeable—namely, that the overwhelming majority of our country's leaders are white. Unlike people with a nondominant identity who usually have to acknowledge the positioning of their identity due to discrimination and prejudice they encounter, people with dominant identities may stay in the unexamined stage for a long time.

In the acceptance stage, a person with a dominant identity passively or actively accepts that some people are treated differently than others but doesn't do anything internally or externally to address it. In the passive acceptance stage, we must be cautious not to blame individuals with dominant identities for internalizing racist, sexist, or heterosexist "norms." The socializing institutions we discussed earlier (family, peers, media, religion, and education) often make oppression seem normal and natural. For example, I have had students who struggle to see that they are in this stage say things like "I know that racism exists, but my parents taught me to be a good person and see everyone as equal." While this is admirable, seeing everyone as equal doesn't make it so. And people who insist that we are all equal may claim that minorities are exaggerating their circumstances or "whining" and just need to "work harder" or "get over it." The person making these statements acknowledges difference but doesn't see their privilege or the institutional perpetuation of various "-isms." Although I've encountered many more people in the passive state of acceptance than the active state, some may progress to an active state where they acknowledge inequality and are proud to be in the "superior" group. In either case, many people never progress from this stage. If they do, it's usually because of repeated encounters with individuals or situations that challenge their acceptance of the status quo, such as befriending someone from a nondominant group or taking a course related to culture.

The resistance stage of dominant identity formation is a major change from the previous in that an individual acknowledges the unearned advantages they are given and feels guilt or shame about it. Having taught about various types of privilege for years, I've encountered many students who want to return their privilege or disown it. These individuals may begin to disassociate with their own dominant group because they feel like a curtain has been opened and their awareness of the inequality makes it difficult for them to interact with others in their dominant group. But it's important to acknowledge that becoming aware of your white privilege, for instance, doesn't mean that every person of color is going to want to accept you as an ally, so retreating to them may not be the most productive move. While moving to this step is a marked improvement in regards to becoming a more aware and socially just person, getting stuck in the resistance stage isn't productive, because people are often retreating rather than trying to address injustice. For some, deciding to share what they've learned with others who share their dominant identity moves them to the next stage.

People in the redefinition stage revise negative views of their identity held in the previous stage and begin to acknowledge their privilege and try to use the power they are granted to work for social justice. They realize that they can claim their dominant identity as heterosexual, able-bodied, male, white, and so on, and perform their identity in ways that counter norms. A male participant in a research project on identity said the following about redefining his male identity:

> I don't want to assert my maleness the same way that maleness is asserted all around us all the time. I don't want to contribute to sexism. So I have to be conscious of that. There's that guilt. But then, I try to utilize my maleness in positive ways, like when I'm talking to other men about male privilege (Jones, Jr., 2009).

The final stage of dominant identity formation is integration. This stage is reached when redefinition is complete and people can integrate their dominant identity into all aspects of their life, finding opportunities to educate others about privilege while also being a responsive ally to people in nondominant identities. As an example, some heterosexual people who find out a friend or family member is gay or lesbian may have to confront their dominant heterosexual identity for the first time, which may lead them through these various stages. As a sign of integration, some may join an organization like PFLAG (Parents, Families, and Friends of Lesbians and Gays), where they can be around others who share their dominant identity as heterosexuals but also empathize with their loved ones.

Knowing more about various types of identities and some common experiences of how dominant and nondominant identities are formed prepares us to delve into more specifics about why difference matters.

Difference Matters

Whenever we encounter someone, we notice similarities and differences. While both are important, it is often the differences that are highlighted and that contribute to communication troubles. We don't only see similarities and differences on an individual level. In fact, we also place people into in-groups and out-groups based on the similarities and differences we perceive. This is important because we then tend to react to someone we perceive as a member of an out-group based on the characteristics we attach to the group rather than the individual (Allen, 2011). In these situations, it is more likely that stereotypes and prejudice will influence our communication. Learning about difference and why it matters will help us be more competent communicators. The flip side of emphasizing difference is to claim that no differences exist and that you see everyone as a human being. Rather than trying to ignore difference and see each person as a unique individual, we should know the history of how differences came to be so socially and culturally significant and how they continue to affect us today.

Culture and identity are complex. You may be wondering how some groups came to be dominant and others nondominant. These differences are not natural, which can be seen as we unpack how various identities have changed over time in the next section. There is, however, an ideology of domination that makes it seem natural and normal to many that some people or groups will always have power over others (Allen, 2011). In fact, hierarchy and domination, although prevalent throughout modern human history, were likely not the norm among early humans. So one of the first reasons difference matters is that people and groups are treated unequally, and better understanding how those differences came to be can help us create a more just society. Difference also matters because demographics and patterns of interaction are changing.

In the United States, the population of people of color is increasing and diversifying, and visibility for people who are gay or lesbian and people with disabilities has also increased. The 2010 Census shows that the Hispanic and Latino/a populations in the United States are now the second largest group in the country, having grown 43 percent since the last census in 2000 (Saenz, 2011). By 2030, racial and ethnic minorities will account for one-third of the population (Allen, 2011). Additionally, legal and social changes have created a more open environment for sexual minorities and people with disabilities. These changes directly affect our interpersonal relationships. The workplace is one context where changing demographics has become increasingly important. Many organizations are striving to comply with changing laws by implementing policies aimed at creating equal access and opportunity. Some organizations are going further than legal compliance to try to create inclusive climates where diversity is valued because of the interpersonal and economic benefits it has the potential to produce.

We can now see that difference matters due to the inequalities that exist among cultural groups and due to changing demographics that affect our personal and social relationships. Unfortunately, there are many obstacles that may impede our valuing of difference (Allen, 2011). Individuals with dominant identities may not validate the experiences of those in nondominant groups because they do not experience the oppression directed at those with nondominant identities. Further, they may find it difficult to acknowledge that not being aware of this oppression is due to privilege associated with their dominant identities. Because of this lack of recognition of oppression, members of dominant groups may minimize, dismiss, or question the experiences of nondominant groups and view them as "complainers" or "whiners." Recall from our earlier discussion of identity formation that people with dominant identities may stay in the unexamined or acceptance stages for a long time. Being stuck in these stages makes it much more difficult to value difference.

Members of nondominant groups may have difficulty valuing difference due to negative experiences with the dominant group, such as not having their experiences validated. Both groups may be restrained from communicating about difference due to norms of political correctness, which may make people feel afraid to speak up because they may be perceived as insensitive or racist. All these obstacles are common and they are valid. However, as we will learn later, developing intercultural communication competence can help us gain new perspectives, become more mindful of our communication, and intervene in some of these negative cycles.

References

Allen, B. J., *Difference Matters: Communicating Social Identity*, 2nd ed. (Long Grove, IL: Waveland, 2011), 4.

Collier, M. J., "Communication Competence Problematics in Ethnic Friendships," *Communication Monographs* 63, no. 4 (1996): 318.

Cullen, L. T., "Employee Diversity Training Doesn't Work," *Time*, April 26, 2007, accessed October 5, 2011, http://www.time.com/time/magazine/article/0,9171,1615183,00.html.

Jones Jr., R. G., "Communicating Queer Identities through Personal Narrative and Intersectional Reflexivity" (PhD diss., University of Denver, 2009), 130–32.

Martin, J. N., and Thomas K. Nakayama, *Intercultural Communication in Contexts*, 5th ed. (Boston, MA: McGraw-Hill, 2010), 166.

Saenz, A., "Census Data Shows a Changed American Landscape," *ABC News*, March 21, 2011, accessed October 9, 2011, http://abcnews.go.com/Politics/census-data-reveals-changed-american-landscape/story?id=13206427.

Shipman, T., "Nerds Get Their Revenge as at Last It's Hip to Be Square," *The Sunday Telegraph*, July 22, 2007, 35.

Spreckels, J. and Helga Kotthoff, "Communicating Identity in Intercultural Communication," in *Handbook of Intercultural Communication*, eds. Helga Kotthoff and Helen Spencer-Oatey (Berlin: Mouton de Gruyter, 2009), 415–19.

Tatum, B. D., "The Complexity of Identity: 'Who Am I?'" in *Readings for Diversity and Social Justice*, eds. Maurianne Adams, Warren J. Blumfeld, Rosie Casteneda, Heather W. Hackman, Madeline L. Peters, Ximena Zuniga (New York: Routledge, 2000), 9.

US Office of Personnel Management, "Guidelines for Conducting Diversity Training," *Training and Development Policy*, accessed October 16, 2011, http://www.opm.gov/hrd/lead/policy/divers97.asp#PART%20B.

Vedantam, S., "Most Diversity Training Ineffective, Study Finds," *The Washington Post*, January 20, 2008, accessed October 5, 2011, http://www.washingtonpost.com/wp-dyn/content/article/2008/01/19/AR2008011901899_pf.html.

Yep, G. A., "My Three Cultures: Navigating the Multicultural Identity Landscape," in *Intercultural Communication: Experiences and Contexts*, eds. Judith

N. Martin, Lisa A. Flores, and Thomas K. Nakayama (Boston, MA: McGraw-Hill, 2002), 61.

6.3 EXPLORING SPECIFIC CULTURAL IDENTITIES

We can get a better understanding of current cultural identities by unpacking how they came to be. By looking at history, we can see how cultural identities that seem to have existed forever actually came to be constructed for various political and social reasons and how they have changed over time. Communication plays a central role in this construction. As we have already discussed, our identities are relational and communicative; they are also constructed. **Social constructionism** is a view that argues the self is formed through our interactions with others and in relationship to social, cultural, and political contexts (Allen, 2011). In this section, we'll explore how the cultural identities of race, gender, sexual orientation and ability have been constructed in the United States and how communication relates to those identities. There are other important identities that could be discussed, like religion, age, nationality, and class. Although they are not given their own section, consider how those identities may intersect with the identities discussed next.

Race

Would it surprise you to know that human beings, regardless of how they are racially classified, share 99.9 percent of their DNA? This finding by the Human Genome Project asserts that race is a social construct, not a biological one. The American Anthropological Association agrees, stating that race is the product of "historical and contemporary social, economic, educational, and political circumstances" (Allen, 2011). Therefore, we'll define **race** as a socially constructed category based on differences in appearance that has been used to create hierarchies that privilege some and disadvantage others.

Race didn't become a socially and culturally recognized marker until European colonial expansion in the 1500s. As Western Europeans traveled to parts of the world previously unknown to them and encountered people who were different from them, a hierarchy of races began to develop that placed lighter skinned Europeans above darker skinned people. At the time, newly developing fields in natural and biological sciences took interest in examining the new locales, including the plant and animal life, natural resources, and native populations. Over the next three hundred years, science that we would now undoubtedly recognize as flawed, biased, and racist legitimated notions that native populations were less evolved than white Europeans, often calling them savages. In fact, there were scientific debates as to whether some of the native populations should be considered human or animal. Racial distinctions have been based largely on phenotypes, or physiological features such as skin color, hair texture, and body/facial features. Western "scientists" used these differences as "proof" that native populations were less evolved than the Europeans, which helped justify colonial expansion, enslavement, genocide, and exploitation on massive scales (Allen, 2011). Even though there is a consensus among experts that race is social rather than biological, we can't deny that race still has meaning in our society and affects people as if it were "real."

Given that race is one of the first things we notice about someone, it's important to know how race and communication relate (Allen, 2011). Discussing race in the United States is difficult for many reasons. One is due to uncertainty about language use. People may be frustrated by their perception that labels change too often or be afraid of using an "improper" term and being viewed as racially insensitive. It is important, however, that we not let political correctness get in the way of meaningful dialogues and learning opportunities related to difference. Learning some of the communicative history of race can make us more competent communicators and open us up to more learning experiences.

Racial classifications used by the government and our regular communication about race in the United States have changed frequently, which further points to the social construction of race. Currently, the primary racial groups in the United States are African American, Asian American, European American, Latino/a, and Native American, but a brief look at changes in how the US Census Bureau has defined race clearly shows that this hasn't always been the case (see graphic below). In the 1900s alone, there were twenty-six different ways that race was categorized on census forms

(Allen, 2011). The way we communicate about race in our regular interactions has also changed, and many people are still hesitant to discuss race for fear of using "the wrong" vocabulary.

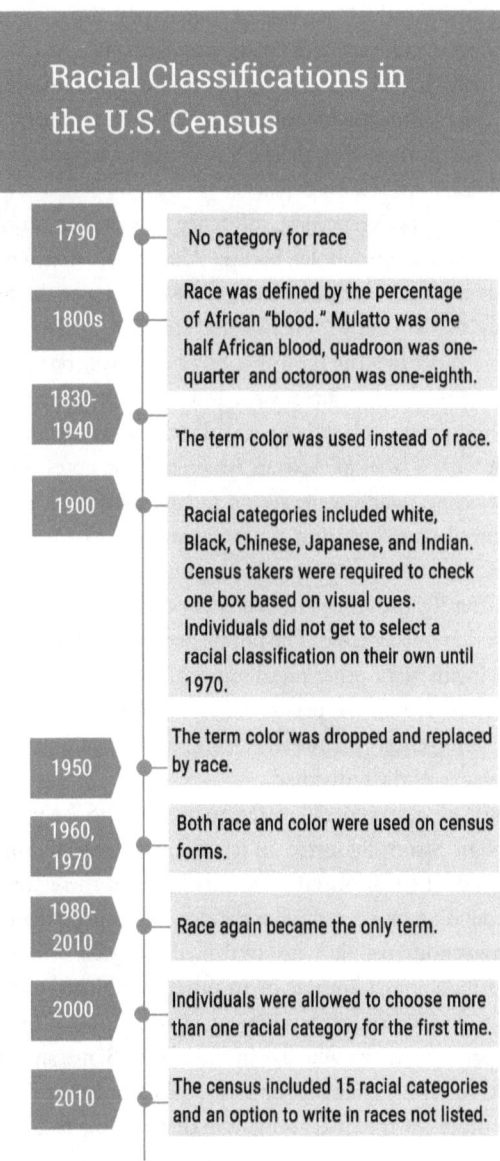

Source: Adapted from Brenda J. Allen, *Difference Matters: Communicating Social Identity* (Long Grove, IL: Waveland Press, 2011), 71–72.

The five primary racial groups noted previously can still be broken down further to specify a particular region, country, or nation. For example, Asian Americans are diverse in terms of country and language of origin and cultural practices. While the category of Asian Americans can be useful when discussing broad trends, it can also generalize among groups, which can lead to stereotypes. You may find that someone identifies as Chinese American or Korean American instead of Asian American. In this case, the label further highlights a person's cultural lineage. We should not assume, however, that someone identifies with his or her cultural lineage, as many people have more in common with their US American peers than a culture that may be one or more generations removed.

History and personal preference also influence how we communicate about race. Culture and communication scholar Brenda Allen notes that when she was born in 1950, her birth certificate included an N for Negro. Later she referred to herself as colored because that's what people in her community referred to themselves as. During and before this time, the term black had negative connotations and would likely have offended someone. There was a movement in the 1960s to reclaim the word black, and the slogan "black is beautiful" was commonly used. Brenda Allen acknowledges the newer label of African American but notes that she still prefers black. The terms colored and Negro are no longer considered appropriate because they were commonly used during a time when black people were blatantly discriminated against. Even though that history may seem far removed to some, it is not to others. Currently, the terms African American and black are frequently used, and both are considered acceptable. The phrase people of color is acceptable for most and is used to be inclusive of other racial minorities. If you are unsure what to use, you could always observe how a person refers to himself or herself, or you could ask for his or her preference. In any case, a competent communicator defers to and respects the preference of the individual.

The label Latin American generally refers to people who live in Central American countries. Although Spain colonized much of what is now South and Central America and parts of the Caribbean, the inhabitants of these areas are now much more diverse. Depending on the region or country, some people primarily trace their lineage to the indigenous people who lived in these areas before colonization, or to a Spanish and indigenous lineage, or to other combinations that may include European, African, and/or indigenous heritage. Latina and Latino are labels that are preferable to Hispanic for many who live in the United States and trace their lineage to South and/or Central America and/or parts of the Caribbean. Scholars who study Latina/o identity often use the label Latina/o in their writing to acknowledge women who avow that identity label (Calafell, 2007). In verbal communication you might say "Latina" when referring to a particular female or "Latino" when referring to a particular male of Latin American heritage. When referring to the group as a whole, you could say "Latinas and Latinos" instead of just "Latinos," which would be more gender inclusive. While Hispanic is used by the US Census, it refers primarily to people of Spanish origin, which doesn't account for the diversity of background of many Latinos/as. The term Hispanic also highlights the colonizer's influence over the indigenous, which erases a history that is important to many. Additionally, there are people who claim Spanish origins and identify culturally as Hispanic but racially as white. Labels such as Puerto Rican or Mexican American, which further specify region or country of origin, may also be used. Just as with other cultural groups, if you are unsure of how to refer to someone, you can always ask for and honor someone's preference.

The history of immigration in the United States also ties to the way that race has been constructed. The metaphor of the melting pot has been used to describe the immigration history of the United States but doesn't capture the experiences of many immigrant groups (Allen, 2011). Generally, immigrant groups who were white, or light skinned, and spoke English were better able to assimilate, or melt into the melting pot. But immigrant groups that we might think of as white today were not always considered so. Irish immigrants were discriminated against and even portrayed as black in cartoons that appeared in newspapers. In some Southern states, Italian immigrants were forced to go to black schools, and it wasn't until 1952 that Asian immigrants were allowed to become citizens of the United States. All this history is important, because it continues to influence communication among races today.

Interracial Communication

Race and communication are related in various ways. Racism influences our communication about race and is not an easy topic for most people to discuss. Today, people tend to view racism as overt acts such as calling someone a derogatory name or discriminating against someone in thought or action. However, there is a difference between racist acts, which we can attach to an individual, and institutional racism, which is not as easily identifiable. It is much easier for people to recognize and decry racist actions than it is to realize that racist patterns and practices go through societal institutions, which means that racism exists and doesn't have to be committed by any one person. As competent communicators and critical thinkers, we must challenge ourselves to be aware of how racism influences our communication at individual and societal levels.

We tend to make assumptions about people's race based on how they talk, and often these assumptions are based on stereotypes. Dominant groups tend to define what is correct or incorrect usage of a language, and since language is so closely tied to identity, labeling a group's use of a language as incorrect or deviant challenges or negates part of their identity (Yancy, 2011). We know there isn't only one way to speak English, but there have been movements to identify a standard. This becomes problematic when we realize that "standard English" refers to a way of speaking English that is based on white, middle-class ideals that do not match up with the experiences of many. When we create a standard for English, we can label anything that deviates from that "nonstandard English." Differences between standard English and what has been called "Black English" have gotten national attention through debates about whether or not instruction in classrooms should accommodate students who do not speak standard English. Education plays an important role in language acquisition, and class relates to access to education. In general, whether someone speaks standard English themselves or not, they tend to negatively judge people whose speech deviates from the standard.

Another national controversy has revolved around the inclusion of Spanish in common language use, such as Spanish as an option at ATMs, or other automated services, and Spanish language instruction in school for students who don't speak or are learning to speak English. As was noted earlier, the Latino/a population in the United States is growing fast, which has necessitated inclusion of Spanish in many areas of public life. This has also created a backlash, which some scholars argue is tied more to the race of the immigrants than the language they speak and a fear that white America could be engulfed by other languages and cultures (Speicher, 2002). This backlash has led to a revived movement to make English the official language of the United States.

The US Constitution does not stipulate a national language, and Congress has not designated one either. While nearly thirty states have passed English-language legislation, it has mostly been symbolic, and court rulings have limited any enforceability (Zuckerman, 2010). The Linguistic Society of America points out that immigrants are very aware of the social and economic advantages of learning English and do not need to be forced. They also point out that the United States has always had many languages represented, that national unity hasn't rested on a single language, and that there are actually benefits to having a population that is multilingual (Linguistic Society of America, 2011). Interracial communication presents some additional verbal challenges.

Code-switching involves changing from one way of speaking to another between or within interactions. Some people of color may engage in code-switching when communicating with dominant group members because they fear they will be negatively judged. Adopting the language practices of the dominant group may minimize perceived differences. This code-switching creates a linguistic dual consciousness in which people are able to maintain their linguistic identities with their in-group peers but can still acquire tools and gain access needed to function in dominant society (Yancy, 2011). White people may also feel anxious about communicating with people of color out of fear of being perceived as racist. In other situations, people in dominant groups may spotlight nondominant members by asking them to comment on or educate others about their race (Allen, 2011). For example, I once taught at a private university that was predominantly white. Students of color talked to me about being asked by professors to weigh in on an issue when discussions of race came up in the classroom. While a professor may have been well-intentioned, spotlighting can make a student feel conspicuous, frustrated, or defensive. Additionally, I bet the professors wouldn't think about asking a white, male, or heterosexual student to give the perspective of their whole group.

Gender

When we first meet a newborn baby, we ask whether it's a boy or a girl. This question illustrates the importance of gender in organizing our social lives and our interpersonal relationships. A Canadian family became aware of the deep emotions people feel about gender and the great discomfort people feel when they can't determine gender when they announced to the world that they were not going to tell anyone the gender of their baby, aside from the baby's siblings. Their desire for their child, named Storm, to be able to experience early life without the boundaries and categories of gender brought criticism from many (Davis & James, 2011). Conversely, many parents consciously or unconsciously "code" their newborns in gendered ways based on our society's associations of pink clothing and accessories with girls and blue with boys. While it's obvious to most people that colors aren't gendered, they take on new meaning when we assign gendered characteristics of masculinity and femininity to them. Just like race, gender is a socially constructed category. While it is true that there are biological differences between who we label male and female, the meaning our society places on those differences is what actually matters in our day-to-day lives. And the biological differences are interpreted differently around the world, which further shows that although we think gender is a natural, normal, stable way of classifying things, it is actually not. There is a long history of appreciation for people who cross gender lines in Native American and South Central Asian cultures, to name just two.

You may have noticed I use the word gender instead of sex. That's because **gender** is an identity based on internalized cultural notions of masculinity and femininity that is constructed through communication and interaction. There are two important parts of this definition to unpack. First, we internalize notions of gender based on socializing institutions, which helps us form our gender identity. Then we attempt to construct that gendered identity through our interactions with others, which is our gender expression. **Sex** is based on biological characteristics, including external genitalia, internal sex organs, chromosomes, and hormones (Wood, 2005). While the biological characteristics between men and women are obviously different, it's the meaning that we create and attach to those characteristics that makes them significant. The cultural differences in how that significance is ascribed are proof that "our way of doing things" is arbitrary. For example, cross-cultural research has found that boys and girls in most cultures show both aggressive and nurturing tendencies, but cultures vary in terms of how they encourage these characteristics between genders. In a group in Africa, young boys are responsible for taking care of babies and are encouraged to be nurturing (Wood, 2005).

Gender has been constructed over the past few centuries in political and deliberate ways that have tended to favor men in terms of power. And various academic fields joined in the quest to "prove" there are "natural" differences between men and women. While the "proof" they presented was credible to many at the time, it seems blatantly sexist and inaccurate today. In the late 1800s and early 1900s, scientists who measure skulls, also known as craiometrists, claimed that men were more intelligent than women because they had larger brains. Leaders in the fast-growing fields of sociology and psychology argued that women were less evolved than men and had more in common with "children and savages" than an adult (white) males (Allen, 2011). Doctors and other decision makers like politicians also used women's menstrual cycles as evidence that they were irrational, or hysterical, and therefore couldn't be trusted to vote, pursue higher education, or be in a leadership position. These are just a few of the many instances of how knowledge was created by seemingly legitimate scientific disciplines that we can now clearly see served to empower men and disempower women. This system is based on the ideology of patriarchy, which is a system of social structures and practices that maintains the values, priorities, and interests of men as a group (Wood, 2005). One of the ways patriarchy is maintained is by its relative invisibility. While women have been the focus of much research on gender differences, males have been largely unexamined. Men have been treated as the "generic" human being to which others are compared. But that ignores that fact that men have a gender, too. Masculinities studies have challenged that notion by examining how masculinities are performed.

There have been challenges to the construction of gender in recent decades. Since the 1960s, scholars and activists have challenged established notions of what it means to be a man or a woman. The women's rights movement in the United States dates back to the 1800s, when the first women's rights convention was held in Seneca Falls, New York, in 1848 (Wood, 2005). Although most women's rights movements have been led by white, middle-class women, there was overlap between those involved in the abolitionist movement to end slavery and the beginnings of the women's rights movement. Although some of the leaders of the early women's rights movement had class and education privilege, they were still taking a risk by organizing and protesting. Black women were even more at risk, and Sojourner Truth, an emancipated slave, faced those risks often and gave a much noted extemporaneous speech at a women's rights gathering in Akron, Ohio, in 1851, which came to be called "Ain't I a Woman?" (Wood, 2005) Her speech highlighted the multiple layers of oppression faced by black women.

Feminism as an intellectual and social movement advanced women's rights and our overall understanding of gender. Feminism has gotten a bad reputation based on how it has been portrayed in the media and by some politicians. When I teach courses about gender, I often ask my students to raise their hand if they consider themselves feminists. I usually only have a few, if any, who do. I've found that students I teach are hesitant to identify as a feminist because of connotations of the word. However, when I ask students to raise their hand if they believe women have been treated unfairly and that there should be more equity, most students raise their hand. Gender and communication scholar Julia Wood has found the same trend and explains that a desire to make a more equitable society for everyone is at the root of feminism. She shares comments from a student that capture this disconnect: (Wood, 2005).

> I would never call myself a feminist, because that word has so many negative connotations. I don't hate men or anything, and I'm not interested in protesting. I don't want to go around with hacked-off hair and no makeup and sit around bashing men. I do think women should have the same kinds of rights, including equal pay for equal work. But I wouldn't call myself a feminist.

It's important to remember that there are many ways to be a feminist and to realize that some of the stereotypes about feminism are rooted in sexism and homophobia, in that feminists are reduced to "men haters" and often presumed to be lesbians. The feminist movement also gave some momentum to the transgender rights movement. **Transgender** is an umbrella term for people whose gender identity and/or expression do not match the gender they were assigned by birth. Transgender people may or may not seek medical intervention like surgery or hormone treatments to help match their physiology with their gender identity. The term transgender includes other labels such as transsexual, transvestite, cross-dresser, and intersex, among others. Terms like hermaphrodite and she-male are not considered appropriate. As with other groups, it is best to allow someone to self-identify first and then honor their preferred label. If you are unsure of which pronouns to use when addressing someone, you can use gender-neutral language or you can use the pronoun that matches with how they are presenting. If someone has long hair, make-up, and a dress on, but you think their biological sex is male due to other cues, it would be polite to address them with female pronouns, since that is the gender identity they are expressing.

Gender as a cultural identity has implications for many aspects of our lives, including real-world contexts like education and work. Schools are primary grounds for socialization, and the educational experience for males and females is different in many ways from preschool through college. Although not always intentional, schools tend to recreate the hierarchies and inequalities that exist in society. Given that we live in a patriarchal society, there are communicative elements present in school that support this (Allen, 2011). For example, teachers are more likely to call on and pay attention to boys in a classroom, giving them more feedback in the form of criticism, praise, and help. This sends an implicit message that boys are more worthy of attention and valuable than girls. Teachers are also more likely to lead girls to focus on feelings and appearance and boys to focus on competition and achievement. The focus on appearance for girls can lead to anxieties about body image. Gender inequalities are also evident in the administrative structure of schools, which puts men in positions of authority more than women. While women make up 75 percent of the educational workforce, only 22 percent of superintendents and 8 percent of high school principals are women. Similar trends exist in colleges and universities, with women only accounting for 26 percent of full professors. These inequalities in schools correspond to larger inequalities in the general workforce. While there are more women in the workforce now than ever before, they still face a glass ceiling, which is a barrier for promotion to upper management. Many of my students have been surprised at the continuing pay gap that exists between men and women. In 2010, women earned about seventy-seven cents to every dollar earned by men (National Committee on Pay Equity, 2011). To put this into perspective, the National Committee on Pay Equity started an event called Equal Pay Day. In 2011, Equal Pay Day was on April 11. This signifies that for a woman to earn the same amount of money a man earned in a year, she would have to work more than three months extra, until April 11, to make up for the difference (National Committee on Pay Equity, 2011).

Sexuality

While race and gender are two of the first things we notice about others, sexuality is often something we view as personal and private. Although many people hold a view that a person's sexuality should be kept private, this isn't a reality for our society. One only needs to observe popular culture and media for a short time to see that sexuality permeates much of our public discourse.

Sexuality relates to culture and identity in important ways that extend beyond sexual orientation, just as race is more than the color of one's skin and gender is more than one's biological and physiological manifestations of masculinity and femininity. Sexuality isn't just physical; it is social in that we communicate with others about sexuality (Allen, 2011). Sexuality is also biological in that it connects to physiological functions that carry significant social and political meaning like puberty, menstruation, and pregnancy. Sexuality connects to public health issues like sexually transmitted infections (STIs), sexual assault, sexual abuse, sexual harassment, and teen pregnancy. Sexuality is at the center of political issues like abortion, sex education, and gay and lesbian rights. While all these contribute to sexuality as a cultural identity, the focus in this section is on sexual orientation.

The most obvious way sexuality relates to identity is through sexual orientation. **Sexual orientation** refers to a person's primary physical and emotional sexual attraction and activity. The terms we most often use to categorize sexual orientation are heterosexual, gay, lesbian, and bisexual. Gays, lesbians, and bisexuals are sometimes referred to as sexual minorities. While the term sexual preference has been used previously, sexual orientation is more appropriate, since preference implies a simple choice. Although someone's preference for a restaurant or actor may change frequently, sexuality is not as simple. The term homosexual can be appropriate in some instances, but it carries with it a clinical and medicalized tone. As you will see in the timeline that follows, the medical community has a recent history of "treating homosexuality" with means that most would view as inhumane today. So many people prefer a term like gay, which was chosen and embraced by gay people, rather than homosexual, which was imposed by a then discriminatory medical system.

The gay and lesbian rights movement became widely recognizable in the United States in the 1950s and continues on today, as evidenced by prominent issues regarding sexual orientation in national news and politics. National and international groups like the Human Rights Campaign advocate for rights for gay, lesbian, bisexual, transgender, and queer (GLBTQ) communities. While these communities are often grouped together within one acronym (GLBTQ), they are different. Gays and lesbians constitute the most visible of the groups and receive the most attention and funding. Bisexuals are rarely visible or included in popular cultural discourses or in social and political movements. Transgender issues have received much more attention in recent years, but transgender identity connects to gender more than it does to sexuality. Last, queer is a term used to describe a group that is diverse in terms of identities but usually takes a more activist and at times radical stance that critiques sexual categories. While queer was long considered a derogatory label, and still is by some, the queer activist movement that emerged in the 1980s and early 1990s reclaimed the word and embraced it as a positive. As you can see, there is a diversity of identities among sexual minorities, just as there is variation within races and genders.

As with other cultural identities, notions of sexuality have been socially constructed in different ways throughout human history. Sexual orientation didn't come into being as an identity category until the late 1800s. Before that, sexuality was viewed in more physical or spiritual senses that were largely separate from a person's identity.The graphic below traces some of the developments relevant to sexuality, identity, and communication that show how this cultural identity has been constructed over the past 3,000 years.

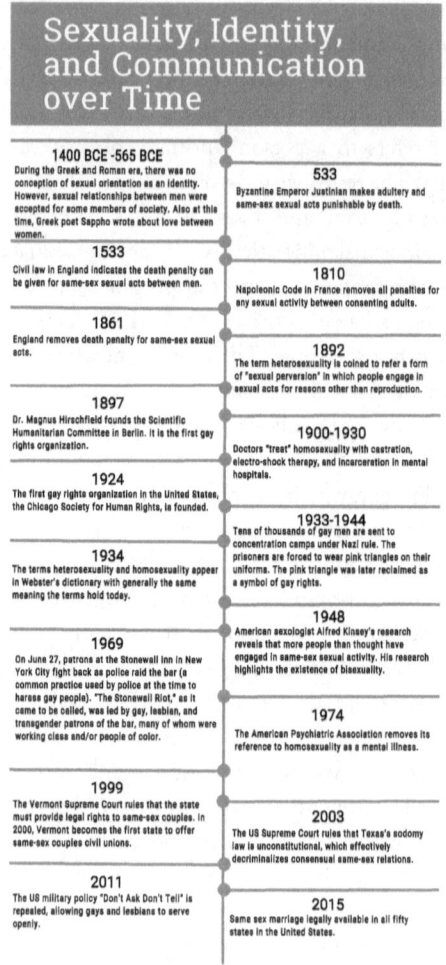

Source: Adapted from Brenda J. Allen, *Difference Matters: Communicating Social Identity* (Long Grove, IL: Waveland Press, 2011), 117–25; and University of Denver Queer and Ally Commission, "Lesbian, Gay, Bisexual, Transgender, Intersex, and Queer History," *Queer Ally Training Manual*, 2008.

Ability

There is resistance to classifying ability as a cultural identity, because we follow a medical model of disability that places disability as an individual and medical rather than social and cultural issue. While much of what distinguishes able-bodied and cognitively able from disabled is rooted in science, biology, and physiology, there are important sociocultural dimensions. The Americans with Disabilities Act (ADA) defines an individual with a disability as "a person who has a physical or mental impairment that substantially limits one or more major life activities, a person who has a history or record of such an impairment, or a person who is perceived by others as having such an impairment" (Allen, 2011). An impairment is defined as "any temporary or permanent loss or abnormality of a body structure or function, whether physiological or psychological" (Allen, 2011). This definition is important because it notes the social aspect of disability in that people's life activities are limited and the relational aspect of disability in that the perception of a disability by others can lead someone to be classified as such. Ascribing an identity of disabled to a person can be problematic. If there is a mental or physical impairment, it should be diagnosed by a credentialed expert. If there isn't an impairment, then the label of disabled can have negative impacts, as this label carries social and cultural significance. People are tracked into various educational programs based on their physical and cognitive abilities, and there are many cases of people being mistakenly labeled disabled who were treated differently despite their protest of the ascribed label. Students who did not speak English as a first language, for example, were—and perhaps still are—sometimes put into special education classes.

Ability, just as the other cultural identities discussed, has institutionalized privileges and disadvantages associated with it. **Ableism** is the system of beliefs and practices that produces a physical and mental standard that is projected as normal for a human being and labels deviations from it abnormal, resulting in unequal treatment and access to resources. Ability privilege refers to the unearned advantages that are provided for people who fit the cognitive and physical norms (Allen, 2011). I once attended a workshop about ability privilege led by a man who was visually impaired. He talked about how, unlike other cultural identities that are typically stable over a lifetime, ability fluctuates for most people. We have all experienced times when we are more or less able.

Perhaps you broke your leg and had to use crutches or a wheelchair for a while. Getting sick for a prolonged period of time also lessens our abilities, but we may fully recover from any of these examples and regain our ability privilege. Whether you've experienced a short-term disability or not, the majority of us will become less physically and cognitively able as we get older.

Statistically, people with disabilities make up the largest minority group in the United States, with an estimated 20 percent of people five years or older living with some form of disability (Allen, 2011). Medical advances have allowed some people with disabilities to live longer and more active lives than before, which has led to an increase in the number of people with disabilities. This number could continue to increase, as we have thousands of veterans returning from the wars in Iraq and Afghanistan with physical disabilities or psychological impairments such as post-traumatic stress disorder.

As disability has been constructed in US history, it has intersected with other cultural identities. For example, people opposed to "political and social equality for women cited their supposed physical, intellectual, and psychological flaws, deficits, and deviations from the male norm." They framed women as emotional, irrational, and unstable, which was used to put them into the "scientific" category of "feeblemindedness," which led them to be institutionalized (Carlson, 2001). Arguments supporting racial inequality and tighter immigration restrictions also drew on notions of disability, framing certain racial groups as prone to mental retardation, mental illness, or uncontrollable emotions and actions. See the graphic below for a timeline of developments related to ability, identity, and communication. These thoughts led to a dark time in US history, as the eugenics movement sought to limit reproduction of people deemed as deficient.

During the early part of the 1900s, the eugenics movement was the epitome of the move to rehabilitate or reject people with disabilities (Allen, 2005). This was a brand of social engineering that was indicative of a strong public support in the rationality of science to cure society's problems (Allen, 2011). A sterilization law written in 1914 "proposed to authorize sterilization of the socially inadequate," which included the "feebleminded, insane, criminalistic, epileptic, inebriate, diseased, blind, deaf, deformed, and dependent" (Lombardo, 2011). During the eugenics movement in the United States, more than sixty thousand people in thirty-three states were involuntarily sterilized (Allen, 2011).

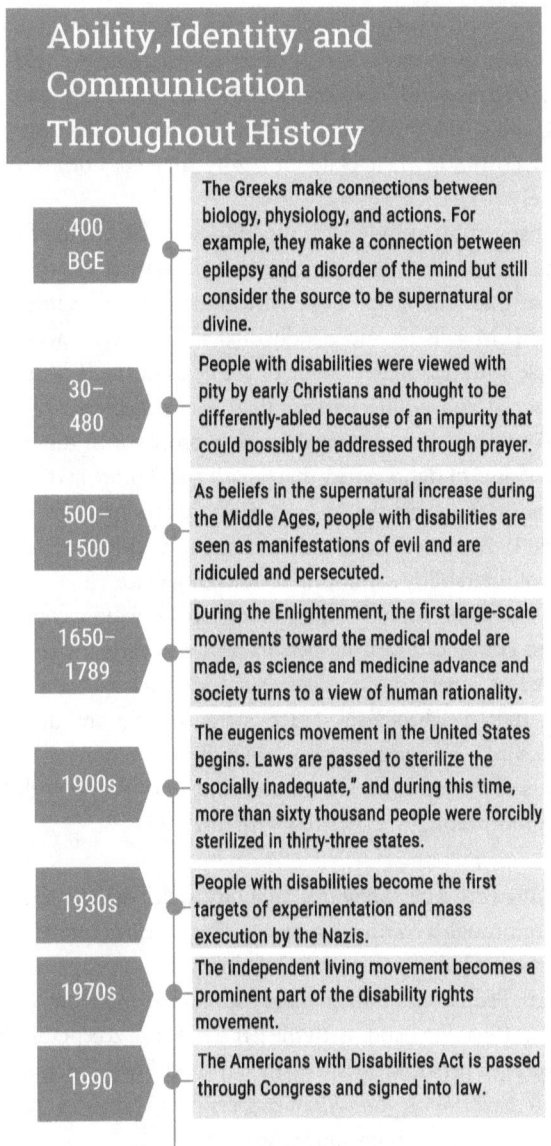

Source: Maggie Shreve, "The Movement for Independent Living: A Brief History," *Independent Living Research Utilization*, accessed October 14, 2011, http://ilru.org/html/publications/infopaks/IL_paradigm.doc.

Although the eugenics movement as it was envisioned and enacted then is unthinkable today, some who have studied the eugenics movement of the early 1900s have issued warnings that a newly packaged version of eugenics could be upon us. As human genome mapping and DNA manipulation become more accessible, advanced genetic testing could enable parents to eliminate undesirable aspects or enhance desirable characteristics of their children before they are born, creating "designer children" (Spice, 2005).

Much has changed for people with disabilities in the United States in the past fifty years. The independent living movement (ILM) was a part of the disability rights movement that took shape along with other social movements of the 1960s and 1970s. The ILM calls for more individual and collective action toward social change by people with disabilities. Some of the goals of the ILM include reframing disability as a social and political rather than just a medical issue, a shift toward changing society rather than just rehabilitating people with disabilities, a view of accommodations as civil rights rather than charity, and more involvement by people with disabilities in the formulation and execution of policies relating to them (Longmore, 2003). As society better adapts to people with disabilities, there will be more instances of interability communication taking place.

Interability communication is communication between people with differing ability levels; for example, a hearing person communicating with someone who is hearing impaired or a person who doesn't use a wheelchair communicating with someone who uses a wheelchair. Since many people are unsure of how to communicate with a person with disabilities, following are the "Ten Commandments of Etiquette for Communicating with People with Disabilities" to help you in communicating with persons with disabilities:[1]

1. When talking with a person with a disability, speak directly to that person rather than through a companion or sign-language interpreter.
2. When introduced to a person with a disability, it is appropriate to offer to shake hands. People with limited hand use or an artificial limb can usually shake hands. (Shaking hands with the left hand is an acceptable greeting.)
3. When meeting a person who is visually impaired, always identify yourself and others who may be with you. When conversing in a group, remember to identify the person to whom you are speaking.

---

1. "Effective Interaction: Communication with and about People with Disabilities in the Workplace," accessed November 5, 2012, http://www.dol.gov/odep/pubs/fact/effectiveinteraction.htm#.UJgp8RjqJJ8.

4. If you offer assistance, wait until the offer is accepted. Then listen to or ask for instructions.
5. Treat adults as adults. Address people who have disabilities by their first names only when extending the same familiarity to all others. (Never patronize people who use wheelchairs by patting them on the head or shoulder.)
6. Leaning on or hanging on to a person's wheelchair is similar to leaning or hanging on to a person and is generally considered annoying. The chair is part of the personal body space of the person who uses it.
7. Listen attentively when you're talking with a person who has difficulty speaking. Be patient and wait for the person to finish, rather than correcting or speaking for the person. If necessary, ask short questions that require short answers, a nod, or a shake of the head. Never pretend to understand if you are having difficulty doing so. Instead, repeat what you have understood and allow the person to respond. The response will clue you in and guide your understanding.
8. When speaking with a person who uses a wheelchair or a person who uses crutches, place yourself at eye level in front of the person to facilitate the conversation.
9. To get the attention of a person who is deaf, tap the person on the shoulder or wave your hand. Look directly at the person and speak clearly, slowly, and expressively to determine if the person can read your lips. Not all people who are deaf can read lips. For those who do lip read, be sensitive to their needs by placing yourself so that you face the light source and keep hands, cigarettes, and food away from your mouth when speaking.
10. Relax. Don't be embarrassed if you happen to use accepted, common expressions such as "See you later" or "Did you hear about that?" that seem to relate to a person's disability. Don't be afraid to ask questions when you're unsure of what to do.

References

Allen, B. J., *Difference Matters: Communicating Social Identity* (Long Grove, IL: Waveland, 2005), 145.

Allen, B. J., *Difference Matters: Communicating Social Identity*, 2nd ed. (Long Grove, IL: Waveland, 2011), 12.

Allen, G. E., "Social Origins of Eugenics," *Eugenics Archive*, accessed October 16, 2011, http://www.eugenicsarchive.org/eugenics/list2.pl.

Calafell, B. M., *Latina/o Communication Studies: Theorizing Performance* (New York: Peter Lang, 2007), 1–9.

Carlson, L., "Cognitive Ableism and Disability Studies: Feminist Reflections on the History of Mental Retardation," *Hypatia* 16, no. 4 (2001): 127.

Davis, L., and Susan Donaldson James, "Canadian Mother Raising Her 'Genderless' Baby, Storm, Defends Her Family's Decision," *ABC News*, May 30, 2011, accessed October 12, 2011, http://abcnews.go.com/Health/genderless-baby-controversy-mom-defends-choice-reveal-sex/story?id=13718047.

Linguistic Society of America, "Resolution: English Only," December 28, 1986, accessed October 12, 2011, http://www.lsadc.org/info/lsa-res-english.cfm.

Lombardo, P., "Eugenic Sterilization Laws," *Eugenics Archive*, accessed October 16, 2011, http://www.eugenicsarchive.org/eugenics/list2.pl.

Longmore, P. K., *Why I Burned My Book and Other Essays on Disability* (Philadelphia, PA: Temple University Press, 2003), 114.

National Committee on Pay Equity, "Wage Gap over Time," accessed October 12, 2011, http://www.pay-equity.org/info-time.html.

Speicher, B. L., "Problems with English-Only Policies," *Management Communication Quarterly* 15, no. 4 (2002): 621.

Spice, B., "Duquesne Focuses on the Perils of Modern 'Eugenics'" *Pittsburgh Post-Gazette*, February 7, 2005, accessed October 16, 2011, http://www.post-gazette.com/pg/05038/453781.stm.

Wood, J. T., *Gendered Lives: Communication, Gender, and Culture*, 5th ed. (Belmont, CA: Thomas Wadsworth, 2005), 19.

Yancy, G., "The Scholar Who Coined the Term Ebonics: A Conversation with Dr. Robert L. Williams," *Journal of Language, Identity, and Education* 10, no. 1 (2011): 41–51.

Zuckerman, M. A., "Constitutional Clash: When English-Only Meets Voting Rights," *Yale Law and Policy Review* 28 (2010): 353–54.

6.4 INTERCULTURAL COMMUNICATION

"The beauty of the world lies in the diversity of its people." -Unknown

It is through intercultural communication that we come to create, understand, and transform culture and identity. **Intercultural communication** is communication between people with differing cultural identities. One reason we should study intercultural communication is to foster greater self-awareness (Martin & Nakayama, 2010). Our thought process regarding culture is often "other focused," meaning that the culture of the other person or group is what stands out in our perception. However, the old adage "know thyself" is appropriate, as we become more aware of our own culture by better understanding other cultures and perspectives. Intercultural communication can allow us to step outside of our comfortable, usual frame of reference and see our culture through a different lens. Additionally, as we become more self-aware, we may also become more ethical communicators as we challenge our **ethnocentrism**, or our tendency to view our own culture as superior to other cultures.

Difference matters, and studying intercultural communication can help us better negotiate our changing world. Changing economies and technologies intersect with culture in meaningful ways (Martin & Nakayama). As was noted earlier, technology has created for some a global village where vast distances are now much shorter due to new technology that make travel and communication more accessible and convenient (McLuhan, 1967). However, as the following "Getting Plugged In" box indicates, there is also a **digital divide**, which refers to the unequal access to technology and related skills that exists in much of the world. People in most fields will be more successful if they are prepared to work in a globalized world. Obviously, the global market sets up the need to have intercultural competence for employees who travel between locations of a multinational corporation. Perhaps less obvious may be the need for teachers to work with students who do not speak English as their first language and for police officers, lawyers, managers, and medical personnel to be able to work with people who have various cultural identities.

Intercultural Communication: A Dialectical Approach

Intercultural communication is complicated, messy, and at times contradictory. Therefore it is not always easy to conceptualize or study. Taking a dialectical approach allows us to capture the dynamism of intercultural communication. A **dialectic** is a relationship between two opposing concepts that constantly push and pull one another (Martin & Nakayama, 2010). To put it another way, thinking dialectically helps us realize that our experiences often occur in between two different phenomena. This perspective is especially useful for interpersonal and intercultural communication, because when we think dialectically, we think relationally. This means we look at the relationship between aspects of intercultural communication rather than viewing them in isolation. Intercultural communication occurs as a dynamic in-betweenness that, while connected to the individuals in an encounter, goes beyond the individuals, creating something unique. Holding a dialectical perspective may be challenging for some Westerners, as it asks us to hold two contradictory ideas simultaneously, which goes against much of what we are taught in our formal education. Thinking dialectically helps us see the complexity in culture and identity because it doesn't allow for dichotomies. **Dichotomies** are dualistic ways of thinking that highlight opposites, reducing the ability to see gradations that exist in between concepts. Dichotomies such as good/evil, wrong/right, objective/subjective, male/female, in-group/out-group, black/white, and so on form the basis of much of our thoughts on ethics, culture, and general philosophy, but this isn't the only way of thinking (Marin & Nakayama, 1999). Many Eastern cultures acknowledge that the world isn't dualistic. Rather, they accept as part of their reality that things that seem opposite are actually interdependent and complement each other. I argue that a dialectical approach is useful in studying intercultural communication because it gets us out of our comfortable and familiar ways of thinking. Since so much of understanding culture and identity is understanding ourselves, having an unfamiliar lens through which to view culture can offer us insights that our familiar lenses will not. Specifically, we can better understand intercultural communication by examining six dialectics (see the graphic below) (Martin & Nakayama, 1999).

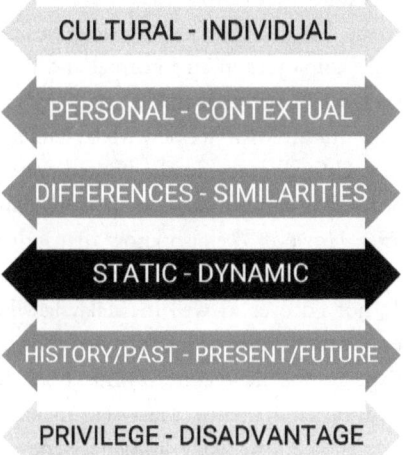

Cultural-Individual Dialectic

The cultural-individual dialectic captures the interplay between patterned behaviors learned from a cultural group and individual behaviors that may be variations on or counter to those of the larger culture. This dialectic is useful because it helps us account for exceptions to cultural norms. For example, earlier we learned that the United States is said to be a low-context culture, which means that we value verbal communication as our primary, meaning-rich form of communication. Conversely, Japan is said to be a high-context culture, which means they often look for nonverbal clues like tone, silence, or what is not said for meaning. However, you can find people in the United States who intentionally put much meaning into *how* they say things, perhaps because they are not as comfortable speaking directly what's on their mind. We often do this in situations where we may hurt someone's feelings or damage a relationship. Does that mean we come from a high-context culture? Does the Japanese man who speaks more than is socially acceptable come from a low-context culture? The answer to both questions is no. Neither the behaviors of a small percentage of individuals nor occasional situational choices constitute a cultural pattern.

Personal-Contextual Dialectic

The personal-contextual dialectic highlights the connection between our personal patterns of and preferences for communicating and how various contexts influence the personal. In some cases, our communication patterns and preferences will stay the same across many contexts. In other cases, a context shift may lead us to alter our communication and adapt. For example, an American businesswoman may prefer to communicate with her employees in an informal and laid-back manner. When she is promoted to manage a department in her company's office in Malaysia, she may again prefer to communicate with her new Malaysian employees the same way she did with those in the United States. In the United States, we know that there are some accepted norms that communication in work contexts is more formal than in personal contexts. However, we also know that individual managers often adapt these expectations to suit their own personal tastes. This type of managerial discretion would likely not go over as well in Malaysia where there is a greater emphasis put on power distance (Hofstede, 1991). So while the American manager may not know to adapt to the new context unless she has a high degree of intercultural communication competence, Malaysian managers would realize that this is an instance where the context likely influences communication more than personal preferences.

Differences-Similarities Dialectic

The differences-similarities dialectic allows us to examine how we are simultaneously similar to and different from others. As was noted earlier, it's easy to fall into a view of intercultural communication as "other oriented" and set up dichotomies between "us" and "them." When we over-focus on differences, we can end up polarizing groups that actually have things in common. When we over-focus on similarities, we **essentialize**, or reduce/overlook important variations within a group. This tendency is evident in most of the popular, and some of the academic, conversations regarding "gender differences." The book *Men Are from Mars and Women Are from Venus* makes it seem like men and women aren't even species that hail from the same planet. The media is quick to include a blurb from a research study indicating again how men and women are "wired" to communicate differently. However, the overwhelming majority of current research on gender and communication finds that while there are differences between how men and women communicate, there are far more similarities (Allen, 2011). Even the language we use to describe the genders sets up dichotomies. That's why I suggest that my students use the term *other gender* instead of the commonly used *opposite sex*. I have a mom, a sister, and plenty of female friends, and I don't feel like any of them are the opposite of me. Perhaps a better title for a book would be *Women and Men Are Both from Earth*.

Static-Dynamic Dialectic

The static-dynamic dialectic suggests that culture and communication change over time yet often appear to be and are experienced as stable. Although it is true that our cultural beliefs and practices are rooted in the past, we have already discussed how cultural categories that most of us assume to be stable, like race and gender, have changed dramatically in just the past fifty years. Some cultural values remain relatively consistent over time, which allows us to make some generalizations about a culture. For example, cultures have different orientations to time. The Chinese have a longer-term orientation to time than do Europeans (Lustig & Koester, 2006). This is evidenced in something that dates back as far as astrology. The Chinese zodiac is done annually (The Year of the Monkey, etc.), while European astrology was organized by month (Taurus, etc.). While this cultural orientation to time has been around for generations, as China becomes more Westernized in terms of technology, business, and commerce, it could also adopt some views on time that are more short term.

History/Past-Present/Future Dialectic

The history/past-present/future dialectic reminds us to understand that while current cultural conditions are important and that our actions now will inevitably affect our future, those conditions are not without a history. We always view history through the lens of the present. Perhaps no example is more entrenched in our past and avoided in our present as the history of slavery in the United States. Where I grew up in the Southern United States, race was something that came up frequently. The high school I attended was 30 percent minorities (mostly African American) and also had a noticeable number of white teens (mostly male) who proudly displayed Confederate flags on their clothing or vehicles.

I remember an instance in a history class where we were discussing slavery and the subject of repatriation, or compensation for descendants of slaves, came up. A white male student in the class proclaimed, "I've never owned slaves. Why should I have to care about this now?" While his statement about not owning slaves is valid, it doesn't acknowledge that effects of slavery still linger today and that the repercussions of such a long and unjust period of our history don't disappear over the course of a few generations.

Privileges-Disadvantages Dialectic

The privileges-disadvantages dialectic captures the complex interrelation of unearned, systemic advantages and disadvantages that operate among our various identities. As was discussed earlier, our society consists of dominant and nondominant groups. Our cultures and identities have certain privileges and/or disadvantages. To understand this dialectic, we must view culture and identity through a lens of **intersectionality**, which asks us to acknowledge that we each have multiple cultures and identities that intersect with each other. Because our identities are complex, no one is completely privileged and no one is completely disadvantaged. For example, while we may think of a white, heterosexual male as being very privileged, he may also have a disability that leaves him without the able-bodied privilege that a Latina woman has. This is often a difficult dialectic for my students to understand, because they are quick to point out exceptions that they think challenge this notion. For example, many people like to point out Oprah Winfrey as a powerful African American woman. While she is definitely now quite privileged despite her disadvantaged identities, her trajectory isn't the norm. When we view privilege and disadvantage at the cultural level, we cannot let individual exceptions distract from the systemic and institutionalized ways in which some people in our society are disadvantaged while others are privileged.

As these dialectics reiterate, culture and communication are complex systems that intersect with and diverge from many contexts. A better understanding of all these dialectics helps us be more critical thinkers and competent communicators in a changing world.

Intercultural Communication and Relationships

Intercultural relationships are formed between people with different cultural identities and include friends, romantic partners, family, and coworkers. Intercultural relationships have benefits and drawbacks. Some of the benefits include increasing cultural knowledge, challenging previously held stereotypes, and learning new skills (Martin & Nakayama, 2010). For example, I learned about the Vietnamese New Year celebration Tet from a friend I made in graduate school. This same friend also taught me how to make some delicious Vietnamese foods that I continue to cook today. I likely would not have gained this cultural knowledge or skill without the benefits of my intercultural friendship. Intercultural relationships also present challenges, however.

The dialectics discussed earlier affect our intercultural relationships. The similarities-differences dialectic in particular may present challenges to relationship formation (Martin & Nakayama, 2010). While differences between people's cultural identities may be obvious, it takes some effort to uncover commonalities that can form the basis of a relationship. Perceived differences in general also create anxiety and uncertainty that is not as present in intracultural relationships. Once some similarities are found, the tension within the dialectic begins to balance out and uncertainty and anxiety lessen. Negative stereotypes may also hinder progress toward relational development, especially if the individuals are not open to adjusting their preexisting beliefs. Intercultural relationships may also take more work to nurture and maintain. The benefit of increased cultural awareness is often achieved, because the relational partners explain their cultures to each other. This type of explaining requires time, effort, and patience and may be an extra burden that some are not willing to carry. Last, engaging in intercultural relationships can lead to questioning or even backlash from one's own group. I experienced this type of backlash from my white classmates in middle school who teased me for hanging out with the African American kids on my bus. While these challenges range from mild inconveniences to more serious repercussions, they are important to be aware of. As noted earlier, intercultural relationships can take many forms. The focus of this section is on friendships and romantic relationships, but much of the following discussion can be extended to other relationship types.

Intercultural Friendships

Even within the United States, views of friendship vary based on cultural identities. Research on friendship has shown that Latinos/as value relational support and positive feedback, Asian Americans emphasize exchanges of ideas like offering feedback or asking for guidance, African Americans value respect and mutual acceptance, and European Americans value recognition of each other as individuals (Coller, 1996). Despite the differences in emphasis, research also shows that the overall definition of a close friend is similar across cultures. A close friend is thought of as someone who is helpful and nonjudgmental, who you enjoy spending time with but can also be independent, and who shares similar interests and personality traits (Lee, 2006).

Intercultural friendship formation may face challenges that other friendships do not. Prior intercultural experience and overcoming language barriers increase the likelihood of intercultural friendship formation (Sias et al., 2008). In some cases, previous intercultural experience, like studying abroad in college or living in a diverse place, may motivate someone to pursue intercultural friendships once they are no longer in that context. When friendships cross nationality, it may be necessary to invest more time in common understanding, due to language barriers. With sufficient motivation and language skills, communication exchanges through self-disclosure can then further relational formation. Research has shown that individuals from different countries in intercultural friendships differ in terms of the topics and depth of self-disclosure, but that as the friendship progresses, self-disclosure increases in depth and breadth (Chen & Nakazawa, 2009). Further, as people overcome initial challenges to initiating an intercultural friendship and move toward mutual self-disclosure, the relationship becomes more intimate, which helps friends work through and move beyond their cultural differences to focus on maintaining their relationship. In this sense, intercultural friendships can be just as strong and enduring as other friendships (Lee, 2006).

The potential for broadening one's perspective and learning more about cultural identities is not always balanced, however. In some instances, members of a dominant culture may be more interested in sharing their culture with their intercultural friend than they are in learning about their friend's culture, which illustrates how context and power influence friendships (Lee, 2006). A research study found a similar power dynamic, as European Americans in intercultural friendships stated they were open to exploring everyone's culture but also communicated that culture wasn't a big part of their intercultural friendships, as they just saw their friends as people. As the researcher states, "These types of responses may demonstrate that it is easiest for the group with the most socioeconomic and sociocultural power to ignore the rules, assume they have the power as individuals to change the rules, or assume that no rules exist, since others are adapting to them rather than vice versa" (Collier, 1996). Again, intercultural friendships illustrate the complexity of culture and the importance of remaining mindful of your communication and the contexts in which it occurs.

Culture and Romantic Relationships

Romantic relationships are influenced by society and culture, and still today some people face discrimination based on who they love. Specifically, sexual orientation and race affect societal views of romantic relationships. Although the United States, as a whole, is becoming more accepting of gay and lesbian relationships, there is still a climate of prejudice and discrimination that individuals in same-gender romantic relationships must face. Despite some physical and virtual meeting places for gay and lesbian people, there are challenges for meeting and starting romantic relationships that are not experienced for most heterosexual people (Peplau & Spalding, 2000).

As we've already discussed, romantic relationships are likely to begin due to merely being exposed to another person at work, through a friend, and so on. But some gay and lesbian people may feel pressured into or just feel more comfortable not disclosing or displaying their sexual orientation at work or perhaps even to some family and friends, which closes off important social networks through which most romantic relationships begin. This pressure to refrain from disclosing one's gay or lesbian sexual orientation in the workplace is not unfounded, as it is still legal in twenty-nine states (as of November 2012) to fire someone for being gay or lesbian (Human Rights Campaign, 2012). There are also some challenges faced by gay and lesbian partners regarding relationship termination. Gay and lesbian couples do not have the same legal and societal resources to manage their relationships as heterosexual couples; for example, gay and lesbian relationships are not legally recognized in most states, it is more difficult for a gay or lesbian couple to jointly own property or share custody of children than heterosexual couples, and there is little public funding for relationship counseling or couples therapy for gay and lesbian couples.

While this lack of barriers may make it easier for gay and lesbian partners to break out of an unhappy or unhealthy relationship, it could also lead couples to termination who may have been helped by the sociolegal support systems available to heterosexuals (Peplau & Spalding, 2000).

Despite these challenges, relationships between gay and lesbian people are similar in other ways to those between heterosexuals. Gay, lesbian, and heterosexual people seek similar qualities in a potential mate, and once relationships are established, all these groups experience similar degrees of relational satisfaction (Peplau & Spalding, 2000). Despite the myth that one person plays the man and one plays the woman in a relationship, gay and lesbian partners do not have set preferences in terms of gender role. In fact, research shows that while women in heterosexual relationships tend to do more of the housework, gay and lesbian couples were more likely to divide tasks so that each person has an equal share of responsibility (Peplau & Spalding, 2000). A gay or lesbian couple doesn't necessarily constitute an intercultural relationship, but as we have already discussed, sexuality is an important part of an individual's identity and connects to larger social and cultural systems. Keeping in mind that identity and culture are complex, we can see that gay and lesbian relationships can also be intercultural if the partners are of different racial or ethnic backgrounds.

While interracial relationships have occurred throughout history, there have been more historical taboos in the United States regarding relationships between African Americans and white people than other racial groups. Antimiscegenation laws were common in states and made it illegal for people of different racial/ethnic groups to marry. It wasn't until 1967 that the Supreme Court ruled in the case of Loving versus Virginia, declaring these laws to be unconstitutional (Pratt, 1995). It wasn't until 1998 and 2000, however, that South Carolina and Alabama removed such language from their state constitutions (Lovingday.org, 2011). The organization and website lovingday.org commemorates the landmark case and works to end racial prejudice through education.

Even after these changes, there were more Asian-white and Latino/a-white relationships than there were African American–white relationships (Gaines Jr. & Brennan, 2011). Having already discussed the importance of similarity in attraction to mates, it's important to note that partners in an interracial relationship, although culturally different, tend to be similar in occupation and income. This can likely be explained by the situational influences on our relationship formation we discussed earlier—namely, that work tends to be a starting ground for many of our relationships, and we usually work with people who have similar backgrounds to us.

There has been much research on interracial couples that counters the popular notion that partners may be less satisfied in their relationships due to cultural differences. In fact, relational satisfaction isn't significantly different for interracial partners, although the challenges they may face in finding acceptance from other people could lead to stressors that are not as strong for intracultural partners (Gaines Jr. & Brennan, 2011). Although partners in interracial relationships certainly face challenges, there are positives. For example, some mention that they've experienced personal growth by learning about their partner's cultural background, which helps them gain alternative perspectives. Specifically, white people in interracial relationships have cited an awareness of and empathy for racism that still exists, which they may not have been aware of before (Gaines Jr. & Liu, 2000).

References

Allen, B. J., *Difference Matters: Communicating Social Identity*, 2nd ed. (Long Grove, IL: Waveland, 2011), 55.

ben-Aaron, D., "Bringing Broadband to Finland's Bookdocks," *Bloomberg Businessweek*, July 19, 2010, 42.

Chen, Y. and Masato Nakazawa, "Influences of Culture on Self-Disclosure as Relationally Situated in Intercultural and Interracial Friendships from a Social Penetration Perspective," *Journal of Intercultural Communication Research* 38, no. 2 (2009): 94. doi:10.1080/17475750903395408.

Coller, M. J., "Communication Competence Problematics in Ethnic Friendships," *Communication Monographs* 63, no. 4 (1996): 324–25.

De La Baume, M. and J. David Goodman, "First Fines over Wearing Veils in France," *The New York Times* (*The Lede: Blogging the News*), September 22, 2011, accessed October 10, 2011, http://thelede.blogs.nytimes.com/2011/09/22/first-fines-over-wearing-full-veils-in-france.

Fraser, C., "The Women Defying France's Fall-Face Veil Ban," *BBC News*,

September 22, 2011, accessed October 10, 2011, http://www.bbc.co.uk/news/world-europe-15023308.

Gaines Jr. S. O., and Kelly A. Brennan, "Establishing and Maintaining Satisfaction in Multicultural Relationships," in *Close Romantic Relationships: Maintenance and Enhancement*, eds. John Harvey and Amy Wenzel (Mahwah, NJ: Lawrence Erlbaum, 2011), 239.

Stanley O. Gaines Jr., S. O., and James H. Liu, "Multicultural/Multiracial Relationships," in *Close Relationships: A Sourcebook*, eds. Clyde Hendrick and Susan S. Hendrick (Thousand Oaks, CA: Sage, 2000), 105.

Hofstede, G., *Cultures and Organizations: Softwares of the Mind* (London: McGraw-Hill, 1991), 26.

Human Rights Campaign, "Pass ENDA NOW", accessed November 5, 2012, http://www.hrc.org/campaigns/employment-non-discrimination-act.

Lee, P., "Bridging Cultures: Understanding the Construction of Relational Identity in Intercultural Friendships," *Journal of Intercultural Communication Research* 35, no. 1 (2006): 11. doi:10.1080/17475740600739156.

Loving Day, "The Last Laws to Go," *Lovingday.org*, accessed October 11, 2011, http://lovingday.org/last-laws-to-go.

Lustig, M. W., and Jolene Koester, *Intercultural Competence: Interpersonal Communication across Cultures*, 2nd ed. (Boston, MA: Pearson, 2006), 128–29.

Martin, J. N., and Thomas K. Nakayama, *Intercultural Communication in Contexts*, 5th ed. (Boston, MA: McGraw-Hill, 2010), 4.

Martin, J. N., and Thomas K. Nakayama, "Thinking Dialectically about Culture and Communication," *Communication Theory* 9, no. 1 (1999): 14.

McLuhan, M., *The Medium Is the Message* (New York: Bantam Books, 1967).

Peplau, L. A. and Leah R. Spalding, "The Close Relationships of Lesbians, Gay Men, and Bisexuals," in *Close Relationships: A Sourcebook*, eds. Clyde Hendrick and Susan S. Hendrick (Thousand Oaks, CA: Sage, 2000), 113.

Pratt, R. A., "Crossing the Color Line: A Historical Assessment and Personal Narrative of *Loving v. Virginia*," *Howard Law Journal* 41, no. 2 (1995): 229–36.

Sias, P. M., Jolanta A. Drzewiecka, Mary Meares, Rhiannon Bent, Yoko Konomi, Maria Ortega, and Colene White, "Intercultural Friendship Development," *Communication Reports* 21, no. 1 (2008): 9. doi:10.1080/08934210701643750.

Smith, P., "The Digital Divide," *New York Times Upfront*, May 9, 2011, 6.

Sylvester, D. E., and Adam J. McGlynn, "The Digital Divide, Political Participation, and Place," *Social Science Computer Review* 28, no. 1 (2010): 64–65. doi:10.1177/0894439309335148.

van Deursen, A. and Jan van Dijk, "Internet Skills and the Digital Divide," *New Media and Society* 13, no. 6 (2010): 893. doi:10.1177/1461444810386774.

6.5 INTERCULTURAL COMMUNICATION COMPETENCE

Throughout this chapter we have been putting various tools in our communication toolbox to improve our communication competence. Many of these tools can be translated into intercultural contexts. While building any form of competence requires effort, building intercultural communication competence often requires us to take more risks. Some of these risks require us to leave our comfort zones and adapt to new and uncertain situations. In this section, we will learn some of the skills needed to be an interculturally competent communicator.

Components of Intercultural Communication Competence

Intercultural communication competence (ICC) is the ability to communicate effectively and appropriately in various cultural contexts. There are numerous components of ICC. Some key components include motivation, self- and other knowledge, and tolerance for uncertainty.

Motivation

Initially, a person's motivation for communicating with people from other cultures must be considered. Motivation refers to the root of a person's desire to foster intercultural relationships and can be intrinsic or extrinsic (Martin & Nakayama, 2010). Put simply, if a person isn't motivated to communicate with people from different cultures, then the components of ICC discussed next don't really matter. If a person has a healthy curiosity that drives him or her toward intercultural encounters in order to learn more about self and others, then there is a foundation from which to build additional competence-relevant attitudes and skills. This intrinsic motivation makes intercultural communication a voluntary, rewarding, and lifelong learning process. Motivation can also be extrinsic, meaning that the desire for intercultural communication is driven by an outside reward like money, power, or recognition. While both types of motivation can contribute to ICC, context may further enhance or impede a person's motivation to communicate across cultures.

Members of dominant groups are often less motivated, intrinsically and extrinsically, toward intercultural communication than members of nondominant groups, because they don't see the incentives for doing so. Having more power in communication encounters can create an unbalanced situation where the individual from the nondominant group is expected to exhibit competence, or the ability to adapt to the communication behaviors and attitudes of the other. Even in situations where extrinsic rewards like securing an overseas business investment are at stake, it is likely that the foreign investor is much more accustomed to adapting to United States business customs and communication than vice versa. This expectation that others will adapt to our communication can be unconscious, but later ICC skills we will learn will help bring it to awareness.

The unbalanced situation I just described is a daily reality for many individuals with nondominant identities. Their motivation toward intercultural communication may be driven by survival in terms of functioning effectively in dominant contexts. Recall the phenomenon known as code-switching discussed earlier, in which individuals from nondominant groups adapt their communication to fit in with the dominant group. In such instances, African Americans may "talk white" by conforming to what is called "standard English," women in corporate environments may adapt masculine communication patterns, people who are gay or lesbian may self-censor and avoid discussing their same-gender partners with coworkers, and people with nonvisible disabilities may not disclose them in order to avoid judgment.

While intrinsic motivation captures an idealistic view of intercultural communication as rewarding in its own right, many contexts create extrinsic motivation. In either case, there is a risk that an individual's motivation can still lead to incompetent communication. For example, it would be exploitative for an extrinsically motivated person to pursue intercultural communication solely for an external reward and then abandon the intercultural relationship once the reward is attained. These situations highlight the relational aspect of ICC, meaning that the motivation of all parties should be considered. Motivation alone cannot create ICC.

Self and Other-Knowledge

Knowledge supplements motivation and is an important part of building ICC. Knowledge includes self- and other-awareness, mindfulness, and cognitive flexibility. Building knowledge of our own cultures, identities, and communication patterns takes more than passive experience (Martin & Nakayama). We learn who we are through our interactions with others. Developing cultural self-awareness often requires us to get out of our comfort zones. Listening to people who are different from us is a key component of developing self-knowledge. This may be uncomfortable, because we may realize that people think of our identities differently than we thought. For example, when I lived in Sweden, my Swedish roommates often discussed how they were wary of befriending students from the United States. They perceived US Americans to be shallow because they were friendly and exciting while they were in Sweden but didn't remain friends once they left. Although I was initially upset by their assessment, I came to see the truth in it. Swedes are generally more reserved than US Americans and take longer to form close friendships. The comparatively extroverted nature of the Americans led some of the Swedes to overestimate the depth of their relationship, which ultimately hurt them when the Americans didn't stay in touch. This made me more aware of how my communication was perceived, enhancing my self-knowledge. I also learned more about communication behaviors of the Swedes, which contributed to my other-knowledge.

The most effective way to develop other-knowledge is by direct and thoughtful encounters with other cultures. However, people may not readily have these opportunities for a variety of reasons. Despite the overall diversity in the United States, many people still only interact with people who are similar to them. Even in a racially diverse educational setting, for example, people often group off with people of their own race. While a heterosexual person may have a gay or lesbian friend or relative, they likely spend most of their time with other heterosexuals. Unless you interact with people with disabilities as part of your job or have a person with a disability in your friend or family group, you likely spend most of your time interacting with able-bodied people. Living in a rural area may limit your ability to interact with a range of cultures, and most people do not travel internationally regularly. Because of this, we may have to make a determined effort to interact with other cultures or rely on educational sources like college classes, books, or documentaries. Learning another language is also a good way to learn about a culture, because you can then read the news or watch movies in the native language, which can offer insights that are lost in translation. It is important to note though that we must evaluate the credibility of the source of our knowledge, whether it is a book, person, or other source. Also, knowledge of another language does not automatically equate to ICC.

Developing self- and other-knowledge is an ongoing process that will continue to adapt and grow as we encounter new experiences. Mindfulness and cognitive complexity will help as we continue to build our ICC (Pusch, 2009). Mindfulness is a state of self- and other-monitoring that informs later reflection on communication interactions. As mindful communicators we should ask questions that focus on the interactive process like "How is our communication going? What are my reactions? What are their reactions?" Being able to adapt our communication in the moment based on our answers to these questions is a skill that comes with a high level of ICC. Reflecting on the communication encounter later to see what can be learned is also a way to build ICC. We should then be able to incorporate what we learned into our communication frameworks, which requires cognitive flexibility. Cognitive flexibility refers to the ability to continually supplement and revise existing knowledge to create new categories rather than forcing new knowledge into old categories. Cognitive flexibility helps prevent our knowledge from becoming stale and also prevents the formation of stereotypes and can help us avoid prejudging an encounter or jumping to conclusions. In summary, to be better intercultural communicators, we should know much about others and ourselves and be able to reflect on and adapt our knowledge as we gain new experiences.

Tolerance of Uncertainty

Motivation and knowledge can inform us as we gain new experiences, but how we feel in the moment of intercultural encounters is also important. Tolerance for uncertainty refers to an individual's attitude about and level of comfort in uncertain situations (Martin & Nakayama, 2010). Some people perform better in uncertain situations than others, and intercultural encounters often bring up uncertainty. Whether communicating with someone of a different gender, race, or nationality, we are often wondering what we should or shouldn't do or say. Situations of uncertainty most often become clearer as they progress, but the anxiety that an individual with a low tolerance for uncertainty feels may lead them to leave the situation or otherwise communicate in a less competent manner. Individuals with a high tolerance for uncertainty may exhibit more patience, waiting on new information to become available or seeking out information, which may then increase the understanding of the situation and lead to a more successful outcome (Pusch, 2009). Individuals who are intrinsically motivated toward intercultural communication may have a higher tolerance for uncertainty, in that their curiosity leads them to engage with others who are different because they find the self- and other-knowledge gained rewarding.

Cultivating Intercultural Communication Competence

How can ICC be built and achieved? This is a key question we will address in this section. Two main ways to build ICC are through experiential learning and reflective practices (Bednarz, 2010). We must first realize that competence isn't any one thing. Part of being competent means that you can assess new situations and adapt your existing knowledge to the new contexts. What it means to be competent will vary depending on your physical location, your role (personal, professional, etc.), and your life stage, among other things. Sometimes we will know or be able to figure out what is expected of us in a given situation, but sometimes we may need to act in unexpected ways to meet the needs of a situation. Competence enables us to better cope with the unexpected, adapt to the nonroutine, and connect to uncommon frameworks. I have always told my students that ICC is less about a list of rules and more about a box of tools.

Three ways to cultivate ICC are to foster attitudes that motivate us, discover knowledge that informs us, and develop skills that enable us (Bennett, 2009). To foster attitudes that motivate us, we must develop a sense of wonder about culture. This sense of wonder can lead to feeling overwhelmed, humbled, or awed (Opdal, 2001). This sense of wonder may correlate to a high tolerance for uncertainty, which can help us turn potentially frustrating experiences we have into teachable moments. I've had many such moments in my intercultural encounters at home and abroad. One such moment came the first time I tried to cook a frozen pizza in the oven in the shared kitchen of my apartment in Sweden. The information on the packaging was written in Swedish, but like many college students, I had a wealth of experience cooking frozen pizzas to draw from. As I went to set the oven dial to preheat, I noticed it was strange that the oven didn't go up to my usual 425–450 degrees. Not to be deterred, I cranked the dial up as far as it would go, waited a few minutes, put my pizza in, and walked down the hall to my room to wait for about fifteen minutes until the pizza was done. The smell of smoke drew me from my room before the fifteen minutes was up, and I walked into a corridor filled with smoke and the smell of burnt pizza. I pulled the pizza out and was puzzled for a few minutes while I tried to figure out why the pizza burned so quickly, when one of my corridor-mates gently pointed out that the oven temperatures in Sweden are listed in Celsius, not Fahrenheit! Despite almost burning the kitchen down, I learned a valuable lesson about assuming my map for temperatures and frozen pizzas was the same as everyone else's.

Discovering knowledge that informs us is another step that can build on our motivation. One tool involves learning more about our cognitive style, or how we learn. Our cognitive style consists of our preferred patterns for "gathering information, constructing meaning, and organizing and applying knowledge" (Bennett, 2009). As we explore cognitive styles, we discover that there are differences in how people attend to and perceive the world, explain events, organize the world, and use rules of logic (Nisbett, 2003). Some cultures have a cognitive style that focuses more on tasks, analytic and objective thinking, details and precision, inner direction, and independence, while others focus on relationships and people over tasks and things, concrete and metaphorical thinking, and a group consciousness and harmony.

Developing ICC is a complex learning process. At the basic level of learning, we accumulate knowledge and assimilate it into our existing frameworks. But accumulated knowledge doesn't necessarily help us in situations where we have to apply that knowledge. Transformative learning takes place at the highest levels and occurs when we encounter situations that challenge our accumulated knowledge and our ability to accommodate that knowledge to manage a real-world situation. The cognitive dissonance that results in these situations is often uncomfortable and can lead to a hesitance to repeat such an engagement. One tip for cultivating ICC that can help manage these challenges is to find a community of like-minded people who are also motivated to develop ICC. In my graduate program, I lived in the international dormitory in order to experience the cultural diversity that I had enjoyed so much studying abroad a few years earlier. I was surrounded by international students and US American students who were more or less interested in cultural diversity. This ended up being a tremendous learning experience, and I worked on research about identity and communication between international and American students.

Developing skills that enable us is another part of ICC. Some of the skills important to ICC are the ability to empathize, accumulate cultural information, listen, resolve conflict, and manage anxiety (Bennett, 2009). Again, you are already developing a foundation for these skills by reading this book, but you can expand those skills to intercultural settings with the motivation and knowledge already described. Contact alone does not increase intercultural skills; there must be more deliberate measures taken to fully capitalize on those encounters. While research now shows that intercultural contact does decrease prejudices, this is not enough to become interculturally competent. The ability to empathize and manage anxiety enhances prejudice reduction, and these two skills have been shown to enhance the overall impact of intercultural contact even more than acquiring cultural knowledge. There is intercultural training available for people who are interested. If you can't access training, you may choose to research intercultural training on your own, as there are many books, articles, and manuals written on the subject.

Reflective practices can also help us process through rewards and challenges associated with developing ICC. As we open ourselves to new experiences, we are likely to have both positive and negative reactions. It can be very useful to take note of negative or defensive reactions you have. This can help you identify certain triggers that may create barriers to effective intercultural interaction. Noting positive experiences can also help you identify triggers for learning that you could seek out or recreate to enhance the positive (Bednarz, 2010). A more complex method of reflection is called intersectional reflexivity. Intersectional reflexivity is a reflective practice by which we acknowledge intersecting identities, both privileged and disadvantaged, and implicate ourselves in social hierarchies and inequalities (Jones Jr., 2010). This method brings in the concepts of dominant and nondominant groups and the privileges/disadvantages dialectic we discussed earlier.

While formal intercultural experiences like studying abroad or volunteering for the Special Olympics or a shelter for gay, lesbian, bisexual, transgender, and queer (GLBTQ) youth can result in learning, informal experiences are also important. We may be less likely to include informal experiences in our reflection if we don't see them as legitimate. Reflection should also include "critical incidents" or what I call "a-ha! moments." Think of reflection as a tool for metacompetence that can be useful in bringing the formal and informal together (Bednarz, 2010).

References

Allen, B. J., *Difference Matters: Communicating Social Identity*, 2nd ed. (Long Grove, IL: Waveland, 2011), 9, 65, 186–87.

Bednarz, F., "Building Up Intercultural Competences: Challenges and Learning Processes," in *Building Intercultural Competencies: A Handbook for Professionals in Education, Social Work, and Health Care*, eds. Maria Giovanna Onorati and Furio Bednarz (Leuven, Belgium: Acco, 2010), 39.

Bennett, J. M., "Cultivating Intercultural Competence," in *The Sage Handbook of Intercultural Competence*, ed. Darla K. Deardorff (Thousand Oaks, CA: Sage, 2009), 127–34.

Jones Jr., R. G., "Putting Privilege into Practice through 'Intersectional Reflexivity': Ruminations, Interventions, and Possibilities," *Reflections: Narratives of Professional Helping* 16, no. 1 (2010): 122.

Martin, J. N., and Thomas K. Nakayama, *Intercultural Communication in Contexts*, 5th ed. (Boston, MA: McGraw-Hill, 2010), 465.

Nisbett, R. E., *The Geography of Thought: How Asians and Westerners Think Differently...and Why* (New York: Free Press, 2003), 44–45.

Opdal, P. M., "Curiosity, Wonder, and Education Seen as Perspective," *Studies in Philosophy and Education* 20 (2001): 331–44.

Pusch, M. D., "The Interculturally Competent Global Leader," in *The Sage Handbook of Intercultural Competence*, ed. Darla K. Deardorff (Thousand Oaks, CA: Sage, 2009), 69.

6.6 ENRICHMENT

Discussion Questions

1. How would you adjust your preparation to speak in a public setting with a more diverse audience compared to your preparation to speak to your public speaking class?
2. List some of your personal, social, and cultural identities. Are there any that relate? If so, how? For your cultural identities, which ones are dominant and which ones are nondominant?
3. Describe a situation in which someone ascribed an identity to you that did not match with your avowed identities. Why do you think the person ascribed the identity to you? Were there any stereotypes involved?

Activities

1. Share three interesting facts or ideas about your culture (Section 6:3 Exploring Specific Cultural Identities) that would help classmates better understand the culture.
2. Take one to three photographs that illustrate or represent your own culture (attitudes, beliefs, values, behaviors, etc.).

7 ORGANIZING AND OUTLINING

Learning Objectives

- Select a topic appropriate to the audience and occasion.
- Formulate a specific purpose statement that identifies precisely what you will do in your speech.
- Craft a thesis statement (central idea) that clearly and succinctly summarizes the argument you will make in your speech.
- Identify and arrange the main points of your speech according to one of many organizational styles discussed in this chapter.
- Connect the points of your speech to one another.
- Create a preparation and speaking outline for your speech.

Learning Objectives

- **Causal Pattern**
- **Chronological Pattern**
- **Coordination**
- **Division**
- **Main Points**
- **Parallelism**
- **Preparation Outline**
- **Preview Statement**

- **Purpose Statement**
- **SignPost**
- **Spatial Pattern**
- **Speaking Outline**
- **Specific Purpose Statement**
- **Subordination**
- **Thesis**
- **Topical Pattern**
- **Transitional Statements**

7.1 WHY IS ORGANIZING AND OUTLINING IMPORTANT?

"If you don't know what you want to achieve in your presentation, your audience never will." -Harvey Diamond

Introduction to Organizing and Outlining

Meg jaunted to the front of the classroom—her trusty index cards in one hand and her water bottle in the other. It was the mid-term presentation in her entomology class, a course she enjoyed more than her other classes. The night before, Meg had spent hours scouring the web for information on the Woody Adelgid, an insect that has ravaged hemlock tree populations in the United States in recent years. But when she made it to the podium and finished her well-written and captivating introduction, her speech began to fall apart. Her index cards were a jumble of unorganized information, not linked together by any unifying theme or purpose. As she stumbled through lists of facts, Meg—along with her peers and instructor—quickly realized that her presentation had all the necessary parts to be compelling, but that those parts were not organized into a coherent and convincing speech.

Giving a speech or presentation can be a daunting task for anyone, especially inexperienced public speakers or students in introductory speech courses. Speaking to an audience can also be a rewarding experience for speakers who are willing to put in the extra effort needed to craft rhetorical masterpieces. Indeed, speeches and presentations must be crafted. Such a design requires that speakers do a great deal of preparatory work, like selecting a specific topic and deciding on a particular purpose for their speech. Once the topic and purpose have been decided on, a thesis statement, or central idea, can be prepared. After these things are established, speakers must select the main points of their speech, which should be organized in a way that illuminates the speaker's perspective, or approach to their speech. In a nutshell, effective public speeches are focused on particular topics and contain main points that are relevant to both the topic and the audience. For all of these components to come together convincingly, organizing and outlining must be done prior to giving a speech.

This chapter addresses a variety of strategies needed to craft the body of public speeches. The chapter begins at the initial stages of speechwriting— selecting an important and relevant topic for your audience. The more difficult task of formulating a purpose statement is discussed next. A purpose statement drives the organization of the speech since different purposes (e.g., informative or persuasive) necessitate different types of evidence and presentation styles. Next, the chapter offers a variety of organizational strategies for the body of your speech. Not every strategy will be appropriate for every speech, so the strengths and weaknesses of the organizational styles are also addressed. The chapter then discusses ways to connect your main points and to draw links between your main points and the purpose you have chosen. In the final section of this chapter, one of the most important steps in speechwriting, outlining your speech, is discussed. The chapter provides the correct format for outlines as well as information on how to write a preparation outline and a speaking outline.

Pete's Patterns

Pistol Pete found himself preparing for an informative speech about the traditions that define the spirit of OSU. The speech was an opportunity to share with his audience, composed of students, faculty, and alumni, the rich history and cherished customs of their beloved university.

First, he started with his *specific purpose* statement. Given the nature of his speech, he chose a specific purpose that was both audience-centered and measurable: "After hearing my speech, the audience will be able to identify specific OSU traditions that not only strengthen our community but also perpetuate our Orange Pride."

Next, he moved on to formulating his *thesis*. He wanted a statement that encapsulated the essence of his speech and served as the anchor point for all the information he would present. He decided on the following: "The traditions at Oklahoma State University, steeped in history and driven by a collective spirit, are instrumental in fostering a sense of unity, instilling pride, and creating lasting memories for everyone who is part of the Cowboy family."

With his specific purpose and thesis defined, Pete moved on to *identify the three main points* that would form the structure of his presentation:

1. Historical Traditions: Here, Pete planned to delve into the history of OSU's longstanding traditions, sharing the origin and evolution of customs such as the Homecoming Celebration, America's Greatest Homecoming, the waving

of the "Waving Song" after victories, and the ringing of the Old Central bell.
2. Symbolic Traditions: Pete would discuss the symbolic significance of traditions like the Sea of Orange Parade and the use of the OSU Spirit Rider to lead the football team onto the field. He wanted his audience to appreciate how these traditions encapsulate the spirit of OSU and its community.
3. Impact of Traditions: Lastly, Pete would address how these traditions enhance the OSU experience, foster a sense of belonging, and serve as a bonding factor for students, faculty, alumni, and fans alike.

By laying out this roadmap for his speech, Pistol Pete felt prepared and excited to share the cherished traditions of Oklahoma State University. He looked forward to not only informing his audience about these customs but also sparking a sense of pride and unity amongst his fellow Cowboys and Cowgirls.

What do you think of Pete's planning for his informative speech? Would you do anything different?

7.2 THE TOPIC, GENERAL PURPOSE, SPECIFIC PURPOSE, AND THESIS

Before any work can be done on crafting the body of your speech or presentation, you must first do some prep work—selecting a topic, formulating a general purpose, a specific purpose statement, and crafting a central idea, or thesis statement. In doing so, you lay the foundation for your speech by making important decisions about what you will speak about and for what purpose you will speak. These decisions will influence and guide the entire speechwriting process, so it is wise to think carefully and critically during these beginning stages.

Selecting a Topic

Generally, speakers focus on one or more interrelated topics—relatively broad concepts, ideas, or problems that are relevant for particular audiences. The most common way that speakers discover topics is by simply observing what is happening around them—at their school, in their local government, or around the world. Student government leaders, for example, speak or write to other students when their campus is facing tuition or fee increases, or when students have achieved something spectacular, like lobbying campus administrators for lower student fees and succeeding. In either case, it is the situation that makes their speeches appropriate and useful for their audience of students and university employees. More importantly, they speak when there is an opportunity to change a university policy or to alter the way students think or behave in relation to a particular event on campus.

But you need not run for president or student government in order to give a meaningful speech. On the contrary, opportunities abound for those interested in engaging speech as a tool for change. Perhaps the simplest way to find a topic is to ask yourself a few questions, including:

- What important events are occurring locally, nationally and internationally?
- What do I care about most?
- Is there someone or something I can advocate for?
- What makes me angry/happy?
- What beliefs/attitudes do I want to share?
- Is there some information the audience needs to know?

Students speak about what is interesting to them and their audiences. What topics do you think are relevant today? There are other questions you might ask yourself, too, but these should lead you to at least a few topical choices. The most important work that these questions do is to locate topics within your pre-existing sphere of knowledge and interest. David Zarefsky (2010) also identifies brainstorming as a way to develop speech topics, a strategy that can be helpful if the questions listed above did not yield an appropriate or interesting topic. Starting with a topic you are already interested in will likely make writing and presenting your speech a more enjoyable and meaningful experience. It means that your entire speechwriting process will focus on something you find important and that you can present this information to people who stand to benefit from your speech.

Once you have answered these questions and narrowed your responses, you are still not done selecting your topic. For instance, you might have decided that you really care about breeds of dogs. This is a very broad topic and could easily lead to a dozen different speeches. To resolve this problem, speakers must also consider the audience to whom they will speak, the scope of their presentation, and the outcome they wish to achieve.

Formulating the Purpose Statements

By honing in on a very specific topic, you begin the work of formulating your

purpose statement. In short, a purpose statement clearly states what it is you would like to achieve. Purpose statements are especially helpful for guiding you as you prepare your speech. When deciding which main points, facts, and examples to include, you should simply ask yourself whether they are relevant not only to the topic you have selected, but also whether they support the goal you outlined in your purpose statement. The general purpose statement of a speech may be to inform, to persuade, to celebrate, or to entertain. Thus, it is common to frame a **specific purpose statement** around one of these goals. According to O'Hair, Stewart, and Rubenstein, a specific purpose statement "expresses both the topic and the general speech purpose in action form and in terms of the specific objectives you hope to achieve" (2004). For instance, the home design enthusiast might write the following specific purpose statement: At the end of my speech, the audience will learn the pro's and con's of flipping houses. In short, the general purpose statement lays out the broader goal of the speech while the specific purpose statement describes precisely what the speech is intended to do. Some of your professors may ask that you include the general purpose and add the specific purpose.

Writing the Thesis Statement

The specific purpose statement is a tool that you will use as you write your talk, but it is unlikely that it will appear verbatim in your speech. Instead, you will want to convert the specific purpose statement into a central idea, or **thesis** statement that you will share with your audience.

Depending on your instructor's approach, a thesis statement may be written two different ways. A thesis statement may encapsulate the main points of a speech in just a sentence or two, and be designed to give audiences a quick preview of what the entire speech will be about. The thesis statement for a speech, like the thesis of a research-based essay, should be easily identifiable and ought to very succinctly sum up the main points you will present. Some instructors prefer that your thesis, or central idea, be a single, declarative statement providing the audience with an overall statement that provides the essence of the speech, followed by a separate preview statement.

If you are a Harry Potter enthusiast, you may write a thesis statement (central idea) the following way using the above approach: *J.K. Rowling is a renowned author of the Harry Potter series with a Cinderella like story having gone from relatively humble beginnings, through personal struggles, and finally success and fame.*

Writing the Preview Statement

However, some instructors prefer that you separate your thesis from your **preview statement**. A preview statement (or series of statements) is a guide to your speech. This is the part of the speech that literally tells the audience exactly what main points you will cover. If you were to open your Waze app, it would tell you exactly how to get there. Best of all, you would know what to look for! So, if we take our J.K Rowling example, let's rewrite that using this approach separating out the thesis and preview:

J.K. Rowling is a renowned author of the Harry Potter series with a Cinderella like rags to riches story. First, I will tell you about J.K. Rowling's humble beginnings. Then, I will describe her personal struggles as a single mom. Finally, I will explain how she overcame adversity and became one of the richest women in the United Kingdom.

There is no best way to approach this. This is up to your instructor.

Writing the Body of Your Speech

Once you have finished the important work of deciding what your speech will be about, as well as formulating the purpose statement and crafting the thesis, you should turn your attention to writing the body of your speech. All of your main points are contained in the body, and normally this section is prepared well before you ever write the introduction or conclusion. The body of your speech will consume the largest amount of time to present; and it is the opportunity for you to elaborate on facts, evidence, examples, and opinions that support your thesis statement and do the work you have outlined in the specific purpose statement. Combining these various elements into a cohesive and compelling speech, however, is not without its difficulties, the first of which is deciding which elements to include and how they ought to be organized to best suit your purpose.

7.3 ORGANIZATIONAL PATTERNS OF ARRANGEMENT

After deciding which main points and subpoints you must include, you can get to work writing up the speech. Before you do so, however, it is helpful to consider how you will organize the ideas. There are many ways you can organize speeches, and these approaches will be different depending on whether you are preparing an informative or persuasive speech. These are referred to as organizational patterns for arranging your main points in a speech. The **chronological** (or temporal), **topical**, **spatial**, or **causal patterns** may be better suited to informative speeches, whereas the Problem-Solution, Monroe's Motivated Sequence (Monroe, 1949), Claim-to-Proof (Mudd & Sillar, 1962), or Refutation pattern would work best for persuasive speeches. Sample outlines for persuasive speeches can be found in Chapter 17.

Chronological Pattern

When you speak about events that are linked together by time, it is sensible to engage the chronological organization pattern. In a chronological speech, main points are delivered according to when they happened and could be traced on a calendar or clock. Some professors use the term temporal to reflect any speech pattern dealing with taking the audience through time. Arranging main points in chronological order can be helpful when describing historical events to an audience as well as when the order of events is necessary to understand what you wish to convey. Informative speeches about a series of events most commonly engage the chronological style, as do many process speeches (e.g., how to bake a cake or build an airplane). Another time when the chronological style makes sense is when you tell the story of someone's life or career. For instance, a speech about Oprah Winfrey might be arranged chronologically. In this case, the main points are arranged by following Winfrey's life from birth to the present time. Life events (e.g., early life, her early career, her life after ending the Oprah Winfrey Show) are connected together according to when they happened and highlight the progression of Winfrey's career. Organizing the speech in this way illustrates the interconnectedness of life events. Below you will find a way in which you can organize your main points chronologically:

> **Topic**: Oprah Winfrey (Chronological Pattern)
> **Thesis**: Oprah's career can be understood by four key, interconnected life stages.
> **Preview**: First, let's look at Oprah's early life. Then, we will look at her early career, followed by her years during the Oprah Winfrey show. Finally, we will explore what she is doing now.

1. Oprah's childhood was spent in rural Mississippi, where she endured sexual abuse from family members.
2. Oprah's early career was characterized by stints on local radio and television networks in Nashville and Chicago.
3. Oprah's tenure as host of the Oprah Winfrey Show began in 1986 and lasted until 2011, a period of time marked by much success.
4. Oprah's most recent media venture is OWN: The Oprah Winfrey Network, which plays host to a variety of television shows including *Oprah's Next Chapter*.

Topical Pattern

When the main points of your speech center on ideas that are more distinct from one another, a topical organization pattern may be used. In a topical speech, main points are developed according to the different aspects, subtopics or topics within an overall topic. Although they are all part of the overall topic, the order in which they are presented really doesn't matter. For example, you are currently attending college. Within your college, there are various student services that are important for you to use while you are here. You may use the library, The Learning Center (TLC), Student Development office, ASG Computer Lab, and Financial Aid. To organize this speech topically, it doesn't matter which area you speak about first, but here is how you could organize it.

Topic: Student Services at College of the Canyons

Thesis and Preview: College of the Canyons has five important student services, which include the library, TLC, Student Development Office, ASG Computer Lab, and Financial Aid.

I. The library can be accessed five days a week and online and has a multitude of books, periodicals, and other resources to use.

II. The TLC has subject tutors, computers, and study rooms available to use six days a week.

III. The Student Development Office is a place that assists students with their ID cards, but also provides students with discount tickets and other student related needs.

IV. The ASG computer lab is open for students to use for several hours a day, as well as to print up to 15 pages a day for free.

V. Financial Aid is one of the busiest offices on campus, offering students a multitude of methods by which they can supplement their personal finances paying for both tuition and books.

Spatial Pattern

Another way to organize the points of a speech is through a spatial speech, which arranges main points according to their physical and geographic relationships. The spatial style is an especially useful organization pattern when the main point's importance is derived from its location or directional focus. Things can be described from top to bottom, inside to outside, left to right, north to south, and so on. Importantly, speakers using a spatial style should offer commentary about the placement of the main points as they move through the speech, alerting audience members to the location changes. For instance, a speech about The University of Georgia might be arranged spatially; in this example, the spatial organization frames the discussion in terms of the campus layout. The spatial style is fitting since the differences in architecture and uses of space are related to particular geographic areas, making location a central organizing factor. As such, the spatial style highlights these location differences.

Topic: University of Georgia (Spatial Pattern)

Thesis: The University of Georgia is arranged into four distinct sections, which are characterized by architectural and disciplinary differences.

I. In North Campus, one will find the University's oldest building, a sprawling treelined quad, and the famous Arches, all of which are nestled against Athens' downtown district.

II. In West Campus, dozens of dormitories provide housing for the University's large undergraduate population and students can regularly be found lounging outside or at one of the dining halls.

III. In East Campus, students delight in newly constructed, modern buildings and enjoy the benefits of the University's health center, recreational facilities, and science research buildings.

IV. In South Campus, pharmacy, veterinary, and biomedical science students traverse newly constructed parts of campus featuring well-kept landscaping and modern architecture.

Causal Pattern

A causal speech informs audience members about causes and effects that have already happened with respect to some condition, event, etc. One approach can be to share what caused something to happen, and what the effects were. Or, the reverse approach can be taken where a speaker can begin by sharing the effects of something that occurred, and then share what caused it. For example, in 1994, there was a 6.7 magnitude earthquake that occurred in the San Fernando Valley in Northridge, California. Let's look at how we can arrange this speech first by using a cause-effect pattern:

Topic: Northridge Earthquake

Thesis: The Northridge earthquake was a devastating event that was caused by an unknown fault and resulted in the loss of life and billions of dollars of damage.

I. The Northridge earthquake was caused by a fault that was previously unknown and located nine miles beneath Northridge.

II. The Northridge earthquake resulted in the loss of 57 lives and over 40 billion dollars of damage in Northridge and surrounding communities.

Depending on your topic, you may decide it is more impactful to start with the effects, and work back to the causes (effect-cause pattern). Let's take the same example and flip it around:

> **Thesis**: The Northridge earthquake was a devastating event that was that resulted in the loss of life and billions of dollars in damage, and was caused by an unknown fault below Northridge.

    I. The Northridge earthquake resulted in the loss of 57 lives and over 40 billion dollars of damage in Northridge and surrounding communities.
    II. The Northridge earthquake was caused by a fault that was previously unknown and located nine miles beneath Northridge.

Why might you decide to use an effect-cause approach rather than a cause-effect approach? In this particular example, the effects of the earthquake were truly horrible. If you heard all of that information first, you would be much more curious to hear about what caused such devastation. Sometimes natural disasters are not that exciting, even when they are horrible. Why? Unless they affect us directly, we may not have the same attachment to the topic. This is one example where an effect-cause approach may be very impactful.

7.4 OUTLINING YOUR SPEECH

Most speakers and audience members would agree that an organized speech is both easier to present as well as more persuasive. Public speaking teachers especially believe in the power of organizing your speech, which is why they encourage (and often require) that you create an outline for your speech. Outlines, or textual arrangements of all the various elements of a speech, are a very common way of organizing a speech before it is delivered. Most extemporaneous speakers keep their outlines with them during the speech as a way to ensure that they do not leave out any important elements and to keep them on track. Writing an outline is also important to the speechwriting process since doing so forces the speakers to think about the main ideas, known as main points, and subpoints, the examples they wish to include, and the ways in which these elements correspond to one another. In short, the outline functions both as an organization tool and as a reference for delivering a speech.

Outline Types

There are two types of outlines, the preparation outline and the speaking outline.

Preparation Outline

The first outline you will write is called the **preparation outline**. Also called a skeletal, working, practice, or rough outline, the preparation outline is used to work through the various components of your speech in an organized format. Stephen E. Lucas (2004) put it simply: "The preparation outline is just what its name implies—an outline that helps you prepare the speech." When writing the preparation outline, you should focus on finalizing the specific purpose and thesis statement, logically ordering your main points, deciding where supporting material should be included, and refining the overall organizational pattern of your speech. As you write the preparation outline, you may find it necessary to rearrange your points or to add or subtract supporting material. You may also realize that some of your main points are sufficiently supported while others are lacking. The final draft of your preparation outline should include full sentences. In most cases, however, the preparation outline is reserved for planning purposes only and is translated into a speaking outline before you deliver the speech. Keep in mind though, even a full sentence outline is not an essay.

Speaking Outline

A **speaking outline** is the outline you will prepare for use when delivering the speech. The speaking outline is much more succinct than the preparation outline and includes brief phrases or words that remind the speakers of the points they need to make, plus supporting material and signposts (Beebe & Beebe, 2003). The words or phrases used on the speaking outline should briefly encapsulate all of the information needed to prompt the speaker to accurately deliver the speech. Although some cases call for reading a speech verbatim from the full-sentence outline, in most cases speakers will simply refer to their speaking outline for quick reminders and to ensure that they do not omit any important information. Because it uses just words or short phrases, and not full sentences, the speaking outline can easily be transferred to index cards that can be referenced during a speech. However, check with your instructor regarding what you will be allowed to use for your speech.

Components of Outlines

The main components of the outlines are the main points, subordination and coordination, parallelism, division, and the connection of main points.

Main Points

Main points are the main ideas in the speech. In other words, the main points are what your audience should remember from your talk, and they are phrased as single, declarative sentences. These are never phrased as a question, nor can they be a quote or form of citation. Any supporting material you have will be put in your outline as a subpoint. Since this is a public speaking class, your instructor will decide how long your speeches will be, but in general, you can assume that no speech will be longer than 10 minutes in length. Given that alone, we can make one assumption. All speeches will fall between 2 to 5 main points based simply on length. If you are working on an outline and you have ten main points, something is wrong, and you need to revisit your ideas to see how you need to reorganize your points.

All main points are preceded by Roman numerals (I, II, III, etc.). Subpoints are preceded by capital letters (A, B, C, etc.), then Arabic numerals (1, 2, 3, etc.), lowercase letters (a, b, c, etc.). You can subordinate further than this. Speak with your instructor regarding his or her specific instructions. Each level of subordination is also differentiated from its predecessor by indenting a few spaces. Indenting makes it easy to find your main points, subpoints, and the supporting points and examples below them.

Let's work on understanding how to take main points and break them into smaller ideas by subordinating them further and further as we go by using the following outline example:

Topic: Dog
    Specific Purpose: To inform my audience about characteristics of dogs
    Thesis: There are many types of dogs that individuals can select from before deciding which
would make the best family pet.
    Preview: First, I will describe the characteristics of large breed dogs, and then I will discuss characteristics of small breed dogs.
    I. First, let's look at the characteristics of large breed dogs
        A. Some large breed dogs need daily activity.
        B. Some large breed dogs are dog friendly.
        C. Some large breed dogs drool.
            1. If you are particularly neat, you may not want one of these.
                a. Bloodhounds drool the most.
                    1) After eating is one of the times drooling is bad.
                    2) The drooling is horrible after they drink, so beware!
                b. English bloodhounds drool a lot as well.
            2. If you live in an apartment, these breeds could pose a problem.

II. Next, let's look at the characteristics of small breed dogs.
    A. Some small breed dogs need daily activity.
    B. Some small breed dogs are dog friendly.
    C. Some small breed dogs are friendly to strangers.
        1. Welsh Terriers love strangers.
            a. They will jump on people.
            b. They will wag their tails and nuzzle.
        2. Beagles love strangers.
        3. Cockapoos also love strangers.

Subordination and Coordination

You should have noticed that as ideas were broken down, or subordinated, there was a hierarchy to the order. To check your outline for coherence, think of the outline as a staircase. All of the points that are beneath and on a diagonal to the points above them are subordinate points. So using the above example, points A, B, and C dealt with characteristics of large breed dogs, and those points are all subordinate to main point I. Similarly, points 1 and 2 under point C both dealt with drool, so those are subordinate. This is the **subordination** of points. If we had discussed food under point C, you would know that something didn't make sense. You will also see that there is **coordination** of points. As part of the hierarchy, coordination simply means that all of the numbers or letters should represent the same idea. In this example, A, B, and C were all characteristics, so those are all coordinate to each other. Had C been "German Shepherd," then the outline would have been incorrect because that is a type of dog, not a characteristic.

Parallelism

Another important rule in outlining is known as **parallelism**. This means that when possible, you begin your sentences in a similar way, using a similar grammatical structure. For example, in the previous example on dogs, some of the sentences began "some large breed dogs." This type of structure adds clarity to your speaking. Students often worry that parallelism will sound boring. It's actually the opposite! It adds clarity. However, if you had ten sentences in a row, we would never recommend you begin them all the same way. That is where transitions come into the picture and break up any monotony that could occur.

Division

The principle of **division** is an important part of outlining. When you have a main point, you will be explaining it. You should have enough meaningful information that you can divide it into two subpoints A and B. If subpoint A has enough information that you can explain it, then it, too, should be able to be divided into two subpoints. So, division means this: If you have an A, then you need a B; if you have a 1, then you need a 2, and so on. What if you cannot divided the point? In a case like that you would simply incorporate the information in the point above.

Connecting Your Main Points

One way to connect points is to include **transitional statements**. Transitional statements are phrases or sentences that lead from one distinct- but-connected idea to another. They are used to alert the audience to the fact that you are getting ready to discuss something else. When moving from one point to another, your transition may just be a word or short phrase, known as a sign post. For instance, you might say "next," "also," or "moreover." You can also enumerate your speech points and signal transitions by starting each point with "First," "Second," "Third," et cetera. You might also incorporate non-verbal transitions, such as brief pauses or a movement across the stage. Pausing to look at your audience, stepping out from behind a podium, or even raising or lowering the rate of your voice can signal to audience members that you are transitioning.

Another way to incorporate transitions into your speech is by offering internal summaries and internal previews within your speech. Summaries provide a recap of what has already been said, making it more likely that audiences will remember the points that they hear again. For example, an internal summary may sound like this:

So far, we have seen that the pencil has a long and interesting history. We also looked at the many uses the pencil has that you may not have known about previously.

Like the name implies, internal previews lay out what will occur next in your speech. They are longer than transitional words or **signposts**.

Next, let us explore what types of pencils there are to pick from that will be best for your specific project.

Additionally, summaries can be combined with internal previews to alert audience members that the next point builds on those that they have already heard.

Now that I have told you about the history of the pencil, as well as its many uses, let's look at what types of pencils you can pick from that might be best for your project.

It is important to understand that if you use an internal summary and internal preview between main points, you need to state a clear main point following the internal preview. Here's an example integrating all of the points on the pencil:

I. First, let me tell you about the history of the pencil.
So far we have seen that the pencil has a long and interesting history. Now, we can look at how the pencil can be used (internal summary, signpost, and internal preview).

II. The pencil has many different uses, ranging from writing to many types of drawing.
Now that I have told you about the history of the pencil, as well as its many uses, let's look at what types of pencils you can pick from that might be best for your project (Signpost, internal summary and preview).

III. There are over fifteen different types of pencils to choose from ranging in hardness and color.

Conclusion

Had Meg, the student mentioned in the opening anecdote, taken some time to work through the organizational process, it is likely her speech would have gone much more smoothly when she finished her introduction. It is very common for beginning speakers to spend a great deal of their time preparing catchy introductions, fancy PowerPoint presentations, and nice conclusions, which are all very important. However, the body of any speech is where the speaker must make effective arguments, provide helpful information, entertain, and the like, so it makes sense that speakers should devote a proportionate amount of time to these areas as well. By following this chapter, as well as studying the other chapters in this text, you should be prepared to craft interesting, compelling, and organized speeches.

Discussion Questions

1. Think back to your previous presentations. How did you select topics appropriate to the audience and occasion? How would you select a persuasive topic for an audience of senior adults? How would you select a persuasive topic for an audience of young adults?
2. How does the thesis statement differ from the specific purpose statement?
3. How does the specific purpose help determine the pattern of organization?
4. Explain how the pattern of organization is significant to a presentation.
5. What are some specific ways we can ensure the audience remembers our main ideas?
6. Why is it important to construct an outline of your presentation?

Activities

1. With your group, write a general purpose, specific purpose, thesis statement, and preview statement for the topic you are assigned. Be creative! Share your terrific responses with the class.
2. On a sheet of paper, write down a topic you find interesting. Suppose you are to give an informative presentation about this topic. Write three (3) main points for each of the following patterns of organization: chronological, topical, spatial, and causal.

8 RESEARCHING YOUR SPEECH

Learning Objectives

- Explain why research is fun and useful.
- Differentiate between primary and secondary research.
- Describe how to establish research needs before beginning research.
- Identify appropriate academic and nonacademic sources.
- Explain the steps for citing sources within a speech.
- Differentiate between direct quotations and paraphrases of information within a speech.
- Describe how to use sources ethically in a speech.
- Explain twelve strategies for avoiding plagiarism.

Learning Objectives

- **Academic Books**
- **APA style**
- **Backtracking**
- **Direct Quotation**
- **Encyclopedias**
- **Fact**
- **Generalizability**

- General-Interest Periodicals
- Interlibrary Loan
- MLA style
- Paraphrase
- Primary Research
- Project Life Cycle
- Research
- Research Log
- Secondary Research
- Special-Interest Periodicals
- Style
- Textbooks
- Theory

8.1 LIBRARY RESOURCES

*Research is formalized curiosity. It is poking and prying with a purpose.
-Zora Neale Hurston (cited in Wilson, 2013, p.111).*

Whether you are dealing with a librarian at a public library or an academic library, librarians have many tricks and shortcuts up their sleeves to make hunting for information easier and faster (George, 2008). You may find it odd that we decided to start a chapter on research discussing librarians, but we strongly believe that interacting with librarians and using libraries effectively is the first step to good research.

To help make your interactions with research librarians more fulfilling, we sent out an e-mail to research librarians who belong to the American Library Association asking them for tips on working with a research librarian. Thankfully, the research librarians were very willing to help us help you. Listed below are some of the top tips we received from research librarians (in no particular order)Author Note: We wish to thank the numerous reference librarians who went out of their way to help us develop our top eighteen tips to working with reference librarians. We opted to keep their comments anonymous, but we want to thank them here.

- Debra Rollins, Louisiana State University-Alexandria
- William Badke, Trinity Western University
- Ingrid Hendrix, University of New Mexico
- Ward Price, Ivy Tech Community College, Northeast
- Tracy L. Stout, Missouri State University
- Sandra J. Ley, Pima Community College
- Annie Smith, Utah Valley University Library
- Sharlee Jeser-Skaggs, Richland College Library
- Leslie N. Todd, University of the Incarnate Word
- Susan G Ryberg, Mount Olive College
- Kathleen A. Hana, Indiana University-Purdue University Indianapolis University Library
- Red Wassenich, Austin Community College
- Elizabeth Kettell, University of Rochester Medical Center

1. Research is a process, not an event. Good research takes time and, while there are shortcuts, students should still expect to spend some time with a librarian and to sort through the sources they find.
2. Your librarian is just as knowledgeable about information resources and the research process as your professor is about his or her discipline. Collaborate with your librarian so that you can benefit from his or her knowledge.
3. Try to learn from the librarian so that you can increase your research skills. You'll need these skills as you advance in your academic coursework, and you'll rely on these skills when you're in the workplace.
4. The librarian can lead you to the resources, but you have to select the best sources for your particular project. This takes time and effort on your part.
5. Reference librarians are professional searchers who went to graduate school to learn how to do research. Reference librarians are here to help no matter how novice a student thinks her or his question is.
6. Students should also know that we ask questions like, "Where have you looked so far?" and "Have you had a library workshop before?" for a reason. It may sound like we're deferring the question, but what we're trying to do is gauge how much experience the student has with research and to avoid going over the same ground twice.
7. Students should approach a librarian sooner rather than later. If a student isn't

finding what they need within fifteen minutes or so, they need to come find a librarian. Getting help early will save the student a lot of time and energy.
8. If you don't have a well-defined topic to research, or if you don't know what information resources you're hoping to find, come to the reference desk with a copy of your class assignment. The librarian will be glad to help you to select a topic that's suitable for your assignment and to help you access the resources you need. Having at least a general topic in mind and knowing what the assignment entails (peer-reviewed only, three different types of sources, etc.) helps immensely.
9. Most academic librarians are willing to schedule in-depth research consultations with students. If you feel you'll need more time and attention than you might normally receive at the reference desk or if you're shy about discussing your research interest in a public area, ask the librarian for an appointment.
10. Students, if they know their topic, should be as specific as possible in what they ask for. Students who are struggling with identifying a narrow topic should seek help from either their professors or librarians. We can help you find sources if your topic is clear.
11. Students should know that many questions do not have ready-made or one-stop answers. Students are encouraged to understand that an interface with a reference librarian is a dialog and part of a recursive, repetitive process. Consider making time for this process and take an active role in the exchange.
12. Be sure to show appreciation to the librarian for their assistance.

Pete's Path

Ready to delve into the rich traditions of Oklahoma State University, Pistol Pete set off towards the Edmon Low Library, the hub of knowledge and research on campus. As he approached the grand structure, he felt a sense of excitement, knowing that the resources within its walls held the information he sought for his upcoming speech.

Upon entering the library, he headed straight for the help desk, where a friendly librarian welcomed him. Pistol Pete explained his mission: to gather substantial and credible information about OSU traditions for his speech. The librarian guided him through the process of using the library's comprehensive digital archives and databases, showing him how to navigate the vast reservoir of information.

His first step was to explore the OSU digital collections. Through this, Pete found historical documents, photographs, and even archived newsletters that offered a glimpse into the traditions of the past. He meticulously went through these sources, taking notes and saving the documents that offered unique insights about the traditions.

Next, he accessed the OSU institutional repository, which stored scholarly works from the university. He found several academic papers and research articles detailing the history and significance of OSU traditions. These scholarly sources provided a deeper understanding and a robust academic perspective, reinforcing the information he had gathered from the digital collections.

Pete then decided to explore some print resources. The librarian directed him to several books in the library that dealt with the history and traditions of Oklahoma State University. With each book he flipped through, Pete discovered more details, anecdotes, and explanations about the cherished customs of OSU.

Lastly, the librarian suggested a valuable source that Pete had not considered – the university yearbooks. Stored in the library's special collections, these yearbooks were a treasure trove of information, providing firsthand accounts of the traditions as they evolved through the years. Pete spent hours poring over these yearbooks, captivated by the vivid pictures and descriptions they contained.

With a substantial list of sources, Pistol Pete felt confident and well-equipped to craft his speech. He had not only gathered valuable information about OSU traditions but also understood their historical context and significance more deeply. With a sense of accomplishment, Pete thanked the librarian for her assistance and left the Edmon Low Library, ready to use his newfound knowledge to create a compelling and informative speech. How important is finding diverse forms of source material for your informative presentation? Will you visit Edmon Low Library like Pete?

References

George, M. W. (2008). *The elements of library research: What every student needs to know*. Princeton, NJ: Princeton University Press.

8.2 WHAT IS RESEARCH?

Say it with me: "Research is fun!" OK, now we know that some of you just looked at that sentence and totally disagree, but we're here to tell you that research is fun. Now, this doesn't mean that research is easy. In fact, research can be quite difficult and time consuming, but it's most definitely fun. Let us explain why. First, when conducting research you get to ask questions and actually find answers. If you have ever wondered what the best strategies are when being interviewed for a job, research will tell you. If you've ever wondered what it takes to be a NASCAR driver, an astronaut, a marine biologist, or a university professor, once again, research is one of the easiest ways to find answers to questions you're interested in knowing. Second, research can open a world you never knew existed. We often find ideas we had never considered and learn facts we never knew when we go through the research process. Lastly, research can lead you to new ideas and activities. Maybe you want to learn how to compose music, draw, learn a foreign language, or write a screenplay; research is always the best step toward learning anything.

For the purposes of this book, we define **research** as scholarly investigation into a topic in order to discover, revise, or report facts, theories, and applications. Now you'll notice that there are three distinct parts of research: discovering, revising, and reporting. The first type of research is when people conduct some kind of study and find something completely new. For example, in 1928 Alexander Fleming accidentally discovered the first antibiotic, penicillin. Before this discovery, there were no antibiotics and simple infections killed people regularly. In this case, Fleming conducted research and discovered something not known to scientists before that time.

The second type of research occurs when people revise existing facts, theories, and applications. The bulk of the work of modern scientists is not really in discovering new things, but rather trying to improve older discoveries. For example, to improve upon the work of Fleming's first antibiotic, a group of Croatian researchers created azithromycin. Today azithromycin is licensed by Pfizer Inc. under the name Zithromax. In essence, the Croatian scientists built on the work of Fleming and ultimately revised our ability to treat infectious diseases. Today, azithromycin is one of the most prescribed antibiotics in the world.

The last part of research is called the reporting function of research. This is the phase when you accumulate information about a topic and report that information to others. For example, in the previous two paragraphs, we conducted research on the history of antibiotics and provided you with that information. We did not discover anything, nor did we revise anything; we are just reporting the research.

In addition to the three functions of research, there are also three end results that researchers strive toward: facts, theories, and applications. First, a **fact** is a truth that is arrived at through the scientific process. For example, in the world of psychology, it is a fact that the human brain influences human behavior. Centuries ago, people believed that human behavior was a result of various combinations of black and yellow biles running through our bodies. However, research failed to find support for this idea, whereas research increasingly found support for the connection between the brain and behavior. Facts are difficult to attain—it can take generations of research before a theory gains acceptance as a scientific fact.

Second, researchers conduct research to understand, contradict, or support theories. A **theory** is a proposed explanation for a phenomenon that can be tested scientifically. Scientists work with theories for a very long time, testing them under a variety of conditions attempting to replicate earlier findings or to identify conditions under which earlier findings do not hold true. For example, one theory that often surprises people is the universal theory of gravity. Many people believe that our understanding of gravity is set in stone, and much of physics relies on the assumption that gravity exists, but gravity is not a fact. The fact that the theory of gravity explains is that if I hold my keys out and let go, they will fall to the floor. Physicists are still debating how gravity actually functions and speculating about other explanations for why my keys will fall to the floor. So from a researcher's perspective, very few things are scientific facts.

Lastly, researchers often look for new applications for something that already exists. For example, botulism was at one point a dreaded bacterium that plagued the US food supply and led to many deaths. In the 1980s, an ophthalmologist named

Allan Scott started using a version of botulism to treat muscle spasms in a drug called onabotulinumtoxinA—better known by the brand name Botox (Williamson, 2011). Richard Clark, a plastic surgeon, reported in a 1989 article that the drug also had the side effect of decreasing wrinkles (Clark & Berris, 1989). From deadly bacteria to medical cure to one of the most commonly used cosmetic drugs in the world, the history of Botox has been a constant stream of new applications.

Primary Research

Research generally falls into one of two categories: primary and secondary. **Primary research** is carried out to discover or revise facts, theories, and applications and is reported by the person conducting the research. Primary research can be considered an active form of research because the researcher is actually conducting the research for the purpose of creating new knowledge. For the purposes of your speech, you may utilize two basic categories of primary research: surveys and interviews.

Surveys You Conduct

The first type of primary research you might conduct is a survey. A survey is a collection of facts, figures, or opinions gathered from participants used to indicate how everyone within a target group may respond. Maybe you're going to be speaking before a board of education about its plans to build a new library, so you create a survey and distribute it to all your neighbors seeking their feedback on the project. During your speech, you could then discuss your survey and the results you found.

Depending on the amount of time you have and the funding available, there are a number of different ways you could survey people. The most expensive method of surveying is sending surveys through the postal system. Unfortunately, most people do not respond to surveys they receive through the mail, so the number of completed surveys you get back tends to be very low (often under 20 percent).

To make surveying cheaper, many people prefer to use the Internet or to approach people face-to-face and ask them to participate. Internet surveying can be very useful and cheap, but you'll still have the same problem mail surveys do—getting people to fill out your survey. Face-to-face surveying, on the other hand, is time consuming but generally results in a higher number of completed surveys.

Ultimately, when determining whether you should conduct a survey, Wrench, Thomas-Maddox, Richmond, and McCroskey suggest that you ask yourself four basic questions (Wrench et al., 2008). First, "Do you know what you want to ask?" Surveys, by their very nature, are concrete—once you've handed it to one person, you need to hand out the same form to every person to be able to compare results.

If you're not sure what questions need to be asked, then a survey is not appropriate. Second, "Do you really need to collect data?" Often you can find information in textbooks, scholarly articles, magazines, and other places. If the information already exists, then why are you duplicating the information? Third, "Do your participants know the information you want to find out, or if they do know, will they tell you?" One of the biggest mistakes novice survey researchers make is to ask questions that their participants can't or won't answer. Asking a young child for her or his parents' gross income doesn't make sense, but then neither does asking an adult how many times they've been to see a physician in the past ten years. The flip side to this question is, "Will your participants tell you?" If the information could be potentially damaging, people are more likely to either lie on a survey or leave the question blank.

The last question is, "Is your goal generalizable?" **Generalizability** occurs when we attempt to survey a small number of people in the hopes of representing a much larger group of people. For example, maybe you want to find out how people in your community feel about a new swimming pool. The whole community may contain one thousand families, but it would be impractical to try to survey all those families, so you decide to survey two hundred families instead. The ultimate question for researchers is whether those two hundred families can be generalized to the one thousand families. The number may be large enough (as opposed to surveying, say, twenty families), but if the two hundred families you survey only represent the rich part of town, then your sample (the two hundred families) is not generalizable to the entire population (one thousand families).

Interviews You Conduct

The second type of primary research you might conduct is an interview. An interview is a conversation in which the interviewer asks a series of questions aimed at learning facts, figures, or opinions from one or more respondents. As with a survey, an interviewer generally has a list of prepared questions to ask; but unlike a survey, an interview allows for follow-up questions that can aid in understanding why a respondent gave a certain answer. Sometimes interviews are conducted on a one-on-one basis, but other times interviews are conducted with a larger group, which is commonly referred to as a focus group.

One-on-one interviews enable an interviewer to receive information about a given topic with little or no interference from others. Focus groups are good for eliciting information, but they are also good for seeing how groups of people interact and perceive topics. Often information that is elicited in a one-on-one interview is different from the information gained from a group of people interacting.

If you're preparing for a speech on implementing project management skills for student organizations, you may want to interview a handful of student organization leaders for their input. You may also want to get a group of students who have led successful projects for their student organizations and see what they did right. You could also get a group of students who have had bad project outcomes and try to understand what went wrong. Ultimately, you could use all this information not only to help you understand the needs student organizations have concerning project management but also to provide support for the recommendations you make during your speech.

Secondary Research

Secondary research is carried out to discover or revise facts, theories, and applications—similar to primary research—but it is reported by someone not involved in conducting the actual research. Most of what we consider "research" falls into the category of secondary research. If you've ever written a paper for one of your classes and had to cite sources, then you've conducted secondary research. Secondary research is when you report the results of someone else's primary research. If you read an academic article about an experiment that a group of researchers conducted and then tell your audience about that study, you are delivering information secondhand to your audience. You as the speaker did not conduct the study, so you are reporting what someone else has written.

One place where secondary research can get people into trouble is when they attempt to use someone else's secondary research. In a book titled Unleashing the Power of PR: A Contrarian's Guide to Marketing and Communication, Mark Weiner cites research conducted by the investment firm Veronis Suhler Stevenson Partners (Weiner, 2006). It might be tempting to leave out Weiner's book and just cite the Veronis Suhler Stevenson Partners' research instead. While this may be easier, it's not exactly ethical. Mark Weiner spent time conducting research and locating primary research; when you steal one of his sources, it's like you're stealing part of the work he's done. Your secondary research should still be your research. If you haven't laid eyes on the original study (e.g., Veronis Suhler Stevenson Partners' study), you shouldn't give your audience the impression that you have. An exception to this rule is if you are citing a translation of something originally written in a foreign language—and in that case, you still need to mention that you're using a translation and not the original.

Aside from the ethics of telling your audience where you got your information, you need to be aware that published sources sometimes make mistakes when citing information, so you could find yourself incorrectly providing information based on a mistake in Weiner's book. Think of it like the old game of "Telephone," in which you tell one person a phrase, that person turns to the next person and repeats the phrase, and by the time thirty people have completed the process, the final phrase doesn't remotely resemble the original. When people pass information along without verifying it themselves, there is always an increased likelihood of error.

References

Clark, R. P., & Berris, C. E. (1989, August). Botulinum toxin: A treatment for facial asymmetry caused by facial nerve paralysis. *Plastic & Reconstructive Surgery, 84*(2), 353–355.

Weiner, M. (2006). *Unleashing the power of PR: A contrarian's guide to marketing and communication.* San Francisco, CA: Jossey-Bass and the International Association of Business Communicators.

Williamson, B. (2011, July 12). The wonders and dangers of Botox. *Australian Broadcasting Corporation, Adelaide.* Retrieved July 14, 2011, from http://www.abc.net.au/local/stories/2011/07/11/3266766.htm

Wrench, J. S., Thomas-Maddox, C., Richmond, V. P., & McCroskey, J. C. (2008). *Quantitative methods for communication researchers: A hands on approach.* New York, NY: Oxford University Press.

8.3 DEVELOPING A RESEARCH STRATEGY

In the previous section we discussed what research was and the difference between primary and secondary research. In this section, we are going to explore how to develop a research strategy. Think of a research strategy as your personal map. The end destination is the actual speech, and along the way, there are various steps you need to complete to reach your destination: the speech. From the day you receive your speech assignment, the more clearly you map out the steps you need to take leading up to the date when you will give the speech, the easier your speech development process will be. In the rest of this section, we are going to discuss time management, determining your research needs, finding your sources, and evaluating your sources.

Allotting Time

First and foremost, when starting a new project, no matter how big or small, it is important to seriously consider how much time that project is going to take. To help us discuss the issue of time with regard to preparing your speech, we're going to examine what the Project Management Institute refers to as the **project life cycle**, or "the phases that connect the beginning of a project to its end" (Project Management Institute, 2004). Often in a public speaking class, the time you have is fairly concrete.

You may have two or three weeks between speeches in a semester course or one to two weeks in a quarter course. In either case, from the moment your instructor gives you the assigned speech, the proverbial clock is ticking. With each passing day, you are losing precious time in your speech preparation process. Now, we realize that as a college student you probably have many things vying for your time in life: school, family, jobs, friends, or dating partners. For this reason, you need to really think through how much time it's going to take you to complete your preparation in terms of both research and speech preparation.

Research Time

The first step that takes a good chunk of your time is researching your speech. Whether you are conducting primary research or relying on secondary research sources, you're going to be spending a significant amount of time researching.

As Howard and Taggart point out in their book Research Matters, research is not just a one-and-done task (Howard & Taggart, 2010). As you develop your speech, you may realize that you want to address a question or issue that didn't occur to you during your first round of research, or that you're missing a key piece of information to support one of your points. For these reasons, it's always wise to allow extra time for targeted research later in your schedule.

You also need to take into account the possibility of meeting with a research librarian. Although research librarians have many useful tips and tricks, they have schedules just like anyone else. If you know you are going to need to speak with a librarian, try to set up an appointment ahead of time for the date when you think you'll have your questions organized, and be ready to meet.

A good rule of thumb is to devote no more than one-third of your speech preparation time to research (e.g., if you have three weeks before your speech date, your research should be done by the end of the first week). If you are not careful, you could easily end up spending all your time on research and waiting until the last minute to actually prepare your speech, which is highly inadvisable.

Speech Preparation Time

The second task in speech preparation is to sit down and actually develop your speech. During this time period, you will use the information you collected during your research to fully flesh out your ideas into a complete speech. You may be making arguments using the research or creating visual aids. Whatever you need to complete during this time period, you need to give yourself ample time to actually prepare your speech. One common rule of thumb is one day of speech preparation per one minute of actual speaking time.

By allowing yourself enough time to prepare your speech, you're also buffering yourself against a variety of things that can go wrong both in life and with your speech. Let's face it, life happens. Often events completely outside our control happen, and these events could negatively impact our ability to prepare a good speech. When you give yourself a little time buffer, you're already insulated from the possible negative effects on your speech if something goes wrong.

The last part of speech preparation is practice. Although some try to say that practice makes perfect, we realize that perfection is never realistic because no one is perfect. We prefer this mantra: "Practice makes permanent."

And by "practice," we mean actual rehearsals in which you deliver your speech out loud. Speakers who only script out their speeches or only think through them often forget their thoughts when they stand in front of an audience. Research has shown that when individuals practice, their speech performance in front of an audience is more closely aligned with their practice than people who just think about their speeches. In essence, you need to allow yourself to become comfortable not only with the text of the speech but also with the nonverbal delivery of the speech, so giving yourself plenty of speech preparation time also gives you more practice time. We will discuss speech development and practice further in other chapters.

Determining Your Needs

When starting your research, you want to start by asking yourself what you think you need. Obviously, you'll need to have a good idea about what your topic is before just randomly looking at information in a library or online. Your instructor may provide some very specific guidance for the type of information he or she wants to see in your speech, so that's a good place to start determining your basic needs.

Once you have a general idea of your basic needs, you can start to ask yourself a series of simple questions:

1. What do I, personally, know about my topic?
2. Do I have any clear gaps in my knowledge of my topic?
3. Do I need to conduct primary research for my speech?
4. What type of secondary research do I need?

    ◦ Do I need research related to facts?
    ◦ Do I need research related to theories?
    ◦ Do I need research related to applications?

The clearer you are about the type of research you need at the onset of the research process, the easier it will be to locate specific information.

Finding Resources

Once you have a general idea about the basic needs you have for your research, it's time to start tracking down your secondary sources. Thankfully, we live in a world that is swimming with information. Back in the decades when the authors of this textbook first started researching, we all had to go to a library and search through a physical card catalog to find books. If you wanted to research a topic in magazine or journal articles, you had to look up key terms in a giant book, printed annually, known as an index of periodicals. Researchers could literally spend hours in the library and find just one or two sources that were applicable to their topic.

Today, on the other hand, information is quite literally at our fingertips. Not only is information generally more accessible, it is also considerably easier to access. In fact, we have the opposite problem from a couple of decades ago—we have too much information at our fingertips. In addition, we now have to be more skeptical about where that information is coming from. In this section we're going to discuss how to find information in both nonacademic and academic sources.

Nonacademic Information Sources

Nonacademic information sources are sometimes also called popular press information sources; their primary purpose is to be read by the general public. Most nonacademic information sources are written at a sixth- to eighth-grade reading level, so they are very accessible. Although the information often contained in these sources is often quite limited, the advantage of using nonacademic sources is that they appeal to a broad, general audience.

Books

The first source we have for finding secondary information is books. Now, the authors of your text are admitted bibliophiles—we love books. Fiction, nonfiction, it doesn't really matter, we just love books. And, thankfully, we live in a world where books abound and reading has never been easier. Unless your topic is very cutting-edge, chances are someone has written a book about your topic at some point in history.

Historically, the original purpose of libraries was to house manuscripts that were copied by hand and stored in library collections. After Gutenberg created the printing press, we had the ability to mass produce writing, and the handwritten manuscript gave way to the printed manuscript. In today's modern era, we are seeing another change where printed manuscript is now giving way, to some extent, to the electronic manuscript. Amazon.com's Kindle, Barnes & Noble's Nook, Apple's iPad, and Sony's e-Ink-based readers are examples of the new hardware enabling people to take entire libraries of information with them wherever they go. We now can carry the amount of information that used to be housed in the greatest historic libraries in the palms of our hands. When you sit back and really think about it, that's pretty darn cool!

In today's world, there are three basic types of libraries you should be aware of: physical library, physical/electronic library, and e-online library. The physical library is a library that exists only in the physical world. Many small community or county library collections are available only if you physically go into the library and check out a book. We highly recommend doing this at some point. Libraries today generally model the US Library of Congress's card catalog system. As such, most library layouts are similar. This familiar layout makes it much easier to find information if you are using multiple libraries. Furthermore, because the Library of Congress catalogs information by type, if you find one book that is useful for you, it's very likely that surrounding books on the same shelf will also be useful. When people don't take the time to physically browse in a library, they often miss out on some great information.

The second type of library is the library that has both physical and electronic components. Most college and university libraries have both the physical stacks (where the books are located) and electronic databases containing e-books. The two largest e-book databases are ebrary (http://www.ebrary.com) and NetLibrary (http://www.netlibrary.com). Although these library collections are generally cost-prohibitive for an individual, more and more academic institutions are subscribing to them. Some libraries are also making portions of their collections available online for free: Harvard University's Digital Collections (http://digitalcollections.harvard.edu), New York Public Library's E-book Collection (http://ebooks.nypl.org), The British Library's Online Gallery (http://www.bl.uk/onlinegallery/virtualbooks/index.html#), and the US Library of Congress (http://www.loc.gov).

One of the greatest advantages to using libraries for finding books is that you can search not only their books, but often a wide network of other academic institutions' books as well. Furthermore, in today's world, we have one of the greatest online card catalogs ever created—and it wasn't created for libraries at all! Retail bookseller sites like Amazon.com can be a great source for finding books that may be applicable to your topic, and the best part is, you don't actually need to purchase the book if you use your library, because your library may actually own a copy of a book you find on a bookseller site. You can pick a topic and then search for that topic on a bookseller site. If you find a book that you think may be appropriate, plug that book's title into your school's electronic library catalog. If your library owns the book, you can go to the library and pick it up today.

If your library doesn't own it, do you still have an option other than buying the book? Yes: interlibrary loans. An **interlibrary loan** is a process where librarians are able to search other libraries to locate the book a researcher is trying to find. If another library has that book, then the library asks to borrow it for a short period of time. Depending on how easy a book is to find, your library could receive it in a couple of days or a couple of weeks. Keep in mind that interlibrary loans take time, so do not expect to get a book at the last minute. The more lead time you provide a librarian to find a book you are looking for, the greater the likelihood that the book will be sent through the mail to your library on time.

The final type of library is a relatively new one, the library that exists only online. With the influx of computer technology, we have started to create vast stores of digitized content from around the world. These online libraries contain full-text documents free of charge to everyone. Some online libraries we recommend are Project Gutenberg (http://www.gutenberg.org), Google Books (http://books.google.com), Read Print (http://www.readprint.com), Open Library (http://openlibrary.org), and Get Free e-Books (http://www.getfreeebooks.com). This is a short list of just a handful of the libraries that are now offering free e-content.

General-Interest Periodicals

The second category of information you may seek out includes **general-interest periodicals**. These are magazines and newsletters published on a fairly systematic basis. Some popular magazines in this category include The New Yorker, People, Reader's Digest, Parade, Smithsonian, and The Saturday Evening Post. These magazines are considered "general interest" because most people in the United States could pick up a copy of these magazines and find them interesting and topical.

Special-Interest Periodicals

Special-interest periodicals are magazines and newsletters that are published for a narrower audience. In a 2005 article, Business Wire noted that in the United States there are over ten thousand different magazines published annually, but only two thousand of those magazines have significant circulation1. Some more widely known special-interest periodicals are Sports Illustrated, Bloomberg's Business Week, Gentleman's Quarterly, Vogue, Popular Science, and House and Garden. But for every major magazine, there are a great many other lesser-known magazines like American Coin Op Magazine, Varmint Hunter, Shark Diver Magazine, Pet Product News International, Water Garden News, to name just a few.

Newspapers and Blogs

Another major source of nonacademic information is newspapers and blogs. Thankfully, we live in a society that has a free press. We've opted to include both newspapers and blogs in this category. A few blogs (e.g., The Huffington Post, Talkingpoints Memo, News Max, The Daily Beast, Salon) function similarly to traditional newspapers. Furthermore, in the past few years we've lost many traditional newspapers around the United States; cities that used to have four or five daily papers may now only have one or two.

According to newspapers.com, the top ten newspapers in the United States are USA Today, the Wall Street Journal, the New York Times, the Los Angeles Times, the Washington Post, the New York Daily News, the Chicago Tribune, the New York Post, Long Island Newsday, and the Houston Chronicle. Most colleges and universities subscribe to a number of these newspapers in paper form or have access to them electronically. Furthermore, LexisNexis, a database many colleges and universities subscribe to, has access to full text newspaper articles from these newspapers and many more around the world.

In addition to traditional newspapers, blogs are becoming a mainstay of information in today's society. In fact, since the dawn of the twenty-first century many major news stories have been broken by professional bloggers rather than traditional newspaper reporters (Ochman, 2007). Although anyone can create a blog, there are many reputable blog sites that are run by professional journalists. As such, blogs can be a great source of information. However, as with all information on the Internet, you often have to wade through a lot of junk to find useful, accurate information.

We do not personally endorse any blogs, but according to Technorati.com, the top eight most commonly read blogs in the world (in 2011) are as follows:

1. *The Huffington Post* (http://www.huffingtonpost.com)
2. *Gizmodo* (http://www.gizmodo.com)
3. *TechCrunch* (http://www.techcrunch.com)
4. *Mashable!* (http://mashable.com)
5. *Engadget* (http://www.engadget.com)
6. *Boing Boing* (http://www.boingboing.net)
7. *The Daily Beast* (http://www.thedailybeast.com)
8. *TMZ* (http://www.tmz.com)

Encyclopedias

Another type of source that you may encounter is the encyclopedia. **Encyclopedias** are information sources that provide short, very general information about a topic. Encyclopedias are available in both print and electronic formats, and their content can range from eclectic and general (e.g., Encyclopædia Britannica) to the very specific (e.g., Encyclopedia of 20th Century Architecture, or Encyclopedia of Afterlife Beliefs and Phenomena). It is important to keep in mind that encyclopedias are designed to give only brief, fairly superficial summaries of a topic area. Thus they may be useful for finding out what something is if it is referenced in another source, but they are generally not a useful source for your actual speech. In fact, many instructors do not allow students to use encyclopedias as sources for their speeches for this very reason.

One of the most popular online encyclopedic sources is Wikipedia. Like other encyclopedias, it can be useful for finding out basic information (e.g., what baseball teams did Catfish Hunter play for?) but will not give you the depth of information you need for a speech. Also keep in mind that Wikipedia, unlike the general and specialized encyclopedias available through your library, can be edited by anyone and therefore often contains content errors and biased information. If you are a fan of The Colbert Report, you probably know that host Stephen Colbert has, on several occasions, asked viewers to change Wikipedia content to reflect his views of the world. This is just one example of why one should always be careful of information on the web, but this advice is even more important when considering group-edited sites such as Wikipedia.

Websites

Websites are the last major source of nonacademic information. In the twenty-first century we live in a world where there is a considerable amount of information readily available at our fingertips. Unfortunately, you can spend hours and hours searching for information and never quite find what you're looking for if you don't devise an Internet search strategy. First, you need to select a good search engine to help you find appropriate information. The graphic below contains a list of common search engines and the types of information they are useful for finding.

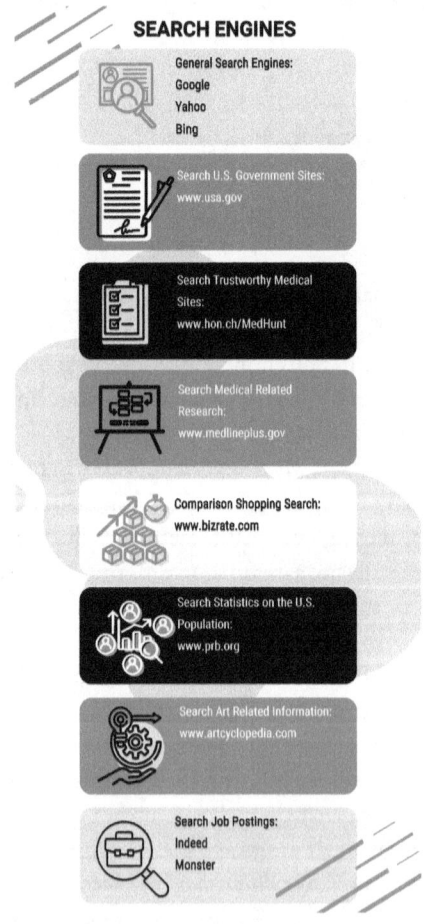

Academic Information Sources

After nonacademic sources, the second major source for finding information comes from academics. The main difference between academic or scholarly information and the information you get from the popular press is oversight. In the nonacademic world, the primary gatekeeper of information is the editor, who may or may not be a content expert. In academia, we have established a way to perform a series of checks to ensure that the information is accurate and follows agreed-upon academic standards. For example, this book, or portions of this book, were read by dozens of academics who provided feedback. Having this extra step in the writing process is time consuming, but it provides an extra level of confidence in the relevance and accuracy of the information. In this section, we will discuss scholarly books and articles, computerized databases, and finding scholarly information on the web.

Scholarly Books

College and university libraries are filled with books written by academics. According to the Text and Academic Authors Association (http://www.taaonline.net), there are two types of scholarly books: textbooks and academic books. **Textbooks** are books that are written about a segment of content within a field of academic study and are written for undergraduate or graduate student audiences. These books tend to be very specifically focused. Take this book, for instance. We are not trying to introduce you to the entire world of human communication, just one small aspect of it: public speaking. Textbooks tend to be written at a fairly easy reading level and are designed to transfer information in a manner that mirrors classroom teaching to some extent. Also, textbooks are secondary sources of information. They are designed to survey the research available in a particular field rather than to present new research.

Academic books are books that are primarily written for other academics for informational and research purposes. Generally speaking, when instructors ask for you to find scholarly books, they are referring to academic books. Thankfully, there are hundreds of thousands of academic books published on almost every topic you can imagine. In the field of communication, there are a handful of major publishers who publish academic books: SAGE (http://www.sagepub.com), Routledge (http://www.routledge.com), Jossey-Bass (http://www.josseybass.com), Pfeiffer (http://www.pfeiffer.com), the American Psychological Association (http://www.apa.org/pubs/books), and the National Communication Association (http://www.ncastore.com), among others. In addition to the major publishers who publish academic books, there are also many university presses who publish academic books: SUNY Press (http://www.sunypress.edu), Oxford University Press (http://www.oup.com/us), University of South Carolina Press (http://www.sc.edu/uscpress), Baylor University Press (http://www.baylorpress.com), University of Illinois Press (http://www.press.uillinois.edu), and the University of Alabama Press (http://www.uapress.ua.edu) are just a few of them.

Scholarly Articles

Because most academic writing comes in the form of scholarly articles or journal articles, that is the best place for finding academic research on a given topic. Every academic subfield has its own journals, so you should never have a problem finding the best and most recent research on a topic. However, scholarly articles are written for a scholarly audience, so reading scholarly articles takes more time than if you were to read a magazine article in the popular press. It's also helpful to realize that there may be parts of the article you simply do not have the background knowledge to understand, and there is nothing wrong with that. Many research studies are conducted by quantitative researchers who rely on statistics to examine phenomena. Unless you have training in understanding the statistics, it is difficult to interpret the statistical information that appears in these articles. Instead, focus on the beginning part of the article where the author(s) will discuss previous research (secondary research), and then focus at the end of the article, where the author(s) explain what was found in their research (primary research).

Computerized Databases

Finding academic research is easier today than it ever has been in the past because of large computer databases containing research. Here's how these databases work. A database company signs contracts with publishers to gain the right to store the publishers' content electronically. The database companies then create thematic databases containing publications related to general areas of knowledge (business, communication, psychology, medicine, etc.). The database companies then sell subscriptions to these databases to libraries.

The largest of these database companies is a group called EBSCO Publishing, which runs both EBSCO Host (an e-journal provider) and NetLibrary (a large e-book library) (http://www.ebscohost.com). Some of the more popular databases that EBSCO provides to colleges and universities are: Academic Search Complete, Business Source Complete, Communication and Mass Media Complete, Education Research Complete, Humanities International Complete, Philosopher's Index, Political Science Complete, PsycArticles, and Vocational and Career Collection. Academic Search Complete is the broadest of all the databases and casts a fairly wide net across numerous fields. Information that you find using databases can contain both nonacademic and academic information, so EBSCO Host has built in a number of filtering options to help you limit the types of information available.

We strongly recommend checking out your library's website to see what databases they have available and if they have any online tutorials for finding sources using the databases to which your library subscribes.

Scholarly Information on the Web

In addition to the subscription databases that exist on the web, there are also a number of great sources for scholarly information on the web. As mentioned earlier, however, finding scholarly information on the web poses a problem because anyone can post information on the web. Fortunately, there are a number of great websites that attempt to help filter this information for us.

Website	Type of Information
http://www.doaj.org	The Directory of Open Access Journals is an online database of all freely available academic journals online.
http://scholar.google.com	Google Scholar attempts to filter out nonacademic information. Unfortunately, it tends to return a large number of for-pay site results.
http://www.cios.org	Communication Institute for Online Scholarship is a clearinghouse for online communication scholarship. This site contains full-text journals and books.
http://xxx.lanl.gov	This is an open access site devoted to making physical science research accessible.
http://www.biomedcentral.com	BioMed Central provides open-access medical research.
http://www.osti.gov/eprints	The E-print Network provides access to a range of scholarly research that interests people working for the Department of Energy.
http://www.freemedicaljournals.com	This site provides the public with free access to medical journals.
http://highwire.stanford.edu	This is the link to Stanford University's free, full-text science archives.
http://www.plosbiology.org	This is the Public Library of Science's journal for biology.
https://dp.la/	The Digital Public Library of America brings together the riches of America's libraries, archives, and museums, and makes them freely available to the world
http://vlib.org	The WWW Virtual Library provides annotated lists of websites compiled by scholars in specific areas.

Tips for Finding Information Sources

Now that we've given you plenty of different places to start looking for research, we need to help you sort through the research. In this section, we're going to provide a series of tips that should make this process easier and help you find appropriate information quickly. And here is our first tip: We cannot recommend Mary George's book The Elements of Library Research: What Every Student Needs to Know more highly. Honestly, we wish this book had been around when we were just learning how to research.

Create a Research Log

Nothing is more disheartening than when you find yourself at 1:00 a.m. asking, "Haven't I already read this?" We've all learned the tough lessons of research, and this is one that keeps coming back to bite us in the backside if we're not careful. According to a very useful book called The Elements of Library Research by M. W. George, a **research log** is a "step-by-step account of the process of identifying, obtaining, and evaluating sources for a specific project, similar to a lab note-book in an experimental setting" (George, 2008). In essence, George believes that keeping a log of what you've done is very helpful because it can help you keep track of what you've read thus far. You can use a good old-fashioned notebook, or if you carry around your laptop or netbook with you, you can always keep it digitally. While there are expensive programs like Microsoft Office OneNote that can be used for note keeping, there are also a number of free tools that could be adapted as well.

Start with Background Information

It's not unusual for students to try to jump right into the meat of a topic, only to find out that there is a lot of technical language they just don't understand. For this reason, you may want to start your research with sources written for the general public. Generally, these lower-level sources are great for background information on a topic and are helpful when trying to learn the basic vocabulary of a subject area.

Search Your Library's Computers

Once you've started getting a general grasp of the broad content area you want to investigate, it's time to sit down and see what your school's library has to offer. If you do not have much experience in using your library's website, see if the website contains an online tutorial. Most schools offer online tutorials to show students the resources that students can access. If your school doesn't have an online tutorial, you may want to call your library and schedule an appointment with a research librarian to learn how to use the school's computers. Also, if you tell your librarian that you want to learn how to use the library, he or she may be able to direct you to online resources that you may have missed.

Try to search as many different databases as possible. Look for relevant books, e-books, newspaper articles, magazine articles, journal articles, and media files. Modern college and university libraries have a ton of sources, and one search may not find everything you are looking for on the first pass. Furthermore, don't forget to think about synonyms for topics. The more synonyms you can generate for your topic, the better you'll be at finding information.

Learn to Skim

If you sit down and try to completely read every article or book you find, it will take you a very long time to get through all the information. Start by reading the introductory paragraphs. Generally, the first few paragraphs will give you a good idea about the overall topic. If you're reading a research article, start by reading the abstract. If the first few paragraphs or abstract don't sound like they're applicable, there's a good chance the source won't be useful for you. Second, look for highlighted, italicized, or bulleted information. Generally, authors use highlighting, italics, and bullets to separate information to make it jump out for readers. Third, look for tables, charts, graphs, and figures. All these forms are separated from the text to make the information more easily understandable for a reader, so seeing if the content is relevant is a way to see if it helps you. Fourth, look at headings and subheadings. Headings and subheadings show you how an author has grouped information into meaningful segments. If you read the headings and subheadings and nothing jumps out as relevant, that's another indication that there may not be anything useful in that source. Lastly, take good notes while you're skimming. One way to take good notes is to attach a sticky note to each source. If you find relevant information, write that information on the sticky note along with the page number. If you don't find useful information in a source, just write "nothing" on the sticky note and move on to the next source. This way when you need to sort through your information, you'll be able to quickly see what information was useful and locate the information. Other people prefer to create a series of note cards to help them organize their information. Whatever works best for you is what you should use.

Read Bibliographies/Reference Pages

After you've finished reading useful sources, see who those sources cited on their bibliographies or reference pages. We call this method **backtracking**. Often the sources cited by others can lead us to even better sources than the ones we found initially.

Ask for Help

Don't be afraid to ask for help. As we said earlier in this chapter, reference librarians are your friends. They won't do your work for you, but they are more than willing to help if you ask.

Evaluating Resources

The final step in research occurs once you've found resources relevant to your topic: evaluating the quality of those resources. Below is a list of six questions to ask yourself about the sources you've collected; these are drawn from the book The Elements of Library Research by M. W. George (Geogrge, 2008).

What Is the Date of Publication?

The first question you need to ask yourself is the date of the source's publication. Although there may be classic studies that you want to cite in your speech, generally, the more recent the information, the better your presentation will be. As an example, if you want to talk about the current state of women's education in the United States, relying on information from the 1950s that debated whether "coeds" should attend class along with male students is clearly not appropriate. Instead you'd want to use information published within the past five to ten years.

Who Is the Author?

The next question you want to ask yourself is about the author. Who is the author? What are her or his credentials? Does he or she work for a corporation, college, or university? Is a political or commercial agenda apparent in the writing? The more information we can learn about an author, the better our understanding and treatment of that author's work will be. Furthermore, if we know that an author is clearly biased in a specific manner, ethically we must tell our audience members. If we pretend an author is unbiased when we know better, we are essentially lying to our audience.

Who Is the Publisher?

In addition to knowing who the author is, we also want to know who the publisher is. While there are many mainstream publishers and academic press publishers, there are also many fringe publishers. For example, maybe you're reading a research report published by the Cato Institute. While the Cato Institute may sound like a regular publisher, it is actually a libertarian think tank (http://www.cato.org). As such, you can be sure that the information in its publications will have a specific political bias. While the person writing the research report may be an upstanding author with numerous credits, the Cato Institute only publishes reports that adhere to its political philosophy. Generally, a cursory examination of a publisher's website is a good indication of the specific political bias. Most websites will have an "About" section or an "FAQ" section that will explain who the publisher is.

Is It Academic or Nonacademic?

The next question you want to ask yourself is whether the information comes from an academic or a nonacademic source. Because of the enhanced scrutiny academic sources go through, we argue that you can generally rely more on the information contained in academic sources than nonacademic sources. One very notorious example of the difference between academic versus nonacademic information can be seen in the problem of popular-culture author John Gray, author of Men are From Mars, Women are From Venus. Gray, who received a PhD via a correspondence program from Columbia Pacific University in 1982, has written numerous books on the topic of men and women. Unfortunately, the academic research on the subject of sex and gender differences is often very much at odds with Gray's writing. For a great critique of Gray's writings, check out Julia Wood's article in the Southern Communication Journal (Wood, 2002). Ultimately, we strongly believe that using academic publications is always in your best interest because they generally contain the most reliable information.

What Is the Quality of the Bibliography/Reference Page?

Another great indicator of a well-thought-out and researched source is the quality of its bibliography or reference page. If you look at a source's bibliography or reference page and it has only a couple of citations, then you can assume that either the information was not properly cited or it was largely made up by someone. Even popular-press books can contain great bibliographies and reference pages, so checking them out is a great way to see if an author has done her or his homework prior to writing a text. As noted above, it is also an excellent way to find additional resources on a topic.

Do People Cite the Work?

The last question to ask about a source is, "Are other people actively citing the work?" One way to find out whether a given source is widely accepted is to see if numerous people are citing it. If you find an article that has been cited by many other authors, then clearly the work has been viewed as credible and useful. If you're doing research and you keep running across the same source over and over again, that is an indication that it's an important study that you should probably take a look at. Many colleges and universities also subscribe to Science Citation Index (SCI), Social Sciences Citation Index (SSCI), or the Arts and Humanities Citation Index (AHCI), which are run through Institute for Scientific Information's Web of Knowledge database service (http://isiwebofknowledge.com). All these databases help you find out where information has been cited by other researchers.

[1]Total number of magazines published in the US is greater than 10,000 but only about 2,000 have significant circulation. (2005, September 21). *Business Wire*. Retrieved from http://findarticles.com.

References

George, M. W. (2008). *The elements of library research: What every student needs to know*. Princeton, NJ: Princeton University Press, p. 183.

Howard, R. M., & Taggart, A. R. (2010). *Research matters*. New York: McGraw-Hill, pp. 102–103.

Ochman, B. L. (2007, June 29). The top 10 news stories broken by bloggers. *TechNewsWorld*. [Web log post]. Retrieved July 14, 2011, from http://www.mpdailyfix.com/technewsworld-the-top-10-news-stories-broken-by-bloggers.

Project Management Institute. (2004). *A guide to the project management body of knowledge: PMBOK® guide* (3rd ed.). Newton Square, PA: Author, p. 19.

Wood, J. T. (2002). A critical response to John Gray's Mars and Venus portrayals of men and women. *Southern Communication Journal, 67*, 201–210.

8.4 CITING SOURCES

By this point you're probably exhausted after looking at countless sources, but there's still a lot of work that needs to be done. Most public speaking teachers will require you to turn in either a bibliography or a reference page with your speeches. In this section, we're going to explore how to properly cite your sources for a Modern Language Association (MLA) list of works cited or an American Psychological Association (APA) reference list. We're also going to discuss plagiarism and how to avoid it.

Why Citing Is Important

Citing is important because it enables readers to see where you found information cited within a speech, article, or book. Furthermore, not citing information properly is considered plagiarism, so ethically we want to make sure that we give credit to the authors we use in a speech. While there are numerous citation styles to choose from, the two most common style choices for public speaking are APA and MLA.

APA versus MLA Source Citations

Style refers to those components or features of a literary composition or oral presentation that have to do with the form of expression rather than the content expressed (e.g., language, punctuation, parenthetical citations, and endnotes). The APA and the MLA have created the two most commonly used style guides in academia today. Generally speaking, scholars in the various social science fields (e.g., psychology, human communication, business) are more likely to use **APA style**, and scholars in the various humanities fields (e.g., English, philosophy, rhetoric) are more likely to use **MLA style**. The two styles are quite different from each other, so learning them does take time.

APA Citations

The first common reference style your teacher may ask for is APA. As of October 2019, the American Psychological Association published the seventh edition of the Publication Manual of the American Psychological Association (http://www.apastyle.org) . The seventh edition provides considerable guidance on working with and citing Internet sources.

MLA Citations

The second common reference style your teacher may ask for is MLA. In March 2009, the Modern Language Association published the seventh edition of the MLA Handbook for Writers of Research Papers (Modern Language Association, 2009) (http://www.mla.org/style). The seventh edition provides considerable guidance for citing online sources and new media such as graphic narratives.

Citing Sources in a Speech

Once you have decided what sources best help you explain important terms and ideas in your speech or help you build your arguments, it's time to place them into your speech. In this section, we're going to quickly talk about using your research effectively within your speeches. Citing sources within a speech is a three-step process: set up the citation, give the citation, and explain the citation.

First, you want to set up your audience for the citation. The setup is one or two sentences that are general statements that lead to the specific information you are going to discuss from your source. Here's an example: "Workplace bullying is becoming an increasing problem for US organizations." Notice that this statement doesn't provide a specific citation yet, but the statement introduces the basic topic.

Second, you want to deliver the source; whether it is a direct quotation or a paraphrase of information from a source doesn't matter at this point. A **direct quotation** is when you cite the actual words from a source with no changes. To **paraphrase** is to take a source's basic idea and condense it using your own words. Here's an example of both:

Direct Quotation	In a 2009 report titled *Bullying: Getting Away With It*, the Workplace Bullying Institute wrote, "Doing nothing to the bully (ensuring impunity) was the most common employer tactic (54%)."
Paraphrase	According to a 2009 study by the Workplace Bullying Institute titled *Bullying: Getting Away With It*, when employees reported bullying, 54 percent of employers did nothing at all.

You'll notice that in both of these cases, we started by citing the author of the study—in this case, the Workplace Bullying Institute. We then provided the title of the study. You could also provide the name of the article, book, podcast, movie, or other source. In the direct quotation example, we took information right from the report. In the second example, we summarized the same information (Workplace Bullying Institute, 2009).

Let's look at another example of direct quotations and paraphrases, this time using a person, rather than an institution, as the author.

Direct Quotation	In her book *The Elements of Library Research: What Every Student Needs to Know*, Mary George, senior reference librarian at Princeton University's library, defines insight as something that "occurs at an unpredictable point in the research process and leads to the formulation of a thesis statement and argument. Also called an 'Aha' moment or focus."
Paraphrase	In her book *The Elements of Library Research: What Every Student Needs to Know*, Mary George, senior reference librarian at Princeton University's library, tells us that insight is likely to come unexpectedly during the research process; it will be an "aha!" moment when we suddenly have a clear vision of the point we want to make.

Notice that the same basic pattern for citing sources was followed in both cases.

The final step in correct source citation within a speech is the explanation. One of the biggest mistakes of novice public speakers (and research writers) is that they include a source citation and then do nothing with the citation at all. Instead, take the time to explain the quotation or paraphrase to put into the context of your speech. Do not let your audience draw their own conclusions about the quotation or paraphrase. Instead, help them make the connections you want them to make. Here are two examples using the examples above:

Bullying Example	Clearly, organizations need to be held accountable for investigating bullying allegations. If organizations will not voluntarily improve their handling of this problem, the legal system may be required to step in and enforce sanctions for bullying, much as it has done with sexual harassment.
Aha! Example	As many of us know, reaching that "aha!" moment does not always come quickly, but there are definitely some strategies one can take to help speed up this process.

Notice how in both of our explanations we took the source's information and then added to the information to direct it for our specific purpose. In the case of the bullying citation, we then propose that businesses should either adopt workplace bullying guidelines or face legal intervention. In the case of the "aha!" example, we turn the quotation into a section on helping people find their thesis or topic. In both cases, we were able to use the information to further our speech.

Using Sources Ethically

The last section of this chapter is about using sources in an ethical manner. Whether you are using primary or secondary research, there are five basic ethical issues you need to consider.

Avoid Plagiarism

First, and foremost, if the idea isn't yours, you need to cite where the information came from during your speech. Having the citation listed on a bibliography or reference page is only half of the correct citation. You must provide correct citations for all your sources within the speech as well. In a very helpful book called *Avoiding Plagiarism: A Student Guide to Writing Your Own Work*, Menager-Beeley and Paulos provide a list of twelve strategies for avoiding plagiarism (Menager-Beeley & Paulos, 2009):

1. *Do your own work, and use your own words.* One of the goals of a public speaking class is to develop skills that you'll use in the world outside academia. When you are in the workplace and the "real world," you'll be expected to think for yourself, so you might as well start learning this skill now.
2. *Allow yourself enough time to research the assignment.* One of the most commonly cited excuses students give for plagiarism is that they didn't have enough time to do the research. In this chapter, we've stressed the necessity of giving yourself plenty of time. The more complete your research strategy is

from the very beginning, the more successful your research endeavors will be in the long run. Remember, not having adequate time to prepare is no excuse for plagiarism.

3. *Keep careful track of your sources.* A common mistake that people can make is that they forget where information came from when they start creating the speech itself. Chances are you're going to look at dozens of sources when preparing your speech, and it is very easy to suddenly find yourself believing that a piece of information is "common knowledge" and not citing that information within a speech. When you keep track of your sources, you're less likely to inadvertently lose sources and not cite them correctly.

4. *Take careful notes.* However you decide to keep track of the information you collect (old-fashioned pen and notebook or a computer software program), the more careful your note-taking is, the less likely you'll find yourself inadvertently not citing information or citing the information incorrectly. It doesn't matter what method you choose for taking research notes, but whatever you do, you need to be systematic to avoid plagiarizing.

5. *Assemble your thoughts, and make it clear who is speaking.* When creating your speech, you need to make sure that you clearly differentiate your voice in the speech from the voice of specific authors of the sources you quote. The easiest way to do this is to set up a direct quotation or a paraphrase, as we've described in the preceding sections. Remember, audience members cannot see where the quotation marks are located within your speech text, so you need to clearly articulate with words and vocal tone when you are using someone else's ideas within your speech.

6. *If you use an idea, a quotation, paraphrase, or summary, then credit the source.* We can't reiterate it enough: if it is not your idea, you need to tell your audience where the information came from. Giving credit is especially important when your speech includes a statistic, an original theory, or a fact that is not common knowledge.

7. *Learn how to cite sources correctly both in the body of your paper and in your List of Works Cited (Reference Page).* Most public speaking teachers will require that you turn in either a bibliography or reference page on the day you deliver a speech. Many students make the mistake of thinking that the bibliography or reference page is all they need to cite information, and then they don't cite any of the material within the speech itself. A bibliography or reference page enables a reader or listener to find those sources after the fact, but you must also correctly cite those sources within the speech itself; otherwise, you are plagiarizing.

8. *Quote accurately and sparingly.* A public speech should be based on factual information and references, but it shouldn't be a string of direct quotations strung together. Experts recommend that no more than 10 percent of a paper

or speech be direct quotations (Menager-Beeley & Paulos, 2009). When selecting direct quotations, always ask yourself if the material could be paraphrased in a manner that would make it clearer for your audience. If the author wrote a sentence in a way that is just perfect, and you don't want to tamper with it, then by all means directly quote the sentence. But if you're just quoting because it's easier than putting the ideas into your own words, this is not a legitimate reason for including direct quotations.

9. *Paraphrase carefully.* Modifying an author's words in this way is not simply a matter of replacing some of the words with synonyms. Instead, as Howard and Taggart explain in *Research Matters*, "paraphrasing force[s] you to understand your sources and to capture their meaning accurately in original words and sentences" (Howard & Taggart, 2010). Incorrect paraphrasing is one of the most common forms of inadvertent plagiarism by students. First and foremost, paraphrasing is putting the author's argument, intent, or ideas into *your* own words.

10. *Do not patchwrite (patchspeak).* Menager-Beeley and Paulos define patchwriting as consisting "of mixing several references together and arranging paraphrases and quotations to constitute much of the paper. In essence, the student has assembled others' work with a bit of embroidery here and there but with little original thinking or expression" (Menager-Beeley & Paulos, 2009). Just as students can patchwrite, they can also engage in patchspeaking. In patchspeaking, students rely completely on taking quotations and paraphrases and weaving them together in a manner that is devoid of the student's original thinking.

11. *Summarize, don't auto-summarize.* Some students have learned that most word processing features have an auto-summary function. The auto-summary function will take a ten-page document and summarize the information into a short paragraph. When someone uses the auto-summary function, the words that remain in the summary are still those of the original author, so this is not an ethical form of paraphrasing.

12. *Do not rework another student's paper (speech) or buy paper mill papers (speech mill speeches).* In today's Internet environment, there are a number of storehouses of student speeches on the Internet. Some of these speeches are freely available, while other websites charge money for getting access to one of their canned speeches. Whether you use a speech that is freely available or pay money for a speech, you are engaging in plagiarism. This is also true if the main substance of your speech was copied from a web page. Any time you try to present someone else's ideas as your own during a speech, you are plagiarizing.

Avoid Academic Fraud

While there are numerous websites where you can download free speeches for your class, this is tantamount to fraud. If you didn't do the research and write your own speech, then you are fraudulently trying to pass off someone else's work as your own. In addition to being unethical, many institutions have student codes that forbid such activity. Penalties for academic fraud can be as severe as suspension or expulsion from your institution.

Don't Mislead Your Audience

If you know a source is clearly biased, and you don't spell this out for your audience, then you are purposefully trying to mislead or manipulate your audience. Instead, if the information may be biased, tell your audience that the information may be biased and allow your audience to decide whether to accept or disregard the information.

Give Author Credentials

You should always provide the author's credentials. In a world where anyone can say anything and have it published on the Internet or even publish it in a book, we have to be skeptical of the information we see and hear. For this reason, it's very important to provide your audience with background about the credentials of the authors you cite.

Use Primary Research Ethically

Lastly, if you are using primary research within your speech, you need to use it ethically as well. For example, if you tell your survey participants that the research is anonymous or confidential, then you need to make sure that you maintain their anonymity or confidentiality when you present those results. Furthermore, you also need to be respectful if someone says something is "off the record" during an interview. We must always maintain the privacy and confidentiality of participants during primary research, unless we have their express permission to reveal their names or other identifying information.

Pete's Proper Citation

Having gathered a wealth of information from various sources for his speech on Oklahoma State University's traditions, Pistol Pete realized he needed to correctly orally cite these sources during his presentation. While he was familiar with written citations, he was unsure about the best way to acknowledge these sources out loud without disrupting the flow of his speech.

Pete decided to consult with his public speaking professor, an expert in the art of oral communication. His professor explained that the key to orally citing sources was to seamlessly integrate the citations into the narrative of the speech. She advised Pete to briefly mention the author or source while presenting the information, making sure it felt natural and didn't distract from the overall message.

With this advice in mind, Pete practiced his speech, making sure to give due credit to his sources. For instance, when discussing the history of OSU traditions, Pete might say, "As noted in Dr. Johnson's comprehensive history of Oklahoma State University found in the podcast "Just Poking Around" in July of 2022..." or "According to an article from the university archives from the Oklahoma State official website in 2002..."

Pete also learned the importance of giving context for the cited information. When citing a yearbook or an archived newsletter, he could say something like, "As described in the 1960 OSU yearbook..." or "As an issue of the OSU newsletter from the 1980s recounts..."

With careful practice, Pistol Pete found he was able to cite his sources naturally and effectively, maintaining the narrative flow of his speech. He felt more confident, knowing he was respecting the work of his sources while also providing his audience with well-researched and accurate information about OSU's beloved traditions. Armed with his well-prepared speech, Pete was ready to inspire his fellow Cowboys and Cowgirls with the rich heritage of their university. What are some transitional phrases, like "According to..." that you can use to seamlessly incorporate your source citations?

References

American Psychological Association. (2010). *Publication manual of the American Psychological Association* (6th ed.). Washington, DC: Author. See also American Psychological Association. (2010). *Concise rules of APA Style: The official pocket style guide from the American Psychological Association* (6th ed.). Washington, DC: Author.

Howard, R. M., & Taggart, A. R. (2010). *Research matters*. New York, NY: McGraw-Hill, p. 131.

Menager-Beeley, R., & Paulos, L. (2009). *Understanding plagiarism: A student guide to writing your own work*. Boston, MA: Houghton Mifflin Harcourt, pp. 5–8.

Modern Language Association. (2009). *MLA handbook for writers of research papers* (7th ed.). New York, NY: Modern Language Association.

Workplace Bullying Institute. (2009). Bullying: Getting away with it WBI Labor Day Study—September, 2009. Retrieved July 14, 2011, from http://www.workplacebullying.org/res/WBI2009-B-Survey.html

8.5 ENRICHMENT

Discussion Questions

1. How do academic sources convey more credibility? What is the value of nonacademic sources?
2. When are primary sources more suitable than secondary sources? When are secondary sources more beneficial?
3. If a book is published by a major publishing company, is it an academic source? Why or why not?
4. What are the consequences of plagiarism here at OSU?

Activities

1. With a partner, find a politically-oriented website and analyze the material using George's (2008) six questions for evaluating sources found in section 8.3. What does your analysis say about the material on the website? Discuss.
2. With a group of classmates, discuss which of Menager-Beeley and Paulos (2009) twelve strategies in section 8.4 for avoiding plagiarism you think might be most useful during speech writing? What can you do to overcome and avoid plagiarism?
3. With a partner, find an academic and a nonacademic source about the same topic. Discuss the differences in the writing style. How useful is the content in each source? Which source has more authority? Why?

Case Study

With a group of classmates, read the following scenario below and respond to the questions. Jonathan sat staring at his computer screen. The previous two days had been the most disastrous weekend of his entire life. First, his girlfriend broke up with him on Friday and informed him that she was dating his best friend behind his back. Then he got a phone call from his mother informing him that his childhood dog had been hit by a car. And if that was not enough, his car died on the way to work, and since it was his third unexcused absence from work, he was fired.

In the midst of all these crises, Jonathan was supposed to be preparing his persuasive speech for his public speaking class. Admittedly, Jonathan had two weeks to work on the speech, but he had not made time to get around to it and thought he could pull it together over the weekend. Now at 1:00 a.m. on Monday morning, he finally got a chance to sit down at his computer to prepare the speech he was giving in nine and a half hours.

His topic was prison reform. He searched through a number of websites and finally found one that seemed really relevant. As he read through the first paragraph, he thought to himself, this is exactly what I want to say. After two paragraphs the information just stopped, and the website asked him to pay $29.95 for the rest of the speech. Without even realizing it, Jonathan had found a speech mill website. Jonathan found himself reaching for his wallet thinking, well it says what I want it to say, so why not?

- If you were a student in Jonathan's class and he confided in you that he had used a speech mill for his speech, how would you react?
- If you were Jonathan, what ethical choices could you have made?
- Is it ever ethical to use a speech written by a speech mill?

9 SUPPORTING IDEAS AND BUILDING ARGUMENTS

Learning Objectives

- Define the term "support" and describe three reasons we use support in speeches.
- Explain four criteria used to evaluate support options.
- Describe how speakers can use statistics to support their speeches.
- Differentiate among the five types of definitions and among the four types of supportive examples.
- Explain how narratives can be used to support informative, persuasive, and entertaining speeches.
- Differentiate between the two forms of testimony and between the two types of analogies that can be used for support.
- Explain how to distinguish between useful and nonuseful forms of support.
- Describe the five ways support is used within a speech.
- Describe the purpose of a reverse outline.
- Explain why it is important to use support for every claim made within a speech.
- Evaluate the three-step process for using support within a speech.

9 SUPPORTING IDEAS AND BUILDING ARGUMENTS

Learning Objectives

- Analysis
- Argument
- Best Example
- Bias
- Conclusion
- Direct Quotation
- Entertaining Narratives
- Execution
- Expertise
- Expert Testimony
- Eyewitness Testimony
- Fact
- Figurative Analogies
- Informative Narratives
- Lexical Definition
- Literal Analogies
- Narratives
- Negative Example
- Nonexample
- Numerical Support
- Paraphrase
- Persuasive Definitions
- Persuasive Narratives
- Pictographic Support
- Positive Example
- Premise
- Reverse Outline
- Setup
- Statistics

9 SUPPORTING IDEAS AND BUILDING ARGUMENTS | 295

- **Stipulative Definition**
- **Summary of Support**
- **Support**
- **Support-Manipulation**
- **Theoretical Definitions**
- **Vividness**

9.1 CRAFTING SUPPORTING IDEAS

"Learn, compare, collect the facts! Always have the courage to say to yourself 'I am ignorant.'" -Ivan Petrovich Pavlov

Every day, all around the country, people give speeches that contain generalities and vagueness. Students on your campus might claim that local policies are biased against students, but may not explain why. Politicians may make claims in their speeches about "family values" without defining what those values are or throw out statistics without giving credit to where they found those numbers. Indeed, the nonpartisan websites FactCheck.org and Politifact.com are dedicated to investigating and dispelling the claims that politicians make in their speeches.

In this chapter, we explore the nature of supporting ideas in public speaking and why support is essential to effective presentations. We will then discuss how to use support to build stronger arguments within a speech.

Pete's Piles

Pistol Pete sat in his room, surrounded by the piles of information he had gathered from the Edmon Low Library. He had a variety of sources, each one offering a different perspective on the traditions of Oklahoma State University. But with such a wealth of information, Pete faced a new challenge – sorting through the research and deciding what forms of support to incorporate into his presentation.

First, Pete decided to go through each source and highlight the most compelling information, keeping his audience and the objectives of his speech in mind. He knew he wanted to provide an informative and engaging narrative, and for that, he needed to balance different types of support in his presentation.

Definitions and explanations were important to give context to the audience, especially for traditions that might not be well-known or understood. For instance, he decided to provide a clear explanation of the significance behind the Sea of Orange Parade, detailing its history and purpose.

Facts and statistics were essential for credibility and demonstrating the impact of the traditions. From historical documents and scholarly papers, he extracted data on how many years specific traditions have been held, how many people participate, and how these customs have evolved over time.

Testimonies, particularly from the yearbooks, brought a personal touch to his speech. They allowed him to share firsthand accounts of the traditions, making the narrative more relatable and engaging for his audience.

Pete recognized the power of stories, and so narratives were an integral part of his speech. He decided to weave in stories from alumni and students that highlighted their experiences with the traditions and the meaning these events held for them.

Finally, considering the visual appeal of his presentation, Pete decided to use visual aids. He had discovered some fascinating photographs in the university's digital collections that showcased the traditions vividly. He knew that including these pictures in his presentation would help bring the traditions to life.

Pistol Pete spent hours reviewing, selecting, and organizing the information, mindful of creating a balanced and engaging narrative. Through careful consideration and a keen understanding of his audience, Pete was able to determine the best forms of support to use in his speech, ensuring a well-rounded and compelling presentation about the traditions at Oklahoma State University.

What forms of support do you think will best suit your informative presentation?

9.2 USING RESEARCH AS SUPPORT

In public speaking, the word "**support**" refers to a range of strategies that are used to develop the central idea and specific purpose by providing corroborating evidence. Whether you are speaking to inform, persuade, or entertain, using support helps you create a more substantive and polished speech. We sometimes use the words "support" or "evidence" synonymously or interchangeably because both are designed to help ground a speech's specific purpose. However, "evidence" tends to be associated specifically with persuasive speeches, so we opt to use the more general term "support" for most of this chapter. In this section, we are going to explore why speakers use support.

Why We Use Support

Speakers use support to help provide a foundation for their message. You can think of support as the legs on a table. Without the legs, the table becomes a slab of wood or glass lying on the ground; as such, it cannot fully serve the purpose of a table. In the same way, without support, a speech is nothing more than fluff. Audience members may ignore the speech's message, dismissing it as just so much hot air. In addition to being the foundation that a speech stands on, support also helps us clarify content, increase speaker credibility, and make the speech more vivid.

To Clarify Content

The first reason to use support in a speech is to clarify content. Speakers often choose a piece of support because a previous writer or speaker has phrased something in a way that evokes a clear mental picture of the point they want to make. For example, suppose you're preparing a speech about hazing in college fraternities. You may read your school's code of student conduct to find out how your campus defines hazing. You could use this definition to make sure your audience understands what hazing is and what types of behaviors your campus identifies as hazing.

To Add Credibility

Another important reason to use support is because it adds to your credibility as a speaker. The less an audience perceives you as an expert on a given topic, the more important it is to use a range of support. By doing so, you let your audience know that you've done your homework on the topic.

At the same time, you could hurt your credibility if you use inadequate support or support from questionable sources. Your credibility will also suffer if you distort the intent of a source to try to force it to support a point that the previous author did not address. For example, the famous 1798 publication by Thomas Malthus, An Essay on the Principle of Population, has been used as support for various arguments far beyond what Malthus could have intended. Malthus's thesis was that as the human population increases at a greater rate than food production, societies will go to war over scarce food resources (Malthus, 1798). Some modern writers have suggested that, according to the Malthusian line of thinking, almost anything that leads to a food shortage could lead to nuclear war. For example, better health care leads to longer life spans, which leads to an increased need for food, leading to food shortages, which lead to nuclear war. Clearly, this argument makes some giant leaps of logic that would be hard for an audience to accept.

For this reason, it is important to evaluate your support to ensure that it will not detract from your credibility as a speaker. Here are four characteristics to evaluate when looking at support options: accuracy, authority, currency, and objectivity.

Accuracy

One of the quickest ways to lose credibility in the eyes of your audience is to use support that is inaccurate or even questionably accurate. Admittedly, determining the accuracy of support can be difficult if you are not an expert in a given area, but here are some questions to ask yourself to help assess a source's accuracy:

Does the information within one piece of supporting evidence completely contradict other supporting evidence you've seen?

If the support is using a statistic, does the supporting evidence explain where that statistic came from and how it was determined?

Does the logic behind the support make sense?

One of this book's authors recently observed a speech in which a student said, "The amount of pollution produced by using paper towels instead of hand dryers is equivalent to driving a car from the east coast to St. Louis." The other students in the class, as well as the instructor, recognized that this information sounded wrong and asked questions about the information source, the amount of time it would take to produce this much pollution, and the number of hand dryers used. The audience demonstrated strong listening skills by questioning the information, but the speaker lost credibility by being unable to answer their questions.

Authority

The second way to use support in building your credibility is to cite authoritative sources—those who are experts on the topic. In today's world, there are all kinds of people who call themselves "experts" on a range of topics. There are even books that tell you how to get people to regard you as an expert in a given industry (Lizotte, 2007). Today there are "experts" on every street corner or website spouting off information that some listeners will view as legitimate.

So what truly makes someone an expert? Bruce D. Weinstein, a professor at West Virginia University's Center for Health Ethics and Law, defined **expertise** as having two senses. In his definition, the first sense of expertise is "knowledge in or about a particular field, and statements about it generally take the form, 'S is an expert in or about D.'... The second sense of expertise refers to domains of demonstrable skills, and statements about it generally take the form, 'S is an expert at skill D (Weinstein, 1993).'" Thus, to be an expert, someone needs to have considerable knowledge on a topic or considerable skill in accomplishing something.

As a novice researcher, how can you determine whether an individual is truly an expert? Unfortunately, there is no clear-cut way to wade through the masses of "experts" and determine each one's legitimacy quickly. However, Table 9.1 "Who Is an Expert?" presents a list of questions based on the research of Marie-Line Germain that you can ask yourself to help determine whether someone is an expert (Germain, 2006).

You don't have to answer "yes" to all the preceding questions to conclude that a source is credible, but a string of "no" answers should be a warning signal. In a *Columbia Journalism Review* article, Allisa Quart raised the question of expert credibility regarding the sensitive subject of autism. Specifically, Quart questioned whether the celebrity spokesperson and autism advocate Jennifer McCarthy (http://www.generationrescue.org/) qualifies as an expert. Quart notes that McCarthy "insists that vaccines caused her son's neurological disorder, a claim that has near-zero support in scientific literature" (Quart, 2010). Providing an opposing view is a widely read blog called *Respectful Insolence* (http://scienceblogs.com/

insolence/), whose author is allegedly a surgeon/scientist who often speaks out about autism and "antivaccination lunacy." Respectful Insolence received the 2008 Best Weblog Award from *MedGagdet: The Internet Journal of Emerging Medical Technologies*. We used the word "allegedly" when referring to the author of *Respectful Insolence* because as the website explains that the author's name, Orac, is the "*nom de* blog of a (not so) humble pseudonymous surgeon/scientist with an ego just big enough to delude himself that someone, somewhere might actually give a rodent's posterior about his miscellaneous verbal meanderings, but just barely small enough to admit to himself that few will" (ScienceBlogs LLC).

When comparing the celebrity Jenny McCarthy to the blogger Orac, who do you think is the better expert? Were you able to answer "yes" to the questions in the graphic above for both "experts"? If not, why not? Overall, determining the authority of support is clearly a complicated task, and one that you should spend time thinking about as you prepare the support for your speech.

Currency

The third consideration in using support to build your credibility is how current the information is. Some ideas stay fairly consistent over time, like the date of the Japanese attack on Pearl Harbor or the mathematical formula for finding the area of a circle, but other ideas change wildly in a short period of time, including ideas about technology, health treatments, and laws.

Although we never want to discount classic supporting information that has withstood the test of time, as a general rule for most topics, we recommend that information be less than five years old. Obviously, this is just a general guideline and can change depending on the topic. If you're giving a speech on the history of mining in West Virginia, then you may use support from sources that are much older. However, if you're discussing a medical topic, then your support information should probably be from the past five years or less. Some industries change even faster, so the best support may come from the past month. For example, if are speaking about advances in word processing, using information about Microsoft Word from 2003 would be woefully out-of-date because two upgrades have been released since 2003 (2007 and 2010). As a credible speaker, it is your responsibility to give your audience up-to-date information.

Objectivity

The last question you should ask yourself when examining support is whether the person or organization behind the information is objective or biased. **Bias** refers to a predisposition or preconception of a topic that prevents impartiality. Although there is a certain logic to the view that every one of us is innately biased, as a credible speaker, you want to avoid just passing along someone's unfounded bias in your speech. Ideally you would use support that is unbiased; the graphic below provides some questions to ask yourself when evaluating a potential piece of support to detect bias.

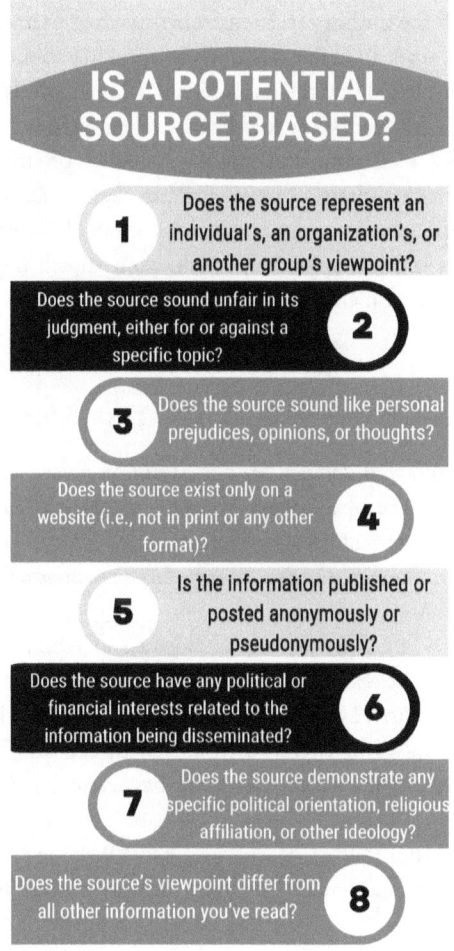

As with the questions in the graphic covering "Who is an Expert?" about expertise, you don't have to have all "no" or "yes" responses to decide on bias. However, being aware of the possibility of bias and where your audience might see bias will help you to select the best possible support to include in your speech.

To Add Vividness

In addition to clarifying content and enhancing credibility, support helps make a speech more vivid. **Vividness** refers to a speaker's ability to present information in a striking, exciting manner. The goal of vividness is to make your speech more memorable. One of the authors still remembers a vivid example from a student speech given several years ago. The student was speaking about the importance of wearing seat belts and stated that the impact from hitting a windshield at just twenty miles per hour without a seat belt would be equivalent to falling out of the window of their second-floor classroom and landing face-first on the pavement below. Because they were in that classroom several times each week, students were easily able to visualize the speaker's analogy and it was successful at creating an image that is remembered years later. Support helps make your speech more interesting and memorable to an audience member.

References

Germain, M. L. (2006). *Development and preliminary validation of a psychometric measure of expertise: The generalized expertise measure (GEM)*. (Unpublished doctoral dissertation). Barry University, Florida.

Lizotte, K. (2007). *The expert's edge: Become the go-to authority people turn to every time*. New York, NY: McGraw-Hill.

Malthus, T. R. (1798). *An essay on the principle of population as it affects the future improvement of society, with remarks on the speculations of Mr. Godwin, M. Condorcet, and other writers*. London, England: J. Johnson, in St. Paul's Churchyard.

Quart, A. (2010, July/August). The trouble with experts: The web allows us to question authority in new ways. *Columbia Journalism Review*. Retrieved from http://www.cjr.org.

ScienceBlogs LLC (n.d.). Who (or what) is Orac? [Web log post]. Retrieved from http://scienceblogs.com/insolence/; see also http://scienceblogs.com/insolence/medicine/autism

Weinstein, B. D. (1993). What is an expert? *Theoretical Medicine, 14*, 57–93.

9.3 EXPLORING TYPES OF SUPPORT

Now that we've explained why support is important, let's examine the various types of support that speakers often use within a speech: facts and statistics, definitions, examples, narratives, testimony, and analogies.

Facts and Statistics

A **fact** is a truth that is arrived at through the scientific process. Speakers often support a point or specific purpose by citing facts that their audience may not know. A typical way to introduce a fact orally is "Did you know that...?"

Many of the facts that speakers cite are based on statistics. **Statistics** is the mathematical subfield that gathers, analyzes, and makes inferences about collected data. Data can come in a wide range of forms—the number of people who buy a certain magazine, the average number of telephone calls made in a month, the incidence of a certain disease. Though few people realize it, much of our daily lives are governed by statistics. Everything from seat-belt laws, to the food we eat, to the amount of money public schools receive, to the medications you are prescribed are based on the collection and interpretation of numerical data.

It is important to realize that a public speaking textbook cannot begin to cover statistics in depth. If you plan to do statistical research yourself, or gain an understanding of the intricacies of such research, we strongly recommend taking a basic class in statistics or quantitative research methods. These courses will better prepare you to understand the various statistics you will encounter.

However, even without a background in statistics, finding useful statistical information related to your topic is quite easy. The table below provides a list of some websites where you can find a range of statistical information that may be useful for your speeches.

Statistics-Oriented Websites

Website	Type of Information
http://www.bls.gov/bls/other.htm	Bureau of Labor Statistics provides links to a range of websites for labor issues related to a vast range of countries.
http://bjs.gov	Bureau of Justice Statistics provides information on crime statistics in the United States.
http://www.census.gov	US Census Bureau provides a wide range of information about people living in the United States.
https://www.cdc.gov/nchs/	National Center for Health Statistics is a program conducted by the US Centers for Disease Control and Prevention. It provides information on a range of health issues in the United States.
http://www.stats.org	STATS is a nonprofit organization that helps people understand quantitative data. It also provides a range of data on its website.
http://ropercenter.cornell.edu/	Roper Center for Public Opinion provides data related to a range of issues in the United States.
http://www.nielsen.com	Nielsen provides data on consumer use of various media forms.
http://www.gallup.com	Gallup provides public opinion data on a range of social and political issues in the United States and around the world.
http://www.adherents.com	Adherents provides both domestic and international data related to religious affiliation.
http://people-press.org	Pew Research Center provides public opinion data on a range of social and political issues in the United States and around the world.

Statistics are probably the most used—and misused—form of support in any type of speaking. People like numbers. People are impressed by numbers. However, most people do not know how to correctly interpret numbers. Unfortunately, there are many speakers who do not know how to interpret them either or who intentionally manipulate them to mislead their listeners. As the saying popularized by Mark Twain goes, "There are three kinds of lies: lies, damned lies, and statistics" (Twain, 1924).

To avoid misusing statistics when you speak in public, do three things. First, be honest with yourself and your audience. If you are distorting a statistic or leaving out other statistics that contradict your point, you are not living up to the level of honesty your audience is entitled to expect. Second, run a few basic calculations to see if a statistic is believable. Sometimes a source may contain a mistake—for example, a decimal point may be in the wrong place or a verbal expression like "increased by 50 percent" may conflict with data showing an increase of 100 percent. Third, evaluate sources (even those in the table above which are generally reputable) according to the criteria discussed earlier in the chapter: accuracy, authority, currency, and objectivity.

Definitions

Imagine that you gave a speech about the use of presidential veto and your audience did not know the meaning of the word "veto." In order for your speech to be effective, you would need to define what a veto is and what it does. Making sure everyone is "on the same page" is a fundamental task of any communication. As speakers, we often need to clearly define what we are talking about to make sure that our audience understands our meaning. The goal of a definition is to help speakers communicate a word or idea in a manner that makes it understandable for their audiences. For the purposes of public speaking, there are four different types of definitions that may be used as support: lexical, persuasive, stipulative, and theoretical.

Lexical Definitions

A **lexical definition** is one that specifically states how a word is used within a specific language. For example, if you go to Dictionary.com and type in the word "speech," here is the lexical definition you will receive:

> **Speech**
> –noun
>   the faculty or power of speaking; oral communication; ability to express one's thoughts and emotions by speech sounds and gesture: *Losing her speech made her feel isolated from humanity.*
>   the act of speaking: *He expresses himself better in speech than in writing.*

something that is spoken; an utterance, remark, or declaration: *We waited for some speech that would indicate her true feelings.*

a form of communication in spoken language, made by a speaker before an audience for a given purpose: a fiery speech.

any single utterance of an actor in the course of a play, motion picture, etc.

the form of utterance characteristic of a particular people or region; a language or dialect.

manner of speaking, as of a person: *Your slovenly speech is holding back your career.*

a field of study devoted to the theory and practice of oral communication.

Lexical definitions are useful when a word may be unfamiliar to an audience and you want to ensure that the audience has a basic understanding of the word. However, our ability to understand lexical definitions often hinges on our knowledge of other words that are used in the definition, so it is usually a good idea to follow a lexical definition with a clear explanation of what it means in your own words.

Persuasive Definitions

Persuasive definitions are designed to motivate an audience to think in a specific manner about the word or term. Political figures are often very good at defining terms in a way that are persuasive. Frank Luntz, a linguist and political strategist, is widely regarded as one of the most effective creators of persuasive definitions (Luntz, 2007). Luntz has the ability to take terms that people don't like and repackage them into persuasive definitions that give the original term a much more positive feel. Here are some of Luntz's more famous persuasive definitions:

Oil drilling → energy exploration
Estate tax → death tax
School vouchers → opportunity scholarships
Eavesdropping → electronic intercepts
Global warming → climate change

Luntz has essentially defined the terms in a new way that has a clear political bent and that may make the term more acceptable to some audiences, especially those who do not question the lexical meaning of the new term. For example, "oil drilling" may have negative connotations among citizens who are concerned about the environmental impact of drilling, whereas "energy exploration" may have much more positive connotations among the same group.

Stipulative Definitions

A **stipulative definition** is a definition assigned to a word or term by the person who coins that word or term for the first time. In 1969, Laurence Peter and Raymond Hull wrote a book called The Peter Principle: Why Things Always Go Wrong. In this book, they defined the "Peter Principle" as "In a Hierarchy Every Employee Tends to Rise to His [sic] Level of Incompetence" (Peter & Hull, 1969). Because Peter and Hull coined the term "Peter Principle," it was up to them to define the term as they saw fit. You cannot argue with this definition; it simply is the definition that was stipulated.

Theoretical Definitions

Theoretical definitions are used to describe all parts related to a particular type of idea or object. Admittedly, these definitions are frequently ambiguous and difficult to fully comprehend. For example, if you attempted to define the word "peace" in a manner that could be used to describe all aspects of peace, then you would be using a theoretical definition. These definitions are considered theoretical because the definitions attempt to create an all-encompassing theory of the word itself.

In an interpersonal communication course, one of our coauthors asked a group of random people online to define the term "falling in love." Here are some of the theoretical definitions they provided:

> I think falling in love would be the act of feeling attracted to a person, with mutual respect given to each other, a strong desire to be close and near a person,...and more.

> Being content with the person you are with and missing them every minute they are gone.

> Um...falling in love is finding a guy with lots of credit cards and no balances owing.

> Falling in love is when you take away the feeling, the passion, and the romance in a relationship and find out you still care for that person.

> Meeting someone who makes your heart sing.

> Skydiving for someone's lips.

Definitions are important to provide clarity for your audience. Effective speakers strike a balance between using definitions where they are needed to increase audience understanding and leaving out definitions of terms that the audience is likely to know. For example, you may need to define what a "claw hammer" is when speaking to a group of Cub Scouts learning about basic tools, but you would appear foolish—or even condescending—if you defined it in a speech to a group of carpenters who use claw hammers every day. On the other hand, just assuming that others know the terms you are using can lead to ineffective communication as well. Medical doctors are often criticized for using technical terms while talking to their patients without taking time to define those terms. Patients may then walk away not really understanding what their health situation is or what needs to be done about it.

Examples

Another often-used type of support is examples. An example is a specific situation, problem, or story designed to help illustrate a principle, method, or phenomenon. Examples are useful because they can help make an abstract idea more concrete for an audience by providing a specific case. Let's examine four common types of examples used as support: positive, negative, nonexamples, and best examples.

Positive Examples

A **positive example** is used to clarify or clearly illustrate a principle, method, or phenomenon. A speaker discussing crisis management could talk about how a local politician handled herself when a local newspaper reported that her husband was having an affair or give an example of a professional baseball player who immediately came clean about steroid use. These examples would provide a positive model for how a corporation in the first instance, and an individual in the second instance, should behave in crisis management. The purpose of a positive example is to show a desirable solution, decision, or course of action.

Negative Examples

Negative examples, by contrast, are used to illustrate what not to do. On the same theme of crisis management, a speaker could discuss the lack of communication from Union Carbide during the 1984 tragedy in Bhopal, India, or the many problems with how the US government responded to Hurricane Katrina in 2005. The purpose of a negative example is to show an undesirable solution, decision, or course of action.

Nonexamples

A **nonexample** is used to explain what something is not. On the subject of crisis management, you might mention a press release for a new Adobe Acrobat software upgrade as an example of corporate communication that is not crisis management. The press release nonexample helps the audience differentiate between crisis management and other forms of corporate communication.

Best Examples

The final type of example is called the **best example** because it is held up as the "best" way someone should behave within a specific context. On the crisis management theme, a speaker could show a clip of an effective CEO speaking during a press conference to show how one should behave both verbally and nonverbally during a crisis. While positive examples show appropriate ways to behave, best examples illustrate the best way to behave in a specific context.

Although examples can be very effective at helping an audience to understand abstract or unfamiliar concepts, they do have one major drawback: some audience members may dismiss them as unusual cases that do not represent what happens most of the time. For example, some opponents of wearing seat belts claim that not wearing your seat belt can help you be thrown from a car and save you from fire or other hazards in the wrecked automobile. Even if a speaker has a specific example of an accident where this was true, many audience members would see this example as a rare case and thus not view it as strong support.

Simply finding an example to use, then, is not enough. An effective speaker needs to consider how the audience will respond to the example and how the example fits with what else the audience knows, as discussed under the heading of accuracy earlier in this chapter.

Narratives

A fourth form of support are **narratives**, or stories that help an audience understand the speaker's message. Narratives are similar to examples except that narratives are generally longer and take on the form of a story with a clear arc (beginning, middle, and end). People like stories. In fact, narratives are so important that communication scholar Walter Fisher believes humans are innately storytelling animals, so appealing to people through stories is a great way to support one's speech (Fisher, 1987).

However, you have an ethical responsibility as a speaker to clearly identify whether the narrative you are sharing is real or hypothetical. In 1981, Washington Post reporter Janet Cooke was awarded a Pulitzer Prize for her story of an eight-year-old heroin addict (Cooke, 1980). After acknowledging that her story was a fake, she lost her job and the prize was rescinded (Green, 1981). In 2009, Louisiana Governor Bobby Jindal gave a nationally televised speech where he recounted a story of his interaction with a local sheriff in getting help for Hurricane Katrina victims. His story was later found to be false; Jindal admitted that he had heard the sheriff tell the story after it happened but he had not really been present at the time (Finch, 2009).

Obviously, we are advocating that you select narratives that are truthful when you use this form of support in a speech. Clella Jaffe explains that narratives are a fundamental part of public speaking and that narratives can be used for support in all three general purposes of speaking: informative, persuasive, and entertaining (Jaffe, 2010).

Informative Narratives

Jaffe defines **informative narratives** as those that provide information or explanations about a speaker's topic (Jaffe, 2010). Informative narratives can help audiences understand nature and natural phenomena, for example. Often the most complicated science and mathematical issues in our world can be understood through the use of story. While many people may not know all the mathematics behind gravity, most of us have grown up with the story of how Sir Isaac Newton was hit on the head by an apple and developed the theory of gravity. Even if the story is not precisely accurate, it serves as a way to help people grasp the basic concept of gravity.

Persuasive Narratives

Persuasive narratives are stories used to persuade people to accept or reject a specific attitude, value, belief, or behavior. Religious texts are filled with persuasive narratives designed to teach followers various attitudes, values, beliefs, and behaviors. Parables or fables are designed to teach people basic lessons about life. For example, read the following fable from Aesop (http://www.aesopfables.com): "One winter a farmer found a snake stiff and frozen with cold. He had compassion on it, and taking it up, placed it in his bosom. The Snake was quickly revived by the warmth, and resuming its natural instincts, bit its benefactor, inflicting on him a mortal wound. 'Oh,' cried the Farmer with his last breath, 'I am rightly served for pitying a scoundrel.'" This persuasive narrative is designed to warn people that just because you help someone in need doesn't mean the other person will respond in kind.

Entertaining Narratives

Entertaining narratives are stories designed purely to delight an audience and transport them from their daily concerns. Some professional speakers make a very good career by telling their own stories of success or how they overcame life's adversities. Comedians such as Jeff Foxworthy tell stories that are ostensibly about their own lives in a manner designed to make the audience laugh. While entertaining narratives may be a lot of fun, people should use them sparingly as support for a more serious topic or for a traditional informative or persuasive speech.

Testimony

Another form of support you may employ during a speech is testimony. When we use the word "testimony" in this text, we are specifically referring to expert opinion or direct accounts of witnesses to provide support for your speech. Notice that within this definition, we refer to both expert and eyewitness testimony.

Expert Testimony

Expert testimony accompanies the discussion we had earlier in this chapter related to what qualifies someone as an expert. In essence, **expert testimony** expresses the attitudes, values, beliefs, or behaviors recommended by someone who is an acknowledged expert on a topic. For example, imagine that you're going to give a speech on why physical education should be mandatory for all grades K–12 in public schools. During the course of your research, you come across The Surgeon General's Vision for a Fit and Healthy Nation (http://www.surgeongeneral.gov/library/obesityvision/obesityvision2010.pdf). You might decide to cite information from within the report written by US Surgeon General Dr. Regina Benjamin about her strategies for combating the problem of childhood obesity within the United States. If so, you are using the words from Dr. Benjamin, as a noted expert on the subject, to support your speech's basic premise. Her expertise is being used to give credibility to your claims.

Eyewitness Testimony

Eyewitness testimony, on the other hand, is given by someone who has direct contact with the phenomenon of your speech topic. Imagine that you are giving a speech on the effects of the 2010 "Deepwater Horizon" disaster in the Gulf of Mexico. Perhaps one of your friends happened to be on a flight that passed over the Gulf of Mexico and the pilot pointed out where the platform was. You could tell your listeners about your friend's testimony of what she saw as she was flying over the spill.

However, using eyewitness testimony as support can be a little tricky because you are relying on someone's firsthand account, and firsthand accounts may not always be reliable. As such, you evaluate the credibility of your witness and the recency of the testimony.

To evaluate your witness's credibility, you should first consider how you received the testimony. Did you ask the person for the testimony, or did he or she give you the information without being asked? Second, consider whether your witness has anything to gain from his or her testimony. Basically, you want to know that your witness isn't biased.

Second, consider whether your witness' account was recent or something that happened some time ago. With a situation like the BP oil spill, the date when the spill was seen from the air makes a big difference. If the witness saw the oil spill when the oil was still localized, he or she could not have seen the eventual scope of the disaster.

Overall, the more detail you can give about the witness and when the witness made his or her observation, the more useful that witness testimony will be when attempting to create a solid argument. However, never rely completely on eyewitness testimony because this form of support is not always the most reliable and may still be perceived as biased by a segment of your audience.

Analogies

An analogy is a figure of speech that compares two ideas or objects, showing how they are similar in some way. Analogies, for public speaking purposes, can also be based in logic. The logical notion of analogies starts with the idea that two ideas or objects are similar, and because of this similarity, the two ideas or objects must be similar in other ways as well. There are two different types of analogies that speakers can employ: figurative and literal.

Figurative Analogies

Figurative analogies compare two ideas or objects from two different classes. For the purposes of understanding analogies, a "class" refers to a group that has common attributes, characteristics, qualities, or traits. For example, you can compare a new airplane to an eagle. In this case, airplanes and eagles clearly are not the same type of objects. While both may have the ability to fly, airplanes are made by humans and eagles exist in nature.

Alternatively, you could attempt to compare ideas such as the struggle of The Church of Reality (http://www.churchofreality.org/wisdom/welcome_home/, a group that sees the use of marijuana as a religious sacrament) to the struggle of the civil rights movement. Is a church's attempt to get marijuana legalized truly the same as the 1960s civil rights movement? Probably not, in most people's view, as fighting for human rights is not typically seen as equivalent to being able to use a controlled substance.

Figurative analogies are innately problematic because people often hear them and immediately dismiss them as far-fetched. While figurative analogies may be very vivid and help a listener create a mental picture, they do not really help a listener determine the validity of the information being presented. Furthermore, speakers often overly rely on figurative analogies when they really don't have any other solid evidence. Overall, while figurative analogies may be useful, we recommend solidifying them with other, more tangible support.

Literal Analogies

Literal analogies, on the other hand, compare two objects or ideas that clearly belong to the same class. The goal of the literal analogy is to demonstrate that the two objects or ideas are similar; therefore, they should have further similarities that support your argument. For example, maybe you're giving a speech on a new fast-food brand that you think will be a great investment. You could easily compare that new fast-food brand to preexisting brands like McDonald's, Subway, or Taco Bell. If you can show that the new start-up brand functions similarly to other brands, you can use that logic to suggest that the new brand will also have the same kind of success as the existing brands.

When using literal analogies related to ideas, make sure that the ideas are closely related and can be viewed as similar. For example, take the Church of Reality discussed above. You could compare the Church of Reality's use of marijuana to the Native American Church's legal exemption to use peyote in its religious practices. In this instance, comparing two different religious groups' use of illegal drugs and demonstrating that one has legal exemption supports the idea that the other should have an exemption, too.

As with figurative analogies, make sure that the audience can see a reasonable connection between the two ideas or objects being compared. If your audience sees your new fast-food brand as very different from McDonald's or Subway, then they will not accept your analogy. You are basically asking your audience to confirm the logic of your comparison, so if they don't see the comparison as valid, it won't help to support your message.

References

Cooke, J. (1980, September 28). Jimmy's world. *The Washington Post*, p. A1.

Finch, S. (2009, Feb 27). Bobby Jindal's fishy Katrina story. *Daily Kos*. Retrieved from http://www.dailykos.com/story/2009/02/27/702671/-Bobby-Jindals-Fishy-Katrina-Story

Fisher, W. R. (1987). *Human communication as narration: Toward a philosophy of reason, value, and action*. Columbia, SC: University of South Carolina Press.

Green, B. (1981, April 19). The confession: At the end, there were the questions, then the tears. *The Washington Post*, p. A14.

Jaffe, C. (2010). *Public speaking: Concepts and skills for a diverse society* (6th ed.). Boston, MA: Cengage.

Luntz, F. (2007). *Words that work: It's not what you say, it's what people hear*. New York, NY: Hyperion.

Peter, L. J., & Hull, R. (1969). *The Peter principle: Why things always go wrong*. New York, NY: William Morrow & Company, p. 15.

Twain, M. (1924). *Autobiography* (Vol. 1). New York, NY: Harper & Bros., p. 538.

9.4 USING SUPPORT AND CREATING ARGUMENTS

Supporting one's ideas with a range of facts and statistics, definitions, examples, narratives, testimony, and analogies can make the difference between a boring speech your audience will soon forget and one that has a lasting effect on their lives.

Although the research process is designed to help you find effective support, you still need to think through how you will use the support you have accumulated. In this section, we will examine how to use support effectively in one's speech, first by examining the types of support one needs in a speech and then by seeing how support can be used to enhance one's argument.

Understanding Arguments

You may associate the word "argument" with a situation in which two people are having some kind of conflict. But in this context we are using a definition for the word **argument** that goes back to the ancient Greeks, who saw arguments as a set of logical premises leading to a clear conclusion. While we lack the time for an entire treatise on the nature and study of arguments, we do want to highlight some of the basic principles in argumentation.

First, all arguments are based on a series of statements that are divided into two basic categories: premises and conclusions. A **premise** is a statement that is designed to provide support or evidence, whereas the **conclusion** is a statement that can be clearly drawn from the provided premises. Let's look at an example and then explain this in more detail:

> Premise 1: Eating fast food has been linked to childhood obesity.
>
> Premise 2: Childhood obesity is clearly linked to early onset type 2 diabetes, which can have many negative health ramifications.
>
> Conclusion: Therefore, for children to avoid developing early onset type 2 diabetes, they must have their fast-food intake limited.

In this example, the first two statements are premises linking fast food to childhood obesity to diabetes. Once we've made this logical connection, we can then provide a logical conclusion that one important way of preventing type 2 diabetes is to limit, if not eliminate, fast food from children's diets. While this may not necessary be a popular notion for many people, the argument itself is logically sound.

How, then, does this ultimately matter for you and your future public speaking endeavors? Well, a great deal of persuasive speaking is built on creating arguments that your listeners can understand and that will eventually influence their ideas or behaviors. In essence, creating strong arguments is a fundamental part of public speaking.

Now, in the example above, we are clearly missing one important part of the argument process—support or evidence. So far we have presented two premises that many people may believe, but we need support or evidence for those premises if we are going to persuade people who do not already believe those statements. As such, when creating logical arguments (unless you are a noted expert on a subject), you must provide support to ensure that your arguments will be seen as credible. And that is what we will discuss next.

Sifting Through Your Support

When researching a topic, you're going to find a range of different types of supporting evidence. You may find examples of all six types of support: facts and statistics, definitions, examples, narratives, testimony, and analogies. Sooner or later, you are going to have to make some decisions as to which pieces of support you will use and which you won't. While there is no one way to select your support, here are some helpful suggestions.

Use a Variety of Support Types

One of the most important parts of using support is variety. Nothing will kill a speech faster than if you use the same type of support over and over again. Try to use as much support as needed to make your point without going overboard. You might decide to begin with a couple of definitions and rely on a gripping piece of eyewitness testimony as your other major support. Or you might use a combination of facts, examples, and narratives. In another case, statistics and examples might be most effective. Audience members are likely to have different preferences for support; some may like statistics while others really find narratives compelling. By using a variety of forms of support, you are likely to appeal to a broader range of audience members and thus effectively adapt to your audience. Even if your audience members prefer a specific form of support, providing multiple types of support is important to keep them interested. To use an analogy, even people who love ice cream would get tired of it if they ate only ice cream every day for a week, so variety is important.

Choose Appropriate Forms of Support

Depending on the type of speech you are giving, your speech's context, and your audience, different types of evidence may or may not be appropriate. While speeches using precise lexical definitions may be useful for the courtroom, they may not be useful in an after-dinner speech to entertain. At the same time, entertaining narratives may be great for a speech whose general purpose is to entertain, but may decrease a speaker's credibility when attempting to persuade an audience about a serious topic.

Check for Relevance

Another consideration about potential support is whether or not it is relevant. Each piece of supporting material you select needs to support the specific purpose of your speech. You may find the coolest quotation, but if that quotation doesn't really help your core argument in your speech, you need to leave it out. If you start using too many irrelevant support sources, your audience will quickly catch on and your credibility will drop through the floor.

Your support materials should be relevant not only to your topic but also to your audience. If you are giving a speech to an audience of sixty-year-olds, you may be able to begin with "Think back to where you were when you heard that President Kennedy had been shot," but this would be meaningless with an audience of twenty-five-year-olds. Similarly, references to music download sites or the latest popular band may not be effective with audiences who are not interested in music.

Don't Go Overboard

In addition to being relevant, supporting materials need to help you support your speech's specific purpose without interfering with your speech. You may find three different sources that support your speech's purpose in the same way. If that happens, you shouldn't include all three forms of support. Instead, pick the form of support that is the most beneficial for your speech. Remember, the goal is to support your speech, not to have the support become your speech.

Don't Manipulate Your Support

The last factor related to shifting through your support involves a very important ethical area called **support-manipulation**. Often speakers will attempt to find support that says exactly what they want it to say despite the fact that the overwhelming majority of evidence says the exact opposite. When you go out of your way to pull the wool over your audience's eyes, you are being unethical and not treating your audience with respect. Here are some very important guidelines to consider to avoiding support-manipulation:

- Do not overlook significant factors or individuals related to your topic.
- Do not ignore evidence that does not support your speech's specific purpose.
- Do not jump to conclusions that are simply not justified based on the supporting evidence you have.
- Do not use evidence to support faulty logic.
- Do not use out-of-date evidence that is no longer supported.
- Do not use evidence out of its original context.
- Do not knowingly use evidence from a source that is clearly biased.
- Make sure you clearly cite all your supporting evidence within your speech.

Using Support within Your Speech

Now that we've described ways to sift through your evidence, it's important to discuss how to use your evidence within your speech. In the previous sections of this chapter, we've talked about the various types of support you can use (facts and statistics, definitions, examples, narratives, testimonies, and analogies). In this section, we're going to examine how these types of evidence are actually used within a speech. Then we will discuss ways to think through the support you need for a speech and also how to actually use support while speaking.

Forms of Speech Support

Let's begin by examining the forms that support can take in a speech: quotations, paraphrases, summaries, numerical support, and pictographic support.

Quotations

The first common form of support utilized in a speech is direct quotation. **Direct quotations** occur when Speaker A uses the exact wording by another speaker or writer within his or her new speech. Quotations are very helpful and can definitely provide you a tool for supporting your speech's specific purpose. Here are five tips for using quotations within a speech:

1. Use a direct quotation if the original author's words are witty, engaging, distinct, or particularly vivid.
2. Use a direct quotation if you want to highlight a specific expert and his or her expertise within your speech.
3. Use a direct quotation if you are going to specifically analyze something that is said within the quotation. If your analysis depends on the exact wording of the quotation, then it is important to use the quotation.

4. Keep quotations to a minimum. One of the biggest mistakes some speakers make is just stringing together a series of quotations and calling it a speech. Remember, a speech is your unique insight into a topic, not just a series of quotations.
5. Keep quotations short. Long quotations can lose an audience, and the connection between your support and your argument can get lost.

Paraphrases

The second form support takes on during a speech is paraphrasing. **Paraphrasing** involves taking the general idea or theme from another speaker or author and condensing the idea or theme in your own words. A mistake that some speakers make is dropping a couple of words or rearranging some words within a direct quotation and thinking that is a paraphrase. When paraphrasing you need to understand the other speaker or author's ideas well enough to relate them without looking back at the original. Here are four tips for using paraphrases in your speeches:

1. Paraphrase when you can say it more concisely than the original speaker or author.
2. Paraphrase when the exact wording from the original speaker or author won't improve your audience's understanding of the support.
3. Paraphrase when you want to adapt an example, analogy, or narrative by another speaker or author to make its relevance more evident.
4. Paraphrase information that is not likely to be questioned by your audience. If you think your audience may question your support, then relying on a direct quotation may be more effective.

Summaries

Whereas quotations and paraphrases are taking a whole text and singling out a couple of lines or a section, a **summary** involves condensing or encapsulating the entire text as a form of support. Summaries are helpful when you want to clearly spell out the intent behind a speaker's or author's text. Here are three suggestions for using summaries within your speech.

1. Summarize when you need another speaker or author's complete argument to understand the argument within your speech.
2. Summarize when explaining possible counterarguments to the one posed within your speech.
3. Summarize when you need to cite a number of different sources effectively and

efficiently to support a specific argument.

Numerical Support

Speakers often have a need to use **numerical support**, or citing data and numbers within a speech. The most common reason for using numerical support comes when a speaker needs to cite statistics. When using data to support your speech, you need to make sure that your audience can accurately interpret the numbers in the same way you are doing. Here are three tips for using numerical support:

1. Clearly state the numbers used and where they came from.
2. Make sure you explain what the numbers mean and how you think they should be interpreted.
3. If the numbers are overly complicated or if you use a variety of numbers within a speech, consider turning this support into a visual aid to enhance your audience's understanding of the numerical support.

Pictographic Support

The last form of support commonly used in speeches we label pictographic support, but it is more commonly referred to as visual aids. **Pictographic support** is any drawn or visual representation of an object or process. For the purposes of this chapter, we call visual aids pictographic support in order to stress that we are using images as a form of support taken from a source. For example, if you're giving a speech on how to swing a golf club, you could bring in a golf club and demonstrate exactly how to use the golf club. While the golf club in this instance is a visual aid, it is not pictographic support. If you showed a diagram illustrating the steps for an effective golf swing, the diagram is an example of pictographic support. So while all forms of pictographic support are visual aids, not all visual aids are pictographic support. Here are five suggestions for effectively using pictographic support in your speech:

1. Use pictographic support when it would be easier and shorter than orally explaining an object or process.
2. Use pictographic support when you really want to emphasize the importance of the support. Audiences recall information more readily when they both see and hear it than if they see or hear the information.
3. Make sure that pictographic support is aesthetically pleasing.
4. Pictographic support should be easy to understand, and it should take less time to use than words alone.

5. Make sure everyone in your audience can easily see your pictographic support. If listeners cannot see it, then it will not help them understand how it is supposed to help your speech's specific purpose.

Is Your Support Adequate?

Now that we've examined the ways to use support in your speech, how do you know if you have enough support?

Use a Reverse Outline

One recommendation we have for selecting the appropriate support for your speech is what we call a reverse outline. A **reverse outline** is a tool you can use to determine the adequacy of your speech's support by starting with your conclusion and logically working backward through your speech to determine if the support you provided is appropriate and comprehensive. In essence, we recommend that you think of your speech in terms of the conclusion first and then work your way backward showing how you get to the conclusion. By forcing yourself to think about logic in reverse, you're more likely to find missteps along the way. This technique is not only helpful for analyzing the overall flow of your speech, but it can also let you see if different sections of your speech are not completely supported individually.

Support Your Claims

When selecting the different types of support for your speech, you need to make sure that every claim you make within the speech can be supported within the speech. For example, if you state, "The majority of Americans want immigration reform," you need to make sure that you have a source that actually says this. As noted at the beginning of this chapter, too often people make claims within a speech that they have no support for whatsoever. When you go through your speech, you need to make sure that each and every claim that you make is adequately supported by the evidence you have selected to use within the speech.

Oral Presentation

Finally, after you have selected and evaluated your forms of support, it is time to plan how you will present your support orally within your speech. How will you present the information to make it effective? To help you think about using support, we recommend a three-step process: setup, execution, and analysis.

Setup

The first step in using support within a speech is what we call the setup. The **setup** is a sentence or phrase in which you explain to your audience where the information you are using came from. Note that if you found the information on a website, it is not sufficient to merely give your audience the URL. Depending on the source of your support, all the following information could be useful: name of source, location of source, date of source, name of author, and identification of author. First, you need to tell your audience the name of your source. Whether you are using a song or an article from a magazine, you need to tell your audience the name of the person who wrote it and its title. Second, if your source comes from a larger work, you need to include the location of the source. For example, a single article (name of source) may come from a magazine (the location). Third, you need to specify the date of the source. Depending on the type of source you are using, you may need to provide just a year or the day and month as well. You should provide as much information on the date as is provided on the copyright information page of the source.

Thus far we've talked only about the information you need to provide specifically about the source; let's now switch gears and talk about the author. When discussing the author, you need to clearly explain not only who the author is but also why the author is an expert (if appropriate). Some sources are written by authors who are not experts, so you really don't need to explain their expertise. In other cases, your audience will already know why the source is an expert, so there is less need to explain why the source is an expert. For example, if giving a speech on current politics in the United States, you probably do not need to explain the expertise of Barack Obama or John Boehner. However, when you don't provide information on an author's expertise and your audience does not already know why the source is an expert, your audience will question the validity of your support.

Now that we've explained the basic information necessary for using support within a speech, here are two different examples:

> According to Melanie Smithfield in an article titled "Do It Right, or Do It Now," published in the June 18, 2009, issue of *Time Magazine*...
>
> According to Roland Smith, a legendary civil rights activist and former chair of the Civil Rights Defense League, in his 2001 book *The Path of Peace*...

In the first example we have an author who wrote an article in a magazine, and in the second one we have an author of a book. In both cases, we provided the information that was necessary to understand where the source was located. The more information we can provide our audiences about our support, the more information our audiences have to evaluate the strength of our arguments.

Execution

Once we have set up the support, the second part of using support is what we call execution. The **execution** of support involves actually reading a quotation, paraphrasing a speaker or author's words, summarizing a speaker or author's ideas, providing numerical support, or showing pictographic support. Effective execution should be seamless and flow easily within the context of your speech. While you want your evidence to make an impact, you also don't want it to seem overly disjointed. One mistake that some novice public speakers make is that when they start providing evidence, their whole performance changes and the use of evidence looks and sounds awkward. Make sure you practice the execution of your evidence when you rehearse your speech.

Analysis

The final stage of using support effectively is the one which many speakers forget: **analysis** of the support. Too often speakers use support without ever explaining to an audience how they should interpret it. While we don't want to "talk down" to our listeners, audiences often need to be shown the connection between the support provided and the argument made. Here are three basic steps you can take to ensure your audience will make the connection between your support and your argument:

1. Summarize the support in your own words (unless you started with a summary).
2. Specifically tell your audience how the support relates to the argument.
3. Draw a sensible conclusion based on your support. We cannot leave an audience hanging, so drawing a conclusion helps complete the support package.

9.5 ENRICHMENT

Discussion Questions

1. What are the ethical implications of using evidence from biased sources? Is this form of support manipulation?
2. During a 2014 TED Talk, Zak Ebrahim begins his talk with a powerful narrative, the revelation that his father helped plan the 1993 World Trade Center bombing. His audience is gripped from the beginning, as he begins to recount the events of his childhood and the path he took after his father's conviction. Is it an effective strategy to begin your narrative in the peak of the action, before starting at the beginning to explain how you got there?
3. Discuss a time that a narrative made an impact on you during a presentation.

Activities

1. Search, choose and analyze a speech from the top one hundred speeches given during the twentieth century. Write about how this speaker goes through the three-step process for using support.
2. You have been asked to give a speech on child labor laws within the United States. Provide a list of possible examples you could use in your speech. You should have one from each of the four categories: positive, negative, non, and best.
3. Find and analyze a newspaper opposition editorial piece or letter to the editor that takes a position on an issue. Next find an article on the same issue from a general news source. Which types of support does each writer use? How effective and convincing do you think the use of support is for each article? Why?

Case Study

While preparing a speech on the Department of Homeland Security (DHS), Aban runs across a website that has a lot of useful information. The website has numerous articles and links that all discuss the importance of the different functions of the DHS. Being a good speaker, Aban delves into the website to determine the credibility of the information being provided.

Aban quickly realizes that the group sponsoring the website is a fringe-militia group that believes no immigrants should be allowed into the United States. While the information Aban is interested in has nothing to do with immigration, he wonders if all the information provided on the website has been distorted to support the organization's basic cause.

With a group of classmates, discuss the following:

- Should Aban use the useful information about DHS even though the other information on the website is from an extremist group?
- Are all sources on the extremist group's website automatically suspect because of the group's stated anti-immigration stance?
- Is it ethical for Aban to use any of the information from this website?
- If Aban was a friend of yours and he showed you the website, how would you tell him to proceed?

10 INTRODUCTIONS AND CONCLUSIONS

Learning Objectives

- Identify key elements of an effective introduction.
- List methods of grabbing the audience's attention.
- Identify key elements of an effective conclusion.

Learning Objectives

- **Attention-Getter**
- **Brakelight**
- **Character**
- **Competence**
- **Credibility**
- **Note of Finality**
- **Preview**
- **Summary**
- **Thesis**

10.1 INTRODUCTIONS

"Never lose the first impression which has moved you." -Jean-Baptiste-Camille Corot

The very first words out of your mouth when you start a speech create a first impression for the audience that either encourages them to listen or tune out. While this is usually a short part of your presentation, it is important to take your time developing the introduction because you are creating a first impression of yourself and the topic. There are four important tasks that must be accomplished during the first few minutes of a speech. You must:

1. Capture the audience's attention.
2. Self introduce and establish your credibility/ethos.
3. Reveal the topic of the speech through a clear thesis and relate it to the audience.
4. Preview the body of the speech by specifically outlining the main points you

will cover.

Capture the Audience's Attention.

Audience members do not attend a presentation with the intention of losing interest or being bored to tears. Truth be told, audience members do not give a speaker a terribly long time to win them over either. You may only have several sentences and, possibly, a chance to actually introduce the topic of the speech before the audience mentally votes "Yes, I want to listen further " or "No, I'm tuning out and thinking about lunch. " This opening statement is known as an **attention getter**.

Depending on the overall time limit of a presentation, an ideal introduction should last no more than around one or two minutes -and this includes your thesis and preview of your main points. This seems like a long time, but in truth, it is not. Hence, you have a short, yet precious window, to lure your audience and hope to keep them there. Here are top attention-gaining strategies to try in your upcoming speeches:

Ask a Question

Ask insightful, meaningful questions. Better yet, ask a series of questions designed to draw the audience further and further into your speech.

When you ask your audience a question, they have to think. In the process of thinking, they are paying attention. Even if your question does not call for an oral reply, they will be thinking what they would answer if called upon.

> "How many of you would categorize yourselves as 'givers'? How many of you search for the perfect Christmas or birthday gift each year for your best friend or perhaps your Mom? You go all out, right? Then, how many of you have signed up to be an organ donor? Isn't that the ultimate gift? The gift of life?
>
> "How many of you have ever had a couple of glasses of wine while dining with friends, then driven yourself home? Did you ever consider that you might not be 'okay' to 'make it home?' Is it possible that you were over the legal limit?"

Find a Quotation

It could be a historical quote, a humorous one, even a song lyric. Ensure you credit the originator of the quote. Ensure the quote is relevant to your topic. A word of caution here is to be careful to avoid reading to your audience. If you use a quote, it should be impactful and cause your audience to want to hear more. When used effectively, the quote is relatively short and memorized by the speaker.

> "Make sure you have finished speaking before your audience has finished listening. "
> – Dorothy Sarnoff

> "Courage is being scared to death- but saddling up anyway. "
> – John Wayne

Shock the Audience

Use a startling statistic or a shocking statement. Share a personal revelation.

> "During the five minutes of my speech, seven individuals will die of AIDS or HIV-related complications in the world. "
>
> "Statistics show that one in every four women will be assaulted in her lifetime. "
>
> "Today, I want to talk to you about a recent loss I've had. I lost my best friend, my consoler, my buddy who could always be counted on to party all night. I lost all of that when I finally accepted that I am an alcoholic. Six months ago, I gave up alcohol. "

Find a Direct Connection to the Audience

Reference a local event, place, or activity. Use a recent news story, tragedy, or occurrence that your audience would be sure to recall.

> "I'm sure all of you will recall the news story a few months back in which a car went over the Buckman Bridge, sideswiped by a drunk driver. Today, I want to discuss how you can be a defensive driver -and hopefully -save yourself from becoming the next headline. "

Tell a Story

Engage us, draw us in, and make the details of the story vivid and real to us.

> "When I was four years old, I became separated from my parents while visiting the zoo. One minute they were there; the next, they were gone. While you might imagine that I was frightened, I wasn't. I continued to look at the snakes in each display, fascinated. I tagged along with other visitors following the same path, staring in awe at each new exhibit. I certainly didn't realize then what we all know now. How dangerous the world can be for a child alone. "

If you ever listened to a scary story told by a camp counselor at night when all were sitting near a camp fire, you know the power of a good story. Religious leaders know the power of a good story also. That is why they often include Bible stories in their sermons. Plan to tell your audience a story, and you will have them listening as attentively to you as campers listen to a counselor's scary story. Use vivid details; paint a mental picture in the minds of your listeners. You want them to relate -to smell the cookies baking, to see the tears in your Grandmother's eyes, to feel the softness of a baby in your arms.

Find a Compelling Visual Aid

- Poignant, shocking, funny. A picture IS worth a thousand words.
- A photo of a homeless child
- A picture of a crystal clear lake and mountain range
- A cartoon depicting a political news story

Self Introduce and Establish Your Credibility.

An audience may or may not have a preconceived notion about you when you stand before them, but you can bet that your audience will make up its mind about you quickly. Humans are notoriously quick to judge and often form a first impression about a date, a stranger, or a speaker within the first 30 seconds. It becomes imperative, then, for you to introduce yourself and establish your **credibility** after you have grabbed the audience's attention. While some in your audience will form a first impression of you based upon your outfit or your smile, **most will judge your credibility based upon two crucial factors: your perceived competence and character** .

Competence ensures your audience that you know your subject well. You have a strong knowledge base, and you are well prepared to share the topic with your listeners. Reveal your expertise in the introduction, so your audience knows from the beginning that you can be trusted. If you have a special relationship to the topic, either personal or professional or by association, the beginning of your presentation is the time to share that. If you do not have in-depth knowledge of the topic, it's time to hit the books, access the Internet, or talk with the experts. You have the ability to become a minor expert on most any topic by doing some research. Then ensure that your audience knows of your research; they want to know that your information is valid.

A second component of credibility comes from the audience's *assessment of your character*. Can you be trusted? Do you have their best interests at heart? Will the information you provide be useful and relevant to their lives or do you have your own agenda? This aspect of credibility is often referred to as "ethos" -simply the Greek word for character. A great example is the stereotype of a used car salesman. You need a car, but you are not sure which one is right for you and which one you can really afford. The salesman knows all the necessary information -gas consumption, mileage, and accessories. But you just do not trust that s/he has your best interest at heart. Is s/he trying to get rid of a particular car or make more commission? Is the car you are being shown best for you or best for the salesman? While you feel confident of the salesperson's competence, you are doubtful of his/her character. It is important that you show your audience that you are credible in both areas (Banks).

Reveal the Topic of the Speech Through a Thesis Statement & Preview the Body of the Speech.

After you grab your audience's attention and before you reach the actual body of the speech, you will reveal your **thesis** statement. Remember, a thesis statement is a singular thought that tells the audience what the speech is about. It should be a strong, single, declarative sentence that captures the main point of your presentation. For example, if you are giving an informative speech on how to properly use a fire extinguisher, your thesis may be:

"Knowing how to operate a fire extinguisher by following four simple steps can be beneficial and potentially life saving."

OR

"Using a fire extinguisher can be accomplished by following four simple steps."

A **preview** statement is also an important component of your introduction. While many people attempt to combine the thesis and preview statement, it is more thorough to include them as separate distinct items. The preview statement is usually the last sentence of the introduction. The preview is like giving your audience a map for a car trip: They will have an overview of where you will be taking them. It will be easier for them to pay attention as you present your information and it will help them retain the main points of your presentation.

Using the same topic as used above, a preview statement might sound like:

"Today we will cover four specific steps that you should follow when using a fire

extinguisher, specifically, pull, aim, squeeze, and sweep, easily remembered by the acronym, PASS."

Or perhaps it will be spoken this way:

"In our time today, we will discuss how you should pull the pin, aim the nozzle, squeeze the trigger and use a sweeping motion when using a fire extinguisher in an emergency situation."

Notice that in each case, the speaker laid out the roadmap for what was going to be presented during the presentation. The audience had a framework to fill in when the supporting material was presented.

To prepare yourself, review the main points you intend to cover and write one sentence that previews each of those points, separated by commas. You can also write three shorter sentences and use periods. *Beware of going into the details reserved for the main body of the speech while previewing your topic.* This will confuse the audience, and they will wonder what else you plan to discuss.

Pete's Pride

Pistol Pete found himself nestled in a quiet corner of the Edmon Low Library, a notepad in front of him filled with facts, stories, and quotes about Oklahoma State

University's traditions. Now that he had done his research, it was time for Pete to craft a compelling speech. He knew he needed to start with an attention-getter — a memorable opening that would capture the audience's interest right from the start.

As he racked his brain for ideas, he thought about what defines OSU — the Cowboy spirit, the community, and of course, the traditions. Suddenly, an idea came to him. One of the most loved traditions at OSU was the singing of the alma mater song, with its captivating melody and heartfelt lyrics that captured the spirit of the university.

For his attention-getter, Pete envisioned starting his speech with the powerful strains of the alma mater song playing softly in the background. As the audience recognized the familiar tune, they would be immediately engaged, their attention piqued.

Then, Pete would step onto the stage, and with the music still playing, he would recite the first few lines of the song: "Proud and immortal, Bright shines your name, Oklahoma State, we herald your fame." As he spoke, the music would fade, leaving the audience with the resonating words and the emotions they stirred.

With this, Pete would have not only caught the attention of his audience but also connected with them on a deeper, emotional level. And most importantly, he would have set the stage for his speech, immersing his audience in the spirit of OSU traditions right from the start.

Feeling a rush of excitement at his idea, Pete jotted it down on his notepad, eager to shape the rest of his speech. He knew that with this attention-getting opener, his audience would be hooked, ready to join him on the journey through OSU's cherished traditions. What do you think of Pete's attention getter?

10.2 CONCLUSIONS

"The end of a melody is not its goal: but nonetheless, had the melody not reached its end it would not have reached its goal either. " -Friedrich Nietzsche

You have riveted your audience with an engaging introduction. Your introduction led to a compellingly written and logically organized speech. Now, it is time to wrap up the entire experience, but how? Do not make the mistake of thinking, "Well, my speech is just about over at this point, so it doesn't matter how I end it. " You need a conclusion just as dynamic and memorable as your speech opener. How do you feel when a movie has a disappointing ending that does not wrap up the story or, worse, simply leaves you hanging? You feel frustrated, quite possibly like you wasted your money and time. Your audience will feel the same way if your closing remarks do not provide effective closure for your speech. Too many speakers do not realize that when a speech fizzles out, the audience is left with a negative impression. Your speech introduction and body may have included the most profound words known to man, but it could be said that a speaker is only as strong as her/his last sentence. You want your final sentences to be ones that are remembered and valued.

What a Speech Conclusion Is Meant to Do

The speech conclusion has four basic missions:

1. Wraps things up- This portion is often referred to as a "**Brakelight**". Much like brake lights on a car warn us the car will be stopping, this "brakelight" or transitional statement warns the audience that the speech is coming to a close.
2. Summarizes- A solid conclusion briefly restates the preview statement in past tense to remind the audience of the main points that were covered in the presentation.
3. Tells the audience where to go from here- Depending on the purpose of your presentation, this component may play different roles. If your goal was to inform the audience, this is where you might tell them of a rich source they can go to for more information if their curiosity was piqued. If your goal is to persuade, this spot serves as a great opportunity to challenge the audience to take action based on the goals of your speech. Tell them what you want them to do now that they heard your speech.
4. Closes the speech- The note of finality, clincher, closing statement or whatever you want to call it is an important element that leaves the audience reflecting on the topic.

Wrapping things up: It says, "We are nearing the end!"

Hopefully, your audience will want you to speak for an hour, rather than just five or eight minutes. However, when you transition into your conclusion and use appropriate signposting, your audience realizes that the speech will come full-circle. Usually the first transitional phrase is a "brakelight" of sorts. It lets the audience know that you are starting to wrap up your presentation. You may use a transitional statement to illustrate this such as, "In conclusion…", "In summary…" or "To wrap things up…".

The Summary: It tells the audience, "Here's what I told you."

Just as you used a mapping statement to preview your main points, now you will **summarize** your points within your conclusion. Often simply rewording -or even restating -your original thesis statement or preview statement in the past tense will effectively summarize your speech. While this will feel very repetitive to you as a speaker, it is useful in helping the audience understand and retain the information you covered. While you may be tempted to revisit all the details of your speech, this element is best served by a clear concise declarative sentence that restates the main points you addressed.

Where to go from here: It says, "Here's What To Do Now!"

The conclusion is the last chance you have to speak to the audience about this topic. Depending on your general purpose, this portion of the speech will vary. Informative speaking often creates an interest in the audience to learn more about your topic. It's best to give the audience a good resource to check out if they want to learn more information. Avoid telling the audience "to google it". We all know how to do that. Since you've done the research, tell us the best one you found. An example is, "If you'd like to learn more about the history of Stillwater, I recommend visiting The Sheerar Museum at 702 South Duncan here in Stillwater." Persuasive presentation conclusions want to utilize the last opportunity to challenge the listeners to action. This portion gives you a specific opportunity to tell them what you hope they do as a result of hearing your speech. You may say something like, "As you leave here today, I challenge you to pick up five pieces of trash as you walk back to your dorm or car."

Note of finality: It let's the audience know, "The speech is over."

Your speech conclusion is a mental takeaway for the audience, and you will want a strong **note of finality**. Your conclusion should contain enough memorable words and phrases that will help the audience positively recall the experience – and even recollect certain points that you made. Do not forget to include that "ta-da " moment. The last statement of your presentation should be thoroughly planned to let the audience know you are done. Many speakers, who do not come up with a strong closing statement, will end their presentation with, "Thank you." While it is polite to thank the audience, it doesn't really serve as the best closing statement. You want your final statement to leave a strong lasting impact. It should leave the audience reflecting on your topic and your information. Some speech writers like to reference the attention getter as a nice way to bring the speech full circle by revisiting a story, question, or video clip they used originally to grab the audience's attention. After your closing statement and applause from the audience, you are, of course, welcome to thank them for their attention and/or attendance.

Pete's Passion

After hours of diligent research and meticulous preparation, Pistol Pete had managed to weave together a compelling narrative for his speech about the traditions of Oklahoma State University. However, he understood that a strong speech needed an equally powerful conclusion to leave a lasting impression on his audience. So, he sat down once again, this time to brainstorm ideas for a closing statement that would bring his speech full circle.

Pete thought about the essence of his speech – the shared history, pride, and sense of community that OSU's traditions inspired. His goal was to leave his audience not only better informed about these traditions but also feeling more connected to the Cowboy spirit and to each other.

An idea gradually began to take shape in his mind. Pete remembered a phrase from the OSU Alma Mater that had always resonated with him, "Ever you'll find us, loyal and true." This line, he felt, perfectly encapsulated the enduring spirit of loyalty and pride in the OSU community, tying back to the traditions he had highlighted in his speech.

For his closing statement, Pete decided to weave this phrase into his narrative since it lined up well with his attention getter. He would conclude by saying, "As we delve into our traditions, as we sing our songs and wear our colors with pride, we embody these words – 'Ever you'll find us, loyal and true.' This is the essence of our traditions, the heart of our Cowboy spirit. And as we carry these traditions forward, we ensure that the spirit of Oklahoma State University – its unity, its pride, and its enduring legacy – continues to shine bright, now and for generations to come."

Satisfied with his idea, Pete felt a sense of accomplishment. He had a strong closing statement that not only tied back to his attention-getter but also underscored the core message of his speech. With his closing statement in place, Pete was confident that he would leave his audience inspired and more deeply connected to the traditions and spirit of Oklahoma State University. Does Pete's final words of his presentation leave an impression on you? Why?

10.3 ENRICHMENT

Discussion Questions

1. There are many ways to capture the audience's attention. Imagine you are giving a speech informing your audience about sea turtles. Give examples of two options for an attention getter.
2. Credibility is built from two components: competence and character. Give an example for how to establish each of these components.
3. Discuss the differences between a thesis statement and a preview statement.
4. A note of finality is an important aspect to the ending of a speech. What are two distinctive, gripping ways you could provide a powerful note of finality?

Activities

1. Think of your favorite color. You will have one minute to convince a partner your favorite color is the best. The goal here is to establish your credibility so they believe you. Include language that enhances your competence and character.
2. Elvis is alive! With a partner, come up with the most effective attention getter you could use for this speech. Remember to be creative and engaging. Share with the class and discuss.

11 THE IMPORTANCE OF LISTENING

Learning Objectives

- Describe the differences between listening and hearing.
- Explain the benefits of listening.
- Discern between the different listening styles.
- Identify the types of noise that can affect a listener's ability to attend to a message.
- Describe how a listener's attention span can limit the listener's ability to attend to a speaker's message.
- Analyze how a listener's personal biases can influence her or his ability to attend to a message.
- Define receiver apprehension and the impact it can have on a listener's ability to attend to a message.
- List and explain the different stages of listening.
- Understand the two types of feedback listeners give to speakers.
- Define and explain critical listening and its importance in the public speaking context.
- Understand six distinct ways to improve your ability to critically listen to speeches.
- Evaluate what it means to be an ethical listener.

Key Terms

- Action-Oriented Listeners
- Assumptions
- Content-Oriented Listeners
- Critical Listening
- Ethical Listening
- Evaluating
- Hearing
- Listening
- Listening or Receiver Apprehension
- Noise
- People-Oriented Listeners
- Physical Noise
- Physiological Noise
- Psychological Noise
- Receiver Biases
- Receiving
- Remembering
- Responding
- Semantic Noise
- Time-Oriented Listeners
- Understanding

11.1 IMPORTANCE OF LISTENING

"Most people don't listen with the intent to understand; they listen with the intent to reply." -Steven R. Covey

"Are you listening to me?" This question is often asked because the speaker thinks the listener is nodding off or daydreaming. We sometimes think that listening means we only have to sit back, stay barely awake, and let a speaker's words wash over us. While many Americans look upon being active as something to admire, to engage in, and to excel at, listening is often understood as a "passive" activity. More recently, *O, the Oprah Magazine* featured a cover article with the title, "How to Talk So People *Really* Listen: Four Ways to Make Yourself Heard." This title leads us to expect a list of ways to leave the listening to others and insist that they do so, but the article contains a surprise ending. The final piece of advice is this: "You can't go wrong by showing interest in what other people say and making them feel important. In other words, the better *you* listen, the more you'll be listened to" (Jarvis, 2009).

You may have heard the adage, "We have two ears but only one mouth"—an easy way to remember that listening can be twice as important as talking. As a student, you most likely spend many hours in a classroom doing a large amount of focused listening, yet sometimes it is difficult to apply those efforts to communication in other areas of your life. As a result, your listening skills may not be all they could be. In this chapter, we will examine listening versus hearing, listening styles, listening difficulties, listening stages, and listening critically.

Pete's Peers

Even though Pistol Pete had always been more comfortable in the spotlight, cheering on the crowds at Oklahoma State University, he found himself in a different role in his public speaking class. Rather than being the center of attention, Pete was often in the audience, listening to his peers present their speeches.

While some speeches were riveting and engaging, others didn't quite pique his interest. Regardless, Pete understood the importance of being a good listener and a supportive audience member. He remembered his own nervousness when delivering speeches and knew how much it mattered to have an attentive audience.

Pete decided to practice effective listening skills, focusing his attention entirely on the speaker, no matter the topic. He made a conscious effort to maintain eye contact, giving the speaker non-verbal feedback and showing his engagement. He understood that eye contact was a simple yet effective way to show respect and encourage the speaker.

Additionally, Pete worked on keeping his mind from wandering, a common challenge when the speech wasn't particularly interesting. He found that taking notes helped him stay focused. He jotted down key points, interesting ideas, or questions that came to his mind, keeping his brain active and engaged throughout the speech.

He also made sure to provide positive feedback after each presentation, appreciating the speaker's effort and highlighting parts of the speech that stood out to him. Even if the topic wasn't of personal interest, he knew that every speaker had put in effort and deserved recognition.

Moreover, Pete refrained from any disruptive behavior, such as talking, using his phone, or doing other tasks during speeches. He realized that being respectful was not just about paying attention but also about creating a supportive environment that allowed the speaker to deliver their speech without unnecessary distractions.

Through these conscious efforts, Pistol Pete became a model audience member in his speech class. Despite the content of the speeches, he managed to stay engaged and supportive, understanding that being a good listener was as crucial as being a good speaker. His actions set a positive example for his classmates, fostering a respectful and encouraging atmosphere for everyone in the class. Are you an effective listener in class? Are you a supportive listener when peers are presenting? How can you improve your listening skills to be more like Pete?

References

Jarvis, T. (2009, November). How to talk so people *really* listen: Four ways to make yourself heard. *O, the Oprah Magazine.* Retrieved from http://www.oprah.com/relationships/Communication-Skills-How-to-Make-Yourself-Heard

11.2 LISTENING VS. HEARING

Hearing is an accidental and automatic brain response to sound that requires no effort. We are surrounded by sounds most of the time. For example, we are accustomed to the sounds of airplanes, lawn mowers, furnace blowers, the rattling of pots and pans, and so on.

HEARING VS. LISTENING

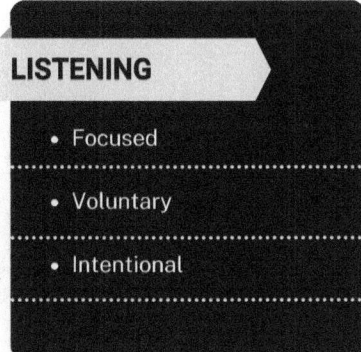

We hear those incidental sounds and, unless we have a reason to do otherwise, we train ourselves to ignore them. We learn to filter out sounds that mean little to us, just as we choose to hear our ringing cell phones and other sounds that are more important to us.

Listening, on the other hand, is purposeful and focused rather than accidental. As a result, it requires motivation and effort. **Listening**, at its best, is active, focused, concentrated attention for the purpose of understanding the meanings expressed by a speaker. We do not always listen at our best, however, and later in this chapter we will examine some of the reasons why and some strategies for becoming more active critical listeners.

Benefits of Listening

Listening should not be taken for granted. Before the invention of writing, people conveyed virtually all knowledge through some combination of showing and telling. Elders recited tribal histories to attentive audiences. Listeners received religious teachings enthusiastically. Myths, legends, folktales, and stories for entertainment survived only because audiences were eager to listen. Nowadays, however, you can gain information and entertainment through reading and electronic recordings rather than through real-time listening. If you become distracted and let your attention wander, you can go back and replay a recording. Despite that fact, you can still gain at least four compelling benefits by becoming more active and competent at real-time listening.

You Become a Better Student

When you focus on the material presented in a classroom, you will be able to identify not only the words used in a lecture but their emphasis and their more complex meanings.

You will take better notes, and you will more accurately remember the instructor's claims, information, and conclusions. Many times, instructors give verbal cues about what information is important, specific expectations about assignments, and even what material is likely to be on an exam, so careful listening can be beneficial.

You Become a Better Friend

When you give your best attention to people expressing thoughts and experiences that are important to them, those individuals are likely to see you as someone who cares about their well-being.

This fact is especially true when you give your attention only and refrain from interjecting opinions, judgments, and advice.

People Will Perceive You as Intelligent and Perceptive

When you listen well to others, you reveal yourself as being curious and interested in people and events.

In addition, your ability to understand the meanings of what you hear will make you a more knowledgeable and thoughtful person.

Good Listening Can Help Your Public Speaking

When you listen well to others, you start to pick up more on the stylistic components related to how people form arguments and present information.

As a result, you have the ability to analyze what you think works and doesn't work in others' speeches, which can help you transform your speeches in the process. For example, really paying attention to how others cite sources orally during their speeches may give you ideas about how to more effectively cite sources in your presentation.

11.3 LISTENING STYLES

If listening were easy, and if all people went about it in the same way, the task for a public speaker would be much easier. Even Aristotle, as long ago as 325 BC, recognized that listeners in his audience were varied in listening style. He differentiated them as follows:

> Rhetoric falls into three divisions, determined by the three classes of listeners to speeches. For of the three elements in speech-making—speaker, subject, and person addressed—it is the last one, the hearer, that determines the speech's end and object. The hearer must be either a judge, with a decision to make about things past or future, or an observer. A member of the assembly decides about future events, a juryman about past events: while those who merely decide on the orator's skill are observers (Aristotle, c. 350 BCE).

Thus Aristotle classified listeners into those who would be using the speech to make decisions about past events, those who would make decisions affecting the future, and those who would evaluate the speaker's skills. This is all the more remarkable when we consider that Aristotle's audiences were composed exclusively of male citizens of one city-state, all prosperous property owners.

Our audiences today are likely to be much more heterogeneous. Think about the classroom audience that will listen to your speeches in this course. Your classmates come from many religious and ethnic backgrounds. Some of them may speak English as a second language. Some might be survivors of war-torn parts of the world such as Bosnia, Darfur, or northwest China. Being mindful of such differences will help you prepare a speech in which you minimize the potential for misunderstanding.

Part of the potential for misunderstanding is the difference in listening styles. In an article in the *International Journal of Listening*, Watson, Barker, and Weaver (Watson, et al., 1995) identified four listening styles: people, action, content, and time.

People

The **people-oriented listener** is interested in the speaker. People-oriented listeners listen to the message in order to learn how the speaker thinks and how they feel about their message. For instance, when people-oriented listeners listen to an interview with a famous rap artist, they are likely to be more curious about the artist as an individual than about music, even though the people-oriented listener might also appreciate the artist's work. If you are a people-oriented listener, you might have certain questions you hope will be answered, such as: Does the artist feel successful? What's it like to be famous? What kind of educational background does he or she have? In the same way, if we're listening to a doctor who responded to the earthquake crisis in Haiti, we might be more interested in the doctor as a person than in the state of affairs for Haitians. Why did he or she go to Haiti? How did he or she get away from his or her normal practice and patients? How many lives did he or she save? We might be less interested in the equally important and urgent needs for food, shelter, and sanitation following the earthquake.

The people-oriented listener is likely to be more attentive to the speaker than to the message. If you tend to be such a listener, understand that the message is about what is important to the speaker.

Action

Action-oriented listeners are primarily interested in finding out what the speaker wants. Does the speaker want votes, donations, volunteers, or something else? It's sometimes difficult for an action-oriented speaker to listen through the descriptions, evidence, and explanations with which a speaker builds his or her case.

Action-oriented listening is sometimes called task-oriented listening. In it, the listener seeks a clear message about what needs to be done, and might have less patience for listening to the reasons behind the task. This can be especially true if the reasons are complicated. For example, when you're a passenger on an airplane waiting to push back from the gate, a flight attendant delivers a brief speech called the preflight safety briefing. The flight attendant does not read the findings of a safety study or the regulations about seat belts. The flight attendant doesn't explain that the content of his or her speech is actually mandated by the Federal Aviation Administration. Instead, the attendant says only to buckle up so we can leave. An action-oriented listener finds "buckling up" a more compelling message than a message about the underlying reasons.

Content

Content-oriented listeners are interested in the message itself, whether it makes sense, what it means, and whether it's accurate. When you give a speech, many members of your classroom audience will be content-oriented listeners who will be interested in learning from you. You therefore have an obligation to represent the truth in the fullest way you can. You can emphasize an idea, but if you exaggerate, you could lose credibility in the minds of your content-oriented audience. You can advocate ideas that are important to you, but if you omit important limitations, you are withholding part of the truth and could leave your audience with an inaccurate view.

Imagine you're delivering a speech on the plight of orphans in Africa. If you just talk about the fact that there are over forty-five million orphans in Africa but don't explain why, you'll sound like an infomercial. In such an instance, your audience's response is likely to be less enthusiastic than you might want. Instead, content-oriented listeners want to listen to well-developed information with solid explanations.

Time

People using a **time-oriented listening** style prefer a message that gets to the point quickly. Time-oriented listeners can become impatient with slow delivery or lengthy explanations. This kind of listener may be receptive for only a brief amount of time and may become rude or even hostile if the speaker expects a longer focus of attention. Time-oriented listeners convey their impatience through eye rolling, shifting about in their seats, checking their cell phones, and other inappropriate behaviors. If you've been asked to speak to a group of middle-school students, you need to realize that their attention spans are simply not as long as those of college students. This is an important reason speeches to young audiences must be shorter, or broken up by more variety than speeches to adults.

In your professional future, some of your audience members will have real time constraints, not merely perceived ones. Imagine that you've been asked to deliver a speech on a new project to the board of directors of a local corporation. Chances are the people on the board of directors are all pressed for time. If your speech is long and filled with overly detailed information, time-oriented listeners will simply start to tune you out as you're speaking. Obviously, if time-oriented listeners start tuning you out, they will not be listening to your message. This is not the same thing as being a time-oriented listener who might be less interested in the message content than in its length.

References

Aristotle. (c. 350 BCE). *Rhetoric* (W. Rhys Roberts, Trans.). Book I, Part 3, para. 1. Retrieved from http://classics.mit.edu/Aristotle/rhetoric.1.i.html.

Watson, K. W., Barker, L. L., & Weaver, J. B., III. (1995). The listening styles profile (LSP-16): Development and validation of an instrument to assess four listening styles. *International Journal of Listening, 9*, 1–13.

11.4 WHY LISTENING IS DIFFICULT

At times, everyone has difficulty staying completely focused during a lengthy presentation. We can sometimes have difficulty listening to even relatively brief messages. Some of the factors that interfere with good listening might exist beyond our control, but others are manageable. It's helpful to be aware of these factors so that they interfere as little as possible with understanding the message.

Noise

Noise is one of the biggest factors to interfere with listening; it can be defined as anything that interferes with your ability to attend to and understand a message. There are many kinds of noise, but we will focus on only the four you are most likely to encounter in public speaking situations: physical noise, psychological noise, physiological noise, and semantic noise.

Physical Noise

Physical noise consists of various sounds in an environment that interfere with a source's ability to hear. Construction noises right outside a window, planes flying directly overhead, or loud music in the next room can make it difficult to hear the message being presented by a speaker even if a microphone is being used. It is sometimes possible to manage the context to reduce the noise. Closing a window might be helpful. Asking the people in the next room to turn their music down might be possible. Changing to a new location is more difficult, as it involves finding a new location and having everyone get there.

Psychological Noise

Psychological noise consists of distractions to a speaker's message caused by a receiver's internal thoughts. For example, if you are preoccupied with personal problems, it is difficult to give your full attention to understanding the meanings of a message. The presence of another person to whom you feel attracted, or perhaps a person you dislike intensely, can also be psychosocial noise that draws your attention away from the message.

Physiological Noise

Physiological noise consists of distractions to a speaker's message caused by a listener's own body. Maybe you're listening to a speech in class around noon and you haven't eaten anything. Your stomach may be growling and you are worried your classmates may be able to hear it. Maybe the room is cold and you're thinking more about how to keep warm than about what the speaker is saying. Maybe your head begins to ache and you feel the need to lay down and rest. In any of these cases, your body can distract you from attending to the information being presented.

Semantic Noise

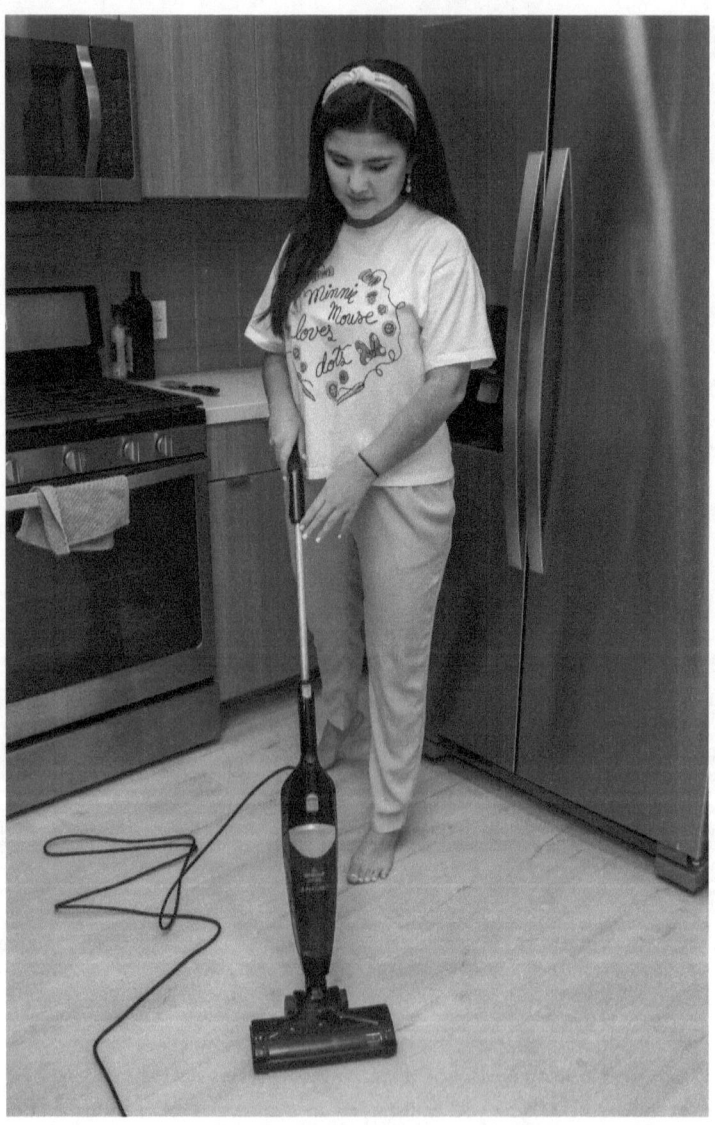

Semantic noise occurs when a receiver experiences confusion over the meaning of a source's word choice. While you are attempting to understand a particular word or phrase, the speaker continues to present the message. While you are struggling with a word interpretation, you are distracted from listening to the rest of the message. One of the authors was listening to a speaker who mentioned using a sweeper to clean carpeting. The author was confused, as she did not see how a broom would be effective in cleaning carpeting. Later, the author found out that the speaker was using the word "sweeper" to refer to a vacuum cleaner; however, in the meantime, her listening was hurt by her inability to understand what the speaker meant. Another example of semantic noise is euphemism. Euphemism is diplomatic language used for delivering unpleasant information. For instance, if someone is said to be "flexible with the truth," it might take us a moment to understand that the speaker means this person sometimes lies.

Many distractions are the fault of neither the listener nor the speaker. However, when you are the speaker, being aware of these sources of noise can help you reduce some of the noise that interferes with your audience's ability to understand you.

Attention Span

A person can only maintain focused attention for a finite length of time. In his 1985 book *Amusing Ourselves to Death: Public Discourse in the Age of Show Business*, New York University's Steinhardt School of Education professor Neil Postman argued that modern audiences have lost the ability to sustain attention to a message (Postman, 1985). More recently, researchers have engaged in an ongoing debate over whether Internet use is detrimental to attention span (Carr, 2010). Whether or not these concerns are well founded, you have probably noticed that even when your attention is "glued" to something in which you are deeply interested, every now and then you pause to do something else, such as getting a drink of water, stretching, or looking out the window.

The limits of the human attention span can interfere with listening, but listeners and speakers can use strategies to prevent this interference. As many classroom instructors know, listeners will readily renew their attention when the presentation includes frequent breaks in pacing (Middendorf & Kalish, 1996). For example, a fifty- to seventy-five-minute class session might include some lecture material alternated with questions for class discussion, video clips, handouts, and demonstrations. Instructors who are adept at holding listeners' attention also move about the front of the room, writing on the board, drawing diagrams, and intermittently using slide transparencies or PowerPoint slides.

If you have instructors who do a good job of keeping your attention, they are positive role models showing strategies you can use to accommodate the limitations of your audience's attention span.

Receiver Biases

Good listening involves keeping an open mind and withholding judgment until the speaker has completed the message. Conversely, biased listening is characterized by jumping to conclusions; the biased listener believes, "I don't need to listen because I already know what I think." **Receiver biases** can refer to two things: biases with reference to the speaker and preconceived ideas and **opinions** about the topic or message. Both can be considered noise. Everyone has biases, but good listeners have learned to hold them in check while listening.

The first type of bias listeners can have is related to the speaker. Often a speaker stands up and an audience member simply doesn't like the speaker, so the audience member may not listen to the speaker's message. Maybe you have a classmate who just gets under your skin for some reason, or maybe you question a classmate's competence on a given topic. When we have preconceived notions about a speaker, those biases can interfere with our ability to listen accurately and competently to the speaker's message.

The second type of bias listeners can have is related to the topic or content of the speech. Maybe the speech topic is one you've heard a thousand times, so you just tune out the speech. Or maybe the speaker is presenting a topic or position you fundamentally disagree with. When listeners have strong preexisting opinions about a topic, such as the death penalty, religious issues, affirmative action, abortion, or global warming, their biases may make it difficult for them to even consider new information about the topic, especially if the new information is inconsistent with what they already believe to be true. As listeners, we have difficulty identifying our biases, especially when they seem to make sense. However, it is worth recognizing that our lives would be very difficult if no one ever considered new points of view or new information. We live in a world where everyone can benefit from clear thinking and open-minded listening.

Listening or Receiver Apprehension

Listening or receiver apprehension is the fear that you might be unable to understand the message or process the information correctly or be able to adapt your thinking to include the new information coherently (Wheeless, 1975). In some situations, you might worry that the information presented will be "over your head"—too complex, technical, or advanced for you to understand adequately.

Many students will actually avoid registering for courses in which they feel certain they will do poorly. In other cases, students will choose to take a challenging course only if it's a requirement. This avoidance might be understandable but is not a good strategy for success. To become educated people, students should take a few courses that can shed light on areas where their knowledge is limited.

As a speaker, you can reduce listener apprehension by defining terms clearly and using simple visual aids to hold the audience's attention. You don't want to underestimate or overestimate your audience's knowledge on a subject, so good audience analysis is always important. If you know your audience doesn't have special knowledge on a given topic, you should start by defining important terms. Research has shown us that when listeners do not feel they understand a speaker's message, their apprehension about receiving the message escalates. Imagine that you are listening to a speech about chemistry and the speaker begins talking about "colligative properties." You may start questioning whether you're even in the right place. When this happens, apprehension clearly interferes with a listener's ability to accurately and competently understand a speaker's message. As a speaker, you can lessen the listener's apprehension by explaining that colligative properties focus on *how much* is dissolved in a solution, not on *what* is dissolved in a solution. You could also give an example that they might readily understand, such as saying that it doesn't matter what kind of salt you use in the winter to melt ice on your driveway, what is important is how much salt you use.

References

Carr, N. (2010, May 24). The Web shatters focus, rewires brains. *Wired Magazine*. Retrieved from http://www.wired.com/magazine/2010/05/ff_nicholas_carr/all/1.

Middendorf, J., & Kalish, A. (1996). The "change-up" in lectures. *The National Teaching and Learning Forum*, 5(2).

Postman, N. (1985). *Amusing ourselves to death: Public discourse in the age of show business*. New York: Viking Press.

Wheeless, L. R. (1975). An investigation of receiver apprehension and social context dimensions of communication apprehension. *Speech Teacher*, 24, 261–268.

This resource is available at no cost at
https://open.library.okstate.edu/speech2713/

11.5 STAGES OF LISTENING

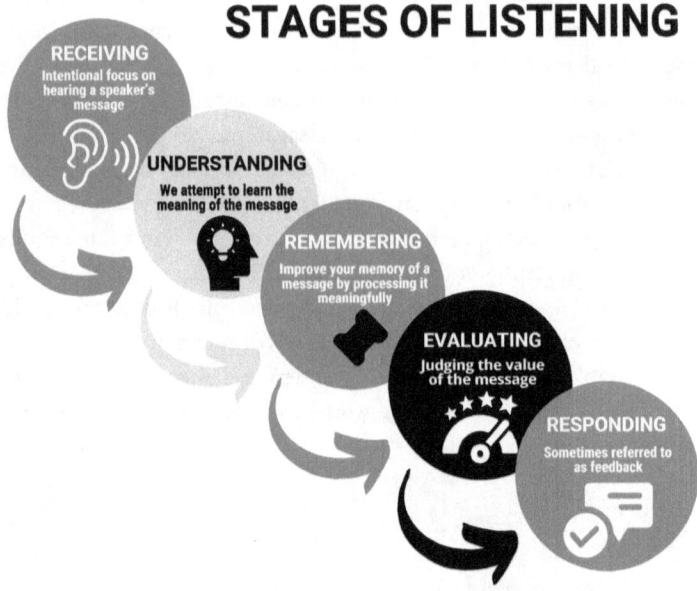

As you read earlier, there are many factors that can interfere with listening, so you need to be able to manage a number of mental tasks at the same time in order to be a successful listener. Author Joseph DeVito has divided the listening process into five stages: receiving, understanding, remembering, evaluating, and responding (DeVito, 2000).

Receiving

Receiving is the intentional focus on hearing a speaker's message, which happens when we filter out other sources so that we can isolate the message and avoid the confusing mixture of incoming stimuli. At this stage, we are still only hearing the message. Notice in Figure 11.3 "Stages of Listening" that this stage is represented by the ear because it is the primary tool involved with this stage of the listening process.

One of the authors of this book recalls attending a political rally for a presidential candidate at which about five thousand people were crowded into an outdoor amphitheater. When the candidate finally started speaking, the cheering and yelling was so loud that the candidate couldn't be heard easily despite using a speaker system. In this example, our coauthor had difficulty receiving the message because of the external noise. This is only one example of the ways that hearing alone can require sincere effort, but you must hear the message before you can continue the process of listening.

Understanding

In the **understanding** stage, we attempt to learn the meaning of the message, which is not always easy. For one thing, if a speaker does not enunciate clearly, it may be difficult to tell what the message was—did your friend say, "I think she'll be late for class," or "my teacher delayed the class"? Notice in Figure 11.3 "Stages of Listening" that stages two, three, and four are represented by the brain because it is the primary tool involved with these stages of the listening process.

Even when we have understood the words in a message, because of the differences in our backgrounds and experience, we sometimes make the mistake of attaching our own meanings to the words of others. For example, say you have made plans with your friends to meet at a certain movie theater, but you arrive and nobody else shows up. Eventually you find out that your friends are at a different theater all the way across town where the same movie is playing. Everyone else understood that the meeting place was the "west side" location, but you wrongly understood it as the "east side" location and therefore missed out on part of the fun.

The consequences of ineffective listening in a classroom can be much worse. When your professor advises students to get an "early start" on your speech, he or she probably hopes that you will begin your research right away and move on to developing a thesis statement and outlining the speech as soon as possible. However, students in your class might misunderstand the instructor's meaning in several ways. One student might interpret the advice to mean that as long as she gets started, the rest of the assignment will have time to develop itself. Another student might instead think that to start early is to start on the Friday before the Monday due date instead of Sunday night.

So much of the way we understand others is influenced by our own perceptions and experiences. Therefore, at the understanding stage of listening we should be on the lookout for places where our perceptions might differ from those of the speaker.

Remembering

Remembering begins with listening; if you can't remember something that was said, you might not have been listening effectively. Wolvin and Coakley note that the most common reason for not remembering a message after the fact is because it wasn't really learned in the first place (Wolvin & Coakley, 1996). However, even when you are listening attentively, some messages are more difficult than others to understand and remember. Highly complex messages that are filled with detail call for highly developed listening skills. Moreover, if something distracts your attention even for a moment, you could miss out on information that explains other new concepts you hear when you begin to listen fully again.

It's also important to know that you can improve your memory of a message by processing it meaningfully—that is, by applying it in ways that are meaningful to you (Gluck, et al., 2008). Instead of simply repeating a new acquaintance's name over and over, for example, you might remember it by associating it with something in your own life. "Emily," you might say, "reminds me of the Emily I knew in middle school," or "Mr. Impiari's name reminds me of the Impala my father drives."

Finally, if understanding has been inaccurate, recollection of the message will be inaccurate too.

Evaluating

The fourth stage in the listening process is **evaluating**, or judging the value of the message. We might be thinking, "This makes sense" or, conversely, "This is very odd." Because everyone embodies biases and perspectives learned from widely diverse sets of life experiences, evaluations of the same message can vary widely from one listener to another. Even the most open-minded listeners will have opinions of a speaker, and those opinions will influence how the message is evaluated. People are more likely to evaluate a message positively if the speaker speaks clearly, presents ideas logically, and gives reasons to support the points made.

Unfortunately, personal opinions sometimes result in prejudiced evaluations. Imagine you're listening to a speech given by someone from another country and this person has an accent that is hard to understand. You may have a hard time simply making out the speaker's message. Some people find a foreign accent to be interesting or even exotic, while others find it annoying or even take it as a sign of ignorance. If a listener has a strong bias against foreign accents, the listener may not even attempt to attend to the message. If you mistrust a speaker because of an accent, you could be rejecting important or personally enriching information. Good listeners have learned to refrain from making these judgments and instead to focus on the speaker's meanings.

Responding

Responding—sometimes referred to as feedback—is the fifth and final stage of the listening process. It's the stage at which you indicate your involvement. Almost anything you do at this stage can be interpreted as feedback. For example, you are giving positive feedback to your instructor if at the end of class you stay behind to finish a sentence in your notes or approach the instructor to ask for clarification. The opposite kind of feedback is given by students who gather their belongings and rush out the door as soon as class is over. Notice in Figure 11.3 "Stages of Listening" that this stage is represented by the lips because we often give feedback in the form of verbal feedback; however, you can just as easily respond nonverbally.

Formative Feedback

Not all response occurs at the end of the message. Formative feedback is a natural part of the ongoing transaction between a speaker and a listener. As the speaker delivers the message, a listener signals his or her involvement with focused attention, note-taking, nodding, and other behaviors that indicate understanding or failure to understand the message. These signals are important to the speaker, who is interested in whether the message is clear and accepted or whether the content of the message is meeting the resistance of preconceived ideas. Speakers can use this feedback to decide whether additional examples, support materials, or explanation is needed.

Summative Feedback

Summative feedback is given at the end of the communication. When you attend a political rally, a presentation given by a speaker you admire, or even a class, there are verbal and nonverbal ways of indicating your appreciation for or your disagreement with the messages or the speakers at the end of the message. Maybe you'll stand up and applaud a speaker you agreed with or just sit staring in silence after listening to a speaker you didn't like. In other cases, a speaker may be attempting to persuade you to donate to a charity, so if the speaker passes a bucket and you make a donation, you are providing feedback on the speaker's effectiveness. At the same time, we do not always listen most carefully to the messages of speakers we admire. Sometimes we simply enjoy being in their presence, and our summative feedback is not about the message but about our attitudes about the speaker. If your feedback is limited to something like, "I just love your voice," you might be indicating that you did not listen carefully to the content of the message.

There is little doubt that by now, you are beginning to understand the complexity of listening and the great potential for errors. By becoming aware of what is involved with active listening and where difficulties might lie, you can prepare yourself both as a listener and as a speaker to minimize listening errors with your own public speeches.

References

DeVito, J. A. (2000). *The elements of public speaking* (7th ed.). New York, NY: Longman.

Gluck, M. A., Mercado, E., & Myers, C. E. (2008). *Learning and memory: From brain to behavior.* New York: Worth Publishers, pp. 172–173.

Wolvin, A., & Coakley, C. G. (1996). *Listening* (5th ed.). Boston, MA: McGraw-Hill.

11.6 LISTENING CRITICALLY

As a student, you are exposed to many kinds of messages. You receive messages conveying academic information, institutional rules, instructions, and warnings; you also receive messages through political discourse, advertisements, gossip, jokes, song lyrics, text messages, invitations, web links, and all other manner of communication. You know it's not all the same, but it isn't always clear how to separate the truth from the messages that are misleading or even blatantly false. Nor is it always clear which messages are intended to help the listener and which ones are merely self-serving for the speaker. Part of being a good listener is to learn when to use caution in evaluating the messages we hear.

Critical listening in this context means using careful, systematic thinking and reasoning to see whether a message makes sense in light of factual evidence. Critical listening can be learned with practice but is not necessarily easy to do. Some people never learn this skill; instead, they take every message at face value even when those messages are in conflict with their knowledge. Problems occur when messages are repeated to others who have not yet developed the skills to discern the difference between a valid message and a mistaken one. Critical listening can be particularly difficult when the message is complex. Unfortunately, some speakers may make their messages intentionally complex to avoid critical scrutiny. For example, a city treasurer giving a budget presentation might use very large words and technical jargon, which make it difficult for listeners to understand the proposed budget and ask probing questions.

Six Ways to Improve Your Critical Listening

Critical listening is first and foremost a skill that can be learned and improved. In this section, we are going to explore six different techniques you can use to become a more critical listener.

Recognizing the Difference between Facts and Opinions

Senator Daniel Patrick Moynihan is credited with saying, "Everyone is entitled to their own opinions, but they are not entitled to their own facts" (Wikiquote). Part of critical listening is learning to separate opinions from facts, and this works two ways: critical listeners are aware of whether a speaker is delivering a factual message or a message based on opinion, and they are also aware of the interplay between their own opinions and facts as they listen to messages.

In American politics, the issue of health care reform is heavily laden with both opinions and facts, and it is extremely difficult to sort some of them out. A clash of fact versus opinion happened on September 9, 2010, during President Obama's nationally televised speech to a joint session of Congress outlining his health care reform plan. In this speech, President Obama responded to several rumors about the plan, including the claim "that our reform effort will insure illegal immigrants. This, too, is false—the reforms I'm proposing would not apply to those who are here illegally." At this point, one congressman yelled out, "You lie!" Clearly, this congressman did not have a very high opinion of either the health care reform plan or the president. However, when the nonpartisan watch group Factcheck.org examined the language of the proposed bill, they found that it had a section titled "No Federal Payment for Undocumented Aliens" (Factcheck.org, 2009).

Often when people have a negative opinion about a topic, they are unwilling to accept facts. Instead, they question all aspects of the speech and have a negative predisposition toward both the speech and the speaker.

This is not to say that speakers should not express their opinions. Many of the greatest speeches in history include personal opinions. Consider, for example, Martin Luther King Jr.'s famous "I Have a Dream" speech, in which he expressed his personal wish for the future of American society. Critical listeners may agree or disagree with a speaker's opinions, but the point is that they know when a message they are hearing is based on opinion and when it is factual.

Uncovering Assumptions

If something is factual, supporting evidence exists. However, we still need to be careful about what evidence does and does not mean. **Assumptions** are gaps in a logical sequence that listeners passively fill with their own ideas and opinions and may or may not be accurate. When listening to a public speech, you may find yourself being asked to assume something is a fact when in reality many people question that fact. For example, suppose you're listening to a speech on weight loss. The speaker talks about how people who are overweight are simply not motivated or lack the self-discipline to lose weight. The speaker has built the speech on the assumption that motivation and self-discipline are the only reasons why people can't lose weight. You may think to yourself, what about genetics? By listening critically, you will be more likely to notice unwarranted assumptions in a speech, which may prompt you to question the speaker if questions are taken or to do further research to examine the validity of the speaker's assumptions. If, however, you sit passively by and let the speaker's assumptions go unchallenged, you may find yourself persuaded by information that is not factual.

When you listen critically to a speech, you might hear information that appears unsupported by evidence. You shouldn't accept that information unconditionally. You would accept it under the condition that the speaker offers credible evidence that directly supports it.

FACTS VS. ASSUMPTIONS

FACTS
- Facts are verified by clear, unambiguous evidence.
- Most facts can be tested.

ASSUMPTIONS
- Assumptions are not supported by evidence.
- Assumptions about the future cannot be tested in the present.

Be Open to New Ideas

Sometimes people are so fully invested in their perceptions of the world that they are unable to listen receptively to messages that make sense and would be of great benefit to them. Human progress has been possible, sometimes against great odds, because of the mental curiosity and discernment of a few people. In the late 1700s when the technique of vaccination to prevent smallpox was introduced, it was opposed by both medical professionals and everyday citizens who staged public protests (Edward Jenner Museum). More than two centuries later, vaccinations against smallpox, diphtheria, polio, and other infectious diseases have saved countless lives, yet popular opposition continues.

In the world of public speaking, we must be open to new ideas. Let's face it, people have a tendency to filter out information they disagree with and to filter in information that supports what they already believe. Nicolaus Copernicus was a sixteenth-century astronomer who dared to publish a treatise explaining that the earth revolves around the sun, which was a violation of Catholic doctrine. Copernicus's astronomical findings were labeled heretical and his treatise banned because a group of people at the time were not open to new ideas. In May of 2010, almost five hundred years after his death, the Roman Catholic Church admitted its error and reburied his remains with the full rites of Catholic burial (Owen, 2010).

While the Copernicus case is a fairly dramatic reversal, listeners should always be open to new ideas. We are not suggesting that you have to agree with every idea that you are faced with in life; rather, we are suggesting that you at least listen to the message and then evaluate the message.

Rely on Reason and Common Sense

If you are listening to a speech and your common sense tells you that the message is illogical, you very well might be right. You should be thinking about whether the speech seems credible and coherent. In this way, your use of common sense can act as a warning system for you.

One of our coauthors once heard a speech on the environmental hazards of fireworks. The speaker argued that fireworks (the public kind, not the personal kind people buy and set off in their backyards) were environmentally hazardous because of litter. Although there is certainly some paper that makes it to the ground before burning up, the amount of litter created by fireworks displays is relatively small compared to other sources of litter, including trash left behind by all the spectators watching fireworks at public parks and other venues. It just does not make sense to identify a few bits of charred paper as a major environmental hazard.

If the message is inconsistent with things you already know, if the argument is illogical, or if the language is exaggerated, you should investigate the issues before accepting or rejecting the message. Often, you will not be able to take this step during the presentation of the message; it may take longer to collect enough knowledge to make that decision for yourself.

However, when you are the speaker, you should not substitute common sense for evidence. That's why during a speech it's necessary to cite the authority of scholars whose research is irrefutable, or at least highly credible. It is all too easy to make a mistake in reasoning, sometimes called fallacy, in stating your case. One of the most common fallacies is *post hoc, ergo propter hoc*, a "common sense" form of logic that translates roughly as "after the fact, therefore because of the fact." The argument says that if A happened first, followed by B, then A caused B. We know the outcome cannot occur earlier than the cause, but we also know that the two events might be related indirectly or that causality works in a different direction. For instance, imagine a speaker arguing that because the sun rises after a rooster's crow, the rooster caused the sun to rise. This argument is clearly illogical because roosters crow many times each day, and the sun's rising and setting do not change according to crowing or lack thereof. But the two events are related in a different way. Roosters tend to wake up and begin crowing at first light, about forty-five minutes before sunrise. Thus it is the impending sunrise that causes the predawn crowing.

What is "common sense" for people of one generation or culture may be quite the opposite for people of a different generation or culture. Thus it is important not to assume that your audience shares the beliefs that are, for you, common sense. Likewise, if the message of your speech is complex or controversial, you should consider the needs of your audience and do your best to explain its complexities factually and logically, not intuitively.

Relate New Ideas to Old Ones

As both a speaker and a listener, one of the most important things you can do to understand a message is to relate new ideas to previously held ideas. Imagine you're giving a speech about biological systems and you need to use the term "homeostasis," which refers to the ability of an organism to maintain stability by making constant adjustments. To help your audience understand homeostasis, you could show how homeostasis is similar to adjustments made by the thermostats that keep our homes at a more or less even temperature. If you set your thermostat for seventy degrees and it gets hotter, the central cooling will kick in and cool your house down. If your house gets below seventy degrees, your heater will kick in and heat your house up. Notice that in both cases your thermostat is making constant adjustments to stay at seventy degrees. Explaining that the body's homeostasis works in a similar way will make it more relevant to your listeners and will likely help them both understand and remember the idea because it links to something they have already experienced.

If you can make effective comparisons while you are listening, it can deepen your understanding of the message. If you can provide those comparisons for your listeners, you make it easier for them to give consideration to your ideas.

Take Notes

Note-taking is a skill that improves with practice. You already know that it's nearly impossible to write down everything a speaker says. In fact, in your attempt to record everything, you might fall behind and wish you had divided your attention differently between writing and listening.

Careful, selective note-taking is important because we want an accurate record that reflects the meanings of the message. However much you might concentrate on the notes, you could inadvertently leave out an important word, such as *not*, and undermine the reliability of your otherwise carefully written notes. Instead, if you give the same care and attention to listening, you are less likely to make that kind of a mistake.

It's important to find a balance between listening well and taking good notes. Many people struggle with this balance for a long time. For example, if you try to write down only key phrases instead of full sentences, you might find that you can't remember how two ideas were related. In that case, too few notes were taken. At the opposite end, extensive note-taking can result in a loss of emphasis on the most important ideas.

To increase your critical listening skills, continue developing your ability to identify the central issues in messages so that you can take accurate notes that represent the meanings intended by the speaker.

Listening Ethically

Ethical listening rests heavily on honest intentions. We should extend to speakers the same respect we want to receive when it's our turn to speak. We should be facing the speaker with our eyes open. We should not be checking our cell phones. We should avoid any behavior that belittles the speaker or the message.

Scholars Stephanie Coopman and James Lull emphasize the creation of a climate of caring and mutual understanding, observing that "respecting others' perspectives is one hallmark of the effective listener" (Coopman & Lull, 2008). Respect, or unconditional positive regard for others, means that you treat others with consideration and decency whether you agree with them or not. Professors Sprague, Stuart, and Bodary (Sprague, et al., 2010). also urge us to treat the speaker with respect even when we disagree, don't understand the message, or find the speech boring.

Doug Lippman (1998) (Lippman, 1998), a storytelling coach, wrote powerfully and sensitively about listening in his book:

> Like so many of us, I used to take listening for granted, glossing over this step as I rushed into the more active, visible ways of being helpful. Now, I am convinced that listening is the single most important element of any helping relationship.
>
> Listening has great power. It draws thoughts and feelings out of people as nothing else can. When someone listens to you well, you become aware of feelings you may not have realized that you felt. You have ideas you may have never thought before. You become more eloquent, more insightful....
>
> As a helpful listener, I do not interrupt you. I do not give advice. I do not do something else while listening to you. I do not convey distraction through nervous mannerisms. I do not finish your sentences for you. In spite of all my attempts to understand you, I do not assume I know what you mean.
>
> I do not convey disapproval, impatience, or condescension. If I am confused, I show a desire for clarification, not dislike for your obtuseness. I do not act vindicated when you misspeak or correct yourself.
>
> I do not sit impassively, withholding participation.
>
> Instead, I project affection, approval, interest, and enthusiasm. I am your partner in communication. I am eager for your imminent success, fascinated by your struggles, forgiving of your mistakes, always expecting the best. I am your delighted listener (Lippman, 1998).

This excerpt expresses the decency with which people should treat each other. It doesn't mean we must accept everything we hear, but ethically, we should refrain from trivializing each other's concerns. We have all had the painful experience of being ignored or misunderstood. This is how we know that one of the greatest gifts one human can give to another is listening.

References

Coopman, S. J., & Lull, J. (2008). *Public speaking: The evolving art*. Cengage Learning, p. 60.

Edward Jenner Museum. (n.d.). Vaccination. Retrieved from http://www.jennermuseum.com/Jenner/vaccination.html

Factcheck.org, a Project of the Annenberg Public Policy Center of the University of Pennsylvania. (2009, September 10). Obama's health care speech. Retrieved from http://www.factcheck.org/2009/09/obamas-health-care-speech

Lippman, D. (1998). *The storytelling coach: How to listen, praise, and bring out people's best*. Little Rock, AR: August House.

Owen, R. (2010, May 23). Catholic church reburies "heretic" Nicolaus

Copernicus with honour. *Times Online*. Retrieved from http://www.timesonline.co.uk/tol/news/world/europe/article7134341.ece

Sprague, J., Stuart, D., & Bodary, D. (2010). *The speaker's handbook* (9th ed.). Boston, MA: Wadsworth Cengage.

Wikiquote. (n.d.). Daniel Patrick Moynihan. Retrieved from http://en.wikiquote.org/wiki/Daniel_Patrick_Moynihan

11.7 ENRICHMENT

Discussion Questions

1. With a partner, discuss how you find out when you have not been listening carefully. What are some of the consequences of poor listening?
2. This chapter discusses different types of listening styles. Under most circumstances, which style best describes you and why?
3. What are the main types of noise that influence your listening in the following areas: home, classroom, work, with friends? How can you begin working to overcome noise in these areas?

Activities

1. In a group, discuss what distracts you most from listening attentively to a speaker. Have you found ways to filter out or manage the distraction? Share with the class to create a list of ways to manage these distractions.
2. Form five groups. Each group is given a different stage in the listening process. Together, create an infographic that describes that stage and the most important concepts in that stage. Each group presents their infographic to the class.
3. Sit back to back with a partner. One is given a simple image (i.e. heart, house, flower, tree, fish, cat, dog, etc.) and the other is given a blank sheet of paper and a pen/pencil. The student with the image must describe it without naming it for the other student to draw. After every pair has finished, share the image and the drawing and discuss the following questions:

    ◦ How did the drawing turn out versus the image?

    ◦ For the listener, what were the most useful things the speaker did to help you get an idea of what you were drawing?

    ◦ For the speaker, what tactics did you use to try to help the listener draw the correct image?

    ◦ What types of noise interfered in this process? How did you overcome that?

- What kinds of listening styles do you think were most used in this activity? How did that help/hurt the process?

- How can you use this experience to improve your listening in the future?

12 LANGUAGE

Learning Objectives

- Explain how language is used for power.
- Describe how languages choices affect the effectiveness of public speaking.
- Explain the standard of clarity.
- Choose clear language that is appropriate for audiences.
- Determine your own language ability in speaking.

Key Terms

- **Abstract Language**
- **Alliteration**
- **Anaphora**
- **Antithesis**
- **Appropriateness**
- **Assonance**
- **Clichés**
- **Connotative**
- **Denotative**
- **Ethnic Identity**

- **Euphemisms**
- **Figurative Language**
- **Hyperbole**
- **Imagery**
- **Irony**
- **Jargon**
- **Language**
- **Literal Language**
- **Metaphors**
- **Parallelism**
- **Similes**
- **Slang**

12.1 WHAT LANGUAGE IS AND DOES

"Words are sacred. They deserve respect. If you get the right ones in the right order you can nudge the world a little." -Tom Stoppard

---

The Ancient Romans who studied and taught rhetoric divided its study and process into five "canons:" invention, disposition, style, memory, and delivery. The term "style" does not refer to clothing styles but language choices. Should a public speaker use very basic language because the audience is unfamiliar with his topic? Or more technical language with many acronyms, abbreviations, and jargon because the audience has expertise in the topic? Or academic language with abstract vocabulary, or flowery, poetic language with lots of metaphors? Perhaps you have never thought about those questions, but they are ones that influence both the clarity of the message as well as the credibility a speaker will gain during the presentation.

However, we would be wrong if we treated language as an "add-on" to the ideas and structure of the speech. Language is a far too complex and foundational aspect of our lives for us to consider it as an afterthought for a speech. In this chapter we will look at how language functions in communication, what standards language choices should meet in public speaking, and how you can become more proficient in using language in public speaking.

Language is any formal system of gestures, signs, sounds, and symbols used or conceived as a means of communicating thought, either through written, enacted, or spoken means. Linguists believe there are far more than 6,900 languages and distinct dialects spoken in the world today (Anderson, 2012). The language spoken by the greatest number of people on the planet is Mandarin (a dialect of Chinese). Other widely spoken languages are English, Spanish, and Arabic. English is spoken widely on every content (thanks to the British Empire) but Mandarin is spoken by the most people. While we tend to think of language in its print form, for most of history and for most of the world, language has been or is spoken, or oral. More than half of spoken languages have not even been put into written form yet (https://www.swarthmore.edu/SocSci/langhotspots/fastfacts.html).

We have already seen in earlier chapters that public speakers have to make adjustments to language for audiences. For example, spoken language is more wordy and repetitive than written language needs to be or should be. It is accompanied by gestures, vocal emphasis, and facial expressions. Additionally, spoken language includes more personal pronouns and more expressive, emotional, colloquial, slang, and nonstandard words.

The study of language is, believe it or not, controversial. If you are an education, social sciences, pre-law, or English major, you will somewhere in your college career come up against this truth. While we use words everyday and don't think about it, scholars in different fields concern themselves with how we choose words, why we choose words, what effect words have on us, and how the powerful people of the world use words. One theory of language, general semantics, says that meaning resides in the person using the word, not in the word ("Basic Understandings," 2015). It is helpful for the public speaker to keep this mind, especially in regard to **denotative** and **connotative** meaning. Wrench, Goding, Johnson, and Attias (2011) use this example to explain the difference:

> portion of the visual spectrum dominated by energy with a wavelength of roughly 440–490 nano-meters. You could also say that the color in question is an equal mixture of both red and green light. While both of these are technically correct ways to interpret the word "blue," we're pretty sure that neither of these definitions is how you thought about the word. When hearing the word "blue," you may have thought of your favorite color, the color of the sky on a spring day, or the color of a really ugly car you saw in the parking lot. When people think about language, there are two different types of meanings that people must be aware of: denotative and connotative. (p. 407)

Denotative meaning is the specific meaning associated with a word. We sometimes refer to denotative meanings as dictionary definitions. The [scientific] definitions provided in the first two sentences of the quotation above are examples of definitions that might be found in a dictionary. Connotative meaning is the idea suggested by or associated with a word at a cultural or personal level. In addition to the examples above, the word "blue" can evoke many other ideas:

- State of depression (feeling blue)
- Indication of winning (a blue ribbon)
- Side during the Civil War (blues vs. grays)
- Sudden event (out of the blue).
- States that lean toward the Democratic Party in their voting
- A slang expression for obscenity (blue comedy)
- In plural form, a genre of music (the blues)

Language is not just something we *use*; it is part of who we are and how we think. When we talk about language, we have to use words to do so, and language is also hard to separate from who we are. Each of us has our own way of expressing ourselves. Even more, it is almost impossible to separate language from thinking. Many people think the federal government should enact a law that only English is spoken in the United States (in government offices, schools, etc.). This is opposed by some groups because it seems discriminatory to immigrants, based on the belief that everyone's language is part of their identity and self-definition.

Not only is language about who we are; it is about power or at least is used by powerful people. In fact, some educational and political theorists believe that language is all about power. For instance, **euphemisms** are often used to make something unpleasant sound more tolerable. In one of the more well-known examples of the use of euphemisms, the government commonly tries to use language to "soften" what many would see as bad. During the Vietnam War, "air support" was invented to cover the real meaning: "bombing." When you hear air support, you probably think "planes bringing supplies in," not "bombing."

Even today, terms like "revenue enhancement" are used instead of "tax increases." The word euphemism has at its core "eu," (which is a prefix from Greek meaning "good" or "pleasant") and "phem" (a root word for speaking). Just as blasphemy is speaking evil about sacred things, "euphemism" is "pleasant speaking about unpleasant things." We use euphemisms every day, but we have to be careful not to obscure meaning or use them deceptively.

There's an old saying in debate, "He who defines the terms wins the debate." In the 1988 election, George H.W. Bush was running against Michael Dukakis, who was the governor of Massachusetts. Vice President Bush was able to stick a label on Dukakis and it stuck, that of "liberal." He not only labeled Governor Dukakis, but he also defined what "liberal" meant. The word was in disuse after that, and you don't hear it as much now. The word in use now is "progressive." Unfortunately, this incident in 1988 politics obscured the fact that the U.S. has always been a "liberal" democratic republic. The word "liberal" has shifted meaning, another trait of language, since meaning exists in the minds of users, not in some protected, never-changing space or form. In the majority of Americans' minds, "liberal" has become associated with specific political positions rather than a form of government in general.

This example brings up another issue with language: words change meaning over time, or more specifically, the meaning we attached to them changes. "Pretty" used to mean "clever" 250 years ago. "Prevent" meant to "precede," not to keep from happening. Language is simply not static, as much as we might like it to be. One of the main reasons we find Shakespeare daunting is that so many of the Elizabethan words are either no longer used or they have changed meanings.

With regard to the use of language for power, even unknowingly, feminists in the 1970s argued that the common way we use English language was biased against women. King-sized means "big and powerful," but "queensized" means "for overweight women." "Master" was not equivalent to "mistress." "Madame" has taken on a negative connotation, even though it should have been equivalent to "sir." Many words referring to women had to add a suffix that was often "less than," such as "-ess" or "-ette" or "co-ed." In the last thirty years we have gotten away from that, so that you often hear a female actor referred to as "actor" rather than "actress," but old habits die hard.

We see another example of power in language in the abortion debate. Prior to 1973, abortions could be obtained legally, to some extent, in three states: California, New York, and Hawaii. After the Roe v. Wade decision in January of 1973, they could, at least theoretically, be obtained in all fifty states. Roe v. Wade did not make abortions legal so much as it made anti-abortion laws illegal or unconstitutional. Practically, the effect was basically the same, but we are often imprecise about language. The people who were against abortion were now on the defensive, and they had to start fighting. It's generally better to be "pro-"something rather than "anti-"something, so they became "pro-life." Those favoring abortion rights then automatically became "pro-death." One side had defined the terms of the debate, and the other had to come up with something comparable. "Pro-choice" takes advantage of the American belief in personal freedoms.

Can you think of how advertisers choose words in a way that is meant to affect your thinking and see an object in different ways? Realtors sell "homes," not houses. McDonald's sells "Happy Meals" even though it is essentially the same food they sell that are not "Happy Meals." As you progress as a public speaker, you will become more aware of the power certain words have over audiences. An ethical communicator will use language in a way that encourages respect for others, freedom of thought, and informed decision making. First, however, a speaker should seek to meet the standards of clarity, effectiveness, appropriateness, and elegance in language, which are discussed in the next section.

Pete's Phrases

As the official mascot of Oklahoma State University, Pistol Pete was a cherished figure, always ready to rally the crowd with his infectious Cowboy spirit and colloquial cowboy lingo. However, during one particular international student orientation, Pete found that his cowboy language didn't always translate as he intended.

Eager to welcome the new students, Pete greeted them with a hearty, "Howdy, partners! Y'all ready to saddle up and ride into the sunset of a great academic journey at OSU?" The crowd responded with a mixture of polite nods and puzzled looks, but there was a palpable sense of confusion among some of the international students unfamiliar with Pete's cowboy vernacular.

Realizing that his message might not have come across as he intended, Pete decided to take a different approach. He remembered that effective communication was about making sure the message was understood, not just about delivering it.

With a friendly smile, he addressed the crowd again, this time opting for more universal language. "Welcome, everyone! Are you excited to begin your amazing academic journey at OSU?" This time, the crowd responded enthusiastically, their faces lighting up with understanding and appreciation.

However, Pete didn't want to completely abandon his unique cowboy lingo, as it was a significant part of his identity and the Oklahoma State spirit. So, he decided to incorporate it in a way that would educate and entertain his listeners.

He explained, "In cowboy speak, when we say 'saddle up,' we mean get ready, and 'ride into the sunset' means to embark on an exciting journey. I know it might sound confusing at first, but don't worry, you'll get the hang of it in no time!" The students laughed and nodded, appreciating Pete's effort to include them in the Cowboy culture.

From that day forward, Pistol Pete made sure to balance his cowboy lingo with clear, universal language, especially when addressing diverse crowds. This experience taught him the importance of adjusting his communication to his audience, ensuring that his messages were not just delivered, but also understood and appreciated. Have you ever used colloquialisms or regional expressions that caused confusion or miscommunication? Why is it important to recognize how our language influences the audience's understanding?

12.2 STANDARDS FOR LANGUAGE IN PUBLIC

Clear language is powerful language. Clarity is the first concern of a public speaker when it comes to choosing how to phrase the ideas of his or her speech. If you are not clear, specific, precise, detailed, and sensory with your language, you won't have to worry about being emotional or persuasive, because you won't be understood. There are many aspects of clarity in language, listed below.

Achieving Clarity

The first aspect of clarity is concreteness. We usually think of concreteness as the opposite of abstraction. Language that evokes many different visual images in the minds of your audience is **abstract language**. Unfortunately, when abstract language is used, the images evoked might not be the ones you really want to evoke. A word such as "creature" is very abstract; it brings up a range of mental pictures or associations: monster, animal, forests, swamps, etc. When asked to identify what an abstract term like "creature" means, twenty people will have twenty different ideas.

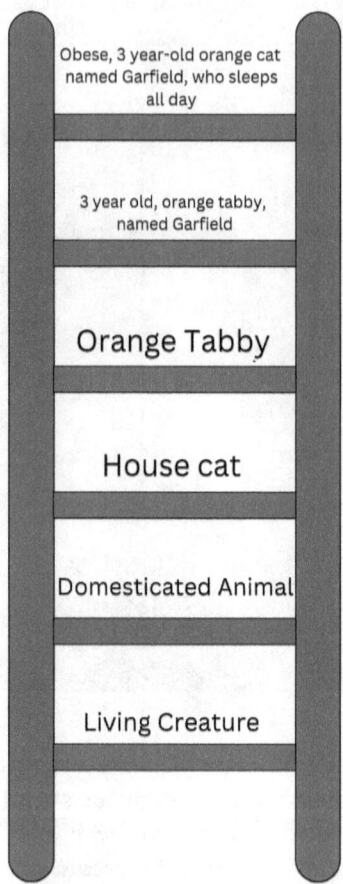

In order to show how language should be more specific, the "ladder of abstraction" (Hayakawa, 1939) was developed. The ladder of abstraction helps us see how our language can range from abstract (general and sometimes vague) to very precise and specific (such as an actual thing that everyone in your audience will know or be able to identify). Instead of saying, "he was a large man," it might provide more clarity if you were specific with your language by saying, "He's 6 foot, four inches tall and weighs about three hundred and fifty pounds."

Or to reference our image above, if you were to tell your audience you have a living creature in your home, it would sound quite mysterious, but it would create more clarity and understanding if they knew you were referencing your three year old, obese, orange tabby who is constantly sleeping or eating. The more specific we can be with our language, the better we can create a mental image for the audience. A picture is worth a thousand words, right?

Related to the issue of specific vs. abstract is the use of the right word. Mark Twain said, "The difference between the right word and the almost right word is the difference between lightning and a lightning bug." For example, the words "prosecute" and "persecute" are commonly confused, but not interchangeable. Two others are peremptory/pre-emptive and prerequisites/perquisites. Can you think of other such word pair confusion?

In the attempt to be clear, which is your first concern, you will also want to be simple and familiar in your language. Familiarity is a factor of attention; familiar language draws in the audience. Simple does not mean simplistic, but the avoidance of multi-syllable words. If a speaker said, "A collection of pre-adolescents fabricated an obese personification comprised of compressed mounds of minute aquatic crystals," you might recognize it as "Some children made a snowman," but maybe not. The language is not simple or familiar and therefore does not communicate well, although the words are correct and do mean the same thing, technically.

Along with language needing to be specific and correct, language can use appropriate similes and metaphors to become clearer. **Literal language** does not use comparisons like similes and metaphors; **figurative language** uses comparisons with objects, animals, activities, roles, or historical or literary figures. Literal says, "The truck is fast." Figurative says "The truck is as fast as..." or "The truck runs like..." or "He drives that truck like Kyle Busch at Daytona." **Similes** use some form of "like" or "as" in the comparisons. **Metaphors** are direct comparisons, such as "He is Kyle Busch at Daytona when he gets behind the wheel of that truck." Here are some more examples of metaphors:

> Love is a *battlefield*.

> Upon hearing the charges, the accused *clammed up* and refused to speak without a lawyer.

> Every year a new crop of activists is *born*.

For rhetorical purposes, metaphors are considered stronger, but both can help you achieve clearer language, if chosen wisely. To think about how metaphor is stronger than simile, think of the difference "Love is a battlefield" and "Love is like a battlefield." Speakers are encouraged to pick and not overuse them. Also, avoid mixed metaphors, as in this example: "That's awfully thin gruel for the right wing to hang their hats on." Or "He found himself up a river and had to change horses." The mixed metaphor here is the use of "up a river" and "change horses" together; you would either need to use an all river-based metaphor (dealing with boats, water, tides, etc.) or a metaphor dealing specifically with horses. The example above about a "new crop" "being born," is actually a mixed metaphor, since crops aren't born, but planted and harvested. Additionally, in choosing metaphors and similes, speakers want to avoid clichés, discussed next.

Clichés are expressions, usually similes, that are predictable. You know what comes next because they are overused and sometimes out of date. Clichés do not have to be linguistic—we often see clichés in movies, such as teen horror films where you know exactly what will happen next! It is not hard to think of clichés: "Scared out of my..." or "When life gives you lemons..." or "All is fair in..." or, when describing a reckless driver, "She drives like a..." If you filled in the blanks with "wits," "make lemonade," "love and war," "or "maniac," those are clichés.

Clichés are not just a problem because they are overused and boring; they also sometimes do not communicate what you need, especially to audiences whose second language is English. "I will give you a ballpark figure" is not as clear as "I will give you an estimate," and assumes the person is familiar with American sports. Therefore, they also will make you appear less credible in the eyes of the audience because you are not analyzing them and taking their knowledge, background, and needs into account. As the United States becomes more diverse, being aware of your audience members whose first language is not English is a valuable tool for a speaker.

Additionally, some clichés are so outdated that no one knows what they mean. "The puppy was as cute as a button" is an example. You might hear your great-grandmother say this, but who really thinks buttons are cute nowadays? Clichés are also imprecise. Although clichés do have a comfort level to them, comfort puts people to sleep. Find fresh ways, or just use basic, literal language. "The bear was big" is imprecise in terms of giving your audience an idea of how frightful an experience faced by a bear would be. "The bear was as big as a house" is a cliché and an exaggeration, therefore imprecise. A better alternative might be, "The bear was two feet taller than I am when he stood on his back legs." The opposite of clichés is clear, vivid, and fresh language.

In trying to avoid clichés, use language with **imagery**, or sensory language. This is language that makes the recipient smell, taste, see, hear, and feel a sensation. Think of the word "ripe." What is "ripe?" Do ripe fruits feel a certain way? Smell a certain way? Taste a certain way? Ripe is a sensory word. Most words just appeal to one sense, like vision. Think of color. How can you make the word "blue" more sensory? How can you make the word "loud" more sensory? How would you describe the current state of your bedroom or dorm room to leave a sensory impression? How would you describe your favorite meal to leave a sensory impression? or a thunderstorm?

Poetry uses much imagery, so to end this section on fresh, clear language, here is a verse from "Daffodils" by William Wordsworth. Notice the metaphors ("daffodils dancing," "host," which brings to mind great heavenly numbers), simile ("as the stars") and the imagery ("golden" rather than "yellow," and other appeals to feeling and sight):

> A host, of golden daffodils;
> Beside the lake, beneath the trees,
> Fluttering and dancing in the breeze.
> Continuous as the stars that shine
> And twinkle on the Milky Way.

Effectiveness

Language achieves effectiveness by communicating the right message to the audience. Clarity contributes to effectiveness, but there are some other aspects of effectiveness. To that end, language should be a means of inclusion and identification, rather than exclusion. Let's establish this truth: Language is for communication; communication is symbolic, and language is the main (but not only) symbol system we use for communication. If language is for communication, then its goal should be to bring people together and to create understanding.

Unfortunately, we habitually use language for exclusion rather than inclusion. We can push people away with our word choices rather than bringing them together. Stereotypes serve as examples of what we're talking about here. What follows are some examples of language that can exclude members of your audience from understanding what you are saying.

Jargon

Jargon used in your profession or hobby should only be used with audiences who share your profession or hobby. Not only will the audience members who don't share your profession or hobby miss your meaning, but they will feel that you are not making an honest effort to communicate or are setting yourself above them in intelligence or rank. Lawyers are often accused of using "legalese," but other professions and groups do the same. If audience members do not understand your references, jargon, or vocabulary, it is unlikely that they will sit there and say, "This person is so smart! I wish I could be smart like this speaker." The audience member is more likely to be thinking, "Why can't this speaker use words we understand and get off the high horse?" (which I admit, is a cliché!)

What this means for you is that you need to be careful about assumptions of your audience's knowledge and their ability to interpret jargon. For example, if you are trying to register for a class at the authors' college and your adviser asks for the CRN, most other people would have no idea what you are talking about (course reference number). Acronyms, such NPO, are common in jargon. Those trained in the medical field know it is based on the Latin for "nothing by mouth." The military has many acronyms, such as MOS (military occupational specialty, or career field in civilian talk). If you are speaking to an audience who does not know the jargon of your field, using it will only make them annoyed by the lack of clarity.

Sometimes we are not even aware of our jargon and its inadvertent effects. A student once complained to one of the authors about her reaction when she heard that she had been "purged." The word sounds much worse than the meaning it had in that context: that her name was taken off the official roll due nonpayment before the beginning of the semester.

Slang

The whole point of **slang** is for a subculture or group to have its own code, almost like secret words. Once slang is understood by the larger culture, it is no longer slang and may be classified as "informal" or "colloquial" language. "Bling" was slang; now it's in the dictionary. Sports have a great deal of slang used by the players and fans that then gets used in everyday language. For example, "That was a slam dunk" is used to describe something easy, not just in basketball.

Complicated Vocabulary

If a speaker used the word "recalcitrant," some audience members would know the meaning or figure it out ("Calci-"is like calcium, calcium is hard, etc.), but many would not. It would make much more sense for them to use a word readily understandable–"stubborn." Especially in oral communication, we should use language that is immediately accessible. However, do not take this to mean "dumb down for your audience." It means being clear and not showing off. For a speaker to say "I am cognizant of the fact that..." instead of "I know" or "I am aware of..." adds nothing to communication.

Profanity and Cursing

It is difficult to think of many examples, other than artistic or comedy venues, where profanity or cursing would be effective or useful with most audiences, so this kind of language is generally discouraged.

Credibility

Another aspect of effectiveness is that your language should enhance your credibility. First, audiences trust speakers who use clear, vivid, respectful, engaging, and honest language. On the other hand, audiences tend not to trust speakers who use language that excludes others or who exhibit uneducated language patterns. All of us make an occasional grammatical or usage error. However, constant verb and pronoun errors and just plain getting words confused will hurt the audience's belief that you are competent and knowledgeable. In addition, a speaker who uses language and references that are not immediately accessible or that are unfamiliar will have diminished credibility. Finally, you should avoid the phrase "I guess" in a speech. Credible speakers should know what they are talking about.

Rhetorical Techniques

There are several traditional techniques that have been used to engage audiences and make ideas more attention-getting and memorable. These are called rhetorical techniques. Although "rhetorical" is associated with persuasive speech, these techniques are also effective with other types of speeches. We will not mention all of them here, but some important ones are listed below. Several of them are based on a form of repetition. You can refer to an Internet source for a full list of the dozens of rhetorical devices.

Assonance is the repetition of vowel sounds in a sentence or passage. As such, it is a kind of rhyme. Minister Tony Campolo said, "When Jesus told his disciples to pray for the kingdom, this was no pie in the sky by and by when you die kind of prayer."

Alliteration is the repetition of initial consonant sounds in a sentence or passage. In his "I Have a Dream Speech," Dr. Martin Luther King said, "I have a dream that my four little children will one day live in a nation where they will not be judged by the color of their skin but by the content of their character." Not only does this sentence use alliteration, it also uses the next rhetorical technique on our list, antithesis.

Antithesis is the juxtaposition of contrasting ideas in balanced or parallel words, phrases, or grammatical structures. Usually antithesis goes: Not this, but this. John F. Kennedy's statement from his 1961 inaugural address is one of the most quoted examples of antithesis: "Ask not what your country can do for you; ask what you can do for your country." In that speech he gave another example, "If a free society cannot help the many who are poor, it cannot save the few who are rich."

Parallelism is the repetition of sentence structures. It can be useful for stating your main ideas. Which one of these sounds better?

> "Give me liberty or I'd rather die."
> "Give me liberty or give me death."

The second one uses parallelism. Quoting again from JFK's inaugural address: "Let every nation know, whether it wishes us well or ill, that we shall pay any price, bear any burden, meet any hardship, support any friend, oppose any foe to assure the survival and the success of liberty." The repetition of the three-word phrases in this sentence (including the word "any" in each) is an example of parallelism.

Anaphora is a succession of sentences beginning with the same word or group of words. In his inaugural address, JFK began several succeeding paragraphs with "To those": "To those old allies," "To those new states," "To those people," etc.

Hyperbole is intentional exaggeration for effect. Sometimes it is for serious purposes, other times for humor. Commonly we use hyperbolic language in our everyday speech to emphasize our emotions, such as when we say "I'm having the worst day ever" or "I would kill for a cup of coffee right now." Neither of those statements is (hopefully) true, but it stresses to others the way you are feeling. Ronald Reagan, who was often disparaged for being the oldest president, would joke about his age. In one case he said, "The chamber is celebrating an important milestone this week: your 70th anniversary. I remember the day you started."

Irony is the expression of one's meaning by using language that normally signifies the opposite, typically for humorous or emphatic effect. Although most people think they understand irony as sarcasm (such as saying to a friend who trips, "That's graceful"), it is a much more complicated topic. A speaker may use it when they profess to say one thing but clearly means something else or say something that is obviously untrue and everyone would recognize that and understand the purpose. Irony in oral communication can be difficult to use in a way that affects everyone in the audience the same way.

Using these techniques alone will not make you an effective speaker. Dr. King and President Kennedy combined them with strong metaphors and images as well; for example, Dr. King described the promises of the founding fathers as a "blank check" returned with the note "insufficient funds" as far as the black Americans of his time were concerned. That was a very concrete, human, and familiar metaphor to his listeners and still speaks to us today.

Appropriateness

Appropriateness relates to several categories involving how persons and groups should be referred to and addressed based on inclusiveness and context. The term "politically correct" has been overused to describe the growing sensitivity to how the power of language can marginalize or exclude individuals and groups. While there are silly extremes such as the term "vertically challenged" for "short," these humorous examples overlook the need to be inclusive about language. Overall, people and groups should be respected and referred to in the way they choose to be. Using inclusive language in your speech will help ensure you aren't alienating or diminishing any members of your audience.

Gender-Inclusive Language

The first common form of non-inclusive language is language that privileges one of the sexes over the other. There are three common problem areas that speakers run into while speaking: using "he" as generic, using "man" to mean all humans, and gender-typing jobs. Consider the statement, "Every morning when an officer of the law puts on his badge, he risks his life to serve and protect his fellow citizens."

Obviously, both male and female police officers risk their lives when they put on their badges.

A better way to word the sentence would be, "Every morning when officers of the law put on their badges, they risk their lives to serve and protect their fellow citizens." Notice that in the better sentence, we made the subject plural ("officers") and used neutral pronouns ("they" and "their") to avoid the generic "he." Likewise, speakers of English have traditionally used terms like "man," and "mankind" when referring to both females and males. Instead of using the word "man," refer to the "human race."

The last common area where speakers get into trouble with gender and language has to do with job titles. It is not unusual for people to assume, for example, that doctors are male and nurses are female. As a result, they may say "she is a woman doctor" or "he is a male nurse" when mentioning someone's occupation, perhaps not realizing that the statements "she is a
doctor" and "he is a nurse" already inform the listener as to the sex of the
person holding that job.

Ethnic Identity

Ethnic identity refers to a group an individual identifies with based on a common culture. For example, within the United States we have numerous ethnic groups, including Italian Americans, Irish Americans, Japanese Americans, Vietnamese

Americans, Cuban Americans, and Mexican Americans. As with the earlier example of "male nurse," avoid statements such as "The committee is made up of four women and a Vietnamese man." All that should be said is, "The committee is made up of five people."

If for some reason gender and ethnicity have to be mentioned—and usually it does not—the gender and ethnicity of each member should be mentioned equally. "The committee is made up of three European-American women, one Latina, and one Vietnamese male." In recent years, there has been a trend toward steering inclusive language away from broad terms like "Asians" and "Hispanics" because these terms are not considered precise labels for the groups they actually represent. If you want to be safe, the best thing you can do is ask a couple of people who belong to an ethnic group how they prefer to be referred to in that context.

Disability

The last category of exclusive versus inclusive language that causes problems for some speakers relates to individuals with physical or intellectual disabilities or forms of mental illness. Sometimes it happens that we take a characteristic of someone and make that the totality or all of what that person is. For example, some people are still uncomfortable around persons who use wheelchairs and don't know how to react. They may totalize and think that the wheelchair defines and therefore limits the user. The person in the wheelchair might be a great guitarist, sculptor, parent, public speaker, or scientist, but those qualities are not seen, only the wheelchair.

Although the terms "visually impaired" and "hearing impaired" are sometimes used for "blind" and "deaf," this is another situation where the person should be referred to as he or she prefers. "Hearing impaired" denotes a wide range of hearing deficit, as does "visually impaired." "Deaf" and "blind" are not generally considered offensive by these groups.

Another example is how to refer to what used to be called "autism." Saying someone is "autistic" is similar to the word "retarded" in that neither is appropriate. Preferable terms are "a person with an autism diagnosis" or "a person on the autism spectrum." In place of "retarded," "a person with intellectual disabilities" should be used. Likewise, slang words for mental illness should always be avoided, such as "crazy" or "mental."

Other Types of Appropriateness

Language in a speech should be appropriate to the speaker and the speaker's background and personality, to the context, to the audience, and to the topic. Let's say that you're an engineering student. If you're giving a presentation in an engineering class, you can use language that other engineering students will know. On the other hand, if you use that engineering vocabulary in a public speaking class, many audience members will not understand you. As another example, if you are speaking about the Great Depression to an audience of young adults or recent immigrants, you can't assume they will know the meaning of terms like "New Deal" and "WPA," which would be familiar to an audience of senior citizens. Audience analysis is a key factor in choosing the language to use in a speech.

12.3 USING EFFECTIVE LANGUAGE IN PUBLIC SPEAKING

At this point, we will make some applications and suggestions about using language as you grow as a public speaker.

First, get in the habit of using "stipulated definitions" with concrete examples (defining operationally). In other words, define your terms for the audience. If you are using jargon, a technical term, a word that has multiple meanings in different contexts, or an often-misunderstood word, you can say at the beginning of the body of your speech, "In this speech I am going to be using the word, "X," and what I mean by it is..." And then the best way to define a word is with a picture or example of what you mean, and perhaps also an example of what you don't mean (visual aids can help here). Don't worry; this is not insulting to most audiences if the word is technical or unfamiliar to them. On the other hand, providing dictionary definitions of common words such as "love" or "loyalty" would be insulting to an audience and pretty boring.

Second, develop specific language. The general semantics movement suggested ways to develop more specific language that reflects the imperfection of our perceptions and the fact that reality changes. You can develop specific language by the following:

- Distinguishing between individuals and the group (that is, avoid stereotyping).

Arab 1 is not Arab 2 is not Arab 3, etc., and none of them are all the Arabs in the world.
- Specifying time and place of behavior instead of making broad statements. What was a true of a person in 1999 is not necessarily true of the person now.
- Using names for jobs or roles ("accountants," "administrative assistants," "instructors") instead of "people" or "workers."
- Avoid "always/never" language. "Always" and "never" usually do not reflect reality and tend to make listeners defensive.
- Avoid confusing opinion for fact. If I say, "Forrest Gump is a stupid movie," I am stating an opinion in the language of fact. If you preface opinions with "I believe," or "It is my opinion" you will be truthful and gain the appearance of being fair-minded and non-dogmatic. What should be said is "The first time I saw Forrest Gump, I didn't realize it was a farce, but after I saw it a second time, I understood it better." This sentence is much more specific and clarifying than "Forrest Gump is a stupid movie." Using this kind of language also helps make the speaker seem less dogmatic and closed-minded.

Third, personalize your language. In a speech it's fine to use personal pronouns as opposed to third person. That means "I," "me," "we," "us," "you," etc. are often helpful in a speech. It gives more immediacy to the speech. Be careful of using "you" for examples that might be embarrassing. "Let's say you are arrested for possession of a concealed weapon," sounds like the audience members are potential criminals.

Finally, develop your vocabulary, but not to show it off. One of the benefits of a college education is that your vocabulary will expand greatly, and it should. A larger vocabulary will give you access to more complicated reading material and allow you to understand the world better. But knowing the meaning of a more complicated word doesn't mean you have to use it with every audience.

Conclusion

Although the placement of this chapter may seem to indicate that language choices, or what the ancient rhetoricians called "style," are not as important as other parts of speaking, language choices are important from the very beginning of your speech preparation, even to your research and choice of search terms. Audience analysis will help you to develop language that is clear, vivid, appropriate, credible, and persuasive.

12.4 ENRICHMENT

Discussion Questions

1. Describe the difference between denotative and connotative meanings of "Wall Street," "proud," and "time of death." Think of other words with different denotative and connotative meanings.
2. Describe a time when you heard a euphemism to describe something negative, like "passed away" or "being let go." How did the language impact the message?
3. Think of a time when you used jargon in conversation and it was misunderstood. What were the results of the misunderstanding? What language could you have used instead of jargon?
4. Why should you avoid using profanity in public speaking? Are there times when profanity might be useful in public speaking? How can we ensure the appropriateness of our language?

Activities

1. Draw a ladder on a piece of paper with several rungs. Think of an abstract word you can start with on the bottom rung. On each level, make it more concrete using each rung of the ladder to create your own "ladder of abstraction" (Hayakawa, 1939) in Section 12.2. For example- Creature–>Domesticated Animal–>Feline—>House cat—> Persian–>Garfield–>red, overweight, Persian name Garfield
2. In a group, pronounce these commonly mispronounced terms: chipotle, colonel, worcestershire, corp, quinoa, dachshund, synecdoche, anemone, pho, acai, niche, gif, tenet, coupe de grace, hyperbole, data. If you are unsure of the correct pronunciation, look them up on your phone/laptop. Can you think of any others? Share with the group. Discuss the consequences of a mispronunciation during a presentation.
3. In small groups, brainstorm and come up with a hyperbole to describe one aspect of your life as a college student (nutrition, exhaustion, learning, cost, living, friends, growth, etc.). Share with the class.

13 PRESENTATION AIDS

Learning Objectives

- List and explain reasons why presentation aids are important in public speaking;
- Explain how presentation aids function in public speaking;
- Describe the various computer-based and non-computer-based types of presentation aids available to the students;
- Explain the correct use of various types of presentation aids;
- Design professional-looking slides using presentation software.

Key Terms

- **Bar Graph**
- **Chart**
- **Diagram**
- **Graph**
- **Gustatory**
- **Line Graph**
- **Olfactory**
- **Pictograph**
- **Pie Graph**
- **Presentation Aids**

- **Tone**

13.1 WHAT ARE PRESENTATION AIDS?

"Well-designed visuals do more than provide information; they bring order to the conversation." -Dale Ludwig

When you give a speech, you are presenting much more than just a collection of words and ideas. Because you are speaking "live and in person," your audience members will experience your speech through all five of their senses: hearing, vision, smell, taste, and touch. In some speaking situations, the speaker appeals only to the sense of hearing. They more or less ignore the other senses except to avoid visual distractions by dressing and presenting themselves in an appropriate manner. But the speaking event can be greatly enriched by appeals to the other senses. This is the role of presentation aids.

Presentation aids are the resources beyond the speech words and delivery that a speaker uses to enhance the message conveyed to the audience. The type of presentation aids that speakers most typically make use of are visual aids: pictures, diagrams, charts and graphs, maps, and the like. Audible aids include musical excerpts, audio speech excerpts, and sound effects. A speaker may also use fragrance samples or food samples as **olfactory** (sense of smell) or **gustatory** (sense of taste) aids. Finally, presentation aids can be three-dimensional objects, animals, and people; they can also change over a period of time, as in the case of a how-to demonstration.

As you can see, the range of possible presentation aids is almost unlimited. However, all presentation aids have one thing in common: To be effective, each presentation aid a speaker uses must be a direct, uncluttered example of a specific element of the speech. It is understandable that someone presenting a speech about Abraham Lincoln might want to include a photograph of him, but because everyone already knows what Lincoln looked like, the picture would not contribute much to the message unless, perhaps, the message was specifically about the changes in Lincoln's appearance during his time in office.

Other visual artifacts are more likely to deliver information more directly relevant to the speech—a diagram of the interior of Ford's Theater where Lincoln was assassinated, a facsimile of the messy and much-edited Gettysburg Address, or a photograph of the Lincoln family, for example. The key is that each presentation aid must directly express an idea in your speech.

Moreover, presentation aids must be used at the time when you are presenting the specific ideas related to the aid. For example, if you are speaking about coral reefs and one of your supporting points is about the location of the world's major reefs, it would make sense to display a map of these reefs while you're talking about location. If you display it while you are explaining what coral actually is, or describing the kinds of fish that feed on a reef, the map will not serve as a useful visual aid—in fact, it's likely to be a distraction.

To be effective, presentation aids must also be easy to use and easy for the listeners to see and understand. In this chapter, we will present some principles and strategies to help you incorporate effective presentation aids into your speech. We will begin by discussing the functions that good presentation aids fulfill. Next, we will explore some of the many types of presentation aids and how best to design and utilize them. We will also describe various media that can be used for presentation aids. We will conclude with tips for successful preparation and use of presentation aids in a speech.

13.1 WHAT ARE PRESENTATION AIDS? | 427

Pete's Presentation Aid

With a clear understanding of the role visual aids play in enhancing a speech, Pistol Pete settled down at his computer to create a slide deck for his upcoming presentation on Oklahoma State University traditions. As he fired up his presentation software, Pete had four criteria in mind to ensure his visuals would be effective: improving understanding, enhancing memory and retention, maintaining audience interest, and establishing speaker credibility.

As he crafted his first slide, Pete decided to set the tone with a captivating image of a vibrant OSU tradition – the Sea of Orange Parade. He chose this image to immediately draw his audience into the world of OSU traditions. He believed that such a vivid depiction of a beloved tradition would not only grab attention but also make a lasting impression, enhancing memory and retention.

For the main body of his presentation, Pete decided to use a combination of **brief** text points and corresponding images. He was mindful to keep the text concise and informative, making sure it aligned with what he was saying verbally. He paired each point with relevant images or short video clips that illustrated the tradition in action. This visual reinforcement of his words aimed to improve the audience's understanding of the traditions.

Pete knew the importance of credibility for a speaker. So, he was careful to orally cite the information referenced on his slides. This not only established his credibility but also provided a reference point for anyone interested in learning more about the traditions at OSU.

To maintain audience interest throughout the speech, Pete decided to infuse elements of surprise into his slide deck. He included a few 'Did you know?' slides at unexpected points, each revealing a fun or little-known fact about OSU traditions. He believed these elements of surprise would keep his audience engaged and attentive throughout his presentation.

As he clicked through his completed slide deck, Pistol Pete felt a surge of satisfaction. He believed he had created a visual aid that not only complemented his speech but would also enhance his audience's understanding, keep them engaged, aid in memory and retention, and demonstrate his credibility. Now all that remained was to deliver his informative speech with the same enthusiasm and passion that had driven his research and preparation. Why do you think it's important to keep text brief and to a minimum on slides? Is it important to include images on each slide?

13.2 FUNCTIONS OF PRESENTATION AIDS

Why should you use presentation aids? If you have prepared and rehearsed your speech adequately, shouldn't a good speech with a good delivery be enough to stand on its own? While it is true that impressive presentation aids will not rescue a poor speech, a good speech can often be made even better by the strategic use of presentation aids. Presentation aids can fulfill several functions: they can serve to improve your audience's understanding of the information you are conveying, enhance audience memory and retention of the message, add variety and interest to your speech, and enhance your credibility as a speaker. Let's examine each of these functions.

Improving Audience Understanding

Human communication is a complex process that often leads to misunderstandings. If you are like most people, you can easily remember incidents when you misunderstood a message or when someone else misunderstood what you said to them. Misunderstandings happen in public speaking just as they do in everyday conversations.

One reason for misunderstandings is the fact that perception and interpretation are highly complex individual processes. Most of us have seen the image in which, depending on your perception, you see either the outline of a vase or the facial profiles of two people facing each other. Or perhaps you have seen the image of the woman who may or may not be young, depending on your frame of reference at the time. This shows how interpretations can differ, and it means that your presentations must be based on careful thought and preparation to maximize the likelihood that your listeners will understand your presentations as you intend them to do so.

As a speaker, one of your basic goals is to help your audience understand your message. To reduce misunderstanding, presentation aids can be used to clarify or to emphasize.

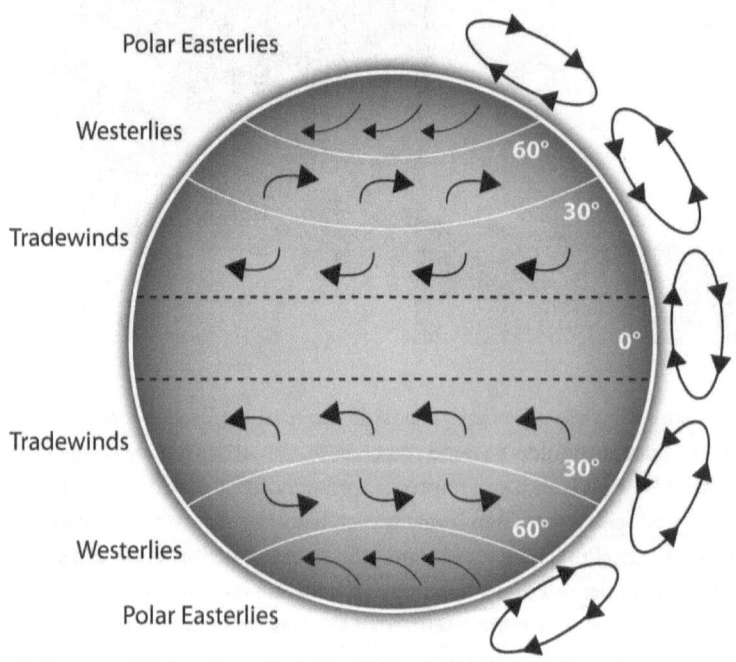

Clarifying

Clarification is important in a speech because if some of the information you convey is unclear, your listeners will come away puzzled or possibly even misled. Presentation aids can help clarify a message if the information is complex or if the point being made is a visual one.

If your speech is about the impact of the Coriolis Effect on tropical storms, for instance, you will have great difficulty clarifying it without a diagram because the process is a complex one. The diagram above would be effective because it shows the audience the interaction between equatorial wind patterns and wind patterns moving in other directions. The diagram allows the audience to process the information in two ways: through your verbal explanation and through the visual elements of the diagram. By the way, the Coriolis Effect is defined as "an effect whereby a mass moving in a rotating system experiences a force (the Coriolis force) acting perpendicular to the direction of motion and to the axis of rotation. On the earth, the effect tends to deflect moving objects to the right in the northern hemisphere and to the left in the southern and is important in the formation of cyclonic weather systems." You can see why a picture really helps with this definition.

Another aspect of clarifying occurs when a speaker wants to help audience members understand a visual concept. For example, if a speaker is talking about the importance of petroglyphs in Native American culture, just describing the petroglyphs won't completely help your audience to visualize what they look like. Instead, showing an example of a petroglyph, such as the one below can more easily help your audience form a clear mental image of your intended meaning.

Emphasizing

When you use a presentational aid for emphasis, you impress your listeners with the importance of an idea. In a speech on water conservation, you might try to show the environmental proportions of the resource. When you use a conceptual drawing like the one below, you show that if the world water supply were equal to ten gallons, only ten drops would be available and drinkable for human or household consumption. This drawing is effective because it emphasizes the scarcity of useful water and thus draws attention to this important information in your speech.

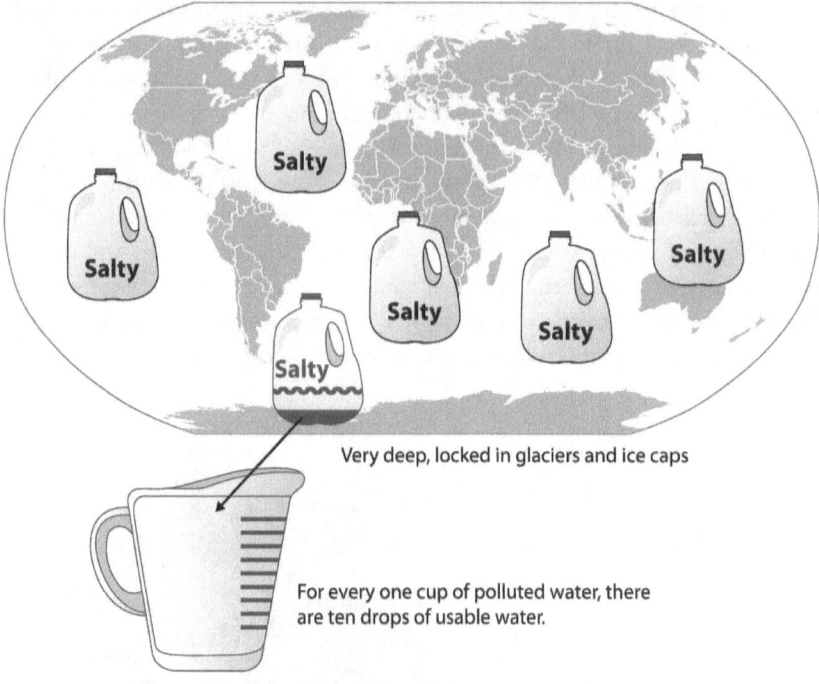

So, clarifying and emphasizing are two roles that support the "Improving Audience Understanding" purpose of presentation aids. What are other purposes?

Aiding Retention and Recall

The second function that presentation aids can serve is to increase the audience's chances of remembering your speech. An article by the U.S. Department of Labor (1996) summarized research on how people learn and remember. The authors found that "83% of human learning occurs visually, and the remaining 17% through the other senses—11% through hearing, 3.5% through smell, 1% through taste, and 1.5% through touch."

For this reason, exposure to an image can serve as a memory aid to your listeners. When your graphic images deliver information effectively and when your listeners understand them clearly, audience members are likely to remember your message long after your speech is over. Moreover, people often are able to remember information that is presented in sequential steps more easily than if that information is presented in an unorganized pattern. When you use a presentation aid to display the organization of your speech (such as can be done with PowerPoint slides), you will help your listeners to observe, follow, and remember the sequence of information you conveyed to them. This is why some instructors display a lecture outline for their students to follow during class and why a slide with a preview of your main points can be helpful as you move into the body of your speech.

An added plus of using presentation aids is that they can boost your memory while you are speaking. Using your presentation aids while you rehearse your speech will familiarize you with the association between a given place in your speech and the presentation aid that accompanies that material.

Adding Variety and Interest

A third function of presentation aids is simply to make your speech more interesting. For example, wouldn't a speech on varieties of roses have greater impact if you accompanied your remarks with a picture of each rose? You can imagine that your audience would be even more enthralled if you had the ability to display an actual flower of each variety in a bud vase. Similarly, if you were speaking to a group of gourmet cooks about Indian spices, you might want to provide tiny samples of spices that they could smell and taste during your speech.

Enhancing a Speaker's Credibility

Presentation aids alone will not be enough to create a professional image. As we mentioned earlier, impressive presentation aids will not rescue a poor speech. Even if you give a good speech, you run the risk of appearing unprofessional if your presentation aids are poorly executed. Conversely, a high quality presentation will contribute to your professional image. This means that in addition to containing important information, your presentation aids must be clear, clean, uncluttered, organized, and large enough for the audience to see and interpret correctly. Misspellings and poorly designed presentation aids can damage your credibility as a speaker.

In addition, make sure that you give proper credit to the source of any presentation aids that you take from other sources. Using a statistical chart or a map without proper credit will detract from your credibility, just as using a quotation in your speech without credit would. This situation will usually take place with digital aids such as PowerPoint slides. The source of a chart or the data shown in a chart form should be cited at the bottom the slide.

If you focus your efforts on producing presentation aids that contribute effectively to your meaning, that look professional, and that are handled well, your audience will most likely appreciate your efforts and pay close attention to your message. That attention will help them learn or understand your topic in a new way and will thus help the audience see you as a knowledgeable, competent, and credible speaker. With the prevalence of digital communication, the audience expectation of quality visual aids has increased.

Avoiding Problems with Presentation Aids

Using presentation aids can come with some risks. However, with a little forethought and adequate practice, you can choose presentation aids that enhance your message and boost your professional appearance in front of an audience. One principle to keep in mind is to use only as many presentation aids as necessary to present your message or to fulfill your classroom assignment. The number and the technical sophistication of your presentation aids should never overshadow your speech.

Another important consideration is technology. Keep your presentation aids within the limits of the working technology available to you. Whether or not your classroom technology works on the day of your speech, you will still have to present. What will you do if the computer file containing your slides is corrupted? What will you do if the easel is broken? What if you had counted on stacking your visuals on a table that disappears right when you need it? Or the Internet connection is down for a YouTube video you plan to show?

You must be prepared to adapt to an uncomfortable and scary situation. This is why we urge students to go to the classroom well ahead of time to test the equipment and ascertain the condition of items they're planning to use. As the speaker, you are responsible for arranging the things you need to make your presentation aids work as intended. Carry a roll of masking tape so you can display your poster even if the easel is gone. Test the computer setup. Have your slides on a flash drive AND send it to yourself as an attachment or upload to a Cloud service. Have an alternative plan prepared in case there is some glitch that prevents your computer-based presentation aids from being usable. And of course, you must know how to use the technology.

More important than the method of delivery is the audience's ability to see and understand the presentation aid. It must deliver clear information, and it must not distract from the message. Avoid overly elaborate presentation aids. Instead, simplify as much as possible, emphasizing the information you want your audience to understand.

Another thing to remember is that presentation aids do not "speak for themselves." When you display a visual aid, you should explain what it shows, pointing out and naming the most important features. If you use an audio aid such as a musical excerpt, you need to tell your audience what to listen for. Similarly, if you use a video clip, it is up to you as the speaker to point out the characteristics in the video that support the point you are making—but probably beforehand, so you are not speaking over the video. At the same time, a visual aid should be quickly accessible to the audience. This is where simplicity comes in. Just as in organization of a speech you would not want to use 20 main points, but more like 3-5, you should limit categories of information on a visual aid.

13.3 TYPES OF PRESENTATION AIDS

Now that we've explored some basic hints for preparing visual aids, let's look at the most common types of visual aids: charts, graphs, representations, objects/models, and people.

Charts

A **chart** is commonly defined as a graphical representation of data (often numerical) or a sketch representing an ordered process. Whether you create your charts or do research to find charts that already exist, it is important for them to exactly match the specific purpose in your speech. The rest of this section will explore three common types of charts: statistical charts, sequence-of-steps chart, and decision trees.

Statistical Charts

For most audiences, statistical presentations must be kept as simple as possible, and they must be explained. Unless you are familiar with statistics, this type of chart may be very confusing. When visually displaying information from a quantitative study, you need to make sure that you understand the material and can successfully and simply explain how one should interpret the data. If you are unsure about the data yourself, then you should probably not use this type of information. This is definitely an example of a visual aid that, though it delivers a limited kind of information, does not speak for itself. On the other hand, if you are presenting to an upper level or graduate class in health sciences or to professionals in health occupations, this chart would be appropriate. As with all other principles of public speaking, KNOW YOUR AUDIENCE.

Sequence-of-Steps Charts

Charts are also useful when you are trying to explain a process that involves several steps. The visual aid below depicts the process of group development using a sequence-of-steps chart. Notice that the chart includes labels to indicate the different phases of group development that you will learn more about in Chapter 15. Additionally, the chart contains a visual that depicts movement through the different stages and contains more specific details about each stage of group development. Adding these more specific details helps your audience understand the process.

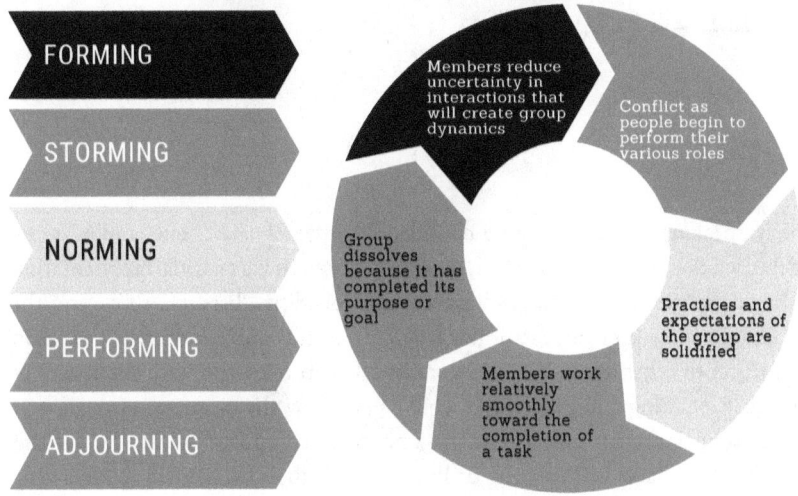

Decision Trees

Decision trees are useful for showing the relationships between ideas. The chart below shows how a decision tree could be used to determine whether or not to drink coffee. As with the other types of charts, you want to be sure that the information in the chart is relevant to the purpose of your speech and that each question and decision is clearly labeled.

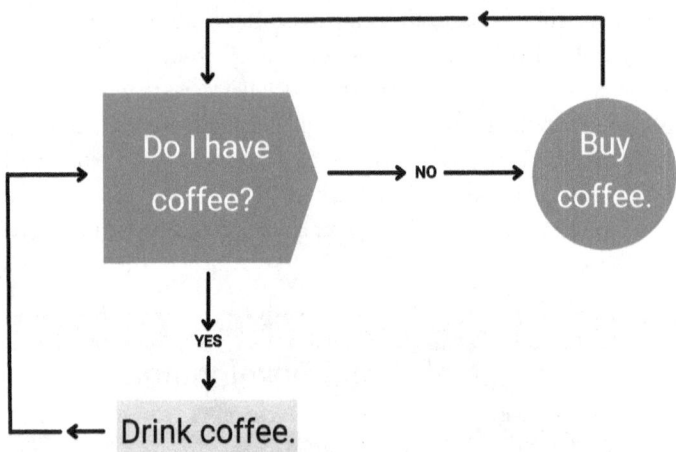

Graphs

Strictly speaking, a graph may be considered a type of chart, but graphs are so widely used that we will discuss them separately. A **graph** is a pictorial representation of the relationships of quantitative data using dots, lines, bars, pie slices, and the like. Graphs show how one factor (such as size, weight, number of items) varies in comparison to other items. Whereas a statistical chart may report the mean ages of individuals entering college, a graph would show how the mean age changes over time. A statistical chart may report the amount of computers sold in the United States, while a graph will use bars or lines to show their breakdown by operating systems such as Windows, Macintosh, and Linux.

Public speakers can show graphs using a range of different formats. Some of those formats are specialized for various professional fields. Very complex graphs often contain too much information that is not related to the purpose of a student's speech. If the graph is cluttered, it becomes difficult to comprehend. In this section, we're going to analyze the common graphs speakers utilize in their speeches: line graphs, bar graphs, pie graphs, and pictographs.

Line Graph

A **line graph** is designed to show trends over time. In the image below, we see a line graph depicting the four-year graduation percentage rate of new freshmen at Oklahoma State. Notice that the four-year graduation rate has seen a steady increase since Fall of 2012. This is far more effective in showing the relationship of numbers than simply reading the numbers aloud.

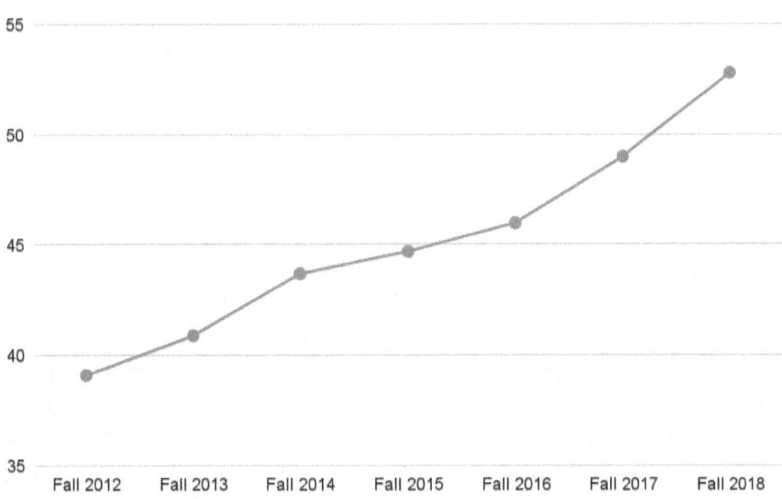

Bar Graph

Bar graphs are useful for showing the differences between quantities. They can be used for population demographics, fuel costs, math ability in different grades, and many other kinds of data. The graph below is well designed. It is relatively simple and is carefully labeled, making it easy for the speaker to guide the audience through the recorded numbers of students enrolled in each college at Oklahoma State in the Spring of 2023. The bar graph is designed to show how many students makes up each college. When you look at the data, the first grouping clearly shows that a large number of students at OSU major in a field in the College of Arts and Sciences.

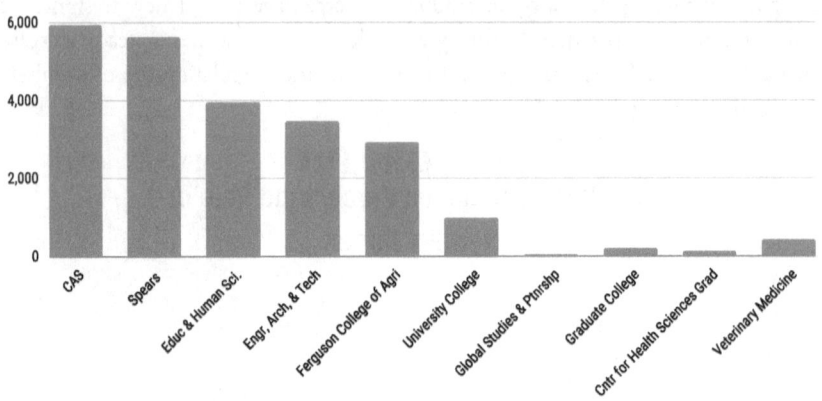

Pie Graph

Pie graphs are usually depicted as circles and are designed to show proportional relationships within sets of data; in other words, they show parts of or percentages of a whole. They should be simplified as much as possible without eliminating important information. As with other graphs, the sections of the pie need to be plotted proportionally. In the pie graph shown below, we see a clear and proportional chart that has been color-coded. Color-coding is useful when it's difficult to fit the explanations in the actual sections of the graph; in that case, you may need to include a legend, or key, to indicate what the colors in the graph mean. In this graph, audience members can see very quickly that Oklahoma State's 2022 student body was mostly made up of white students.

PIE CHART
Race/Ethnicity of OSU's 2022 Student Body

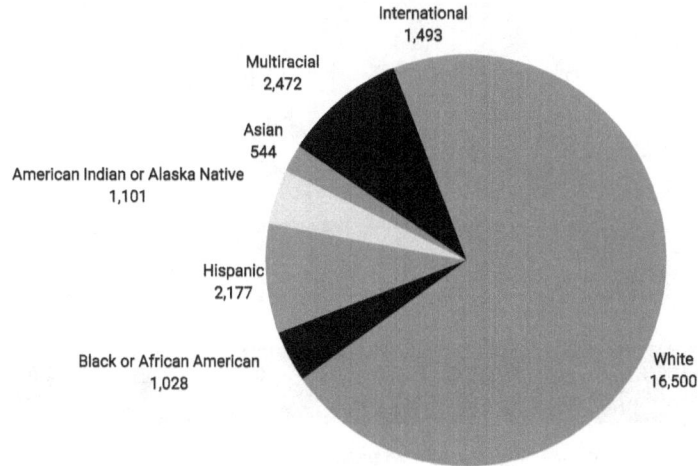

Pictograph

Similar to bar graphs, **pictograph**s use numbers and/or sizes of iconic symbols to dramatize differences in amounts. Check out the example below that displays OSU's undergraduate student classification in the Fall of 2022. Pictographs, although interesting, do not allow for depiction of specific statistical data. If you were trying to show the output of oil from various countries through oil wells, each oil well representing a ten million barrels a day, it might be hard for the audience to see the difference between a third of an oil well and a fourth of one, but that is a significant difference in amounts (3.3 million versus 2.5 million).

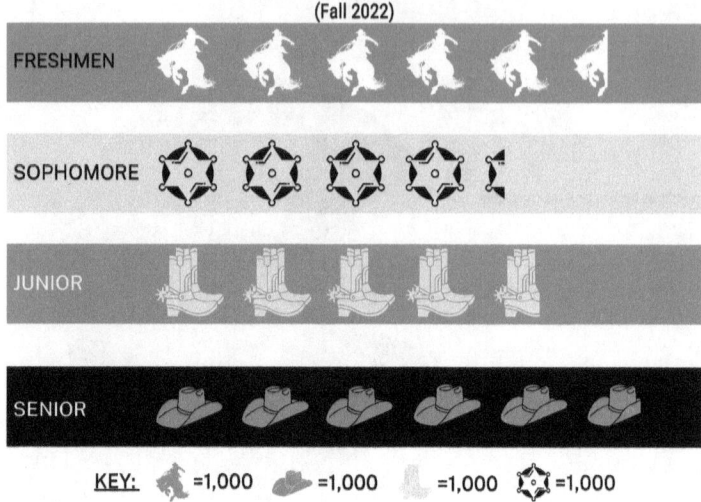

Graphs can present challenges in being effective but also in being ethical. To be both ethical and effective, you need a good understanding of what statistics mean, and you need to create or use graphs that show amounts clearly. For example, if you were showing GPAs of freshmen, sophomore, junior, and senior students at your college, and the bottom number on the graph was 2.25 rather than 0.0, that would result in a visually bigger difference than what really exists .

Diagrams

Diagrams are drawings or sketches that outline and explain the parts of an object, process, or phenomenon that cannot be readily seen. Like graphs, diagrams can be considered a type of chart, as in the case of organizational charts and process-flow charts. When you use a diagram, be sure to explain each part of the phenomenon, paying special attention to elements that are complicated or prone to misunderstanding. You will likely recognize the example below from Chapter One; this diagram describes the linear model of communication. This diagram provides a visual representation of the process of communication as well as the key components in that process.

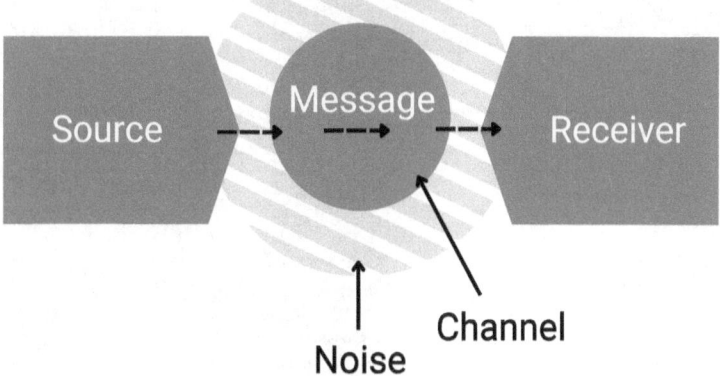

Maps

Maps are extremely useful if the information is clear and limited. There are all kinds of maps, including population, weather, ocean current, political, and economic maps, so you should find the right kind for the purpose of your speech. Choose a map that emphasizes the information you need to deliver. The map shown below ("African Map with Nigerian Emphasis") is simple, showing clearly the geographic location of Nigeria. This can be extremely valuable for some audiences who might not be able to name and locate countries on the continent of Africa. The map also shows the relative size of Nigeria compared to its neighbors.

Below is another example of a map that has been scaled for emphasis. You might recognize this image from OSU's online interactive campus map. You might be especially familiar with the emphasized portion of the map, Boone Pickens Stadium. When using maps for presentation aids, make sure to clarify the aspects of the map that you want the audience to understand.

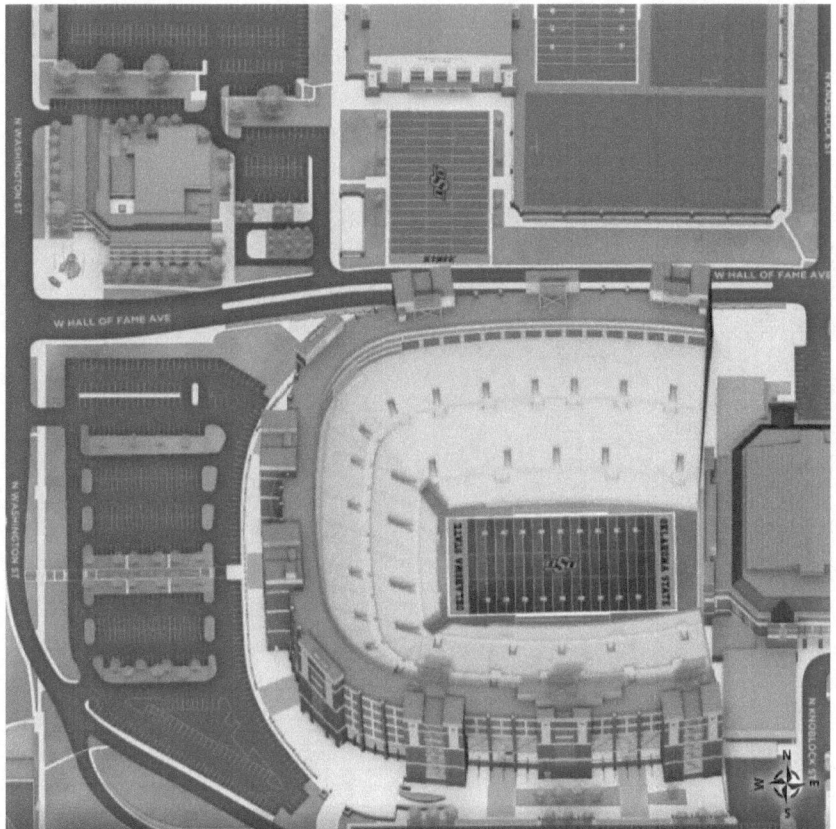

Photographs and Drawings

Sometimes a photograph or a drawing is the best way to show an unfamiliar but important detail. The photograph below pictures the fountain in front of Edmon Low Library after it has been dyed orange for OSU's annual Homecoming celebration. This photograph might be a good presentation aid for a speech about Oklahoma State's Homecoming traditions. Audiences expect high quality in photographs now, and as with all presentation aids they should enhance the speech and not just "be there." It is common to put stock photographs on PowerPoint slides as "clip art," but they should be relevant and not detract from the message of the slide.

Video or Audio Recordings

Another very useful type of presentation aid is a video or audio recording. Whether it is a short video from a website such as YouTube or Vimeo, a segment from a song, or a piece of a podcast, a well-chosen video or audio recording may be a good choice to enhance your speech. Imagine, for example, that you're giving a speech on how Lap-Band surgeries help people lose weight. One of the sections of your speech could explain how the Lap-Band works, so you could easily show a forty-three second video available on YouTube to demonstrate the part of the surgery. Maybe you could include a recording of a real patient explaining why they decided to get the Lap-Band.

There is one major warning to using audio and video clips during a speech: do not forget that they are supposed to be aids to your speech, not the speech itself. In addition, be sure to avoid these five mistakes that speakers often make when using audio and video clips:

- Avoid choosing clips that are too long for the overall length of the speech. Your instructor can give you some guidelines for how long video and audio clips should be for the speeches in your class, if they are allowed (and make sure they are).
- Practice with the audio or video equipment prior to speaking. If you are unfamiliar with the equipment, you'll look foolish trying to figure out how it works. This fiddling around will not only take your audience out of your

speech but also have a negative impact on your credibility. It also wastes valuable time. Finally, be sure that the speakers on the computer are on and at the right volume level.
- Cue the clip to the appropriate place prior to beginning your speech. We cannot tell you the number of times we've seen students spend valuable speech time trying to find a clip on YouTube or a DVD. You need to make sure your clip is ready to go before you start speaking. Later in this chapter we will look at using video links in slides.
- In addition to cuing the clip to the appropriate place, the browser window should be open and ready to go. If there are advertisements before the video, be sure to have the video cued to play after the ad. The audience should not have to sit through a commercial. There is a website called TubeChop that can allow you to cut a segment out of a YouTube video, then creating a new link. It has limitations but can be useful.
- The audience must be given context before a video or audio clip is played, specifically what the clip is and why it relates to the speech. At the same time, the video should not repeat what you have already said, but add to it.

Objects or Models

Objects and models are another form of presentation aid that can be very helpful in getting your audience to understand your message. Objects refer to anything you could hold up and talk about during your speech. If you're talking about the importance of not using plastic water bottles, you might hold up a plastic water bottle and a stainless steel water bottle as examples. Models, on the other hand, are re-creations of physical objects that you cannot have readily available with you during a speech. If you're giving a speech on heart murmurs, you may be able to show how heart murmurs work by holding up a model of the human heart. As will be discussed in the section on handouts below, a speaker should not pass an object or model around during a speech. It is highly distracting.

People and Animals

The next category of presentation aids are people and animals. We can often use ourselves or other people to adequately demonstrate an idea during our speeches.

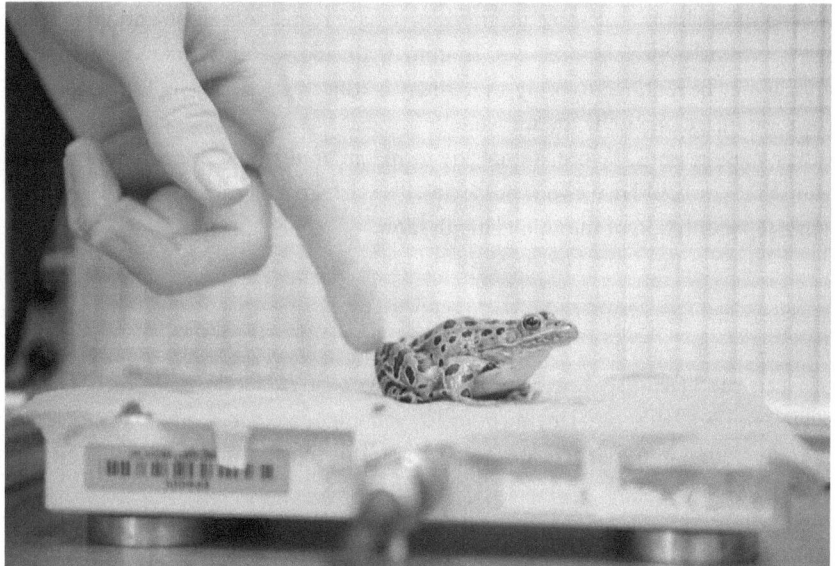

Animals as Presentation Aids

When giving a speech on a topic relating to animals, it is often tempting to bring an animal to serve as your presentation aid. While this can sometimes add a very engaging dimension to the speech, it carries some serious risks that you need to consider.

The first risk is that animal behavior tends to be unpredictable. You may think this won't be a problem if your presentation aid animal is small enough to be kept confined throughout your speech—for example, a goldfish in a bowl or a lizard or bird in a cage. However, even caged animals can be very distracting to your audience if they run about, chirp, or exhibit other agitated behavior. The chances are great that an animal will react to the stress of an unfamiliar situation by displaying behavior that does not contribute positively to your speech or to the cleanliness of the physical environment. Additionally, the animal's behavior may not only affect audience attention during your speech, but potentially during your classmates' speeches as well.

The second risk is that some audience members may respond negatively to a live animal. In addition to common fears and aversions to animals like snakes, spiders, and mice, many people have allergies to various animals. One of the authors had an experience where a student brought his six-foot yellow python to class for a speech. As a result, one of the other students refused to stay in the room because of her snake phobia (the instructor was not too comfortable either).

The third risk is that some locations may have regulations about bringing non-service animals onto the premises. If animals are allowed, the person bringing the animal may be required to bring a veterinary certificate or may be legally responsible for any damage caused by the animal.

For these reasons, before you decide to use an animal as a presentation aid, ask yourself if you could make your point equally well with a picture, model, diagram, or other representation of the animal in question.

Speaker as Presentation Aid

Speakers can often use their own bodies to demonstrate facets of a speech. If your speech is about ballroom dancing or ballet, you might use your body to demonstrate the basic moves in the cha-cha or the five basic ballet positions.

Other People as Presentation Aids

In some cases, such as for a demonstration speech, you might want to ask someone else to serve as your presentation aid. You should arrange ahead of time for a person (or persons) to be an effective aid—do not assume that an audience member will volunteer on the spot. If you plan to demonstrate how to immobilize a broken bone, your volunteer must know ahead of time that you will touch them as much as necessary to splint the break.

You must also make certain that they will arrive dressed presentably and that they will not draw attention away from your message through their appearance or behavior. The transaction between you and your human presentation aid must be appropriate, especially if you are going to demonstrate something like a dance step. In short, make sure your helper will know what is expected of them and consents to it.

13.4 USING PRESENTATION SLIDES

Ever since the 1990s and the mainstreaming of personal computer technology, speakers have had the option of using slide presentation software to accompany their speeches and presentations. The most commonly known one is PowerPoint, although there are several others:

- Prezi, available at www.prezi.com
- Slide Rocket, available at www.sliderocket.com
- Google Slides, available in Google Drive and useful for collaborative assignments
- Keynote, the Apple presentation slide software on MACs
- Impress, an Open Office product (http://www.openoffice.org/product/impress.html)
- PrezentIt
- AdobeAcrobat Presenter
- ThinkFree

These products, some of which are offered free for trial or basic subscriptions (called a "freemium), allow you to present professional-looking slides. Each one is "robust," a word used to mean it has a large number of functions and features, some of which are helpful and some of which are distracting. For example, you can use the full range of fonts, although many of them are not appropriate for presentations because they are hard to read. In this section we will discuss the proper use of presentation slides, with the assumption that you understand the basics of cutting, pasting, inserting, etc. involved in these products. You may have taken a class in high school where you learned to use the technology, but that is not the same as learning to use them for actual presentations.

The Advantages and Disadvantages of Using Presentation Slides

In some industries and businesses, there is an assumption that speakers will use presentation slides. They allow visualization of concepts, they are easily portable, they can be embedded with videos and audio, words can dance around the screen—why wouldn't a speaker use them? You will probably also be expected to have slide presentations in future assignments in college. Knowing how to use them, beyond the basic technology, is vital to being a proficient presenter.

But why not use them? Franck Frommer, a French journalist and communication expert, published the book *How PowerPoint Makes You Stupid* (2012), whose title says it all. He criticizes the "linearity" of PowerPoint and similar presentation software, meaning that audiences are not encouraged to see the relationship of ideas and that PowerPoint hurts critical thinking in the audience. Slide follows slide of bulleted information without one slide being more important or the logical connections being clear.

As recently as the mid-2000s, critics such as well-known graphic expert and NASA consultant Edward Tufte (2005) charged that PowerPoint's tendency to force the user to put a certain number of bullet points on each slide in a certain format was a serious threat to the accurate presentation of data. As Tufte put it, "the rigid slide-by-slide hierarchies, indifferent to content, slice and dice the evidence into arbitrary compartments, producing an anti-narrative with choppy continuity."

Tufte argues that poor decision making, such as was involved with the 2003 space shuttle *Columbia* disaster, may have been related to the shortcomings of such presentation aids in NASA meetings. While more recent versions of PowerPoint and similar programs allow much more creative freedom in designing slides, this freedom comes with a responsibility—the user needs to take responsibility for using the technology to support the speech and not get carried away with the many special effects the software is capable of producing.

It should be mentioned here that Prezi helps address one of the major criticisms of PowerPoint. Because Prezi, in its design stage, looks something like a mind map on a very large canvas with grid lines, it allows you to show the relationship and hierarchy of ideas better. For example, you can see and design the slides so that the "Big Ideas" are in big circles and the subordinate ideas are in smaller ones.

In addition to recognizing the truth behind Frommer's and Tufte's critiques, we have all sat through a presenter who committed the errors of putting far too much text on the slide. When a speaker does this, the audience is confused—do they read the text or listen to the speaker? An audience member cannot do both. Then, the speaker feels the need to read the slides rather than use PowerPoint for what it does best, visual reinforcement and clarification. We have also seen many poorly designed PowerPoint slides, either through haste or lack of knowledge: slides where the graphics are distorted (elongated or squatty), words and graphics not balanced, text too small, words printed over photographs, garish or nauseating colors, or animated figures left up on the screen for too long and distracting the audience. What about you? Can you think about PowerPoint "don'ts" that have hurt your reception of a presentation or lecture? This would be a good discussion for class, and a good way to know what not to do with your own slides.

Creating Quality Slide Shows

Slides should show the principles of good design, which include unity, emphasis or focal point, scale and proportion, balance, and rhythm (Lauer & Pentak, 2000). Presenters should also pay attention to tone and usability. With those principles in mind, here are some tips for creating and then using presentation software.

Unity and Consistency

Generally it is best to use a single font for the text on your visuals so that they look like a unified set. Or you can use two different fonts in consistent ways, such as having all headings and titles in the same font and all bullet points in the same font. Additionally, the background should probably remain consistent, whether you choose one of the many design templates or if you just opt for a background color.

In terms of unity, the adage, "Keep It Simple, Speaker" definitely applies to presentation slides. Each slide should have one message, one photo, one graphic. The audience members should know what they are supposed to look at on the slide. A phrase to remember about presentation slides and the wide range of design elements available is "Just because you can,
doesn't mean you should."

Another area related to unity and consistency, as well as audience response, is the use of animation or movement. There are three types of animation in slideshows. First, you can embed little characters or icons that have movement. These may seem like fun, but they have limited use and should not stay on the screen very long—you can use the second type of animation to take them off the screen.

That second type is the designed movement of text or objects on and off the screen. Although using this function takes up time in preparing your slides, especially if you want to do it well and be creative with it, it is very useful. You can control what your audience is seeing. It also avoids bringing up all the text and material on a slide at one time, which tempts the audience again to pay more attention to the screen than to you. Movement on the screen attracts attention, for better or worse. PowerPoint, for example, allows bouncing words, pulsating text, swirling phrases, even Star Wars scroll, which may or may not serve your purpose.

The third type of animation is called slide transitions, which is the design of how the next slide appears. In PowerPoint you can have the slides appear automatically or as blinds, as little checkerboards, from different sides of the screen, in opening circles, etc. (You can also use sound effects, but that is strongly discouraged.) In Prezi, the slides transition by zooming in and out, which is a clever effect but does make some audience members experience motion sickness. In general, you want to use a consistent and efficient pattern of movement with the second and third types of animation.

Emphasis, Focal Point, and Visibility

Several points should be made about how to make sure the audience sees what they need to see on the slides.

1. It is essential to make sure the information is large enough for the audience to see; and since the display size may vary according to the projector you are using, this is another reason for practicing in advance with the equipment you intend to use.
2. The standard rule is for text is 7 X 7, or sometimes (if the screen is smaller) 6 X 6. Does this mean 49 or 36 words on the slide? No. It means, in the case of 7 X 7, that you should have no more than seven horizontal lines of text (this does not mean bullet points, but lines of text, including the heading) and the longest line should not exceed seven words.
3. Following the 7 X 7 rule will keep you from putting too much information on a slide, and you should also avoid too many slides. Less sometimes really is more. Again, there is no hard and fast rule, but a ten-minute speech probably needs fewer than ten slides, unless you can make a good argument for more based on the content of the speech. If, however, the slides are just text, more than ten is too many.
4. Do not assume that all the templates feature visible text. Text should not be smaller than 22 point font for best visibility, and some of the templates use much smaller fonts than 22 point. This is especially important in those situations where the speaker creates handouts. Text smaller than 22 is very

13.4 USING PRESENTATION SLIDES | 455

difficult to see on handouts of your slides. (However, handouts are not recommended for most situations.)

5. High contrast between the text and slides is extremely important. White fonts against very dark backgrounds and black fonts against very light backgrounds are probably your safest bet here. Remember that the way it looks on your computer screen is not the exactly how it will look when projected—the light is coming from a different place. Avoid words on photos.
6. Also in terms of visibility, most experts say that sans serif fonts such as Arial, Tahoma, and Verdana are better for reading from screens than serif fonts such as Times New Roman, Bookface, Georgia, or Garamond. Merriam-Webster (2018) defines "serif" as "any of the short lines stemming from and at an angle to the upper and lower ends of the strokes of a letter." Serifs are additions to the letters on different fonts that give them a different appearance and help the flow of eye when reading.

> "Communication is the backbone of our society. It allows us to form connections, influence decisions, and motivate change. Without communication skills, the ability to progress in the working world and in life, itself, would be nearly impossible. Public speaking is one of the most important and most dreaded forms of communication." PAN Communications, 2021

How does the slide pictured above stack up beside these rules for visibility? You probably noticed that slide is a "fail" in terms of high contrast between the font and background and the use of a block of text not broken up for easy reading. The audience would feel like they are supposed to read it but not be able to.

Tone

Fonts, color, clip art, photographs, and templates all contribute to **tone**, which is the attitude being conveyed in the slides. If you want a light tone, such as for a speech about cruises, some colors (springtime, pastel, cool, warm, or primary colors) and fonts (such as Comic Sans) and lots of photographs will be more appropriate. For a speech about the Holocaust, more somber colors and design elements would be more fitting, whereas clip art would not be.

Scale and Proportion

Although there are several ways to think about scale and proportion, we will discuss three here. First, bullet points. Bullet points infer that the items in the bulleted list are equal and the sequence doesn't matter. If you want to communicate order or sequence or priority, use numbers. Do not mix outline points or numerical points with bullet points. Also, you should not put your outline (Roman numerals, etc.) on the slide.

Bullet points should be short—not long, full sentences—but at the same time should be long enough to mean something. In a speech on spaying and neutering pets, the bullet point "pain" may be better replaced with "Pet feels little pain." Second, when you are designing your slides, it is best to choose a template and stick with it. If you input all your graphics and material and then change the template, the format of the slide will change, in some cases dramatically, and you will have distorted graphics and words covered up. You will then have to redesign each slide, which can be unnecessarily time-consuming.

The third aspect of scale and proportion is the relationship between the graphics and text in terms of size. This aspect is discussed below in the next section on "Balance." Also, a graphic should be surrounded by some empty space and not just take up the whole slide.

Balance

In general you want symmetrical slides. Below are four examples of slides that are unbalanced; the last one achieves a better symmetry and design.

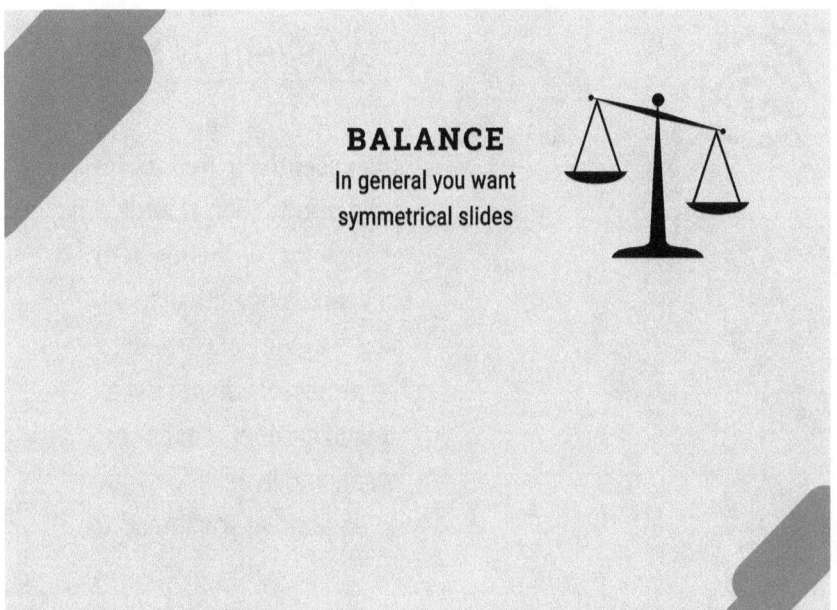

This slide leaves too much "white space" below the text, leaving an imbalance between the text and graphic; the graphic goes up into the title, and the title could be centered.

This slide does not break the text up into bullets and is therefore hard to read; the graphic is strangely small, and the heading is in a different font. Script fonts are often hard to read on screens.

In this slide, similar problems from the one above are repeated, but the text is also too small and the graphic is distorted because it was not sized from the corner.

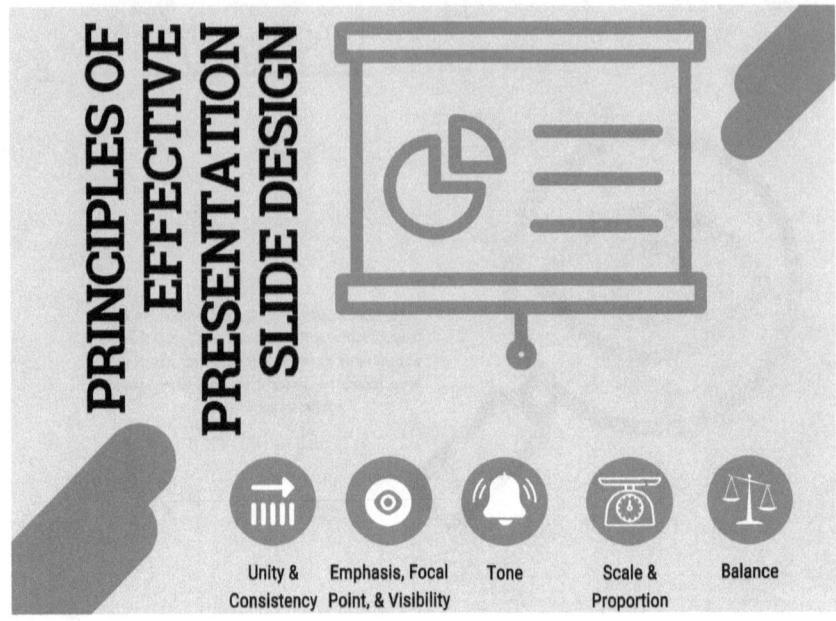

This slide is far too "busy." The additional clip art is not helpful, the font is too small, and the ideas are disconnected. Having text in all caps and presented vertically is also difficult to read.

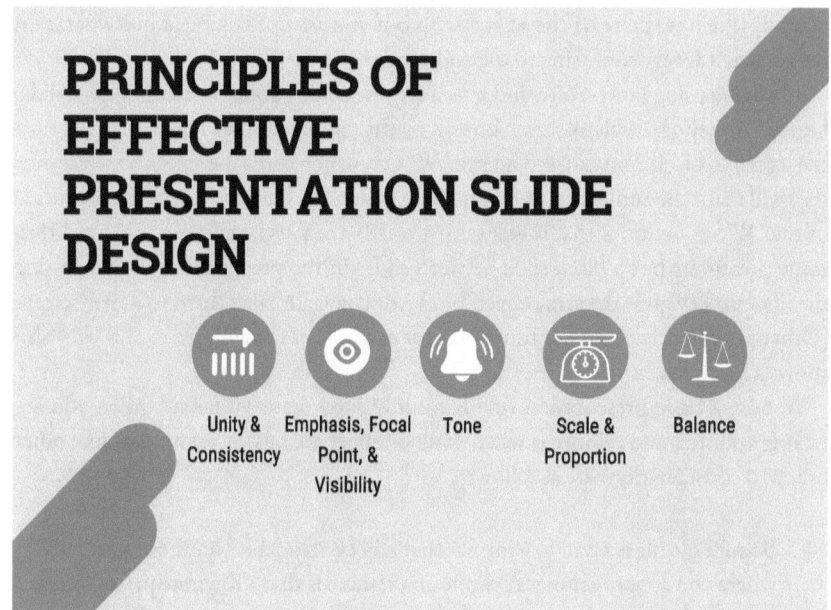

This version provides more visual balance and with better scale and proportion.

Rhythm in Presenting

The rhythm of your slide display should be reasonably consistent—you would not want to display a dozen different slides in the first minute of a five-minute presentation and then display only one slide per minute for the rest of the speech. Timing them so that the audience can actually take them in is important. Presenters often overdo the number of slides, thinking they will get a better grade, but too many slides just causes overkill.

If you can obtain a remote mouse to change slides, that can help you feel independent of the mouse attached to the computer. However, you have to practice with the remote "clicker." But if you have to use the mouse to change slide, keep your hands off of it between clicks. We have seen students wiggle the little arrow all over the screen. It is extremely annoying.

Whether using a remote "clicker" or the attached mouse, you must attend to the connection between what is on the screen and what you are actually talking about at the moment. Put reminders in your notes about when you need to change slides during your speech.

For better or worse, we have become very screen-oriented in our communication, largely because screens change often and that changing teaches us to expect new stimuli, which we crave. If the screen is up but you are not talking about what is on the screen, it is very confusing to the audience.

If you are using PowerPoint and if you are not talking about something on a slide, hit the "B" key or the blank screen button on the remote mouse. This action will turn the screen to black. You can also hit the "W" key, which turns the screen to white, but that will make the audience think something is coming. Unfortunately, the downside of the "B" key action is that it will return you to the previous screen. To avoid this, some presenters put a black slide between slides in the presentation so that hitting the forward key gives the same effect, but hitting it again takes them to a new screen. (Other programs have similar functions; for example, if using Prezi, the "B" key also shows a black screen.)

In fact, a basic presentation rule is to only show your visual aid when you are talking about it, and remove it when you no longer are talking about it. Some other practical considerations are as follows:

1. Be sure the file is saved in a format that will be "readable" on the computer where you are presenting. A common example is that a Keynote presentation (Apple) does not open on all PCs. You can save Keynote as a .ppt file for use on a PC. Likewise, if you chose to use Prezi or other web-based presentation software, you will need a strong, reliable Internet connection to show the slides.
2. Any borrowed graphic must be cited on the slide where it is used; the same would be true of borrowed textual material. Putting your sources only on the last slide is insufficient.
3. A very strong temptation for speakers is to look at the projected image rather than the audience during the speech. This practice cuts down on eye contact, of course, and is distracting for the audience. Two solutions for that are to print your notes from the presentation slides and/or use the slides as your note structure. Also remember that if the image is on the computer monitor in front of you, it is on the screen behind you.
4. Always remember—and this cannot be emphasized enough—technology works for you, not you for the technology. The presentation aids are aids, not the speech itself.
5. As mentioned before, sometimes life happens—technology does not work. It could be that the projector bulb goes out or the Internet connection is down. The show must go on.
6. If you are using a video or audio clip from an Internet source, it is probably best to hyperlink the URL on one of the slides rather than minimize the program and change to the Internet site. You can do this by highlighting a key word on the slide, right clicking to find "hyperlink," and then pasting the URL there. Although you can also embed video in a PowerPoint, it makes the file

extremely large and that may cause problems of its own.
7. Finally, it is common for speakers to think "the slide changes, so the audience know there is a change, so I don't need a verbal transition." Please do not fall into this trap. Verbal transitions are just as, and maybe more, necessary for a speech using slides.

13.5 LOW-TECH PRESENTATION AIDS

One reason for using digital media is that they can't be prone to physical damage in the form of smudges, scratches, dents, and rips. Unlike posters and objects, presentation software can be kept professional looking if you have to carry them through a rainstorm or blizzard. However, there are times when it makes sense to use "low-tech" media for presentations. Here are some directions for those times.

Dry-Erase Board

If you use a chalkboard or dry-erase board, you are not using a prepared presentation aid. Your failure to prepare visuals ahead of time can be interpreted in several ways, mostly negative. If other speakers carefully design, produce, and use attractive visual aids, yours will stand out by contrast. You will be seen as the speaker who does not take the time to prepare even a simple aid. Do not use a chalkboard or dry-erase board and pretend it's a prepared presentation aid.

However, numerous speakers do utilize chalk and dry-erase boards effectively. Typically, these speakers use the chalk or dry-erase board for interactive components of a speech. For example, maybe you're giving a speech in front of a group of executives. You may have a PowerPoint all prepared, but at various points in your speech you want to get your audience's responses. (More recent technologies, such as on iPads, allow you to do the interaction on the screen, but this would have to be supported by the environment.) Chalk or dry-erase boards are very useful when you want to visually show information that you are receiving from your audience. If you ever use a chalk or dry-erase board, follow these four simple rules:

1. Write large enough so that everyone in the room can see (which is harder than it sounds; it is also hard to write and talk at the same time!).
2. Print legibly; don't write in cursive script.
3. Write short phrases; don't take time to write complete sentences.
4. Be sure you have markers that will not go dry, and clean the board afterward.

Flipchart

A flipchart is useful for situations when you want to save what you have written for future reference or to distribute to the audience after the presentation. As with whiteboards, you will need good markers and readable handwriting, as well as a strong easel to keep the flipchart upright.

Posters

You may have the opportunity in your college years to attend or participate in a "poster session." These are times during an academic conference where visitors can view a well-designed poster depicting a research project and discuss it one-on-one with the researcher. These kinds of posters are quite large and involve a great deal of work. They can be generated from PowerPoint but often require a special printer. Otherwise, posters are probably not the best way to approach presentation aids in a speech. There are problems with visibility as well as portability. Avoid producing a presentation aid that looks like you simply cut pictures out of magazines and pasted them on. Slapping some text and images on a board looks unprofessional and will not be viewed as credible or effective.

Handouts

Handouts are appropriate for delivering information that audience members can take away with them. As we will see, handouts require a great deal of management if they are to contribute to your credibility as a speaker.

First, make sure the handout is worth the trouble of making, copying, and distributing it. Does the audience really need the handout? Second, make sure to bring enough copies of the handout for each audience member to get one. Having to share or look on with one's neighbor does not contribute to a professional image. Under no circumstances should you ever provide a single copy of a handout to pass around. It is distracting and everyone will see it at different times in the speech, which is also true about passing any object around the room.

There are three possible times to distribute handouts: before you begin your speech, during the speech, and after your speech is over. Naturally, if you need your listeners to follow along in a handout, you will need to distribute it before your speech begins. If you have access to the room ahead of time, place a copy of the handout at or on each seat in the audience. If not, ask a volunteer to distribute them as quickly as possible while you prepare to begin speaking. If the handout is a "takeaway," leave it on a table near the door so that those audience members who are interested can take one on their way out; in this case, don't forget to tell them to do so as you conclude your speech. It is almost never appropriate to distribute handouts during your speech, as it is distracting, takes up time, and interrupts the pace of your presentation.

Conclusion

To finish this chapter, we will recap and remind you about the principles of effective presentation aids. Whether your aid is a slide show, object, a person, or dry erase board, these standards are essential:

- Presentation aids must be easily seen or heard by your audience. Squinting and head-cocking are not good reactions. Neither should they look at the screen the whole time and ignore the speaker.
- Presentation aids must be portable, easily handled, and efficient.
- Presentation aids should disappear when not in use.
- Presentation aids should be aesthetically pleasing, which includes in good taste. Avoid shock value just for shock value. You might want to show pictures of diseased organs and teeth, deformities, or corpses for your speech to make a point, but context is everything. Will your audience react so strongly that the overall point is missed? Additionally, electronic media today allows you to create very "busy" slides with varieties of fonts, colors, collages of photos, etc. Keep in mind the principles of unity and focal point.
- Color is another aesthetic aspect. Some colors are just more soothing, readable, and appropriate than others. Also, the color on your slides may be different when projected from what is on your computer. Finally, presentation aids must support your speech and have high relevance to your content.

This chapter has covered a wide range of information about all kinds of audio and visual aids, but audiences today expect and appreciate professionally designed and handled presentation aids. The stakes are higher now, but the tools are many.

13.6 ENRICHMENT

Discussion Questions

1. What is the best or worst presentation aid you have seen used by a speaker? What made it effective or ineffective?
2. What are some reasons for using a presentation aid in your speech?
3. You have been asked to give an informative speech on your student organization's accomplishments this year. Which type of presentation aid would be best? Would you include any graphs or charts?
4. When using presentation slides, what are some of the main pitfalls for speakers?
5. Should every speech have a presentation aid? Why or why not?

Activities

1. Form five or six small groups. Each group will choose an informative speech topic and find an appropriate presentation aid for that topic. Finally, each group will present their topic and presentation aid to the class by citing it orally and describing how the presentation aid will be used in the speech. Discuss the following questions:

    - Why did each group make the choices they did?
    - Which presentation aids worked best? Why?
    - Together, list the most important considerations for choosing and implementing effective presentation aids.

2. Form five or six groups. Each group will be given two types of presentation aids listed in Section 13:3: Types of Presentation Aids. Students will then list the pros and cons of using those types of presentations aids and provide examples of speeches in which those aids would be most effective. Finally, groups will present what they have learned to the class.
3. Form five or six groups. Each group will be given sample presentation aids to critique using advice from Section 13:4 Using Presentation Aids and Section 13.5: Low-Tech Presentation Aids. Give each visual aid a rating on a scale from one to ten. Finally, groups share their analysis aloud.

14 INFORMATIVE SPEAKING

Learning Objectives

- Recognize opinion versus factual information.
- Recognize the different types of informative speeches.
- Distinguish the best organizational approach for types of informative speeches.
- Employ proven guidelines for preparing an informative speech.
- Construct an informative speech.

Key Terms

- **Informative Speech**
- **Irrefutable**
- **Opinion**

14.1 WHAT IS AN INFORMATIVE SPEECH?

"The improvement of understanding is for two ends: first our own increase for knowledge; secondly, to enable us to deliver that knowledge to others." -John Locke

Defining what an informative speech is can be both straight-forward and somewhat tricky at the same time. Very simply, an **informative speech** can first be defined as a speech based entirely and exclusively on facts. Basically, an informative speech conveys knowledge, a task that every person engages in every day in some form or another. Whether giving someone who is lost driving directions, explaining the specials of the day as a server, or describing the plot of a movie to friends, people engage in forms of informative speaking daily. Secondly, an informative speech does not attempt to convince the audience that one thing is better than another. It does not advocate a course of action.

Consider the following two statements:

2 + 2 = 4

George Washington was the first President of the United States.

In each case, the statement made is what can be described as **irrefutable**, meaning a statement or claim that cannot be argued. In the first example, even small children are taught that having two apples and then getting two more apples will result in having four apples. This statement is irrefutable in that no one in the world will (or should!) argue this: It is a fact.

Similarly, with the statement "George Washington was the first President of the United States," this again is an irrefutable fact. If you asked one hundred history professors and read one hundred history textbooks, the professors and textbooks would all say the same thing: Washington was the first president. No expert, reliable source, or person with any common sense would argue about this.

(Someone at this point might say, "No, John Hanson was the first president." However, he was president under the Articles of Confederation for a short period—November 5, 1781, to November 3, 1782—not under our present Constitution. This example shows the importance of stating your facts clearly and precisely and being able to cite their origins.)

Therefore, an informative speech should not incorporate **opinion** as its basis. This can be the tricky part of developing an informative speech, because some opinion statements sometimes sound like facts (since they are generally agreed upon by many people), but are really opinion.

For example, in an informative speech on George Washington, you might say, "George Washington was one of the greatest presidents in the history of the United States." While this statement may be agreed upon by most people, it is possible for some people to disagree and argue the opposite point of view. The statement "George Washington was one of the greatest presidents in the history of the United States" is not irrefutable, meaning someone could argue this claim. If, however, you present the opinion as an opinion from a source, that is acceptable: it is a fact that someone (hopefully someone with expertise) holds the opinion. You do not want your central idea, your main points, and the majority of your supporting material to be opinion or argument in an informative speech.

Additionally, you should never take sides on an issue in an informative speech, nor should you "spin" the issue in order to influence the opinions of the listeners. Even if you are informing the audience about differences in views on controversial topics, you should simply and clearly explain the issues. This is not to say, however, that the audience's needs and interests have nothing to do with the informative speech. We come back to the WIIFM principle ("What's in it for me?") because even though an informative speech is fact-based, it still needs to relate to people's lives in order to maintain their attention.

The question may arise here, "If we can find anything on the Internet now, why bother to give an informative speech?" The answer lies in the unique relationship between audience and speaker found in the public speaking context. The speaker can choose to present information that is of most value to the audience. Secondly, the speaker is not just overloading the audience with data. As we have mentioned before, that's not really a good idea because audiences cannot remember great amounts of data and facts after listening. The focus of the content is what matters. This is where the specific purpose and central idea come into play. Remember, public speaking is not a good way to "dump data" on the audience, but to make information meaningful.

Finally, although we have stressed that the informative speech is fact-based and does not have the purpose of persuasion, information still has an indirect effect on someone. If a classmate gives a speech on correctly using the Heimlich Maneuver to help a choking victim, the side effect (and probably desired result) is that the audience would use it when confronted with the situation.

Pete Goes to the Writing Center

With his informative speech about the traditions of OSU looming, Pistol Pete knew he needed to ensure his preparation outline was in tip-top shape. While he was confident about his content, he wanted to make certain his structure was clear and cohesive. Who better to help with that than the experts at the OSU Writing Center?

As he approached the Writing Center, Pete felt a mix of nervousness and excitement. The Writing Center had a reputation for being a resourceful hub, a place where many students had honed their writing skills.

He was greeted warmly by a student consultant named Sarah. "How can I help you today, Pistol Pete?" she asked with a smile. Pete explained his assignment and his desire to refine his preparation outline.

Sarah began by asking Pete about his main objectives for the speech. As he shared his thoughts, she listened attentively, jotting down notes. She then asked to see the current state of his outline. As Pete handed it over, he explained his three main points and how he intended to delve into each one.

Sarah reviewed the outline, making annotations. She noticed that while Pete had a wealth of information, it would be beneficial to reorganize some points to improve flow and cohesiveness. They worked together to structure the outline, ensuring each point logically led to the next.

She also gave Pete tips on effective transitions to maintain audience engagement and create a seamless progression between points. Pete, always eager to learn, scribbled down notes, asking questions when needed.

Noticing that Pete had included a lot of historical details in his outline, Sarah suggested incorporating personal anecdotes or experiences related to the traditions to add a touch of relatability. Pete loved the idea and thought of a couple of personal stories he could weave in.

Before wrapping up, Sarah directed Pete to some online resources available through the Writing Center's website, which could further help him refine his speech. She also reminded him about the importance of rehearsing his speech multiple times to ensure it flowed smoothly with the revised outline.

Pistol Pete left the Writing Center feeling empowered and grateful. Sarah's guidance had transformed his outline into a clear and engaging roadmap for his speech. He felt more prepared than ever to share the rich traditions of OSU with his audience, all thanks to the support he received at the Writing Center. Have you ever visited the Writing Center on campus?

14.2 TYPES OF INFORMATIVE SPEECHES

While the topics to choose from for informative speeches are nearly limitless, they can generally be pared down into five broad categories. Understanding the type of informative speech that you will be giving can help you to figure out the best way to organize, research, and prepare for it, as will be discussed below.

Type 1: History

A common approach to selecting an informative speech topic is to discuss the history or development of something. With so much of human knowledge available via the Internet, finding information about the origins and evolution of almost anything is much easier than it has ever been (with the disclaimer that there are quite a few websites out there with false information). With that in mind, some of the areas that a historical informative speech could cover would include:

Objects

(Example: the baseball; the saxophone). Someone at some point in history was the first to develop what is considered the modern baseball. Who was it? What was it originally made of? How did it evolve into the baseball that is used by Major League Baseball today?

Places

(Example: your college; Disney World). There is a specific year that you college or university opened, a specific number of students who were initially enrolled, and often colleges and universities have name and mission changes. All of these facts can be used to provide an overall understanding of the college and its history. Likewise, the Disney World of today is different from the Disney World of the early 1970s; the design has developed over the last fifty years.

Ideas

(Example: democracy; freedom of speech). It is possible to provide facts on an idea, although in some cases the information may be less precise. For example, while no one can definitively point to a specific date or individual who first developed the concept of democracy, it is known to have been conceived in ancient Greece

(Raaflaub, Ober, & Wallace, 2007). By looking at the civilizations and cultures that adopted forms of democracy throughout history, it is possible to provide an audience with a better understanding of how the idea has been shaped into what it has become today.

Type 2: Biography

A biography is similar to a history, but in this case the subject is specifically a person, whether living or deceased. For the purposes of this class, biographies should focus on people of some note or fame, since doing research on people who are not at least mildly well-known could be difficult. But again, as with histories, there are specific and irrefutable facts that can help provide an overview of someone's life, such as dates that President Lincoln was born (February 12, 1809) and died (April 15, 1865) and the years he was in office as president (1861-1865).

This might be a good place to address research and support. The basic dates of Abraham Lincoln's life could be found in multiple sources and you would not have to cite the source in that case. But if you use the work of a specific historian to explain how Lincoln was able to win the presidency in the tumultuous years before the Civil War, that would need a citation of that author and the publication.

Type 3: Processes

Examples of process speech topics would be how to bake chocolate chip cookies; how to throw a baseball; how a nuclear reactor works; how a bill works its way through Congress.

Process speeches are sometimes referred to as demonstration or "how to" speeches because they often entail demonstrating something. These speeches require you to provide steps that will help your audience understand how to accomplish a specific task or process. However, How To speeches can be tricky in that there are rarely universally agreed upon (i.e. irrefutable) ways to do anything. If your professor asked the students in his or her public speaking class to each bring in a recipe for baking chocolate chip cookies, would all of them be the exact same recipe?

Probably not, but they would all be similar and, most importantly, they would all give you chocolate chip cookies as the end result. Students giving a demonstration speech will want to avoid saying "You *should* bake the cookies for 12 minutes" since that is not how everyone does it. Instead, the student should say something like:

"You can bake the cookies for 10 minutes."

"One option is to bake the cookies for 10 minutes."

"This particular recipe calls for the cookies to be baked for 10 minutes."

Each of the previous three statements is absolutely a fact that no one can argue or disagree with. While some people may say 12 minutes is too long or too short (depending on how soft or hard they like their cookies), no one can reasonably argue that these statements are not true.

On the other hand, there is a second type of process speech that focuses not on how the audience can achieve a result, such as changing oil in their cars or cooking something, but on how a process is achieved. The goal is understanding and not performance. After a speech on how to change a car tire, the audience members could probably do it (they might not want to, but they would know the steps). However, after a speech on how a bill goes through Congress, the audience would understand this important part of democracy but not be ready to serve in Congress.

Type 4: Ideas and Concepts

Sometimes an informative speech is designed to explain an idea or concept. What does democracy mean? What is justice? In this case, you will want to do two things. First, you'll want to define the idea or concept for the audience. The second is to make your concept concrete, real, and specific for your audience with examples.

Type 5: Categories or Divisions

Sometimes an informative speech topic doesn't lend itself to a specific type of approach, and in those cases the topics tend to fall into a "general" category of informative speeches. For example, if a student wanted to give an informative speech on the four "C's" of diamonds (cut, carat, color, and clarity), they certainly wouldn't approach it as if they were providing the history of diamonds, nor would they necessarily be informing anyone on "how to" shop for or buy diamonds or how diamonds are mined. The approach in this case would simply be to inform an audience on the four "C's" and what they mean. Other examples of this type of informative speech would be positions in playing volleyball or the customs to know when traveling in China.

As stated above, identifying the type of informative speech being given can help in several ways (conducting research, writing the introduction and conclusion), but perhaps the biggest benefit is that the type of informative speech being given will help determine, to some degree, the organizational pattern that will need to be used (see Chapter 7). For example, a How To speech must be in chronological order. There really isn't a way (or reason) to present a How To speech other than how the process is done in a time sequence. That is to say, for a speech on how to bake chocolate chip cookies, getting the ingredients (Main Point 1) must come before mixing the ingredients (Main Point 2), which must come before baking them (Main Point 3). Putting them in any other order will only confuse the audience.

Similarly, most Histories and Biographies will be organized chronologically, but not always. It makes sense to explain the history of the baseball from when it was first developed to where it is today, but certain approaches to Histories and Biographies can make that irrelevant. For an informative speech on Benjamin Franklin, a student might choose as his or her three main points: 1) His time as a printer, 2) His time as an inventor, 3) His time as a diplomat. These main points are not in strict chronological order because Franklin was a printer, inventor, and diplomat at the same time during periods of his whole life. However, this example would still be one way to inform an audience about him without using the chronological organizational pattern.

As for general informative speeches, since the topics that can be included in this category are very diverse and cover a range of subject matter, the way they are organized will be varied as well. However, if the topic is "types of" something or "kinds of" something, the organizational pattern would be topical; if it were the layout of a location, such as the White House, it would be spatial.

14.3 GUIDELINES FOR SELECTING AN INFORMATIVE SPEECH TOPIC

Pick a Specific or Focused Topic

Perhaps one of the biggest and most common misconceptions students have about informative speech topics is that the topic needs to be broad in order to fill the time requirements for the speech. It is not uncommon for a student to propose an informative speech topic such as "To inform my audience about the history of music." How is that topic even possible? When does the history of music even begin? The thinking here is that this speech will be easy to research and write since there is so much information available. But the opposite is actually true. A topic this broad makes doing research even harder.

Let's consider the example of a student who proposes the topic "To inform my audience about the Civil War." The Civil War was, conservatively speaking, four years long, resulted in over 750,000 casualties, and arguably changed the course of human history. So to think that it is possible to cover all of that in five to seven minutes is unrealistic. Also, a typical college library has hundreds of books dealing with the Civil War. How will you choose which ones are best suited to use for your speech?

The better approach in this case is to be as specific as possible. A revised specific purpose for this speech might be something like "To inform my audience about the Gettysburg Address." This topic is much more compact (the Gettysburg Address is only a few minutes long), and doing research will now be exponentially easier—although you will still find hundreds of sources on it. Or, an even more specific topic would be like the one in the outline at the end of this chapter: "To inform my classmates of the specific places in Gettysburg, Pennsylvania, that are considered haunted."

Instead of looking through all the books in your campus library on the Civil War, searching through the library's databases and catalog for material on the Gettysburg Address will yield a much more manageable number of books and articles. It may sound counterintuitive, but selecting a speech topic that is very specifically focused will make the research and writing phases of the informative speech much easier.

Avoid Faux or Fake Informative Speech Topics

Sometimes students think that because something sounds like an informative speech topic, it is one. This happens a lot with political issues that are usually partisan in nature. Some students may feel that the speech topic "To inform my audience why William Henry Harrison was a bad president" sounds factual, but really this is an opinion. Similarly, a number of topics that include conspiracy and paranormal subject matter are usually mistaken for good informative topics as well.

It is not uncommon for a student to propose the topic "To inform my audience about the existence of extraterrestrials," thinking it is a good topic. After all, there is plenty of evidence to support the claim, right? There are pictures of unidentified objects in the sky that people claim are from outer space, there are people who claim to have seen extraterrestrials, and most powerful of all, there are people who say that they have been abducted by aliens and taken into space.

The problem here, as you have probably already guessed, is that these facts are not irrefutable. Not every single person who sees something unknown in the sky will agree it is an alien spacecraft, and there can be little doubt that not everyone who claims to have been abducted by a UFO is telling the truth. This isn't to say that you can't still do an informative speech on alien sites. For example, two viable options are "To inform my audience about the SETI Project" or "To inform my audience of the origin of the Area 51 conspiracy." However, these types of speeches can quickly devolve into opinion if you aren't careful, which would then make them persuasive speeches. Even if you start by trying to be objective, unless you can present each side equally, it will end up becoming a persuasive speech. Additionally, when a speaker picks such a topic, it is often because of a latent desire to persuade the audience about them.

14.4 GUIDELINES FOR PREPARING AN INFORMATIVE SPEECH

Don't Be Too Broad

In preparing and writing an informative speech, one of the most common mistakes students make is to think that they must be comprehensive in covering their topic, which isn't realistic. Take for example an informative speech on Abraham Lincoln. Lincoln was 56 years old when he died, so to think that it is possible to cover his entire life's story in 5 to 7 minutes is un-realistic. The better option is to select three aspects of his life and focus on those as a way to provide an overall picture of who he was. So a proposed speech on Lincoln might have the specific purpose: "To inform my audience about Abraham Lincoln's administration of the Civil War." This is still a huge topic in that massive books have been written about it, but it could be addressed in three or four main points such as:

    I. The Civil War began in the aftermath of Lincoln's Election and Inauguration
    II. Finding the right military leaders for the Union was his major challenge at the beginning.
    III. The Emancipation Proclamation changed the nature of the War.
    IV. Lincoln adopted a policy that led to the North's victory.

Regardless of the topic, you will never be able to cover everything that is known about your topic, so don't try. Select the things that will best help the audience gain a general understanding of the topic, that will interest them, and that they hopefully will find valuable.

Be Accurate, Clear, and Interesting

A good informative speech conveys accurate information to the audience in a way that is clear and that keeps the listener interested in the topic. Achieving all three of these goals—accuracy, clarity, and interest—is the key to being an effective speaker. If information is inaccurate, incomplete, or unclear, it will be of limited usefulness to the audience.

Part of being accurate is making sure that your information is current. Even if you know a great deal about your topic or wrote a good paper on the topic in a high school course, you will need to verify the accuracy and completeness of what you know, especially if it is medical or scientific information. Most people understand that technology changes rapidly, so you need to update your information almost constantly. The same is true for topics that, on the surface, may seem to require less updating. For example, the Civil War occurred over 150 years ago, but contemporary research still offers new and emerging theories about the causes of the war and its long-term effects. So even with a topic that seems to be unchanging, carefully check the information to be sure it's accurate and up to date.

What defines "interesting?" In approaching the informative speech, you should keep in mind the good overall principle that the audience is asking, "what's in it for me?" The audience is either consciously or unconsciously wondering "What in this topic for me? How can I use this information? Of what value is this speech content to me? Why should I listen to it?" One reason this textbook uses examples of the Civil War is that the authors' college is located by several Civil War sites and even a major battlefield. Students see reminders of the Civil War on a regular basis.

You might consider it one of the jobs of the introduction to directly or indirectly answer these questions. If you can't, then you need to think about your topic and why you are addressing it. If it's only because the topic is interesting to you, you are missing the point. For example, why should we know about Abraham Lincoln's administration of the Civil War? Obviously, because it had significant, long-term consequences to Americans, and you should articulate that in terms the audience can understand.

Keep in Mind Audience Diversity

Finally, remember that not everyone in your audience is the same, so an informative speech should be prepared with audience diversity in mind. If the information in a speech is too complex or too simplistic, it will not hold the interest of the listeners. Determining the right level of complexity can be hard. Audience analysis is one important way to do this. Do the members of your audience belong to different age groups? Did they all go to public schools in the United States, or are some them international students? Are they all students majoring in the same subject, or is there a mixture of majors? Never assume that just because an audience is made up of students, they all share a knowledge set.

14.5 GIVING INFORMATIVE SPEECHES IN GROUPS

There are instances where you will be called upon to give an informative speech as part of a group of other informative speakers. This situation may be referred to as a panel or as a symposium. The difference is that in a panel, the focus is on a discussion by experts in front of an audience. The expert speakers may start with an opening statement, but typically the panelists are seated and their opening remarks are designed to present their basic position or stance and the bulk of time is spent in question-and-answer from the audience, from the moderator, or from each other. Some tips for panels are given here.

A symposium is more formal and the experts or presenters have put together prepared speeches on different aspects of an overall topic. For example, they may all be experts on juveniles in the criminal justice system, but they have chosen or been assigned a specific informative topic for the audience, who are probably also professionals in that field. One might speak on challenges with legal representation for juveniles, another on family reconciliation, another on educational opportunities, and so on. While there may be time for question and answers at the end, the bulk of the time is taken up by the prepared speeches.

The author has used the symposium format in her teaching of the informative speech for over 25 years. The students at first are skeptical, but usually afterward they see the benefit of the experience in the classroom. For one thing, instead of a class of 25-30 separate and unrelated informative speeches in the class, there are four sets of related speeches that explore a topic in more depth. Some popular topics have been physical and mental health issues (diabetes, breast cancer, pets, schizophrenia, phobias), the arts (musical genres, history of film), travel, and food. In those years, there have been topics that didn't work. Serial killers and sexually transmitted infections were two of them. One speech on that is acceptable. Six or seven, not so much. Just to clarify, the author always assigns the groups but the students pick the topics.

Here are some pointers if you are assigned to give a symposium-style informative speech:

1. Spend ample time discussing the topics so that everyone is supportive of the overall topic and the way the topic is broken down into separate speech topics. Do not let one person run the show and insist on a specific topic. A strong personality can sway the rest of the group and then later the other members become unhappy about the topic and resentful of the persuasive member.
2. Try to develop topics in different ways; for example, let's take the overall topic of phobias. The temptation is for each separate speech to be a specific phobia. While this is all right, it becomes repetitive to the audience. There are other ways to develop the subtopics (origins, different treatment options, phobias related to certain demographic groups) instead of six or seven speeches on different phobias.
3. Be in constant communication with your peers so that you know exactly what their topics are and how they are being developed. You don't want one or two co-presenters to "go rogue" and change their topics without the knowledge of the others in the group. You also do not want to end up overlapping, so that part of your speech is actually in someone else's speech. Share phone numbers so you can text or call each other, if the members are willing.
4. You should appoint a moderator who will introduce the speeches and speakers and close or call for questions when the speeches are completed, and possibly summarize the set of speeches at the end. This member does not have to be the first or last speaker in the group.
5. Be sure the order of speeches is logical, not random.
6. Be sure to get to the class early so you can set up and feel secure that your team members are present.
7. If you are required to have a question-and-answer session at the end, the moderator should try to make sure that the participation is balanced and one talkative person doesn't answer all the questions. There will be questions you cannot answer, so just be honest and say, "I didn't find that answer in my research."

Many instructors use this format because it not only teaches informative speaking skills, but because it emphasizes team work. You will be expected to do many team projects in your educational and professional careers, and this is a good way to start learning effective teamwork skills.

Conclusion

Learning how to give informative speeches will serve you well in your college career and your future work. Keep in mind the principles in this chapter but also those of the previous chapters: relating to the informational needs of the audience, using clear structure, and incorporating interesting and attention-getting supporting evidence.

14.6 SAMPLE INFORMATIVE SPEECH OUTLINE

The Spirit of Tradition: The Heartbeat of Oklahoma State University
January 01, 2023
Pistol Pete
CRN #2713

Informative Presentation
The Spirit of Tradition: The Heartbeat of Oklahoma State University

Specific Purpose: *After hearing my speech, the audience will be able to identify specific OSU traditions that not only strengthen our community but also perpetuate our Orange Pride.*

Thesis statement: The traditions at Oklahoma State University, steeped in history and driven by a collective spirit, are instrumental in fostering a sense of unity, instilling pride, and creating lasting memories for everyone who is part of the Cowboy family.

Audience Analysis: The primary audience for this presentation is undergraduate students at Oklahoma State University. Because this class is a 2000 level course, it is most likely full of first year students and sophomores. This increases the likelihood that the audience members will be somewhat new to OSU traditions, unless they have grown up visiting OSU with parents or grandparents. If the majority of students are from Oklahoma, it is possible they have heard of some of the traditions in a superficial way but may not know the origins or the impact on the university. This audience seems receptive to learning more about our campus community and will be likely to attentively listen to this presentation.

I. Attention/Introduction

    A. Attention getter: (Playing the alma mater softly in the background) "Proud and immortal; Bright shines your name; Oklahoma State, we herald your fame."

    (Music fades)

        1. Ah, yes.

        2. It gets me every time.

        3. You probably recognize those precious words from our Oklahoma State alma mater, written by Robert McCulloh in 1957.

    B. Orientation

        1. Self-introduction: Hi, you all know who I am, but just in case, I'm Pistol Pete, your official mascot for OSU!

        2. Background

            a. According to OSU's official website, our traditions have connected more than 240,000 alumni across the globe!

b. Honestly, I would venture to guess that it's even more than that!

c. The official website also shares that the plan for OSU began on Christmas Eve in 1890, but the first students didn't assemble for classes until December 14, 1891, despite having no buildings, books, or curriculum at the time.

d. As you can see, a lot of things have changed over the last 133 years.

3. Thesis/Central idea: The traditions at Oklahoma State University, rooted in history and driven by collective spirit, foster a sense of unity, instill pride, and create lasting memories for all who are a part of the Cowboy family!

C. Establish SAT Relationship/Credibility (verbally or nonverbally)

1. As a student here, you are a member of that family and will most likely be participating in traditions that make you part of our collective spirit.

2. I have participated in these traditions and witnessed firsthand their impact on our community.

D. Preview statement: Today, I would like to share with you some of the historical traditions, symbolic traditions, and the lasting impact of those traditions.

[Transition: One of the definitions of "tradition", according to Meriam-Webster, is "cultural continuity in social attitudes, customs, and institutions."]

II. Body

A. Main point 1: That helps us understand why I'd first like to address the significance of a couple of the historical traditions at OSU.

1. Probably one of the most iconic traditions we celebrate at OSU is the weeklong America's Greatest Homecoming Celebration.

            a. The week kicks off with dyeing the Edmon Low Library fountain orange on Sunday, a Harvest carnival and chili cookoff on Tuesday, Walk Around and Homecoming & Hoops on Friday and the Sea of Orange Homecoming parade on Saturday before the football game.
            b. The energy in the air during OSU's homecoming is something all OSU fans have to experience firsthand for themselves.
         2. The Waving song is also a historical tradition seen mostly at athletic events.
            a. In an O'Colly article in August 2005, it was reported by longtime OSU band director Hiram Henry that The Waving song originated during the early 1900s when Professor H.G. Seldombridge saw a performance of Victor Herbert's "The Red Mill" while visiting New York.
            b. The same article states that it was first introduced to the student body at the 1908 Varsity Review when lettermen from different sports took to the stage and sang, "O-A-M-C, O-A-M-C, we'll sing your praise tonight!" as they waved goodbye to the audience.
            c. The song, an instant success, had the crowd on their feet, while returning the wave to the athletes.

[Transition: While all traditions are rooted in history, not all have symbolic meanings.]

      B. Main point 2: Some of our traditions continue despite not everyone being aware of their symbolic nature.
         1. One such tradition is the Bedlam bell clapper.

a. The OSU alumni association shares that in 1917 when OSU and OU met in OKC, and the then "Aggies" caused an upset over the Sooners 9-0, the bell in the tower of Old Central rang out across Stillwater letting the town know about the victory over the Sooners.
   b. All night the Old Central bell rang with a student relay taking turns pulling the bell rope.
   c. OU students stole the clapper from the bell during a Bedlam game in 1932, but it didn't keep Cowboy fans from ringing the bell with a sledgehammer when OSU won.
   d. The tradition of the bell clapper continues to this day, but in a different way: a crystal bell is given to the winning school of the Bedlam series.
   e. Unfortunately this may be a tradition that comes to an end since OU has left the Big 12 to play in the SEC.
2. Another important symbolic tradition is the Spirit Rider, which started as a mascot for the band.
   a. According to OSU Athletics' website, the idea came from former band director, Richard Kastendieck.
   b. In 1984, Richard, Eddy Finley, an ag ed professor, and a student named, John Beall, started the tradition.
   c. Beall used his quarter horse, Della, to parade down the field after OSU scored a touchdown.

    d. As it became a staple, in 1998 OSU purchased its own Black horse, which through a student contest, became known as "Bullet."
    e. Bullet appears with the marching band at the beginning of each home game and after each OSU touchdown.
    f. Bullet is a symbol that's rallied fans on game days since the Spirit Rider was founded in 1984.

[Transition: While we've only covered a few of the many traditions that are carried on each year, it becomes apparent the impact these traditions have on us as a community.]

C. Main point 3: These traditions have an incredible and significant impact on our cultural identity, school spirit, and connection.
    1. Most folks'll tell you that being a Cowboy isn't about your clothes, it's your character.
        a. Part of OSU's amazing legacy and traditions involve the kindness and helpfulness you'll find when you communicate with the friendly folks on campus or at a university event.
        b. Being a member of the OSU community means you are a part of something...a culture.
        c. That culture is continued through the traditions and community we share to this day.
    2. Find your way to an athletic event and tell me how your heart grows when you hear the alma mater or wave your hands to the waving song.

        a. These traditions immerse us in school spirit and pride, as well as connection to the other Poke fans sitting around us cheering their hearts out for their beloved team.
        b. There's nothing like loading up with thousands of your closest friends, singing, chanting, waving, and living the cowboy way.
III. Conclusion
   A. Brakelight- In conclusion…
   B. Summary Statement: Today, you learned about some of the historical and symbolic traditions at OSU as well as the impact those traditions have on our community.
   C. Where to go from here: If this presentation sparked your interest, there's still so much more to know about the traditions here on campus.
      1. First, I suggest O-STATE Stories.
         a. It's a project of the Oklahoma Oral History Research Program and can be found through the digital archives at Edmon Low Library.
         b. Oral history interviews were conducted with a variety of folks to document their experiences at OSU over the last hundred years.
      2. Next, I suggest the O'Colly, the OSU Alumni Association, or the OSU official website.
   E. Note of finality
      1. As we delve into our traditions, as we sing our songs and wear our colors with pride, we embody these words: "Ever you'll find us, loyal and true."
      2. This is the essence of our traditions, the heart of our Cowboy Spirit.

Annotated Bibliography

Hillis, T. (2021, June 11). Newest spirit rider set to take saddle for OSU home football games. *KWTV News 9*. Retrieved from https://www.news9.com/story/60c384f299ca0f0bef368a51/newest-spirit-rider-set-to-take-saddle-for-osu-home-football-games

This News 9 story introduces the newest Spirit Rider for Oklahoma State University, Cadlyn Smith. The story gives background information about Smith, a former Miss Oklahoma Rodeo Queen, who used to barrel race in high school. A Meritt native, will be riding Bullet as Spirit Rider for more than 60,000 cheering fans for the 2022 season. This story is relevant and useful for this presentation because it shares historical information about the Spirit Rider and the importance of this role in our OSU traditions.

Merriam-Webster. (2023). Tradition. In *Merriam-Webster.com dictionary*. Retrieved from https://www.merriam-webster.com/dictionary/traditions?utm_campaign=sd&utm_medium=serp&utm_source=jsonld

The Merriam-Webster online dictionary provides definitions for most words, those commonly used and those not as much. Looking up the term, "tradition", helped give me a better idea of the general concept of the entire presentation. While the M-W dictionary gave a variety of definitions that work in their own way, I selected the one that referred to cultural continuity in customs and institutions. I feel this definition will enhance understanding and provide clarity for my audience.

OSU Alumni Association. (2023). University History. *Orangeconnection.org*. Retrieved from https://www.orangeconnection.org/s/860/18/interior.aspx?sid=860&gid=1&pgid=9445

The OSU Alumni association has a lot of great information on the page labeled University History. They outline the beginning of OSU's founding by: discussing the purpose of land grant universities, revealing the history of our school colors, sharing the history of me (Pistol Pete), describing the Spirit Rider, sharing the Songs, Hymns, and Chants, showcasing The OSU band, detailing the origins of Theta Pond, illustrating the history of Edmon Low library, reporting on Athletics, tracing Bedlam and talking about the class ring tradition. This site was extremely relevant and useful for my presentation as it provided historical information on specific traditions I wanted to address in my presentation.

OSU Athletics brings its own wheat wavin' traditions that become part of the experience. (2005, August 17). *The O'Colly*. Retrieved from https://www.ocolly.com/osu-athletics-brings-its-own-wheat-wavin-traditions-that-become-part-of-the-experience/article_708394fa-21bb-5b8b-92dc-d89c72ab01a6.html

In this O'Colly article, from the OSU student newspaper, they discuss some of the characteristics of traditions seen during football season. This article specifically focused on The Fight Songs, like "Ride 'Em Cowboys," "The OSU Chant," "The Waving Song," and the OSU Alma Mater. The article details a rumored history of the songs and provides some historical context that helps us better understand these melodic traditions. Lastly, the article discusses Bullet and the OSU Spirit Rider and it's historical significance. This article gives a lot of important historical information that helps us better understand the background of our cultural traditions.

Oklahoma State University Athletics. (2023). Gameday Traditions. *Okstate.com*. Retrieved from https://okstate.com/sports/2015/3/17/GEN_201401011

The university's official athletic website contains a page titled Gameday Traditions. This page outlines the history of numerous traditions specifically related to gameday. They discuss how names changed from Oklahoma A&M to Oklahoma State University. Outlining how we became the "cowboys", the website offers a thorough historical recounting of the OSU traditions and where they got their start. The website features videos and facts that are useful in understanding traditions. This website is relevant and useful because it directly connects to several of my main points and provides forms of support that will better illustrate the point for my listeners.

14.7 ENRICHMENT

Discussion Questions

1. List as many types of informative speeches that you have heard in your everyday life. What are the common elements of these speeches?
2. Of the informative speeches you have heard before, are there any speakers that stand out to you? Why?
3. What are the most important considerations when choosing an informative speech topic?
4. Why do you think it is important to know the differences between facts and opinions when preparing an informative speech?
5. How would you define and describe a controversial idea, such as assisted suicide for terminally ill patients, without your presentation becoming emotional? Is it possible for an informative speech to be emotional without becoming persuasive? Explain.
6. Have you ever sensed that a speaker who professed to be informing you was actually trying to persuade you? What was it about the presentation that gave you this impression? Did it make you skeptical about the speaker's information?

Activities

1. Form five groups. Each group will be given a type of informative speech listed in Section 14:2: Types of Informative Speeches (history, biography, processes, ideas and concepts, and categories or divisions). Brainstorm to create at least three informative speech topics for the type of speech the group has been given. Each group will share the topics with the class who will then vote on the most and least interesting topics to better understand the audience's interests. Finally, students should brainstorm their own informative speech topic individually and then share with their group members for feedback.
2. Watch a sample informative speech video and use the informative speech grading rubric to evaluate the speech. Discuss your finding with the class.

15 UNDERSTANDING SMALL GROUP COMMUNICATION

Learning Objectives

- Define small group communication.
- Explain the characteristics and functions of small groups.
- Compare and contrast different types of small groups.
- Discuss advantages and disadvantages of small groups.
- Explain the process and characteristics of the stages of group development.
- Explain the relationship between group cohesion and group climate.
- Describe the process of group member socialization.
- Explain the relationship between conformity and groupthink.
- Define various types of group conflict and identify strategies for managing each type.

Key Terms

- **Adjourning**
- **Forming**
- **Group Climate**
- **Group Cohesion**
- **Group Fantasies**

- Group Socialization
- Groupthink
- Interdependence
- Interpersonal Conflict
- Norming
- Performing
- Primary Group
- Primary Tension
- Procedural Conflict
- Relational-Oriented Group
- Secondary Group
- Secondary Tension
- Small Group Communication
- Social Cohesion
- Social Loafing
- Storming
- Substantive Conflict
- Symbolic Convergence
- Synergy
- Task Cohesion
- Task-Oriented Group
- Team
- Virtual Group

15.1 COMMUNICATING IN SMALL GROUPS

"Never doubt that a small group of thoughtful, committed citizens can change the world. Indeed, it is the only thing that ever has." -Margaret Mead

When you think of small groups, you probably think of the much dreaded "group assignment" that you've endured in high school and college. You are less likely to think of the numerous other groups to which you belong that bring more positive experiences, such as your family and friendship groups or shared-interest groups. Group communication scholars are so aware of this common negative sentiment toward group communication that they coined the term *grouphate* to describe it. Susan M. Sorensen, "Group-Hate: A Negative Reaction to Group Work" (paper presented at the annual meeting of the International Communication Association, Minneapolis, MN, May, 1981). Small groups, however, aren't just entities meant to torture students; they have served a central purpose in human history and evolution. Groups make it easier for us to complete a wide variety of tasks; help us establish meaningful social bonds; and help us create, maintain, and change our sense of self (Owen Hargie, *Skilled Interpersonal Interaction: Research, Theory, and Practice*, 5th ed. London: Routledge, 2011, 433). Negative group experiences are often exacerbated by a lack of knowledge about group communication processes. We are just expected to know how to work in groups without much instruction or practice. This lack of knowledge about group communication can lead to negative group interactions, which creates a negative cycle that perpetuates further negative experiences. Fortunately, as with other areas of communication, instruction in group communication can improve people's skills and increase people's satisfaction with their group experiences.

Pete's Small Group Project

The excitement of a new group project in his speech class had Pistol Pete eager to dive in, brainstorm ideas, and collaborate with his group members. However, his enthusiasm was met with silence. Despite his numerous texts and messages on the group discussion board, his teammates had yet to respond.

Faced with this challenge, Pete understood that he had to take initiative to ensure the project moved forward. He knew that he couldn't control the responses of his group members, but he could certainly control his actions.

Firstly, he decided to schedule a group meeting. He sent out an email proposing a few different times and days, hoping that providing options would accommodate everyone's schedules. He emphasized the importance of starting early on the project and the benefits of brainstorming together.

Next, he reached out individually to each member. Sometimes, personal communication can be more effective than group messages. He asked about their schedules, preferences for project roles, and initial ideas for the project.

While waiting for responses, Pete took the initiative to start brainstorming ideas for the project himself. He outlined potential topics, research resources, and a tentative plan of action. He shared this preliminary work with the group, hoping it might spark ideas and kickstart the conversation.

Recognizing that everyone might not be comfortable speaking up in a group setting, Pete suggested creating a shared document where everyone could contribute ideas at their own pace. This way, everyone had an avenue to contribute, and the collective thoughts of the team could start to take shape.

Finally, he considered that his peers might be overwhelmed or unsure about the project. So, Pete offered to help them understand the project better and encouraged them to ask questions. He tried to foster an open and supportive group environment, where everyone felt comfortable sharing their thoughts and concerns.

Throughout this process, Pistol Pete was proactive and patient, understanding that good teamwork often requires good leadership. He was confident that with persistence and a positive attitude, he would be able to rally his group and get the project on track. After all, being a Cowboy wasn't just about spirit and pride, but also about resilience and determination.

15.2 UNDERSTANDING SMALL GROUPS

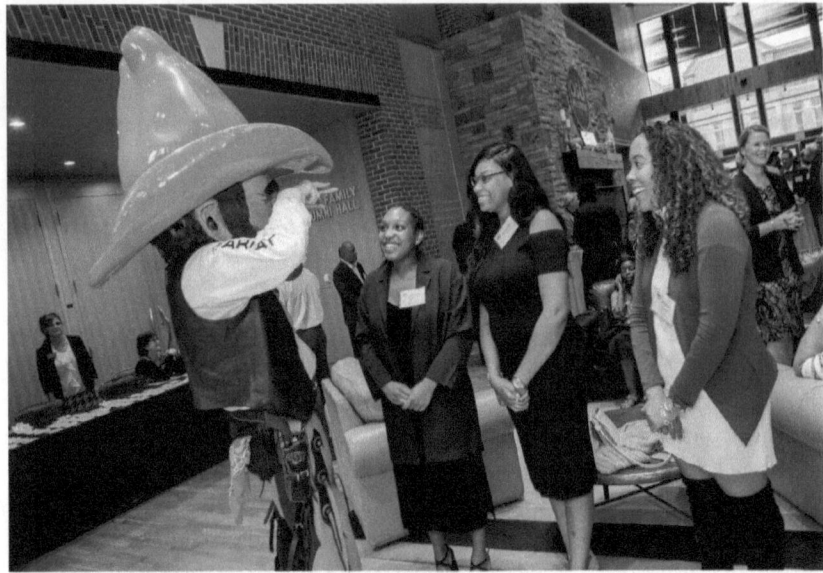

The communication skills most often discussed are directed toward dyadic communication, meaning that they are applied in two-person interactions. While many of these skills can be transferred to and used in small group contexts, the more complex nature of group interaction necessitates some adaptation and some additional skills. **Small group communication** refers to interactions among three or more people who are connected through a common purpose, mutual influence, and a shared identity. In this section, we will learn about the characteristics, functions, and types of small groups.

Characteristics of Small Groups

Different groups have different characteristics, serve different purposes, and can lead to positive, neutral, or negative experiences. While our interpersonal relationships primarily focus on relationship building, small groups usually focus on some sort of task completion or goal accomplishment. A college learning community focused on math and science, a campaign team for a state senator, and a group of local organic farmers are examples of small groups that would all have a different size, structure, identity, and interaction pattern.

Size of Small Groups

There is no set number of members for the ideal small group. A small group requires a minimum of three people (because two people would be a pair or dyad), but the upper range of group size is contingent on the purpose of the group. When groups grow beyond fifteen to twenty members, it becomes difficult to consider them a small group based on the previous definition. An analysis of the number of unique connections between members of small groups shows that they are deceptively complex. For example, within a six-person group, there are fifteen separate potential dyadic connections, and a twelve-person group would have sixty-six potential dyadic connections (Hargie, 2011). As you can see, when we double the number of group members, we more than double the number of connections, which shows that network connection points in small groups grow exponentially as membership increases. So, while there is no set upper limit on the number of group members, it makes sense that the number of group members should be limited to those necessary to accomplish the goal or serve the purpose of the group. Small groups that add too many members increase the potential for group members to feel overwhelmed or disconnected.

Structure of Small Groups

Internal and external influences affect a group's structure. In terms of internal influences, member characteristics play a role in initial group formation. For instance, a person who is well informed about the group's task and/or highly motivated as a group member may emerge as a leader and set into motion internal decision-making processes, such as recruiting new members or assigning group roles, that affect the structure of a group (Ellis & Fisher, 1994). Different members will also gravitate toward different roles within the group and will advocate for certain procedures and courses of action over others. External factors such as group size, task, and resources also affect group structure. Some groups will have more control over these external factors through decision making than others. For example, a commission that is put together by a legislative body to look into ethical violations in athletic organizations will likely have less control over its external factors than a self-created weekly book club.

Group structure is also formed through formal and informal network connections. In terms of formal networks, groups may have clearly defined roles and responsibilities or a hierarchy that shows how members are connected. The group itself may also be a part of an organizational hierarchy that networks the group into a larger organizational structure. This type of formal network is especially important in groups that have to report to external stakeholders. These external stakeholders may influence the group's formal network, leaving the group little or no control over its structure. Conversely, groups have more control over their informal networks, which are connections among individuals within the group and among group members and people outside of the group that aren't official. For example, a group member's friend or relative may be able to secure a space to hold a fundraiser at a discounted rate, which helps the group achieve its task. Both types of networks are important because they may help facilitate information exchange within a group and extend a group's reach in order to access other resources.

Size and structure also affect communication within a group (Ellis & Fisher, 1994). In terms of size, the more people in a group, the more issues with scheduling and coordination of communication. Remember that time is an important resource in most group interactions and a resource that is usually strained. Structure can increase or decrease the flow of communication. Reachability refers to the way in which one member is or isn't connected to other group members. For example, the "Circle" group structure in the graphic below shows that each group member is connected to two other members. This can make coordination easy when only one or two people need to be brought in for a decision. In this case, Erik and Callie are very reachable by Winston, who could easily coordinate with them. However, if Winston needed to coordinate with Bill or Stephanie, he would have to wait on Erik or Callie to reach that person, which could create delays. The circle can be a good structure for groups who are passing along a task and in which each member is expected to progressively build on the others' work. A group of scholars coauthoring a research paper may work in such a manner, with each person adding to the paper and then passing it on to the next person in the circle. In this case, they can ask the previous person questions and write with the next person's area of expertise in mind. The "Wheel" group structure in the graphic below shows an alternative organization pattern. In this structure, Tara is very reachable by all members of the group. This can be a useful structure when Tara is the person with the most expertise in the task or the leader who needs to review and approve work at each step before it is passed along to other group members. But Phillip and Shadow, for example, wouldn't likely work together without Tara being involved.

SMALL GROUP STRUCTURES

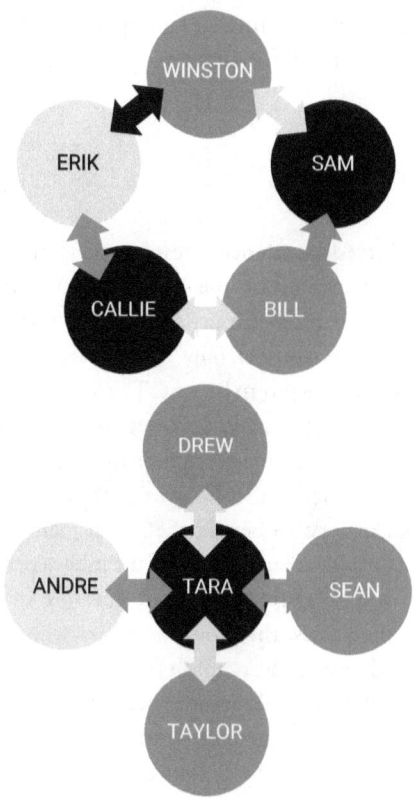

Looking at the group structures, we can make some assumptions about the communication that takes place in them. The wheel is an example of a centralized structure, while the circle is decentralized. Research has shown that centralized groups are better than decentralized groups in terms of speed and efficiency (Ellis & Fisher, 1994). But decentralized groups are more effective at solving complex problems. In centralized groups like the wheel, the person with the most connections, person C, is also more likely to be the leader of the group or at least have more status among group members, largely because that person has a broad perspective of what's going on in the group. The most central person can also act as a gatekeeper. Since this person has access to the most information, which is usually a sign of leadership or status, he or she could consciously decide to limit the flow of information. But in complex tasks, that person could become overwhelmed by the burden of processing and sharing information with all the other group members. The circle structure is more likely to emerge in groups where collaboration is the goal and a specific task and course of action isn't required under time constraints. While the person who initiated the group or has the most expertise in regards to the task may emerge as a leader in a decentralized group, the equal access to information lessens the hierarchy and potential for gatekeeping that is present in the more centralized groups.

Interdependence

Small groups exhibit **interdependence**, meaning they share a common purpose and a common fate. If the actions of one or two group members lead to a group deviating from or not achieving their purpose, then all members of the group are affected. Conversely, if the actions of only a few of the group members lead to success, then all members of the group benefit. This is a major contributor to many college students' dislike of group assignments, because they feel a loss of control and independence that they have when they complete an assignment alone. This concern is valid in that their grades might suffer because of the negative actions of someone else or their hard work may go to benefit the group member who just skated by. Group meeting attendance is a clear example of the interdependent nature of group interaction. Many of us have arrived at a group meeting only to find half of the members present. In some cases, the group members who show up have to leave and reschedule because they can't accomplish their task without the other members present. Group members who attend meetings but withdraw or don't participate can also derail group progress. Although it can be frustrating to have your job, grade, or reputation partially dependent on the actions of others, the interdependent nature of groups can also lead to higher-quality performance and output, especially when group members are accountable for their actions.

Shared Identity

The shared identity of a group manifests in several ways. Groups may have official charters or mission and vision statements that lay out the identity of a group. For example, the Girl Scout mission states that "Girl Scouting builds girls of courage, confidence, and character, who make the world a better place" (Girl Scouts, 2012). The mission for this large organization influences the identities of the thousands of small groups called troops. Group identity is often formed around a shared goal and/or previous accomplishments, which adds dynamism to the group as it looks toward the future and back on the past to inform its present. Shared identity can also be exhibited through group names, slogans, songs, handshakes, clothing, or other symbols. At a family reunion, for example, matching t-shirts specially made for the occasion, dishes made from recipes passed down from generation to generation, and shared stories of family members that have passed away help establish a shared identity and social reality.

A key element of the formation of a shared identity within a group is the establishment of the in-group as opposed to the out-group. The degree to which members share in the in-group identity varies from person to person and group to group. Even within a family, some members may not attend a reunion or get as excited about the matching t-shirts as others. Shared identity also emerges as groups become cohesive, meaning they identify with and like the group's task and other group members. The presence of cohesion and a shared identity leads to a building of trust, which can also positively influence productivity and members' satisfaction.

Functions of Small Groups

Why do we join groups? Even with the challenges of group membership that we have all faced, we still seek out and desire to be a part of numerous groups. In some cases, we join a group because we need a service or access to information. We may also be drawn to a group because we admire the group or its members. Whether we are conscious of it or not, our identities and self-concepts are built on the groups with which we identify. So, to answer the earlier question, we join groups because they function to help us meet instrumental, interpersonal, and identity needs.

Groups Meet Instrumental Needs

Groups have long served the instrumental needs of humans, helping with the most basic elements of survival since ancient humans first evolved. Groups helped humans survive by providing security and protection through increased numbers and access to resources. Today, groups are rarely such a matter of life and death, but they still serve important instrumental functions. Labor unions, for example, pool efforts and resources to attain material security in the form of pay increases and health benefits for their members, which protects them by providing a stable and dependable livelihood. Individual group members must also work to secure the instrumental needs of the group, creating a reciprocal relationship. Members of labor unions pay dues that help support the group's efforts. Some groups also meet our informational needs. Although they may not provide material resources, they enrich our knowledge or provide information that we can use to then meet our own instrumental needs. Many groups provide referrals to resources or offer advice. For example, several consumer protection and advocacy groups have been formed to offer referrals for people who have been the victim of fraudulent business practices. Whether a group forms to provide services to members that they couldn't get otherwise, advocate for changes that will affect members' lives, or provide information, many groups meet some type of instrumental need.

Groups Meet Interpersonal Needs

Group membership meets interpersonal needs by giving us access to inclusion, control, and support. In terms of inclusion, people have a fundamental drive to be a part of a group and to create and maintain social bonds. As we've learned, humans have always lived and worked in small groups. Family and friendship groups, shared-interest groups, and activity groups all provide us with a sense of belonging and being included in an in-group. People also join groups because they want to have some control over a decision-making process or to influence the outcome of a group. Being a part of a group allows people to share opinions and influence others. Conversely, some people join a group to be controlled, because they don't want to be the sole decision maker or leader and instead want to be given a role to follow.

Just as we enter into interpersonal relationships because we like someone, we are drawn toward a group when we are attracted to it and/or its members. Groups also provide support for others in ways that supplement the support that we get from significant others in interpersonal relationships. Some groups, like therapy groups for survivors of sexual assault or support groups for people with cancer, exist primarily to provide emotional support. While these groups may also meet instrumental needs through connections and referrals to resources, they fulfill the interpersonal need for belonging that is a central human need.

Groups Meet Identity Needs

Our affiliations are building blocks for our identities, because group membership allows us to use reference groups for social comparison—in short, identifying us with some groups and characteristics and separating us from others. Some people join groups to be affiliated with people who share similar or desirable characteristics in terms of beliefs, attitudes, values, or cultural identities. For example, people may join the National Organization for Women because they want to affiliate with others who support women's rights or a local chapter of the National Association for the Advancement of Colored People (NAACP) because they want to affiliate with African Americans, people concerned with civil rights, or a combination of the two. Group memberships vary in terms of how much they affect our identity, as some are more prominent than others at various times in our lives. While religious groups as a whole are too large to be considered small groups, the work that people do as a part of a religious community—as a lay leader, deacon, member of a prayer group, or committee—may have deep ties to a person's identity.

The prestige of a group can initially attract us because we want that group's identity to "rub off" on our own identity. Likewise, the achievements we make as a group member can enhance our self-esteem, add to our reputation, and allow us to create or project certain identity characteristics to engage in impression management. For example, a person may take numerous tests to become a part of Mensa, which is an organization for people with high IQs, for no material gain but for the recognition or sense of achievement that the affiliation may bring. Likewise, people may join sports teams, professional organizations, and honor societies for the sense of achievement and affiliation. Such groups allow us opportunities to better ourselves by encouraging further development of skills or knowledge. For example, a person who used to play the oboe in high school may join the community band to continue to improve on his or her ability.

Types of Small Groups

There are many types of small groups, but the most common distinction made between types of small groups is that of task-oriented and relational-oriented groups (Hargie, 2011). **Task-oriented groups** are formed to solve a problem, promote a cause, or generate ideas or information (McKay, Davis, & Fanning, 1995). In such groups, like a committee or study group, interactions and decisions are primarily evaluated based on the quality of the final product or output. The three main types of tasks are production, discussion, and problem-solving tasks (Ellis & Fisher, 1994). Groups faced with production tasks are asked to produce something tangible from their group interactions such as a report, design for a playground, musical performance, or fundraiser event. Groups faced with discussion tasks are asked to talk through something without trying to come up with a right or wrong answer. Examples of this type of group include a support group for people with HIV/AIDS, a book club, or a group for new fathers. Groups faced with problem-solving tasks have to devise a course of action to meet a specific need. These groups also usually include a production and discussion component, but the end goal isn't necessarily a tangible product or a shared social reality through discussion. Instead, the end goal is a well-thought-out idea. Task-oriented groups require honed problem-solving skills to accomplish goals, and the structure of these groups is more rigid than that of relational-oriented groups.

Relational-oriented groups are formed to promote interpersonal connections and are more focused on quality interactions that contribute to the well-being of group members. Decision making is directed at strengthening or repairing relationships rather than completing discrete tasks or debating specific ideas or courses of action. All groups include task and relational elements, so it's best to think of these orientations as two ends of a continuum rather than as mutually exclusive.

For example, although a family unit works together daily to accomplish tasks like getting the kids ready for school and friendship groups may plan a surprise party for one of the members, their primary and most meaningful interactions are still relational.

To more specifically look at the types of small groups that exist, we can examine why groups form. Some groups are formed based on interpersonal relationships. Our family and friends are considered **primary groups**, or long-lasting groups that are formed based on relationships and include significant others. These are the small groups in which we interact most frequently. They form the basis of our society and our individual social realities. Kinship networks provide important support early in life and meet physiological and safety needs, which are essential for survival. They also meet higher-order needs such as social and self-esteem needs. When people do not interact with their biological family, whether voluntarily or involuntarily, they can establish fictive kinship networks, which are composed of people who are not biologically related but fulfill family roles and help provide the same support.

We also interact in many **secondary groups**, which are characterized by less frequent face-to-face interactions, less emotional and relational communication, and more task-related communication than primary groups (Barker, 1991). While we are more likely to participate in secondary groups based on self-interest, our primary-group interactions are often more reciprocal or other oriented. For example, we may join groups because of a shared interest or need.

Groups formed based on shared interest include social groups and leisure groups such as a group of independent film buffs, science fiction fans, or bird watchers. Some groups form to meet the needs of individuals or of a particular group of people. Examples of groups that meet the needs of individuals include study groups or support groups like a weight loss group. These groups are focused on individual needs, even though they meet as a group, and they are also often discussion oriented. Service groups, on the other hand, work to meet the needs of individuals but are task oriented. Service groups include Habitat for Humanity and Rotary Club chapters, among others. Still other groups form around a shared need, and their primary task is advocacy. For example, the Gay Men's Health Crisis is a group that was formed by a small group of eight people in the early 1980s to advocate for resources and support for the still relatively unknown disease that would later be known as AIDS. Similar groups form to advocate for everything from a stop sign at a neighborhood intersection to the end of human trafficking.

As we already learned, other groups are formed primarily to accomplish a task. **Teams** are task-oriented groups in which members are especially loyal and dedicated to the task and other group members (Larson & LaFasto, 1989). In professional and civic contexts, the word *team* has become popularized as a means of drawing on the positive connotations of the term—connotations such as "high-spirited," "cooperative," and "hardworking." Scholars who have spent years studying highly effective teams have identified several common factors related to their success. Successful teams have (Adler & Elmhorst, 2005)

- clear and inspiring shared goals,
- a results-driven structure,
- competent team members,
- a collaborative climate,
- high standards for performance,
- external support and recognition, and
- ethical and accountable leadership.

Increasingly, small groups and teams are engaging in more virtual interaction. **Virtual groups** take advantage of new technologies and meet exclusively or primarily online to achieve their purpose or goal. Some virtual groups may complete their task without ever being physically face-to-face. Virtual groups bring with them distinct advantages and disadvantages.

Advantages and Disadvantages of Small Groups

As with anything, small groups have their advantages and disadvantages. Advantages of small groups include shared decision making, shared resources, synergy, and exposure to diversity. It is within small groups that most of the decisions that guide our country, introduce local laws, and influence our family interactions are made. In a democratic society, participation in decision making is a key part of citizenship. Groups also help in making decisions involving judgment calls that have ethical implications or the potential to negatively affect people. Individuals making such high-stakes decisions in a vacuum could have negative consequences given the lack of feedback, input, questioning, and proposals for alternatives that would come from group interaction. Group members also help expand our social networks, which provide access to more resources. A local community-theater group may be able to put on a production with a limited budget by drawing on these connections to get set-building supplies, props, costumes, actors, and publicity in ways that an individual could not. The increased knowledge, diverse perspectives, and access to resources that groups possess relates to another advantage of small groups—synergy.

Synergy refers to the potential for gains in performance or heightened quality of interactions when complementary members or member characteristics are added to existing ones (Larson Jr., 2010). Because of synergy, the final group product can be better than what any individual could have produced alone. When I worked in housing and residence life, I helped coordinate a "World Cup Soccer Tournament" for the international students that lived in my residence hall. As a group, we created teams representing different countries around the world, made brackets for people to track progress and predict winners, got sponsors, gathered prizes, and ended up with a very successful event that would not have been possible without the synergy created by our collective group membership. The members of this group were also exposed to international diversity that enriched our experiences, which is also an advantage of group communication.

Participating in groups can also increase our exposure to diversity and broaden our perspectives. Although groups vary in the diversity of their members, we can strategically choose groups that expand our diversity, or we can unintentionally end up in a diverse group. When we participate in small groups, we expand our social networks, which increase the possibility to interact with people who have different cultural identities than ourselves. Since group members work together toward a common goal, shared identification with the task or group can give people with diverse backgrounds a sense of commonality that they might not have otherwise. Even when group members share cultural identities, the diversity of experience and opinion within a group can lead to broadened perspectives as alternative ideas are presented and opinions are challenged and defended. One of my favorite parts of facilitating class discussion is when students with different identities and/or perspectives teach one another things in ways that I could not on my own. This example brings together the potential of synergy and diversity. People who are more introverted or just avoid group communication and voluntarily distance themselves from groups—or are rejected from groups—risk losing opportunities to learn more about others and themselves.

There are also disadvantages to small group interaction. In some cases, one person can be just as or more effective than a group of people. Think about a situation in which a highly specialized skill or knowledge is needed to get something done. In this situation, one very knowledgeable person is probably a better fit for the task than a group of less knowledgeable people. Group interaction also has a tendency to slow down the decision-making process. Individuals connected through a hierarchy or chain of command often work better in situations where decisions must be made under time constraints. When group interaction does occur under time constraints, having one "point person" or leader who coordinates action and gives final approval or disapproval on ideas or suggestions for actions is best.

Group communication also presents interpersonal challenges. A common problem is coordinating and planning group meetings due to busy and conflicting schedules. Some people also have difficulty with the other-centeredness and self-sacrifice that some groups require. The interdependence of group members that we discussed earlier can also create some disadvantages. Group members may take advantage of the anonymity of a group and engage in **social loafing**, meaning they contribute less to the group than other members or than they would if working alone (Karau & Williams, 1993). Social loafers expect that no one will notice their behaviors or that others will pick up their slack. It is this potential for social loafing that makes many students and professionals dread group work, especially those who have a tendency to cover for other group members to prevent the social loafer from diminishing the group's productivity or output.

References

Adler, R. B., and Jeanne Marquardt Elmhorst, *Communicating at Work: Principles and Practices for Businesses and the Professions*, 8th ed. (Boston, MA: McGraw-Hill, 2005), 248–50.

Ahuja, M. K., and John E. Galvin, "Socialization in Virtual Groups," *Journal of Management* 29, no. 2 (2003): 163.

Barker, D. B., "The Behavioral Analysis of Interpersonal Intimacy in Group Development," *Small Group Research* 22, no. 1 (1991): 79.

Comer, D. R., "Organizational Newcomers' Acquisition of Information from Peers," *Management Communication Quarterly* 5, no. 1 (1991): 64–89.

Ellis, D. G., and B. Aubrey Fisher, *Small Group Decision Making: Communication and the Group Process*, 4th ed. (New York: McGraw-Hill, 1994), 57.

Girl Scouts, "Facts," accessed July 15, 2012, http://www.girlscouts.org/who_we_are/facts.

Hargie, O., *Skilled Interpersonal Interaction: Research, Theory, and Practice*, 5th ed. (London: Routledge, 2011), 452–53.

Karau, S. J., and Kipling D. Williams, "Social Loafing: A Meta-Analytic Review and Theoretical Integration," *Journal of Personality and Social Psychology* 65, no. 4 (1993): 681.

Larson, C. E., and Frank M. J. LaFasto, *TeamWork: What Must Go Right/What Must Go Wrong* (Newbury Park, CA: Sage, 1989), 73.

Larson Jr., J. R., *In Search of Synergy in Small Group Performance* (New York: Psychology Press, 2010).

McKay, M., Martha Davis, and Patrick Fanning, *Messages: Communication Skills Book*, 2nd ed. (Oakland, CA: New Harbinger Publications, 1995), 254.

Myers, S. A., and Alan K. Goodboy, "A Study of Grouphate in a Course on Small Group Communication," *Psychological Reports* 97, no. 2 (2005): 385.

Walther, J. B., and Ulla Bunz, "The Rules of Virtual Groups: Trust, Liking, and Performance in Computer-Mediated Communication," *Journal of Communication* 55, no. 4 (2005): 830.

Weimer, M., "Why Students Hate Groups," *The Teaching Professor*, July 1, 2008, accessed July 15, 2012, http://www.teachingprofessor.com/articles/teaching-and-learning/why-students-hate-groups.

15.3 SMALL GROUP DEVELOPMENT

Forming

Small groups have to start somewhere. Even established groups go through changes as members come and go, as tasks are started and completed, and as relationships change. In this section, we will learn about the stages of group development, which are forming, storming, norming, performing, and adjourning (Tuckman & Jensen, 1977). As with most models of communication phenomena, although we order the stages and discuss them separately, they are not always experienced in a linear fashion. Additionally, some groups don't experience all five stages, may experience stages multiple times, or may experience more than one stage at a time.

During the **forming** stage, group members begin to reduce uncertainty associated with new relationships and/or new tasks through initial interactions that lay the foundation for later group dynamics. Groups return to the forming stage as group members come and go over the life span of a group. Although there may not be as much uncertainty when one or two new people join a group as there is when a group first forms, groups spend some time in the forming stage every time group membership changes.

Given that interpersonal bonds are likely not yet formed and people are unfamiliar with the purpose of the group or task at hand, there are high levels of uncertainty. Early stages of role negotiation begin and members begin to determine goals for the group and establish rules and norms. Group cohesion also begins to form during this stage. **Group cohesion** refers to the commitment of members to the purpose of the group and the degree of attraction among individuals within the group (Hargie, 2011). The cohesion that begins in this stage sets the group on a trajectory influenced by group members' feelings about one another and their purpose or task. Groups with voluntary membership may exhibit high levels of optimism about what the group can accomplish. Although the optimism can be motivating, unrealistic expectations can lead to disappointment, making it important for group members to balance optimism with realism. Groups with assigned or mandatory membership may include members that carry some degree of resentment toward the group itself or the goals of the group. These members can start the group off on a negative trajectory that will lessen or make difficult group cohesiveness. Groups can still be successful if these members are balanced out by others who are more committed to and positive in regards to the purpose of the group.

Many factors influence how the forming stage of group development plays out. The personalities of the individuals in the group, the skills that members bring, the resources available to the group, the group's size, and the group's charge all contribute to the creation of the early tone of and climate within a group (Ellis & Fisher, 1994). For example, more dominant personalities may take early leadership roles in the group that can affect subsequent decisions. Group members' diverse skill sets and access to resources can also influence the early stages of role differentiation. In terms of size, the bonding that begins in the forming stage becomes difficult when the number of people within the group prevents every person from having a one-on-one connection with every other member of the group. Also, in larger groups, more dominant members tend to assert themselves as leaders and build smaller coalitions within the group, which can start the group on a trajectory toward more conflict during the upcoming storming stage (Ellis & Fisher, 1994).

When a group receives an external charge, meaning that the goal or purpose of the group is decided by people outside the group, there may be less uncertainty related to the task dimensions of the group. Additionally, decisions about what roles people will play including group leaders and other decisions about the workings of the group may come from the outside, which reduces some of the uncertainty inherent in the forming stage. Relational uncertainty can also be diminished when group members have preexisting relationships or familiarity with each other. Although the decreased uncertainty may be beneficial at this stage, too much imposed structure from the outside can create resentment or a feeling of powerlessness among group members. So a manageable amount of uncertainty is actually a good thing for group cohesion and productivity.

Storming

During the **storming** stage of group development, conflict emerges as people begin to perform their various roles, have their ideas heard, and negotiate where they fit in the group's structure. The uncertainty present in the forming stage begins to give way as people begin to occupy specific roles and the purpose, rules, and norms of a group become clearer. Conflict develops when some group members aren't satisfied with the role that they or others are playing or the decisions regarding the purpose or procedures of the group. For example, if a leader begins to emerge or is assigned during the forming stage, some members may feel that the leader is imposing his or her will on other members of the group. As we will learn in our section on group leadership, leaders should expect some degree of resentment from others who wanted to be the leader, have interpersonal conflicts with the leader, or just have general issues with being led.

Although the word *storming* and the concept of conflict have negative connotations, conflict can be positive and productive. Just like storms can replenish water supplies and make crops grow, storming can lead to group growth. While conflict is inevitable and should be experienced by every group, a group that gets stuck at the storming stage will likely not have much success in completing its task or achieving its purpose. Influences from outside the group can also affect the conflict in the storming stage. Interpersonal conflicts that predate the formation of the group may distract the group from the more productive idea- or task-oriented conflict that can be healthy for the group and increase the quality of ideas, decision making, and output.

Norming

During the **norming** stage of group development, the practices and expectations of the group are solidified, which leads to more stability, productivity, and cohesion within the group. Group norms are behaviors that become routine but are not explicitly taught or stated. In short, group norms help set the tone for what group members ought to do and how they ought to behave (Ellis & Fisher, 1994). Many implicit norms are derived from social norms that people follow in their everyday life. Norms within the group about politeness, lateness, and communication patterns are typically similar to those in other contexts. Sometimes a norm needs to be challenged because it is not working for the group, which could lead a group back to the storming stage. Other times, group members challenge norms for no good reason, which can lead to punishment for the group member or create conflict within the group.

15.3 SMALL GROUP DEVELOPMENT

At this stage, there is a growing consensus among group members as to the roles that each person will play, the way group interactions will typically play out, and the direction of the group. Leaders that began to emerge have typically gained the support of other group members, and group identity begins to solidify. The group may now be recognizable by those on the outside, as slogans, branding, or patterns of interaction become associated with the group. This stage of group development is key for the smooth operation of the group. Norms bring a sense of predictability and stability that can allow a group to move on to the performing stage of group development. Norms can also bring with them conformity pressures that can be positive or negative. In general, people go along with a certain amount of pressure to conform out of a drive to avoid being abnormal that is a natural part of our social interaction (Ellis & Fisher, 1994). Too much pressure, however, can lead people to feel isolated and can create a negative group climate. We will learn more about pressure as a group dynamic later in this chapter.

Explicit rules may also guide group interaction. Rules are explicitly stated guidelines for members and may refer to things like expected performance levels or output, attitudes, or dress codes. Rules may be communicated through verbal instructions, employee handbooks, membership policies, or codes of conduct (Hargie, 2011). Groups can even use procedures like Robert's Rules of Order to manage the flow of conversations and decision-making procedures. Group members can contest or subvert group rules just as they can norms. Violations of group rules, however, typically result in more explicit punishments than do violations of norms.

Performing

During the **performing** stage of group development, group members work relatively smoothly toward the completion of a task or achievement of a purpose. Although interactions in the performing stage are task focused, the relational aspects of group interaction provide an underlying support for the group members. Socialization outside of official group time can serve as a needed relief from the group's task. During task-related interactions, group members ideally begin to develop a synergy that results from the pooling of skills, ideas, experiences, and resources. Synergy is positive in that it can lead group members to exceed their expectations and perform better than they could individually. Glitches in the group's performance can lead the group back to previous stages of group development. Changes in membership, member roles, or norms can necessitate a revisiting of aspects of the forming, storming, or norming stages. One way to continue to build group cohesion during the performing stage is to set short-term attainable group goals. Accomplishing something, even if it's small, can boost group morale, which in turn boosts cohesion and productivity.

Adjourning

The **adjourning** stage of group development occurs when a group dissolves because it has completed its purpose or goal, membership is declining and support for the group no longer exists, or it is dissolved because of some other internal or external cause. Some groups may live on indefinitely and not experience the adjourning stage. Other groups may experience so much conflict in the storming stage that they skip norming and performing and dissolve before they can complete their task. For groups with high social cohesion, adjourning may be a difficult emotional experience. However, group members may continue interpersonal relationships that formed even after the group dissolves. In reality, many bonds, even those that were very close, end up fading after the group disbands. This doesn't mean the relationship wasn't genuine; interpersonal relationships often form because of proximity and shared task interaction. Once that force is gone, it becomes difficult to maintain friendships, and many fade away. For groups that had negative experiences, the adjourning stage may be welcomed.

To make the most out of the adjourning stage, it is important that there be some guided and purposeful reflection. Many groups celebrate their accomplishments with a party or ceremony. Even groups that had negative experiences or failed to achieve their purpose can still learn something through reflection in the adjourning stage that may be beneficial for future group interactions. Often, group members leave a group experience with new or more developed skills that can be usefully applied in future group or individual contexts. Even groups that are relational rather than task focused can increase members' interpersonal, listening, or empathetic skills or increase cultural knowledge and introduce new perspectives.

References

Ellis, D. G., and B. Aubrey Fisher, *Small Group Decision Making: Communication and the Group Process*, 4th ed. (New York: McGraw-Hill, 1994), 14.

Hargie, O., *Skilled Interpersonal Interaction: Research, Theory, and Practice*, 5th ed. (London: Routledge, 2011), 445.

Tuckman, B. W., and Mary Ann C. Jensen, "Stages of Small-Group Development Revisited," *Group and Organizational Studies* 2, no. 4 (1977): 419–27.

15.4 SMALL GROUP DYNAMICS

Any time a group of people come together, new dynamics are put into place that differ from the dynamics present in our typical dyadic interactions. The impressions we form about other people's likeability and the way we think about a group's purpose are affected by the climate within a group that is created by all members. Groups also develop norms, and new group members are socialized into a group's climate and norms just as we are socialized into larger social and cultural norms in our everyday life. The pressure to conform to norms becomes more powerful in group situations, and some groups take advantage of these forces with positive and negative results. Last, the potential for productive and destructive conflict increases as multiple individuals come together to accomplish a task or achieve a purpose. This section explores the dynamics mentioned previously in order to better prepare you for future group interactions.

Group Cohesion and Climate

When something is cohesive, it sticks together, and the cohesion within a group helps establish an overall group climate. **Group climate** refers to the relatively enduring tone and quality of group interaction that is experienced similarly by group members. To better understand cohesion and climate, we can examine two types of cohesion: task and social.

Task cohesion refers to the commitment of group members to the purpose and activities of the group. **Social cohesion** refers to the attraction and liking among group members. Ideally, groups would have an appropriate balance between these two types of cohesion relative to the group's purpose, with task-oriented groups having higher task cohesion and relational-oriented groups having higher social cohesion. Even the most task-focused groups need some degree of social cohesion, and vice versa, but the balance will be determined by the purpose of the group and the individual members. For example, a team of workers from the local car dealership may join a local summer softball league because they're good friends and love the game. They may end up beating the team of faculty members from the community college who joined the league just to get to know each other better and have an excuse to get together and drink beer in the afternoon. In this example, the players from the car dealership exhibit high social and task cohesion, while the faculty exhibit high social but low task cohesion.

Cohesion benefits a group in many ways and can be assessed through specific group behaviors and characteristics. Groups with an appropriate level of cohesiveness (Hargie, 2011)

- set goals easily;
- exhibit a high commitment to achieving the purpose of the group;
- are more productive;
- experience fewer attendance issues;
- have group members who are willing to stick with the group during times of difficulty;
- have satisfied group members who identify with, promote, and defend the group;
- have members who are willing to listen to each other and offer support and constructive criticism; and
- experience less anger and tension.

Appropriate levels of group cohesion usually create a positive group climate, since group climate is affected by members' satisfaction with the group. Climate has also been described as group morale. Following are some qualities that contribute to a positive group climate and morale (Marston & Hecht, 1988):

- **Participation.** Group members feel better when they feel included in discussion and a part of the functioning of the group.
- **Messages.** Confirming messages help build relational dimensions within a

group, and clear, organized, and relevant messages help build task dimensions within a group.
- **Feedback.** Positive, constructive, and relevant feedback contribute to group climate.
- **Equity.** Aside from individual participation, group members also like to feel as if participation is managed equally within the group and that appropriate turn taking is used.
- **Clear and accepted roles.** Group members like to know how status and hierarchy operate within a group. Knowing the roles isn't enough to lead to satisfaction, though—members must also be comfortable with and accept those roles.
- **Motivation.** Member motivation is activated by perceived connection to and relevance of the group's goals or purpose.

Group cohesion and climate is also demonstrated through symbolic convergence (Bormann, 1985). **Symbolic convergence** refers to the sense of community or group consciousness that develops in a group through non-task-related communication such as stories and jokes. The originator of symbolic convergence theory, Ernest Bormann, claims that the sharing of group fantasies creates symbolic convergence. Fantasy, in this sense, doesn't refer to fairy tales, sexual desire, or untrue things. In group communication, **group fantasies** are verbalized references to events outside the "here and now" of the group, including references to the group's past, predictions for the future, or other communication about people or events outside the group (Griffin, 2009). For example, as a graduate student, I spent a lot of time talking with others in our small group about research, writing, and other things related to our classes and academia in general. Most of this communication wouldn't lead to symbolic convergence or help establish the strong social bonds that we developed as a group. Instead, it was our grad student "war stories" about excessive reading loads and unreasonable paper requirements we had experienced in earlier years of grad school, horror stories about absent or vindictive thesis advisors, and "you won't believe this" stories from the classes that we were teaching that brought us together.

In any group, you can tell when symbolic convergence is occurring by observing how people share such fantasies and how group members react to them. If group members react positively and agree with or appreciate the teller's effort or other group members are triggered to tell their own related stories, then convergence is happening and cohesion and climate are being established. Over time, these fantasies build a shared vision of the group and what it means to be a member that creates a shared group consciousness. By reviewing and applying the concepts in this section, you can hopefully identify potential difficulties with group cohesion and work to enhance cohesion when needed in order to create more positive group climates and enhance your future group interactions.

Socializing Group Members

Group socialization refers to the process of teaching and learning the norms, rules, and expectations associated with group interaction and group member behaviors. Group norms, rules, and cohesion can only be created and maintained through socialization (Ahuja & Galvin, 2003). It is also through socialization that a shared identity and social reality develops among group members, but this development is dependent on several factors. For example, groups with higher levels of cohesion are more likely to have members that "buy into" rules and norms, which aids in socialization. The need for socialization also changes throughout a group's life span. If membership in a group is stable, long-term members should not need much socialization. However, when new members join a group, existing members must take time to engage in socialization. When a totally new group is formed, socialization will be an ongoing process as group members negotiate rules and procedures, develop norms, and create a shared history over time.

The information exchanged during socialization can be broken down into two general categories: technical and social knowledge (Ahuja & Galvin, 2003). Technical knowledge focuses on skills and information needed to complete a task, and social knowledge focuses on behavioral norms that guide interaction. Each type of information is usually conveyed through a combination of formal and informal means. Technical knowledge can be fairly easily passed along through orientations, trainings, manuals, and documents, because this content is often fairly straightforward. Social knowledge is more ambiguous and is usually conveyed through informal means or passively learned by new members through observation. To return to our earlier terminology, technical knowledge relates more to group rules and social knowledge relates more to group norms.

Companies and social organizations socialize new members in different ways. A new training cohort at an established company may be given technical rule-based information in the form of a manual and a history of the organization and an overview of the organizational culture to help convey social knowledge about group norms. Members of some small groups like fraternities or professional organizations have to take pledges or oaths that may convey a mixture of technical and social knowledge. Social knowledge may be conveyed in interactions that are separate from official group time. For example, literally socializing as a group is a good way to socialize group members. Many large and successful businesses encourage small groups within the company to socialize outside of work time in order to build cohesion and group solidarity.

Socialization continues after initial membership through the enforcement of rules and norms. When someone deviates from the rules and norms and is corrected, it serves as a reminder for all other members and performs a follow-up socializing function. Since rules are explicitly stated and documented, deviation from the rules can have consequences ranging from verbal warnings, to temporary or permanent separation from the group, to fines or other sanctions. And although norms are implicit, deviating from them can still have consequences. Even though someone may not actually verbally correct the deviation, the self-consciousness, embarrassment, or awkwardness that can result from such deviations is often enough to initiate corrective actions. Group norms can be so implicit that they are taken for granted and operate under group members' awareness.

Group rules and norms provide members with a sense of predictability that helps reduce uncertainty and increase a sense of security for one's place within the group. They also guide group members' involvement with the group, help create a shared social reality, and allow the group to function in particular ways without having actual people constantly educating, monitoring, and then correcting member behaviors (Hargie, 2011). Of course, the degree to which this is successful depends on the buy-in from group members.

Group Pressures

There must be some kind of motivating force present within groups in order for the rules and norms to help govern and guide a group. Without such pressure, group members would have no incentive to conform to group norms or buy into the group's identity and values. In this section, we will discuss how rules and norms gain their power through internal and external pressures and how these pressures can have positive and negative effects.

Conformity

In general, some people are more likely to accept norms and rules than others, which can influence the interaction and potential for conflict within a group. While some people may feel a need for social acceptance that leads them to accept a norm or rule with minimal conformity pressure, others may actively resist because they have a valid disagreement or because they have an aggressive or argumentative personality (Ellis & Fisher, 1994). Such personality traits are examples of internal pressures that operate within the individual group member and act as a self-governing mechanism.

When group members discipline themselves and monitor their own behavior, groups need not invest in as many external mechanisms to promote conformity. Deviating from the group's rules and norms that a member internalized during socialization can lead to self-imposed feelings of guilt or shame that can then initiate corrective behaviors and discourage the member from going against the group.

External pressures in the form of group policies, rewards or punishments, or other forces outside of individual group members also exert conformity pressure. In terms of group policies, groups that have an official admission process may have a probation period during which new members' membership is contingent on them conforming to group expectations. Deviation from expectations during this "trial period" could lead to expulsion from the group. Supervisors, mentors, and other types of group leaders are also agents that can impose external pressures toward conformity. These group members often have the ability to provide positive or negative reinforcement in the form of praise or punishment, which are clear attempts to influence behavior.

Conformity pressure can also stem from external forces when the whole group stands to receive a reward or punishment based on its performance, which ties back to the small group characteristic of interdependence. Although these pressures may seem negative, they also have positive results. Groups that exert an appropriate and ethical amount of conformity pressure typically have higher levels of group cohesion, which as we learned leads to increased satisfaction with group membership, better relationships, and better task performance. Groups with a strong but healthy level of conformity also project a strong group image to those outside the group, which can raise the group's profile or reputation (Hargie, 2011). Pressures toward conformity, of course, can go too far, as is evidenced in tragic stories of people driven to suicide because they felt they couldn't live up to the conformity pressure of their group and people injured or killed enduring hazing rituals that take expectations for group conformity to unethical and criminal extremes.

Groupthink

Groupthink is a negative group phenomenon characterized by a lack of critical evaluation of proposed ideas or courses of action that results from high levels of cohesion and/or high conformity pressures (Janis, 1972). We can better understand groupthink by examining its causes and effects. When group members fall victim to groupthink, the effect is uncritical acceptance of decisions or suggestions for plans of action to accomplish a task or goal. Group meetings that appear to go smoothly with only positive interaction among happy, friendly people may seem ideal, but these actions may be symptomatic of groupthink (Ellis & Fisher, 1994). When people rush to agreement or fear argument, groupthink has a tendency to emerge. Decisions made as a result of groupthink may range from a poorly-thought-out presentation method that bores the audience to a mechanical failure resulting in death.

Two primary causes of groupthink are high levels of cohesion and excessive conformity pressures. When groups exhibit high levels of social cohesion, members may be reluctant to criticize or question another group member's ideas or suggestions for fear that it would damage the relationship. When group members have a high level of task cohesion, they may feel invincible and not critically evaluate ideas. High levels of cohesion may actually lessen conformity pressures since group members who identify strongly with the group's members and mission may not feel a need to question the decisions or suggestions made by others. For those who aren't blinded by the high levels of cohesion, internal conformity pressures may still lead them to withhold criticism of an idea because the norm is to defer to decisions made by organization leaders or a majority of group members. External conformity pressures because of impending reward or punishment, time pressures, or an aggressive leader are also factors that can lead to groupthink.

To Avoid Groupthink, Groups Should (Hargie, 2011)

- Divvy up responsibilities between group members so decision-making power isn't in the hands of a few
- Track contributions of group members in such a way that each person's input and output is recorded so that it can be discussed
- Encourage and reward the expression of minority or dissenting opinions

- Allow members to submit ideas prior to a discussion so that opinions aren't swayed by members who propose ideas early in a discussion
- Question each major decision regarding its weaknesses and potential negative consequences relative to competing decisions (encourage members to play "devil's advocate")
- Have decisions reviewed by an outside party that wasn't involved in the decision-making process
- Have a "reflection period" after a decision is made and before it is implemented during which group members can express reservations or second thoughts about the decision

Group Conflict

Conflict can appear in indirect or direct forms within group interaction, just as it can in interpersonal interactions. Group members may openly question each other's ideas or express anger toward or dislike for another person. Group members may also indirectly engage in conflict communication through innuendo, joking, or passive-aggressive behavior. Although we often view conflict negatively, conflict can be beneficial for many reasons. When groups get into a rut, lose creativity, or become complacent, conflict can help get a group out of a bad or mediocre routine. Conversely, conflict can lead to lower group productivity due to strain on the task and social dimensions of a group. There are three main types of conflict within groups: procedural, substantive, and interpersonal (Fujishin, 2001). Each of these types of conflict can vary in intensity, which can affect how much the conflict impacts the group and its members.

Procedural Conflict

Procedural conflict emerges from disagreements or trouble with the mechanics of group operations. In this type of conflict, group members differ in their beliefs about *how* something should be done. Procedural conflict can be handled by a group leader, especially if the leader put group procedures into place or has the individual power to change them. If there is no designated leader or the leader doesn't have sole power to change procedures (or just wants input from group members), proposals can be taken from the group on ways to address a procedural conflict to initiate a procedural change. A vote to reach a consensus or majority can also help resolve procedural conflict.

Substantive Conflict

Substantive conflict focuses on group members' differing beliefs, attitudes, values, or ideas related to the purpose or task of the group. Rather than focusing on questions of *how*, substantive conflicts focus on questions of *what*. Substantive conflicts may emerge as a group tries to determine its purpose or mission. As members figure out how to complete a task or debate which project to start on next, there will undoubtedly be differences of opinion on what something means, what is acceptable in terms of supporting evidence for a proposal, or what is acceptable for a goal or performance standard. Leaders and other group members shouldn't rush to close this type of conflict down. As we learned in our earlier discussion of groupthink, open discussion and debate regarding ideas and suggestions for group action can lead to higher-quality output and may prevent groupthink. Leaders who make final decisions about substantive conflict for the sake of moving on run the risk of creating a win/lose competitive climate in which people feel like their ideas may be shot down, which could lead to less participation. To resolve this type of conflict, group members may want to do research to see what other groups have done in similar situations, as additional information often provides needed context for conflict regarding information and ideas. Once the information is gathered, weigh all proposals and try to discover common ground among perspectives. Civil and open discussions that debate the merits of an idea are more desirable than a climate in which people feel personally judged for their ideas.

Interpersonal Conflict

Interpersonal conflict emerges from conflict between individual members of the group. Whereas procedural conflict deals with *how* and substantive conflict deals with *what*, interpersonal conflict deals with *who*. Such conflict can be completely irrelevant to the functioning or purpose of the group, perhaps focusing instead on personality differences. Interpersonal conflict can be the result of avoided or improperly handled procedural or substantive conflict that festers and becomes personal rather than task focused. This type of conflict can also result from differences in beliefs, attitudes, and values (when such differences are taken personally rather than substantively); different personalities; or different communication styles. While procedural and substantive conflict may be more easily expressed because they do not directly address a person, interpersonal conflict may slowly build as people avoid openly criticizing or confronting others. Passive-aggressive behavior is a sign that interpersonal conflict may be building under the surface, and other group members may want to intervene to avoid escalation and retaliation. Leaders can also meet with people involved in interpersonal conflict privately to help them engage in perception checking and act as mediators, if needed. While people who initiate procedural or substantive conflict may be perceived by other group members as concerned about the group's welfare and seen as competent in their ability to notice areas on which the group could improve, people who initiate interpersonal conflict are often held in ill-regard by other group members (Ellis & Fisher, 1994).

Primary and Secondary Tensions

Relevant to these types of conflict are primary and secondary tensions that emerge in every group (Bormann & Borman, 1988). When the group first comes together, members experience **primary tension**, which is tension based on uncertainty that is a natural part of initial interactions. It is only after group members begin to "break the ice" and get to know each other that the tension can be addressed and group members can proceed with the forming stage of group development. Small talk and politeness help group members manage primary tensions, and there is a relatively high threshold for these conflicts because we have all had experiences with such uncertainty when meeting people for the first time and many of us are optimistic that a little time and effort will allow us to get through the tensions. Since some people are more comfortable initiating conversation than others, it's important for more extroverted group members to include less talkative members. Intentionally or unintentionally excluding people during the negotiation of primary tensions can lead to unexpected secondary tensions later on. During this stage people are also less direct in their communication, using more hedges and vague language than they will later in the group process. The indirect communication and small talk that characterize this part of group development aren't a waste of time, as they help manage primary tensions and lay the foundation for future interactions that may involve more substantive conflict.

Secondary tension emerges after groups have passed the forming stage of group development and begin to have conflict over member roles, differing ideas, and personality conflicts. These tensions are typically evidenced by less reserved and less polite behavior than primary tensions. People also have a lower tolerance threshold for secondary tensions, because rather than being an expected part of initial interaction, these conflicts can be more negative and interfere with the group's task performance. Secondary tensions are inevitable and shouldn't be feared or eliminated. It's not the presence or absence of secondary tension that makes a group successful or not; it's how it handles the tensions when they emerge. A certain level of secondary tension is tolerable, not distracting, and can actually enhance group performance and avoid groupthink. When secondary tensions rise above the tolerance threshold and become distracting, they should be released through direct means such as diplomatic confrontation or indirect means such as appropriate humor or taking a break. While primary tensions eventually disappear (at least until a new member arrives), secondary tensions will come and go and may persist for longer periods of time. For that reason, we will now turn to a discussion of how to manage conflict in group interaction.

Managing Conflict in Small Groups

Some common ways to manage conflict include clear decision-making procedures, third-party mediation, and leader facilitation (Ellis & Fisher, 1994).Commonly used methods for decision making such as majority vote can help or hurt conflict management efforts. While an up-and-down vote can allow a group to finalize a decision and move on, members whose vote fell on the minority side may feel resentment toward other group members. This can create a win/lose climate that leads to further conflict. Having a leader who makes ultimate decisions can also help move a group toward completion of a task, but conflict may only be pushed to the side and left not fully addressed. Third-party mediation can help move a group past a conflict and may create less feelings of animosity, since the person mediating and perhaps making a decision isn't a member of the group. In some cases, the leader can act as an internal third-party mediator to help other group members work productively through their conflict.

Tips for Managing Group Conflict (Ellis & Fisher, 1994)

1. Clarify the issue at hand by getting to the historical roots of the problem. Keep in mind that perception leads us to punctuate interactions differently, so it may be useful to know each person's perspective of when, how, and why the conflict began.
2. Create a positive discussion climate by encouraging and rewarding active listening.
3. Discuss needs rather than solutions. Determine each person's needs to be met and goals for the outcome of the conflict before offering or acting on potential solutions.
4. Set boundaries for discussion and engage in gatekeeping to prevent unproductive interactions like tangents and personal attacks.
5. Use "we" language to maintain existing group cohesion and identity, and use "I" language to help reduce defensiveness.

Remember that a complete lack of conflict in a group is a bad sign, as it indicates either a lack of activity or a lack of commitment on the part of the members (Ellis & Fisher, 1994). Conflict, when properly handled, can lead a group to have a better understanding of the issues they face. For example, substantive conflict brings voice to alternative perspectives that may not have been heard otherwise. Additionally, when people view conflict as healthy, necessary, and productive, they can enter into a conflict episode with an open mind and an aim to learn something. This is especially true when those who initiate substantive conflict are able to share and defend their views in a competent and civil manner. Group cohesion can also increase as a result of well-managed conflict. Occasional experiences of tension and unrest followed by resolutions makes groups feel like they have accomplished something, which can lead them to not dread conflict and give them the confidence to more productively deal with it the next time.

Conflict that goes on for too long or is poorly handled can lead to decreased cohesiveness. Group members who try to avoid a conflict can still feel anger or frustration when the conflict drags on. Members who consistently take task-oriented conflict personally and escalate procedural or substantive conflict to interpersonal conflict are especially unpopular with other group members. Mishandled or chronic conflict can eventually lead to the destruction of a group or to a loss in members as people weigh the costs and rewards of membership (Ellis & Fisher, 1994). Hopefully a skilled leader or other group members can take on conflict resolution roles in order to prevent these disadvantages of conflict.

References

Ahuja, M. K. and John E. Galvin, "Socialization in Virtual Groups," *Journal of Management* 29, no. 2 (2003): 163.

Bormann, E. G. "Symbolic Convergence Theory: A Communication Formulation," *Journal of Communication*, 35, no. 4 (1985): 128–38.

Bormann, E. G., and Nancy C. Borman, *Effective Small Group Communication*, 4th ed. (Santa Rosa, CA: Burgess Publishing, 1988), 72.

Campo, S., Gretchen Poulos, and John W. Sipple, "Prevalence and Profiling: Hazing among College Students and Points of Intervention," *American Journal of Health Behavior* 29, no. 2 (2005): 138.

Cimino, A., "The Evolution of Hazing: Motivational Mechanisms and the Abuse of Newcomers," *Journal of Cognition and Culture* 11, no. 3–4 (2011): 235.

Daniel, L. J., and Charles R. Davis, "What Makes High-Performance Teams Excel?" *Research Technology Management* 52, no. 4 (2009): 40–41.

du Chatenier, E., Jos A. A. M. Verstegen, Harm J. A. Biemans, Martin Mulder, and Onno S. W. F. Omta, "Identification of Competencies in Open Innovation Teams," *Research and Development Management* 40, no. 3 (2010): 271.

Ellis, D. G., and B. Aubrey Fisher, *Small Group Decision Making: Communication and the Group Process*, 4th ed. (New York: McGraw-Hill, 1994), 133.

Fujishin, R., *Creating Effective Groups: The Art of Small Group Communication* (San Francisco, CA: Acada Books, 2001): 160–61.

Griffin, E., *A First Look at Communication Theory*, 7th ed. (Boston, MA: McGraw-Hill, 2009), 28.

Hargie, O., *Skilled Interpersonal Interaction: Research, Theory, and Practice*, 5th ed. (London: Routledge, 2011), 445.

Jain, A. K., Jon M. Thompson, Joseph Chaudry, Shaun McKenzie, and Richard W. Schwartz, "High-Performance Teams for Current and Future Physician Leaders: An Introduction," *Journal of Surgical Education* 65 (2008): 145.

Janis, I. L., *Victims of Groupthink: A Psychological Study of Foreign-Policy Decisions and Fiascos* (New York: Houghton Mifflin, 1972).

Marston, P. J. and Michael L. Hecht, "Group Satisfaction," in *Small Group Communication*, 5th ed., eds. Robert Cathcart and Larry Samovar (Dubuque, IA: Brown, 1988), 236–46.

Richardson, B. K., Zuoming Wang, and Camille A. Hall, "Blowing the Whistle against Greek Hazing: The Theory of Reasoned Action as a Framework for Reporting Intentions," *Communication Studies* 63, no. 2 (2012): 173.

Solansky, S. T., "Team Identification: A Determining Factor of Performance," *Journal of Managerial Psychology* 26, no. 3 (2011): 250.

15.5 ENRICHMENT

Discussion Questions

1. Think back to a recent time when you have had to problem-solve or perform a task in a small group. What went well for your group? What did not go well for your group? How can you use this knowledge to make your small group speech as smooth as possible?
2. Which type of small group from Section 15.2: Understanding Small Groups best describes your group for the small group speech?
3. How can your group use the knowledge of small group development (forming, storming, norming, performing, adjourning) to better understand and improve your group communication?
4. Think back to previous groups again and discuss your experience regarding group climate and socialization? Can you think of specific types of communication that created a positive group climate? How might you use this knowledge to encourage positive group socialization prior to your small group speech?

Activities

1. Small groups work to create a group contract that includes the following information:

    - How will you ensure that each group member has mutual concern for the topic?
    - How will you divide the small group speech to ensure task cohesion? Equitable division of responsibilities?
    - How will you all communicate with each other to ensure group cohesion?
    - How will you ensure group members respond/reply in a timely manner? Provide the minimum number of sources?
    - How will you handle the three types of group conflict?
    - Finally, list important dates (meeting times), specific project requirements, and member responsibilities before signing the contract.

2. With your assigned small group members, create a word tree with "small group

work" as the root word. Assign one group member to be the notetaker and to identify key words from the comments of all group members (including the notetaker). These key words should be added to the tree. The branches of the tree could include concepts such as: (1) some of the advantages of working with a small group; (2) some of the disadvantages of working with a small group; (3) the role of group cohesion; (4) the impact of groupthink; and (5) any other topics that are important to your group. As you conclude this exercise together, talk about how past experiences of group members can benefit the upcoming small group speech project.

3. With your assigned small group members, organize a series of emojis to represent a movie, book, television show, or song. Be creative and make your solution challenging. Submit your "emoji illustration," (or "emoji quiz") to a Canvas Dropbox. As your instructor shares each group's emoji sequence, work together to interpret each group's solution as quickly as possible. The first group to correctly decipher all the "emoji illustrations" wins.

4. As a newly formed problem-solving group, create a list of 10 criteria that make for an amazing group/team member. Which one is most/least important? Why did you select these criteria? Present your list to the class.

5. With your assigned small group members, your instructor will hand out the list of photos required to win the photo scavenger hunt. Groups must stay together and every member must be present in the pictures. You can take a group selfie or you can ask someone from outside the group to take it. The group that gets back to the classroom with the most photos from the list in the required time frame wins. Group members will then write about the group member roles and assign one to each member of the group based on their communication during the exercise.

16 SMALL GROUPS & DECISION MAKING

Learning Objectives

- Discuss the various perspectives on how and why people become leaders.
- Compare and contrast various leadership styles.
- Discuss the types of power a leader may use.
- Identify and discuss task-related group roles and behaviors; maintenance group roles and behaviors; and negative group roles and behaviors.
- Discuss the common components and characteristics of problems.
- Explain the five steps of the group problem-solving process.
- Describe the brainstorming and discussion that should take place before the group makes a decision.
- Compare and contrast the different decision-making techniques.
- Discuss the various influences on decision making.

Key Terms

- **Achievement-Oriented Leaders**
- **Coercive Power**
- **Consensus Rule**
- **Designated Leaders**

- Directive Leaders
- Emergent Leaders
- Expediter
- Expert Power
- Gatekeeper
- Harmonizer
- Information Power
- Information Provider
- Information Seeker
- Interpreter
- Leader
- Leadership
- Legitimate Power
- Majority Rule
- Minority Rule
- Nominal Group Technique
- Participative Leaders
- Problem Question
- Problem Statement
- Recorder
- Referent Power
- Reward Power
- Self-Centered Roles
- Supporter
- Supportive Leaders
- Tension Releaser
- Unproductive Roles

16.1 LEADERSHIP, ROLES, AND PROBLEM SOLVING IN GROUPS

"A single leaf working alone provides no shade." -Chuck Page

What makes a good leader? What are some positive and negative roles that people play in groups? How do groups solve problems and make decisions in order to accomplish their task? This chapter will begin to answer those questions, because leadership and group member roles influence the performance of small groups. Whether you consider yourself a leader or not, all members of a group can perform leadership functions, and being familiar with these behaviors can improve your group's performance. Likewise, knowing the various roles that typically emerge in a group can help you better understand a group's dynamics and hopefully improve your overall group experience.

Pete's Path to Leadership

When Pistol Pete initially found himself facing unresponsiveness from his group members for the speech class project, he was disappointed but not disheartened. Drawing upon his role as the spirited and resourceful mascot of Oklahoma State University, he stepped up, demonstrating effective leadership skills that soon propelled him into the role of the group's leader.

Pete began by setting a clear direction for the project, presenting a tentative plan and outlining potential topics. His initiative served as a starting point, providing a framework for the group's discussions and actions.

Understanding the importance of open communication, he established multiple channels for discussion, from group meetings to a shared document where everyone could contribute ideas at their own pace. This ensured that every member had an opportunity to express their thoughts and ideas.

However, Pete knew that a group wasn't just about the leader but about every individual member. He made it a point to involve every group member, assigning roles and responsibilities based on their strengths and interests. He also encouraged each member to contribute to the shared document, fostering a sense of ownership and involvement.

To ensure everyone stayed on track, Pete set up regular check-ins where they could discuss their progress, address any issues, and adjust their plan if needed. He was always available to provide help and support, maintaining an open and positive communication environment.

But Pete also understood that encouragement and motivation were as important as clear roles and regular communication. He made sure to recognize each member's contributions, highlighting their good work and progress during meetings. This not only boosted their morale but also reinforced the importance of their roles and responsibilities in the project.

Under Pistol Pete's leadership, the group began to show signs of progress. The once-empty shared document started to fill with ideas, discussions became more active and productive, and the project began to take shape.

Despite the initial hurdles, Pistol Pete's effective leadership had steered the group towards cooperation and productivity. His ability to lead, motivate, and involve each member had transformed the group's dynamic, setting them on a path to not just complete their project, but to do it well, embodying the Cowboy spirit of resilience, collaboration, and excellence. How would you have handled a group experience like this one? Would you do it differently than Pete did?

16.2 LEADERSHIP AND SMALL GROUP COMMUNICATION

Leadership is one of the most studied aspects of group communication. Scholars in business, communication, psychology, and many other fields have written extensively about the qualities of leaders, theories of leadership, and how to build leadership skills. It's important to point out that although a group may have only one official leader, other group members play important leadership roles. Making this distinction also helps us differentiate between leaders and leadership (Hargie, 2011). The **leader** is a group role that is associated with a high-status position and may be formally or informally recognized by group members. **Leadership** is a complex of beliefs, communication patterns, and behaviors that influence the functioning of a group and move a group toward the completion of its task. A person in the role of leader may provide no or poor leadership. Likewise, a person who is not recognized as a "leader" in title can provide excellent leadership. In the remainder of this section, we will discuss some approaches to the study of leadership, leadership styles, and leadership and group dynamics.

Why and How People Become Leaders

Throughout human history, some people have grown into, taken, or been given positions as leaders. Many early leaders were believed to be divine in some way. In some indigenous cultures, shamans are considered leaders because they are believed to be bridges that can connect the spiritual and physical realms. Many early kings, queens, and military leaders were said to be approved by a god to lead the people. Today, many leaders are elected or appointed to positions of power, but most of them have already accumulated much experience in leadership roles. Some leaders are well respected, some are feared, some are hated, and many elicit some combination of these reactions. This brief overview illustrates the centrality of leadership throughout human history, but it wasn't until the last hundred years that leadership became an object of systematic study.

Before we move onto specific approaches to studying leadership, let's distinguish between designated and emergent leaders. In general, some people gravitate more toward leadership roles than others, and some leaders are designated while other are emergent (Hargie, 2011). **Designated leaders** are officially recognized in their leadership role and may be appointed or elected by people inside or outside the group. Designated leaders can be especially successful when they are sought out by others to fulfill and are then accepted in leadership roles. On the other hand, some people seek out leadership positions not because they possess leadership skills and have been successful leaders in the past but because they have a drive to hold and wield power. Many groups are initially leaderless and must either designate a leader or wait for one to emerge organically. **Emergent leaders** gain status and respect through engagement with the group and its task and are turned to by others as a resource when leadership is needed. Emergent leaders may play an important role when a designated leader unexpectedly leaves. We will now turn our attention to three common perspectives on why some people are more likely to be designated leaders than others and how leaders emerge in the absence of or in addition to a designated leader.

Leaders Emerge Because of Their Traits

The trait approach to studying leadership distinguishes leaders from followers based on traits, or personal characteristics (Pavitt, 1999). Some traits that leaders, in general, share are related to physical appearance, communication ability, intelligence, and personality (Cragan & Wright, 1991). In terms of physical appearance, designated leaders tend to be taller and more attractive than other group members. This could be because we consciously and/or subconsciously associate a larger size (in terms of height and build, but not body fat) with strength and strength with good leadership. As far as communication abilities, leaders speak more fluently, have a more confident tone, and communicate more often than other group members. Leaders are also moderately more intelligent than other group members, which is attractive because leaders need good problem-solving skills. Interestingly, group members are not as likely to designate or recognize an emergent leader that they perceive to be exceedingly more intelligent than them. Last, leaders are usually more extroverted, assertive, and persistent than other group members. These personality traits help get these group members noticed by others, and expressivity is often seen as attractive and as a sign of communication competence.

The trait approach to studying leaders has provided some useful information regarding how people view ideal leaders, but it has not provided much insight into why some people become and are more successful leaders than others. The list of ideal traits is not final, because excellent leaders can have few, if any, of these traits and poor leaders can possess many. Additionally, these traits are difficult to change or control without much time and effort. Because these traits are enduring, there isn't much room for people to learn and develop leadership skills, which makes this approach less desirable for communication scholars who view leadership as a communication competence. Rather than viewing these traits as a guide for what to look for when choosing your next leader, view them as traits that are made meaningful through context and communication behaviors.

Leaders Emerge Because of the Situation

The emergent approach to studying leadership considers how leaders emerge in groups that are initially leaderless and how situational contexts affect this process (Pavitt, 1999). The situational context that surrounds a group influences what type of leader is best. Situations may be highly structured, highly unstructured, or anywhere in between (Cragan & Wright, 1991). Research has found that leaders with a high task orientation are likely to emerge in both highly structured contexts like a group that works to maintain a completely automated factory unit and highly unstructured contexts like a group that is responding to a crisis. Relational-oriented leaders are more likely to emerge in semistructured contexts that are less formal and in groups composed of people who have specific knowledge and are therefore be trusted to do much of their work independently (Fiedler, 1967). For example, a group of local business owners who form a group for professional networking would likely prefer a leader with a relational-oriented style, since these group members are likely already leaders in their own right and therefore might resent a person who takes a rigid task-oriented style over a more collegial style.

Leaders emerge differently in different groups, but there are two stages common to each scenario (Bormann & Bormann, 1988). The first stage only covers a brief period, perhaps no longer than a portion of one meeting. During this first stage, about half of the group's members are eliminated from the possibility of being the group's leader. Remember that this is an informal and implicit process—not like people being picked for a kickball team or intentionally vetted. But there are some communicative behaviors that influence who makes the cut to the next stage of informal leader consideration. People will likely be eliminated as leader candidates if they do not actively contribute to initial group interactions, if they contribute but communicate poorly, if they contribute but appear too rigid or inflexible in their beliefs, or if they seem uninformed about the task of the group.

The second stage of leader emergence is where a more or less pronounced struggle for leadership begins. In one scenario, a leader candidate picks up an ally in the group who acts as a supporter or lieutenant, reinforcing the ideas and contributions of the candidate. If there are no other leader candidates or the others fail to pick up a supporter, the candidate with the supporter will likely become the leader. In a second scenario, there are two leader candidates who both pick up supporters and who are both qualified leaders. This leads to a more intense and potentially prolonged struggle that can actually be uncomfortable for other group members. Although the two leader candidates don't overtly fight with each other or say, "I should be leader, not you!" they both take strong stances in regards to the group's purpose and try to influence the structure, procedures, and trajectory for the group. Group members not involved in this struggle may not know who to listen to, which can lead to low task and social cohesion and may cause a group to fail. In some cases, one candidate-supporter team will retreat, leaving a clear leader to step up. But the candidate who retreated will still enjoy a relatively high status in the group and be respected for vying for leadership. The second-place candidate may become a nuisance for the new emergent leader, questioning his or her decisions. Rather than excluding or punishing the second-place candidate, the new leader should give him or her responsibilities within the group to make use of the group member's respected status.

Leaders Emerge Based on Communication Skill and

Competence

This final approach to the study of leadership is considered a functional approach, because it focuses on how particular communication behaviors function to create the conditions of leadership. This last approach is the most useful for communication scholars and for people who want to improve their leadership skills, because leadership behaviors (which are learnable and adaptable) rather than traits or situations (which are often beyond our control) are the primary focus of study. As we've already learned, any group member can exhibit leadership behaviors, not just a designated or emergent leader. Therefore leadership behaviors are important for all of us to understand even if we don't anticipate serving in leadership positions (Cragan & Wright, 1991).

The communication behaviors that facilitate effective leadership encompass three main areas of group communication including task, procedural, and relational functions. Although any group member can perform leadership behaviors, groups usually have patterns of and expectations for behaviors once they get to the norming and performing stages of group development. Many groups only meet one or two times, and in these cases it is likely that a designated leader will perform many of the functions to get the group started and then step in to facilitate as needed.

Leadership behaviors that contribute to a group's task-related functions include providing, seeking, and evaluating information. Leaders may want to be cautious about contributing ideas before soliciting ideas from group members, since the leader's contribution may sway or influence others in the group, therefore diminishing the importance of varying perspectives. Likewise a leader may want to solicit evaluation of ideas from members before providing his or her own judgment. In group situations where creativity is needed to generate ideas or solutions to a problem, the task leader may be wise to facilitate brainstorming and discussion.

This can allow the leader to keep his or her eye on the "big picture" and challenge group members to make their ideas more concrete or discuss their implications beyond the group without adding his or her own opinion. To review, some of the key leadership behaviors that contribute to the task-related functions of a group include the following (Cragan & Wright, 1991):

- Contributing ideas
- Seeking ideas
- Evaluating ideas
- Seeking idea evaluation
- Visualizing abstract ideas
- Generalizing from specific ideas

Leadership behaviors that contribute to a group's procedural-related functions help guide the group as it proceeds from idea generation to implementation. Some leaders are better at facilitating and managing ideas than they are at managing the administrative functions of a group. So while a group leader may help establish the goals of the group and set the agenda, another group member with more experience in group operations may step in to periodically revisit and assess progress toward completion of goals and compare the group's performance against its agenda. It's also important to check in between idea-generating sessions to clarify, summarize, and gauge the agreement level of group members. A very skilled and experienced leader may take primary responsibility for all these behaviors, but it's often beneficial to share them with group members to avoid becoming overburdened. To review, some of the key leadership behaviors that contribute to the procedural functions of a group include the following (Cragan & Wright, 1991):

- Goal setting
- Agenda making
- Clarifying
- Summarizing
- Verbalizing consensus
- Generalizing from specific ideas

Leadership behaviors that contribute to a group's relational functions include creating a participative and inclusive climate, establishing norms of reflection and self-analysis, and managing conflict. By encouraging participation among group members, a leader can help quell people who try to monopolize discussion and create an overall climate of openness and equality. Leaders want to make sure that people don't feel personally judged for their ideas and that criticism remains idea centered, not person centered. A safe and positive climate typically leads to higher-quality idea generation and decision making. Leaders also encourage group members to metacommunicate, or talk about the group's communication. This can help the group identify and begin to address any interpersonal or communication issues before they escalate and divert the group away from accomplishing its goal. A group with a well-established participative and inclusive climate will be better prepared to handle conflict when it emerges. Remember that conflict when handled competently can enhance group performance. Leaders may even instigate productive conflict by playing devil's advocate or facilitating civil debate of ideas. To review, some of the key leadership behaviors that contribute to the relational functions of a group include the following (Cragan & Wright, 1991):

- Regulating participation

- Climate making
- Instigating group self-analysis
- Resolving conflict
- Instigating productive conflict

Leadership Styles

Given the large amount of research done on leadership, it is not surprising that there are several different ways to define or categorize leadership styles. In general, effective leaders do not fit solely into one style in any of the following classifications. Instead, they are able to adapt their leadership style to fit the relational and situational context (Wood, 1977). One common way to study leadership style is to make a distinction among autocratic, democratic, and laissez-faire leaders (Lewin, Lippitt, & White, 1939). These leadership styles can be described as follows:

- Autocratic leaders set policies and make decisions primarily on their own, taking advantage of the power present in their title or status to set the agenda for the group.
- Democratic leaders facilitate group discussion and like to take input from all members before making a decision.
- Laissez-faire leaders take a "hands-off" approach, preferring to give group members freedom to reach and implement their own decisions.

While this is a frequently cited model of leadership styles, we will focus in more detail on a model that was developed a few years after this one. I choose to focus on this later model because it offers some more specifics in terms of the communicative elements of each leadership style. The four leadership styles used in this model are directive, participative, supportive, and achievement oriented (House & Mitchell, 1974).

Directive Leaders

Directive leaders help provide psychological structure for their group members by clearly communicating expectations, keeping a schedule and agenda, providing specific guidance as group members work toward the completion of their task, and taking the lead on setting and communicating group rules and procedures. Although this is most similar to the autocratic leadership style mentioned before, it is more nuanced and flexible. The originators of this model note that a leader can be directive without being seen as authoritarian. To do this, directive leaders must be good motivators who encourage productivity through positive reinforcement or reward rather than through the threat of punishment.

A directive leadership style is effective in groups that do not have a history and may require direction to get started on their task. It can also be the most appropriate method during crisis situations in which decisions must be made under time constraints or other extraordinary pressures. When groups have an established history and are composed of people with unique skills and expertise, a directive approach may be seen as "micromanaging." In these groups, a more participative style may be the best option.

Participative Leaders

Participative leaders work to include group members in the decision-making process by soliciting and considering their opinions and suggestions. When group members feel included, their personal goals are more likely to align with the group and organization's goals, which can help productivity. This style of leadership can also aid in group member socialization, as the members feel like they get to help establish group norms and rules, which affects cohesion and climate. When group members participate more, they buy into the group's norms and goals more, which can increase conformity pressures for incoming group members. As we learned earlier, this is good to a point, but it can become negative when the pressures lead to unethical group member behavior. In addition to consulting group members for help with decision making, participative leaders also grant group members more freedom to work independently. This can lead group members to feel trusted and respected for their skills, which can increase their effort and output.

The participative method of leadership is similar to the democratic style discussed earlier, and it is a style of leadership practiced in many organizations that have established work groups that meet consistently over long periods of time. US companies began to adopt a more participative and less directive style of management in the 1980s after organizational scholars researched teamwork and efficiency in Japanese corporations. Japanese managers included employees in decision making, which blurred the line between the leader and other group members and enhanced productivity. These small groups were called quality circles, because they focused on group interaction intended to improve quality and productivity (Cragan & Wright, 1991).

Supportive Leaders

Supportive leaders show concern for their followers' needs and emotions. They want to support group members' welfare through a positive and friendly group climate. These leaders are good at reducing the stress and frustration of the group, which helps create a positive climate and can help increase group members' positive feelings about the task and other group members. As we will learn later, some group roles function to maintain the relational climate of the group, and several group members often perform these role behaviors. With a supportive leader as a model, such behaviors would likely be performed as part of established group norms, which can do much to enhance social cohesion. Supportive leaders do not provide unconditionally positive praise. They also competently provide constructive criticism in order to challenge and enhance group members' contributions.

A supportive leadership style is more likely in groups that are primarily relational rather than task focused. For example, support groups and therapy groups benefit from a supportive leader. While maintaining positive relationships is an important part of any group's functioning, most task-oriented groups need to spend more time on task than social functions in order to efficiently work toward the completion of their task. Skilled directive or participative leaders of task-oriented groups would be wise to employ supportive leadership behaviors when group members experience emotional stress to prevent relational stress from negatively impacting the group's climate and cohesion.

Achievement-Oriented Leaders

Achievement-oriented leaders strive for excellence and set challenging goals, constantly seeking improvement and exhibiting confidence that group members can meet their high expectations. These leaders often engage in systematic social comparison, keeping tabs on other similar high-performing groups to assess their expectations and the group's progress. This type of leadership is similar to what other scholars call transformational or visionary leadership and is often associated with leaders like former Apple CEO Steve Jobs, talk show host and television network CEO Oprah Winfrey, former president Bill Clinton, and business magnate turned philanthropist Warren Buffett. Achievement-oriented leaders are likely less common than the other styles, as this style requires a high level of skill and commitment on the part of the leader and the group. Although rare, these leaders can be found at all levels of groups ranging from local school boards to *Fortune* 500 companies. Certain group dynamics must be in place in order to accommodate this leadership style. Groups for which an achievement-oriented leadership style would be effective are typically intentionally created and are made up of members who are skilled and competent in regards to the group's task. In many cases, the leader is specifically chosen because of his or her reputation and expertise, and even though the group members may not have a history of working with the leader, the members and leader must have a high degree of mutual respect.

Leadership and Power

Leaders help move group members toward the completion of their goal using various motivational strategies. The types of power leaders draw on to motivate have long been a topic of small group study. A leader may possess or draw on any of the following five types of power to varying degrees: legitimate, expert, referent, information, and reward/coercive (French Jr. & Raven, 1959). Effective leaders do not need to possess all five types of power. Instead, competent leaders know how to draw on other group members who may be better able to exercise a type of power in a given situation.

Legitimate Power

The very title of *leader* brings with it **legitimate power**, which is power that flows from the officially recognized position, status, or title of a group member. For example, the leader of the "Social Media Relations Department" of a retail chain receives legitimate power through the title "director of social media relations." It is important to note though that being designated as someone with status or a position of power doesn't mean that the group members respect or recognize that power. Even with a title, leaders must still earn the ability to provide leadership. Of the five types of power, however, the leader alone is most likely to possess legitimate power.

Expert Power

Expert power comes from knowledge, skill, or expertise that a group member possesses and other group members do not. For example, even though all the workers in the Social Media Relations Department have experience with computers, the information technology (IT) officer has expert power when it comes to computer networking and programming. Because of this, even though the director may have a higher status, she or he must defer to the IT officer when the office network crashes. A leader who has legitimate and expert power may be able to take a central role in setting the group's direction, contributing to problem solving, and helping the group achieve its goal. In groups with a designated leader who relies primarily on legitimate power, a member with a significant amount of expert power may emerge as an unofficial secondary leader. A group mmber with expertise in an area relevant to the group's task may draw on expert power to lead the group. For example, a transplant surgeon may lead a team of other doctors and nurses during the surgery while a critical case nurse may take the lead during postsurgery recovery.

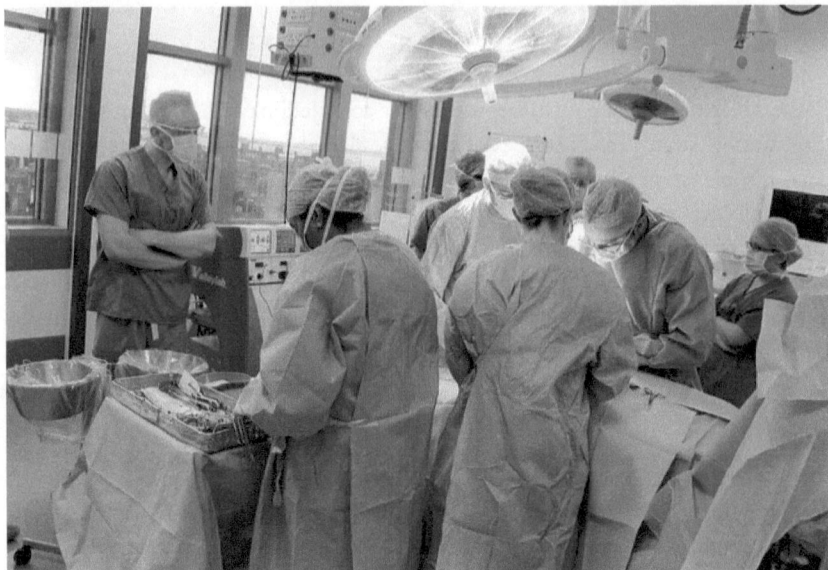

Referent Power

Referent power comes from the attractiveness, likeability, and charisma of the group member. As we learned earlier, more physically attractive people and more outgoing people are often chosen as leaders. This could be due to their referent power. Referent power also derives from a person's reputation. A group member may have referent power if he or she is well respected outside of the group for previous accomplishments or even because he or she is known as a dependable and capable group member. Like legitimate power, the fact that a person possesses referent power doesn't mean he or she has the talent, skill, or other characteristic needed to actually lead the group. A person could just be likable but have no relevant knowledge about the group's task or leadership experience. Some groups actually desire this type of leader, especially if the person is meant to attract external attention and serve as more of a "figurehead" than a regularly functioning group member. For example, a group formed to raise funds for a science and nature museum may choose a former mayor, local celebrity, or NASA astronaut as their leader because of his or her referent power. In this situation it would probably be best for the group to have a secondary leader who attends to task and problem-solving functions within the group.

Information Power

Information power comes from a person's ability to access information that comes through informal channels and well-established social and professional networks. We have already learned that information networks are an important part of a group's structure and can affect a group's access to various resources. When a group member is said to have "know how," they possess information power. The knowledge may not always be official, but it helps the group solve problems and get things done. Individuals develop information power through years of interacting with others, making connections, and building and maintaining interpersonal and instrumental relationships. For example, the group formed to raise funds for the science and nature museum may need to draw on informal information networks to get leads on potential donors, to get information about what local science teachers would recommend for exhibits, or to book a band willing to perform for free at a fundraising concert.

Reward and Coercive Power

The final two types of power, reward and coercive, are related. **Reward power** comes from the ability of a group member to provide a positive incentive as a compliance-gaining strategy, and **coercive power** comes from the ability of a group member to provide a negative incentive. These two types of power can be difficult for leaders and other group members to manage, because their use can lead to interpersonal conflict. Reward power can be used by nearly any group member if he or she gives another group member positive feedback on an idea, an appreciation card for hard work, or a pat on the back. Because of limited resources, many leaders are frustrated by their inability to give worthwhile tangible rewards to group members such as prizes, bonuses, or raises. Additionally, the use of reward power may seem corny or paternalistic to some or may arouse accusations of favoritism or jealousy among group members who don't receive the award.

Coercive power, since it entails punishment or negative incentive, can lead to interpersonal conflict and a negative group climate if it is overused or used improperly. While any leader or group member could make threats to others, leaders with legitimate power are typically in the best position to use coercive power. In such cases, coercive power may manifest in loss of pay and/or privileges, being excluded from the group, or being fired (if the group work is job related). In many volunteer groups or groups that lack formal rules and procedures, leaders have a more difficult time using coercive power, since they can't issue official punishments. Instead, coercive power will likely take the form of interpersonal punishments such as ignoring group members or excluding them from group activities.

References

Bormann, E. G., and Nancy C. Bormann, *Effective Small Group Communication*, 4th ed. (Santa Rosa, CA: Burgess CA, 1988), 130–33.

Cragan, J. F., and David W. Wright, *Communication in Small Group Discussions: An Integrated Approach*, 3rd ed. (St. Paul, MN: West Publishing, 1991), 120.

Deutschman, A., "Exit the King," *The Daily Beast*, September 21, 2011, accessed August 23, 2012, http://www.thedailybeast.com/newsweek/2011/08/28/steve-jobs-american-genius.html.

Fiedler, F. E., *A Theory of Leadership Effectiveness* (New York: McGraw-Hill, 1967).

French Jr., J. R. P., and Bertram Raven, "The Bases of Social Power," in *Studies in Social Power*, ed. Dorwin Cartwright (Ann Arbor, MI: Institute for Social Research, 1959), 150–67.

Hargie, O., *Skilled Interpersonal Interaction: Research, Theory, and Practice* (London: Routledge, 2011), 456.

House, R. J., and Terrence R. Mitchell, "Path-Goal Theory of Leadership," *Journal of Contemporary Business* 3 (1974): 81–97.

Lewin, K., Ronald Lippitt, and Ralph K. White, "Patterns of Aggressive Behavior in Experimentally Created 'Social Climates,'" *Journal of Social Psychology* 10, no. 2 (1939): 269–99.

Pavitt, C., "Theorizing about the Group Communication-Leadership Relationship," in *The Handbook of Group Communication Theory and Research*, ed. Lawrence R. Frey (Thousand Oaks, CA: Sage, 1999), 313.

Wood, J. T., "Leading in Purposive Discussions: A Study of Adaptive Behavior," *Communication Monographs* 44, no. 2 (1977): 152–65.

16.3 GROUP MEMBER ROLES

Just as leaders have been long studied as a part of group communication research, so too have group member roles. Group roles are more dynamic than leadership roles in that a role can be formal or informal and played by more than one group member. Additionally, one group member may exhibit various role behaviors within a single group meeting or play a few consistent roles over the course of his or her involvement with a group. Some people's role behaviors result from their personality traits, while other people act out a certain role because of a short-term mood, as a reaction to another group member, or out of necessity. Group communication scholars have cautioned us to not always think of these roles as neatly bounded all-inclusive categories. After all, we all play multiple roles within a group and must draw on multiple communication behaviors in order to successfully play them. When someone continually exhibits a particular behavior, it may be labeled as a role, but even isolated behaviors can impact group functioning. In this section, we will discuss the three categories of common group roles that were identified by early group communication scholars. These role categories include task-related roles, maintenance roles, and individual roles that are self-centered or unproductive for the group (Benne & Sheats, 1948).

Task-Related Roles and Behaviors

Task roles and their related behaviors contribute directly to the group's completion of a task or achievement of its goal or purpose. Task-related roles typically serve leadership, informational, or procedural functions. In this section we will discuss the following roles and behaviors: task leader, expediter, information provider, information seeker, gatekeeper, and recorder.

Task Leader

Within any group, there may be a task leader who has a high group status because of his or her maturity, problem-solving abilities, knowledge, and/or leadership experience and skills and functions primarily to help the group complete its task (Cragan & Wright, 1991). This person may be a designated or emergent leader, but in either case, task leaders tend to talk more during group interactions than other group members and also tend to do more work in the group. Depending on the number of tasks a group has, there may be more than one task leader, especially if the tasks require different sets of skills or knowledge. Because of the added responsibilities of being a task leader, people in these roles may experience higher levels of stress. A task leader's stresses, however, may be lessened through some of the maintenance role behaviors that we will discuss later.

Task-leader behaviors can be further divided into two types: substantive and procedural (Pavitt, 1999). The substantive leader is the "idea person" who communicates "big picture" thoughts and suggestions that feed group discussion. The procedural leader is the person who gives the most guidance, perhaps following up on the ideas generated by the substantive leader. A skilled and experienced task leader may be able to perform both of these roles, but when the roles are filled by two different people, the person considered the procedural leader is more likely than the substantive leader to be viewed by members as the overall group leader. This indicates that task-focused groups assign more status to the person who actually guides the group toward the completion of the task (a "doer") than the person who comes up with ideas (the "thinker").

Expediter

The **expediter** is a task-related role that functions to keep the group on track toward completing its task by managing the agenda and setting and assessing goals in order to monitor the group's progress. An expediter doesn't push group members mindlessly along toward the completion of their task; an expediter must have a good sense of when a topic has been sufficiently discussed or when a group's extended focus on one area has led to diminishing returns. In such cases, the expediter may say, "Now that we've had a thorough discussion of the pros and cons of switching the office from PCs to Macs, which side do you think has more support?" or "We've spent half of this meeting looking for examples of what other libraries have done and haven't found anything useful. Maybe we should switch gears so we can get something concrete done tonight."

If you've ever worked in a restaurant, you're probably familiar with an expediter's role in the kitchen. The person working "expo" helps make sure that the timing on all the dishes for a meal works out and that each plate is correct before it goes out to the table. This is by no means an easy job, since some entrées cook quicker than others and not everyone orders their burger the same way. So the expediter helps make order out of chaos by calling the food out to the kitchen in a particular order that logically works so that all the food will come up at the same time. Once the food is up, he or she also checks what's on the plate against what's on the ticket to make sure it matches. Expediting in a restaurant and in a small group is like a dance that requires some flexible and creative thinking and an ability to stick to a time frame and assess progress. To avoid the perception that group members are being rushed, a skilled expediter can demonstrate good active-listening skills by paraphrasing what has been discussed and summarizing what has been accomplished in such a way that makes it easier for group members to see the need to move on.

Information Provider

The role of **information provider** includes behaviors that are more evenly shared than in other roles, as ideally, all group members present new ideas, initiate discussions of new topics, and contribute their own relevant knowledge and experiences. When group members are brought together because they each have different types of information, early group meetings may consist of group members taking turns briefing each other on their area of expertise. In other situations, only one person in the group may be chosen because of his or her specialized knowledge and this person may be expected to be the primary information provider for all other group members. For example, I was asked to serve on a university committee that is reviewing our undergraduate learning goals. Since my official role is to serve as the "faculty expert" on the subcommittee related to speaking, I played a more central information-provider function for our group during most of our initial meetings. Since other people on the subcommittee weren't as familiar with speaking and its place within higher education curriculum, it made sense that information-providing behaviors were not as evenly distributed in this case.

Information Seeker

The **information seeker** asks for more information, elaboration, or clarification on items relevant to the group's task. The information sought may include factual information or group member opinions. In general, information seekers ask questions for clarification, but they can also ask questions that help provide an important evaluative function. Most groups could benefit from more critically oriented information-seeking behaviors. As our discussion of groupthink notes, critical questioning helps increase the quality of ideas and group outcomes and helps avoid groupthink. By asking for more information, people have to defend (in a nonadversarial way) and/or support their claims, which can help ensure that the information being discussed is credible, relevant, and thoroughly considered. When information seeking or questioning occurs as a result of poor listening skills, it risks negatively impacting the group. Skilled information providers and seekers are also good active listeners. They increase all group members' knowledge when they paraphrase and ask clarifying questions about the information presented.

Gatekeeper

The **gatekeeper** manages the flow of conversation in a group in order to achieve an appropriate balance so that all group members get to participate in a meaningful way. The gatekeeper may prompt others to provide information by saying something like "Let's each share one idea we have for a movie to show during Black History Month."

He or she may also help correct an imbalance between members who have provided much information already and members who have been quiet by saying something like "Aretha, we've heard a lot from you today. Let's hear from someone else. Beau, what are your thoughts on Aretha's suggestion?" Gatekeepers should be cautious about "calling people out" or at least making them feel that way. Instead of scolding someone for not participating, they should be invitational and ask a member to contribute to something specific instead of just asking if they have anything to add. Since gatekeepers make group members feel included, they also service the relational aspects of the group.

Recorder

The **recorder** takes notes on the discussion and activities that occur during a group meeting. The recorder is the only role that is essentially limited to one person at a time since in most cases it wouldn't be necessary or beneficial to have more than one person recording. At less formal meetings there may be no recorder, while at formal meetings there is almost always a person who records meeting minutes, which are an overview of what occurred at the meeting. Each committee will have different rules or norms regarding the level of detail within and availability of the minutes. While some group's minutes are required by law to be public, others may be strictly confidential. Even though a record of a group meeting may be valuable, the role of recorder is often regarded as a low-status position, since the person in the role may feel or be viewed as subservient to the other members who are able to more actively contribute to the group's functioning. Because of this, it may be desirable to have the role of recorder rotate among members (Cragan & Wright, 1991).

Maintenance Roles and Behaviors

Maintenance roles and their corresponding behaviors function to create and maintain social cohesion and fulfill the interpersonal needs of group members. All these role behaviors require strong and sensitive interpersonal skills. The maintenance roles we will discuss in this section include social-emotional leader, supporter, tension releaser, harmonizer, and interpreter.

Social-Emotional Leader

The social-emotional leader within a group may perform a variety of maintenance roles and is generally someone who is well liked by the other group members and whose role behaviors complement but don't compete with the task leader. The social-emotional leader may also reassure and support the task leader when he or she becomes stressed. In general, the social-emotional leader is a reflective thinker who has good perception skills that he or she uses to analyze the group dynamics and climate and then initiate the appropriate role behaviors to maintain a positive climate. Unlike the role of task leader, this isn't a role that typically shifts from one person to another. While all members of the group perform some maintenance role behaviors at various times, the socioemotional leader reliably functions to support group members and maintain a positive relational climate. Social-emotional leadership functions can actually become detrimental to the group and lead to less satisfaction among members when the maintenance behaviors being performed are seen as redundant or as too distracting from the task (Pavitt, 1999).

Supporter

The role of **supporter** is characterized by communication behaviors that encourage other group members and provide emotional support as needed. The supporter's work primarily occurs in one-on-one exchanges that are more intimate and in-depth than the exchanges that take place during full group meetings. While many group members may make supporting comments publicly at group meetings, these comments are typically superficial and/or brief. A supporter uses active empathetic listening skills to connect with group members who may seem down or frustrated by saying something like "Tayesha, you seemed kind of down today. Is there anything you'd like to talk about?" Supporters also follow up on previous conversations with group members to maintain the connections they've already established by saying things like "Alan, I remember you said your mom is having surgery this weekend. I hope it goes well. Let me know if you need anything." The supporter's communication behaviors are probably the least noticeable of any of the other maintenance roles, which may make this group member's efforts seem overlooked. Leaders and other group members can help support the supporter by acknowledging his or her contributions.

Tension Releaser

The **tension releaser** is someone who is naturally funny and sensitive to the personalities of the group and the dynamics of any given situation and who uses these qualities to manage the frustration level of the group. Being funny is not enough to fulfill this role, as jokes or comments could indeed be humorous to other group members but be delivered at an inopportune time, which ultimately creates rather than releases tension. The healthy use of humor by the tension releaser performs the same maintenance function as the empathy employed by the harmonizer or the social-emotional leader, but it is less intimate and is typically directed toward the whole group instead of just one person. The tension releaser may start serving his or her function during the forming stage of group development when primary tensions are present due to the typical uncertainties present during initial interactions. The tension releaser may help "break the ice" or make others feel at ease during the group's more socially awkward first meetings. When people make a failed attempt to release tension, they may be viewed as a joker, which is a self-centered role we will learn more about later.

Harmonizer

The **harmonizer** role is played by group members who help manage the various types of group conflict that emerge during group communication. They keep their eyes and ears open for signs of conflict among group members and ideally intervene before it escalates. For example, the harmonizer may sense that one group member's critique of another member's idea wasn't received positively, and he or she may be able to rephrase the critique in a more constructive way, which can help diminish the other group member's defensiveness. Harmonizers also deescalate conflict once it has already started—for example, by suggesting that the group take a break and then mediating between group members in a side conversation. These actions can help prevent conflict from spilling over into other group interactions. In cases where the whole group experiences conflict, the harmonizer may help lead the group in perception-checking discussions that help members see an issue from multiple perspectives. For a harmonizer to be effective, it's important that he or she be viewed as impartial and committed to the group as a whole rather than to one side of an issue or one person or faction within the larger group. A special kind of harmonizer that helps manage cultural differences within the group is the interpreter.

Interpreter

An **interpreter** helps manage the diversity within a group by mediating intercultural conflict, articulating common ground between different people, and generally creating a climate where difference is seen as an opportunity rather than as something to be feared. Just as an interpreter at the United Nations acts as a bridge between two different languages, the interpreter can bridge identity differences between group members. Interpreters can help perform the other maintenance roles discussed with a special awareness of and sensitivity toward cultural differences. While a literal interpreter would serve a task-related function within a group, this type of interpreter may help support a person who feels left out of the group because he or she has a different cultural identity than the majority of the group. Interpreters often act as allies to people who are different even though the interpreter doesn't share the specific cultural identity. The interpreter may help manage conflict that arises as a result of diversity, in this case, acting like an ambassador or mediator. Interpreters, because of their cultural sensitivity, may also take a proactive role to help address conflict before it emerges—for example, by taking a group member aside and explaining why his or her behavior or comments may be perceived as offensive.

Negative Roles and Behaviors

Group communication scholars began exploring the negative side of group member roles more than sixty years ago (Benne & Sheats, 1948). Studying these negative roles can help us analyze group interactions and potentially better understand why some groups are more successful than others. It's important to acknowledge that we all perform some negative behaviors within groups but that those behaviors do not necessarily constitute a role. A person may temporarily monopolize a discussion to bring attention to his or her idea. If that behavior gets the attention of the group members and makes them realize they were misinformed or headed in a negative direction, then that behavior may have been warranted. Negative behaviors can be enacted with varying degrees of intensity and regularity, and their effects may range from mild annoyance to group failure. In general, the effects grow increasingly negative as they increase in intensity and frequency. While a single enactment of a negative role behavior may still harm the group, regular enactment of such behaviors would constitute a role, and playing that role is guaranteed to negatively impact the group. We will divide our discussion of negative roles into self-centered and unproductive roles.

Self-Centered Roles

The behaviors associated with all the **self-centered roles** divert attention from the task to the group member exhibiting the behavior. Although all these roles share in their quest to divert attention, they do it in different ways and for different reasons. The self-centered roles we will discuss are the central negative, monopolizer, self-confessor, insecure compliment seeker, and joker (Cragan & Wright, 1991).

Central Negative

The central negative argues against most of the ideas and proposals discussed in the group and often emerges as a result of a leadership challenge during group formation. The failed attempt to lead the group can lead to feelings of resentment toward the leader and/or the purpose of the group, which then manifest in negative behaviors that delay, divert, or block the group's progress toward achieving its goal. This scenario is unfortunate because the central negative is typically a motivated and intelligent group member who can benefit the group if properly handled by the group leader or other members. Group communication scholars suggest that the group leader or leaders actively incorporate central negatives into group tasks and responsibilities to make them feel valued and to help diminish any residual anger, disappointment, or hurt feelings from the leadership conflict (Bormann & Bormann, 1988). Otherwise the central negative will continue to argue against the proposals and decisions of the group, even when they may be in agreement. In some cases, the central negative may unintentionally serve a beneficial function if his or her criticisms prevent groupthink.

Monopolizer

The monopolizer is a group member who makes excessive verbal contributions, preventing equal participation by other group members. In short, monopolizers like to hear the sound of their own voice and do not follow typical norms for conversational turn taking. There are some people who are well informed, charismatic, and competent communicators who can get away with impromptu lectures and long stories, but monopolizers do not possess the magnetic qualities of such people. A group member's excessive verbal contributions are more likely to be labeled as monopolizing when they are not related to the task or when they provide unnecessary or redundant elaboration. Some monopolizers do not intentionally speak for longer than they should. Instead, they think they are making a genuine contribution to the group. These folks likely lack sensitivity to nonverbal cues, or they would see that other group members are tired of listening or annoyed. Other monopolizers just like to talk and don't care what others think. Some may be trying to make up for a lack of knowledge or experience. This type of monopolizer is best described as a dilettante, or an amateur who tries to pass himself or herself off as an expert.

There are some subgroups of behaviors that fall under the monopolizer's role. The "stage hog" monopolizes discussion with excessive verbal contributions and engages in one-upping and narcissistic listening. One-upping is a spotlight-stealing strategy in which people try to verbally "out-do" others by saying something like "You think that's bad? Listen to what happened to me!" They also listen to others in order to find something they can connect back to themselves, not to understand the message. The stage hog is like the diva that refuses to leave the stage to let the next performer begin. Unlike a monopolizer, who may engage in his or her behaviors unknowingly, stage hogs are usually aware of what they're doing.

The "egghead" monopolizes the discussion with excessive contributions that are based in actual knowledge but that exceed the level of understanding of other group members or the needs of the group (Cragan & Wright, 1999). The egghead is different from the dilettante monopolizer discussed earlier because this person has genuine knowledge and expertise on a subject, which may be useful to the group. But like the monopolizer and stage hog, the egghead's excessive contributions draw attention away from the task, slow the group down, and may contribute to a negative group climate. The egghead may be like an absentminded professor who is smart but lacks the social sensitivity to tell when he or she has said enough and is now starting to annoy other group members. This type of egghead naively believes that other group members care as much about the subject as he or she does. The second type of egghead is more pompous and monopolizes the discussion to flaunt his or her intellectual superiority. While the first type of egghead may be tolerated to a point by the group and seen as eccentric but valuable, the second type of egghead is perceived more negatively and more quickly hurts the group. In general, the egghead's advanced knowledge of a subject and excessive contributions can hurt the group's potential for synergy, since other group members may defer to the egghead expert, which can diminish the creativity that comes from outside and nonexpert perspectives.

Self-Confessor

The self-confessor is a group member who tries to use group meetings as therapy sessions for issues not related to the group's task. Self-confessors tend to make personal self-disclosures that are unnecessarily intimate. While it is reasonable to expect that someone experiencing a personal problem may want to consult with the group, especially if that person has formed close relationships with other group members, a self-confessor consistently comes to meetings with drama or a personal problem. A supporter or gatekeeper may be able to manage some degree of self-confessor behavior, but a chronic self-confessor is likely to build frustration among other group members that can lead to interpersonal conflict and a lack of cohesion and productivity. Most groups develop a norm regarding how much personal information is discussed during group meetings, and some limit such disclosures to time before or after the meeting, which may help deter the self-confessor.

Insecure Compliment Seeker

The insecure compliment seeker wants to know that he or she is valued by the group and seeks recognition that is often not task related. For example, they don't want to be told they did a good job compiling a report; they want to know that they're a good person or attractive or smart—even though they might not be any of those things. In short, they try to get validation from their relationships with group members—validation that they may be lacking in relationships outside the group. Or they may be someone who continually seeks the approval of others or tries to overcompensate for insecurity through excessive behaviors aimed at eliciting compliments. For example, if a group member wears a tight-fitting t-shirt in hopes of drawing attention to his physique but doesn't receive any compliments from the group, he may say, "My girlfriend said she could tell I've been working out. What do you think?"

Joker

The joker is a person who consistently uses sarcasm, plays pranks, or tells jokes, which distracts from the overall functioning of the group. In short, the joker is an incompetent tension releaser. Rather than being seen as the witty group member with good timing, the joker is seen as the "class clown." Like the insecure compliment seeker, the joker usually seeks attention and approval because of an underlying insecurity. A group's leader may have to intervene and privately meet with a person engaging in joker behavior to help prevent a toxic or unsafe climate from forming. This may be ineffective, though, if a joker's behaviors are targeted toward the group leader, which could indicate that the joker has a general problem with authority. In the worst-case scenario, a joker may have to be expelled from the group if his or her behavior becomes violent, offensive, illegal, or otherwise unethical.

Unproductive Roles

There are some negative roles in group communication that do not primarily function to divert attention away from the group's task to a specific group member. Instead, these **unproductive roles** just prevent or make it more difficult for the group to make progress. These roles include the blocker, withdrawer, aggressor, and doormat.

Blocker

The blocker intentionally or unintentionally keeps things from getting done in the group. Intentionally, a person may suggest that the group look into a matter further or explore another option before making a final decision even though the group has already thoroughly considered the matter. They may cite a procedural rule or suggest that input be sought from additional people in order to delay progress. Behaviors that lead to more information gathering can be good for the group, but when they are unnecessary they are blocking behaviors. Unintentionally, a group member may set blocking behaviors into motion by missing a meeting or not getting his or her work done on time. People can also block progress by playing the airhead role, which is the opposite of the egghead role discussed earlier. An airhead skirts his or her responsibilities by claiming ignorance when he or she actually understands or intentionally performs poorly on a task so the other group members question his or her intellectual abilities to handle other tasks (Cragan & Wright, 1999). Since exhibiting airhead behaviors gets a person out of performing tasks, they can also be a tactic of a withdrawer, which we will discuss next.

Withdrawer

A withdrawer mentally and/or physically removes herself or himself from group activities and only participates when forced to. When groups exceed five members, the likelihood of having a member exhibit withdrawer behaviors increases. For example, a member may attend meetings and seemingly pay attention but not contribute to discussions or not volunteer to take on tasks, instead waiting on other members to volunteer first. Withdrawers are often responsible for the social loafing that makes other group members dread group work. A member may also avoid eye contact with other group members, sit apart from the group, or orient his or her body away from the group to avoid participation. Withdrawers generally do not exhibit active listening behaviors. At the extreme, a group member may stop attending group meetings completely. Adopting a problem-solving model that requires equal participation, starting to build social cohesion early, and choosing a meeting space and seating arrangement that encourages interactivity can help minimize withdrawing behaviors. Gatekeepers, supporters, and group leaders can also intervene after early signs of withdrawing to try to reengage the group member.

Aggressor

An aggressor exhibits negative behaviors such as putting others' ideas down, attacking others personally when they feel confronted or insecure, competing unnecessarily to "win" at the expense of others within the group, and being outspoken to the point of distraction. An aggressor's behaviors can quickly cross the fine line between being abrasive or dominant and being unethical. For example, a person vigorously defending a position that is relevant and valid is different from a person who claims others' ideas are stupid but has nothing to contribute. As with most behaviors, the aggressor's fall into a continuum based on their intensity. On the more benign end of the continuum is assertive behavior, toward the middle is aggressive behavior, and on the unethical side is bullying behavior. At their worst, an aggressor's behaviors can lead to shouting matches or even physical violence within a group. Establishing group rules and norms that set up a safe climate for discussion and include mechanisms for temporarily or permanently removing a group member who violates that safe space may proactively prevent such behaviors.

Doormat

While we all need to take one for the team sometimes or compromise for the sake of the group, the doormat is a person who is chronically submissive to the point that it hurts the group's progress (Cragan & Wright, 1999). Doormat behaviors include quickly giving in when challenged, self-criticism, and claims of inadequacy. Some people who exhibit doormat behaviors may have difficulty being self-assured and assertive, may be conflict avoidant, or may even feel that their behaviors will make other group members like them. Other people play the martyr and make sure to publicly note their "sacrifices" for the group, hoping to elicit praise or attention. If their sacrifices aren't recognized, they may engage in further negative behaviors such as whining and/or insecure compliment seeking.

References

Benne, K. D., and Paul Sheats, "Functional Roles of Group Members," *Journal of Social Issues* 4, no. 2 (1948): 41–49.

Bormann, E. G., and Nancy C. Bormann, *Effective Small Group Communication*, 4th ed. (Santa Rosa, CA: Burgess CA, 1988).

Cragan, J. F., and David W. Wright, *Communication in Small Group Discussions: An Integrated Approach*, 3rd ed. (St. Paul, MN: West Publishing, 1991), 147.

Pavitt, C., "Theorizing about the Group Communication-Leadership

Relationship," in *The Handbook of Group Communication Theory and Research*, ed. Lawrence R. Frey (Thousand Oaks, CA: Sage, 1999), 317.

16.4 PROBLEM SOLVING AND DECISION MAKING IN GROUPS

"Alone we are smart. Together, we are brilliant." -Steven Anderson

Although the steps of problem solving and decision making that we will discuss next may seem obvious, we often don't think to or choose not to use them. Instead, we start working on a problem and later realize we are lost and have to backtrack. I'm sure we've all reached a point in a project or task and had the "OK, now what?" moment. I've recently taken up some carpentry projects as a functional hobby, and I have developed a great respect for the importance of advanced planning. It's frustrating to get to a crucial point in building or fixing something only to realize that you have to unscrew a support board that you already screwed in, have to drive back to the hardware store to get something that you didn't think to get earlier, or have to completely start over. In this section, we will discuss the group problem-solving process, methods of decision making, and influences on these processes.

Group Problem Solving

The problem-solving process involves thoughts, discussions, actions, and decisions that occur from the first consideration of a problematic situation to the goal. The problems that groups face are varied, but some common problems include budgeting funds, raising funds, planning events, addressing customer or citizen complaints, creating or adapting products or services to fit needs, supporting members, and raising awareness about issues or causes.

Problems of all sorts have three common components (Adams & Galanes, 2009):

1. **An undesirable situation.** When conditions are desirable, there isn't a problem.
2. **A desired situation.** Even though it may only be a vague idea, there is a drive to better the undesirable situation. The vague idea may develop into a more precise goal that can be achieved, although solutions are not yet generated.
3. **Obstacles between undesirable and desirable situation.** These are things that stand in the way between the current situation and the group's goal of addressing it. This component of a problem requires the most work, and it is the part where decision making occurs. Some examples of obstacles include limited funding, resources, personnel, time, or information. Obstacles can also take the form of people who are working against the group, including people resistant to change or people who disagree.

Discussion of these three elements of a problem helps the group tailor its problem-solving process, as each problem will vary. While these three general elements are present in each problem, the group should also address specific characteristics of the problem. Five common and important characteristics to consider are task difficulty, number of possible solutions, group member interest in problem, group member familiarity with problem, and the need for solution acceptance (Adams & Galanes, 2009).

1. **Task difficulty.** Difficult tasks are also typically more complex. Groups should be prepared to spend time researching and discussing a difficult and complex task in order to develop a shared foundational knowledge. This typically requires individual work outside of the group and frequent group meetings to share information.
2. **Number of possible solutions.** There are usually multiple ways to solve a problem or complete a task, but some problems have more potential solutions than others. Figuring out how to prepare a beach house for an approaching hurricane is fairly complex and difficult, but there are still a limited number of

things to do—for example, taping and boarding up windows; turning off water, electricity, and gas; trimming trees; and securing loose outside objects. Other problems may be more creatively based. For example, designing a new restaurant may entail using some standard solutions but could also entail many different types of innovation with layout and design.
3. **Group member interest in problem.** When group members are interested in the problem, they will be more engaged with the problem-solving process and invested in finding a quality solution. Groups with high interest in and knowledge about the problem may want more freedom to develop and implement solutions, while groups with low interest may prefer a leader who provides structure and direction.
4. **Group familiarity with problem.** Some groups encounter a problem regularly, while other problems are more unique or unexpected. A family who has lived in hurricane alley for decades probably has a better idea of how to prepare its house for a hurricane than does a family that just recently moved from the Midwest. Many groups that rely on funding have to revisit a budget every year, and in recent years, groups have had to get more creative with budgets as funding has been cut in nearly every sector. When group members aren't familiar with a problem, they will need to do background research on what similar groups have done and may also need to bring in outside experts.
5. **Need for solution acceptance.** In this step, groups must consider how many people the decision will affect and how much "buy-in" from others the group needs in order for their solution to be successfully implemented. Some small groups have many stakeholders on whom the success of a solution depends. Other groups are answerable only to themselves. When a small group is planning on building a new park in a crowded neighborhood or implementing a new policy in a large business, it can be very difficult to develop solutions that will be accepted by all. In such cases, groups will want to poll those who will be affected by the solution and may want to do a pilot implementation to see how people react. Imposing an excellent solution that doesn't have buy-in from stakeholders can still lead to failure.

Group Problem-Solving Process

There are several variations of similar problem-solving models based on US American scholar John Dewey's reflective thinking process (Bormann & Bormann, 1988). As you read through the steps in the process, think about how you can apply what we learned regarding the general and specific elements of problems. Some of the following steps are straightforward, and they are things we would logically do when faced with a problem. However, taking a deliberate and systematic approach to problem solving has been shown to benefit group functioning and performance. A deliberate approach is especially beneficial for groups that do not have an established history of working together and will only be able to meet occasionally. Although a group should attend to each step of the process, group leaders or other group members who facilitate problem solving should be cautious not to dogmatically follow each element of the process or force a group along. Such a lack of flexibility could limit group member input and negatively affect the group's cohesion and climate.

Step 1: Define the Problem

Define the problem by considering the three elements shared by every problem: the current undesirable situation, the goal or more desirable situation, and obstacles in the way (Adams & Galanes, 2009). At this stage, group members share what they know about the current situation, without proposing solutions or evaluating the information. Here are some good questions to ask during this stage: What is the current difficulty? How did we come to know that the difficulty exists? Who/what is involved? Why is it meaningful/urgent/important? What have the effects been so far? What, if any, elements of the difficulty require clarification? At the end of this stage, the group should be able to compose a single sentence that summarizes the problem called a **problem statement**. Avoid wording in the problem statement or question that hints at potential solutions. A small group formed to investigate ethical violations of city officials could use the following problem statement: "Our state does not currently have a mechanism for citizens to report suspected ethical violations by city officials."

Step 2: Analyze the Problem

During this step a group should analyze the problem and the group's relationship to the problem. Whereas the first step involved exploring the "what" related to the problem, this step focuses on the "why." At this stage, group members can discuss the potential causes of the difficulty. Group members may also want to begin setting out an agenda or timeline for the group's problem-solving process, looking forward to the other steps. To fully analyze the problem, the group can discuss the five common problem variables discussed before. Here are two examples of questions that the group formed to address ethics violations might ask: Why doesn't our city have an ethics reporting mechanism? Do cities of similar size have such a mechanism? Once the problem has been analyzed, the group can pose a **problem question** that will guide the group as it generates possible solutions. "How can citizens report suspected ethical violations of city officials and how will such reports be processed and addressed?" As you can see, the problem question is more complex than the problem statement, since the group has moved on to more in-depth discussion of the problem during step 2.

Step 3: Generate Possible Solutions

During this step, group members generate possible solutions to the problem. Again, solutions should not be evaluated at this point, only proposed and clarified. The question should be what *could* we do to address this problem, not what *should* we do to address it. It is perfectly OK for a group member to question another person's idea by asking something like "What do you mean?" or "Could you explain your reasoning more?" Discussions at this stage may reveal a need to return to previous steps to better define or more fully analyze a problem. Since many problems are multifaceted, it is necessary for group members to generate solutions for each part of the problem separately, making sure to have multiple solutions for each part. Stopping the solution-generating process prematurely can lead to groupthink. For the problem question previously posed, the group would need to generate solutions for all three parts of the problem included in the question. Possible solutions for the first part of the problem (How can citizens report ethical violations?) may include "online reporting system, e-mail, in-person, anonymously, on-the-record," and so on. Possible solutions for the second part of the problem (How will reports be processed?) may include "daily by a newly appointed ethics officer, weekly by a nonpartisan nongovernment employee," and so on. Possible solutions for the third part of the problem (How will reports be addressed?) may include "by a newly appointed ethics commission, by the accused's supervisor, by the city manager," and so on.

Step 4: Evaluate Solutions

During this step, solutions can be critically evaluated based on their credibility, completeness, and worth. Once the potential solutions have been narrowed based on more obvious differences in relevance and/or merit, the group should analyze each solution based on its potential effects—especially negative effects. Groups that are required to report the rationale for their decision or whose decisions may be subject to public scrutiny would be wise to make a set list of criteria for evaluating each solution. Additionally, solutions can be evaluated based on how well they fit with the group's charge and the abilities of the group. To do this, group members may ask, "Does this solution live up to the original purpose or mission of the group?" and "Can the solution actually be implemented with our current resources and connections?" and "How will this solution be supported, funded, enforced, and assessed?" Secondary tensions and substantive conflict, two concepts discussed earlier, emerge during this step of problem solving, and group members will need to employ effective critical thinking and listening skills.

Decision making is part of the larger process of problem solving and it plays a prominent role in this step. While there are several fairly similar models for problem solving, there are many varied decision-making techniques that groups can use. For example, to narrow the list of proposed solutions, group members may decide by majority vote, by weighing the pros and cons, or by discussing them until a consensus is reached. Once the final decision is reached, the group leader or facilitator should confirm that the group is in agreement. It may be beneficial to let the group break for a while or even to delay the final decision until a later meeting to allow people time to evaluate it outside of the group context.

Step 5: Implement and Assess the Solution

Implementing the solution requires some advanced planning, and it should not be rushed unless the group is operating under strict time restraints or delay may lead to some kind of harm. Although some solutions can be implemented immediately, others may take days, months, or years. As was noted earlier, it may be beneficial for groups to poll those who will be affected by the solution as to their opinion of it or even to do a pilot test to observe the effectiveness of the solution and how people react to it. Before implementation, groups should also determine how and when they would assess the effectiveness of the solution by asking, "How will we know if the solution is working or not?" Since solution assessment will vary based on whether or not the group is disbanded, groups should also consider the following questions: If the group disbands after implementation, who will be responsible for assessing the solution? If the solution fails, will the same group reconvene or will a new group be formed?

Certain elements of the solution may need to be delegated out to various people inside and outside the group. Group members may also be assigned to implement a particular part of the solution based on their role in the decision making or because it connects to their area of expertise. Likewise, group members may be tasked with publicizing the solution or "selling" it to a particular group of stakeholders. Last, the group should consider its future. In some cases, the group will get to decide if it will stay together and continue working on other tasks or if it will disband. In other cases, outside forces determine the group's fate.

"None of us is as smart as all of us." -Ken Blanchard

Decision Making in Groups

We all engage in personal decision making daily, and we all know that some decisions are more difficult than others. When we make decisions in groups, we face some challenges that we do not face in our personal decision making, but we also stand to benefit from some advantages of group decision making (Napier & Gershenfeld, 2004). Group decision making can appear fair and democratic but really only be a gesture that covers up the fact that certain group members or the group leader have already decided. Group decision making also takes more time than individual decisions and can be burdensome if some group members do not do their assigned work, divert the group with self-centered or unproductive role behaviors, or miss meetings. Conversely, though, group decisions are often more informed, since all group members develop a shared understanding of a problem through discussion and debate. The shared understanding may also be more complex and deep than what an individual would develop, because the group members are exposed to a variety of viewpoints that can broaden their own perspectives. Group decisions also benefit from synergy, one of the key advantages of group communication that we discussed earlier. Most groups do not use a specific method of decision making, perhaps thinking that they'll work things out as they go. This can lead to unequal participation, social loafing, premature decisions, prolonged discussion, and a host of other negative consequences. So in this section we will learn some practices that will prepare us for good decision making and some specific techniques we can use to help us reach a final decision.

Brainstorming before Decision Making

Before groups can make a decision, they need to generate possible solutions to their problem. The most commonly used method is brainstorming, although most people don't follow the recommended steps of brainstorming. As you'll recall, brainstorming refers to the quick generation of ideas free of evaluation. The originator of the term *brainstorming* said the following four rules must be followed for the technique to be effective (Osborn, 1959):

1. Evaluation of ideas is forbidden.
2. Wild and crazy ideas are encouraged.
3. Quantity of ideas, not quality, is the goal.
4. New combinations of ideas presented are encouraged.

To make brainstorming more of a decision-making method rather than an idea-generating method, group communication scholars have suggested additional steps that precede and follow brainstorming (Cragan & Wright, 1991).

1. **Do a warm-up brainstorming session.** Some people are more apprehensive about publicly communicating their ideas than others are, and a warm-up session can help ease apprehension and prime group members for task-related idea generation. The warm-up can be initiated by anyone in the group and should only go on for a few minutes. To get things started, a person could ask, "If our group formed a band, what would we be called?" or "What other purposes could a mailbox serve?" In the previous examples, the first warm up gets the group's more abstract creative juices flowing, while the second focuses more on practical and concrete ideas.
2. **Do the actual brainstorming session.** This session shouldn't last more than thirty minutes and should follow the four rules of brainstorming mentioned previously. To ensure that the fourth rule is realized, the facilitator could encourage people to piggyback off each other's ideas.
3. **Eliminate duplicate ideas.** After the brainstorming session is over, group members can eliminate (without evaluating) ideas that are the same or very similar.
4. **Clarify, organize, and evaluate ideas.** Before evaluation, see if any ideas need clarification. Then try to theme or group ideas together in some orderly

fashion. Since "wild and crazy" ideas are encouraged, some suggestions may need clarification. If it becomes clear that there isn't really a foundation to an idea and that it is too vague or abstract and can't be clarified, it may be eliminated. As a caution though, it may be wise to not throw out off-the-wall ideas that are hard to categorize and to instead put them in a miscellaneous or "wild and crazy" category.

Discussion before Decision Making

The **nominal group technique** guides decision making through a four-step process that includes idea generation and evaluation and seeks to elicit equal contributions from all group members (Delbecq & Ven de Ven, 1971). This method is useful because the procedure involves all group members systematically, which fixes the problem of uneven participation during discussions. Since everyone contributes to the discussion, this method can also help reduce instances of social loafing. To use the nominal group technique, do the following:

1. Silently and individually list ideas.
2. Create a master list of ideas.
3. Clarify ideas as needed.
4. Take a secret vote to rank group members' acceptance of ideas.

During the first step, have group members work quietly, in the same space, to write down every idea they have to address the task or problem they face. This shouldn't take more than twenty minutes. Whoever is facilitating the discussion should remind group members to use brainstorming techniques, which means they shouldn't evaluate ideas as they are generated. Ask group members to remain silent once they've finished their list so they do not distract others.

During the second step, the facilitator goes around the group in a consistent order asking each person to share one idea at a time. As the idea is shared, the facilitator records it on a master list that everyone can see. Keep track of how many times each idea comes up, as that could be an idea that warrants more discussion. Continue this process until all the ideas have been shared. As a note to facilitators, some group members may begin to edit their list or self-censor when asked to provide one of their ideas. To limit a person's apprehension with sharing his or her ideas and to ensure that each idea is shared, I have asked group members to exchange lists with someone else so they can share ideas from the list they receive without fear of being personally judged.

During step three, the facilitator should note that group members can now ask for clarification on ideas on the master list. Do not let this discussion stray into evaluation of ideas. To help avoid an unnecessarily long discussion, it may be useful to go from one person to the next to ask which ideas need clarifying and then go to the originator(s) of the idea in question for clarification.

During the fourth step, members use a voting ballot to rank the acceptability of the ideas on the master list. If the list is long, you may ask group members to rank only their top five or so choices. The facilitator then takes up the secret ballots and reviews them in a random order, noting the rankings of each idea. Ideally, the highest ranked idea can then be discussed and decided on. The nominal group technique does not carry a group all the way through to the point of decision; rather, it sets the group up for a roundtable discussion or use of some other method to evaluate the merits of the top ideas.

Specific Decision-Making Techniques

Some decision-making techniques involve determining a course of action based on the level of agreement among the group members. These methods include majority, expert, authority, and consensus rule. Table 16.1 "Pros and Cons of Agreement-Based Decision-Making Techniques" reviews the pros and cons of each of these methods.

Majority rule is a commonly used decision-making technique in which a majority (one-half plus one) must agree before a decision is made. A show-of-hands vote, a paper ballot, or an electronic voting system can determine the majority choice. Many decision-making bodies, including the US House of Representatives, Senate, and Supreme Court, use majority rule to make decisions, which shows that it is often associated with democratic decision making, since each person gets one vote and each vote counts equally. Of course, other individuals and mediated messages can influence a person's vote, but since the voting power is spread out over all group members, it is not easy for one person or party to take control of the decision-making process. In some cases—for example, to override a presidential veto or to amend the constitution—a super majority of two-thirds may be required to make a decision.

Minority rule is a decision-making technique in which a designated authority or expert has final say over a decision and may or may not consider the input of other group members. When a designated expert makes a decision by minority rule, there may be buy-in from others in the group, especially if the members of the group didn't have relevant knowledge or expertise. When a designated authority makes decisions, buy-in will vary based on group members' level of respect for the authority. For example, decisions made by an elected authority may be more accepted by those who elected him or her than by those who didn't. As with majority rule, this technique can be time saving. Unlike majority rule, one person or party can have control over the decision-making process. This type of decision making is more similar to that used by monarchs and dictators. An obvious negative consequence of this method is that the needs or wants of one person can override the needs and wants of the majority. A minority deciding for the majority has led to negative consequences throughout history. The white Afrikaner minority that ruled South Africa for decades instituted apartheid, which was a system of racial segregation that disenfranchised and oppressed the majority population. The quality of the decision and its fairness really depends on the designated expert or authority.

Consensus rule is a decision-making technique in which all members of the group must agree on the same decision. On rare occasions, a decision may be ideal for all group members, which can lead to unanimous agreement without further debate and discussion. Although this can be positive, be cautious that this isn't a sign of groupthink. More typically, consensus is reached only after lengthy discussion. On the plus side, consensus often leads to high-quality decisions due to the time and effort it takes to get everyone in agreement. Group members are also more likely to be committed to the decision because of their investment in reaching it. On the negative side, the ultimate decision is often one that all group members can live with but not one that's ideal for all members. Additionally, the process of arriving at consensus also includes conflict, as people debate ideas and negotiate the interpersonal tensions that may result.

PROS & CONS OF DECISION MAKING TECHNIQUES

Technique	PROS	CONS
Majority Rule Technique	• Quick • Efficient in large groups • Each vote counts equally	• Close decisions (5–4) may reduce internal and external "buy-in" • Doesn't take advantage of group synergy to develop alternatives that more members can support • Minority may feel alienated
Minority Rule by Expert	• Quick • Decision quality is better than what less knowledgeable people could produce • Experts are typically objective and less easy to influence	• Expertise must be verified • Experts can be difficult to find / pay for • Group members may feel useless
Minority Rule by Authority	• Quick • Buy-in could be high if authority is respected	• Authority may not be seen as legitimate, leading to less buy-in • Group members may try to sway the authority or compete for his or her attention • Unethical authorities could make decisions that benefit them and harm group members
Consensus Rule	• High-quality decisions due to time invested • Higher level of commitment because of participation in decision • Satisfaction with decision because of shared agreement	• Time consuming • Difficult to manage idea and personal conflict that can emerge as ideas are debated • Decision may be OK but not ideal

Influences on Decision Making

Many factors influence the decision-making process. For example, how might a group's independence or access to resources affect the decisions they make? What potential advantages and disadvantages come with decisions made by groups that are more or less similar in terms of personality and cultural identities? In this section, we will explore how situational, personality, and cultural influences affect decision making in groups.

Situational Influences on Decision Making

A group's situational context affects decision making. One key situational element is the degree of freedom that the group has to make its own decisions, secure its own resources, and initiate its own actions. Some groups have to go through multiple approval processes before they can do anything, while others are self-directed, self-governing, and self-sustaining. Another situational influence is uncertainty. In general, groups deal with more uncertainty in decision making than do individuals because of the increased number of variables that comes with adding more people to a situation. Individual group members can't know what other group members are thinking, whether or not they are doing their work, and how committed they are to the group. So the size of a group is a powerful situational influence, as it adds to uncertainty and complicates communication.

Access to information also influences a group. First, the nature of the group's task or problem affects its ability to get information. Group members can more easily make decisions about a problem when other groups have similarly experienced it. Even if the problem is complex and serious, the group can learn from other situations and apply what it learns. Second, the group must have access to flows of information. Access to archives, electronic databases, and individuals with relevant experience is necessary to obtain any relevant information about similar problems or to do research on a new or unique problem. In this regard, group members' formal and information network connections also become important situational influences.

The origin and urgency of a problem are also situational factors that influence decision making. In terms of origin, problems usually occur in one of four ways:

1. **Something goes wrong.** Group members must decide how to fix or stop something. Example—a firehouse crew finds out that half of the building is contaminated with mold and must be closed down.
2. **Expectations change or increase.** Group members must innovate more efficient or effective ways of doing something. Example—a firehouse crew finds out that the district they are responsible for is being expanded.
3. **Something goes wrong and expectations change or increase.** Group members must fix/stop and become more efficient/effective. Example—the firehouse crew has to close half the building and must start responding to more calls due to the expanding district.
4. **The problem existed from the beginning.** Group members must go back to the origins of the situation and walk through and analyze the steps again to decide what can be done differently. Example—a firehouse crew has consistently had to work with minimal resources in terms of building space

and firefighting tools.

In each of the cases, the need for a decision may be more or less urgent depending on how badly something is going wrong, how high the expectations have been raised, or the degree to which people are fed up with a broken system. Decisions must be made in situations ranging from crisis level to mundane.

Personality Influences on Decision Making

A long-studied typology of value orientations that affect decision making consists of the following types of decision maker: the economic, the aesthetic, the theoretical, the social, the political, and the religious (Spranger, 1928).

- The *economic* decision maker makes decisions based on what is practical and useful.
- The *aesthetic* decision maker makes decisions based on form and harmony, desiring a solution that is elegant and in sync with the surroundings.
- The *theoretical* decision maker wants to discover the truth through rationality.
- The *social* decision maker emphasizes the personal impact of a decision and sympathizes with those who may be affected by it.
- The *political* decision maker is interested in power and influence and views people and/or property as divided into groups that have different value.
- The *religious* decision maker seeks to identify with a larger purpose, works to unify others under that goal, and commits to a viewpoint, often denying one side and being dedicated to the other.

In the United States, economic, political, and theoretical decision making tend to be more prevalent decision-making orientations, which likely corresponds to the individualistic cultural orientation with its emphasis on competition and efficiency. But situational context, as we discussed before, can also influence our decision making.

The personalities of group members, especially leaders and other active members, affect the climate of the group. Group member personalities can be categorized based on where they fall on a continuum anchored by the following descriptors: dominant/submissive, friendly/unfriendly, and instrumental/emotional (Cragan & Wright, 1999). The more group members there are in any extreme of these categories, the more likely that the group climate will also shift to resemble those characteristics.

- **Dominant versus submissive.** Group members that are more dominant act more independently and directly, initiate conversations, take up more space,

make more direct eye contact, seek leadership positions, and take control over decision-making processes. More submissive members are reserved, contribute to the group only when asked to, avoid eye contact, and leave their personal needs and thoughts unvoiced or give into the suggestions of others.
- **Friendly versus unfriendly.** Group members on the friendly side of the continuum find a balance between talking and listening, don't try to win at the expense of other group members, are flexible but not weak, and value democratic decision making. Unfriendly group members are disagreeable, indifferent, withdrawn, and selfish, which leads them to either not invest in decision making or direct it in their own interest rather than in the interest of the group.
- **Instrumental versus emotional.** Instrumental group members are emotionally neutral, objective, analytical, task-oriented, and committed followers, which leads them to work hard and contribute to the group's decision making as long as it is orderly and follows agreed-on rules. Emotional group members are creative, playful, independent, unpredictable, and expressive, which leads them to make rash decisions, resist group norms or decision-making structures, and switch often from relational to task focus.

Cultural Context and Decision Making

Just like neighborhoods, schools, and countries, small groups vary in terms of their degree of similarity and difference. Demographic changes in the United States and increases in technology that can bring different people together make it more likely that we will be interacting in more and more heterogeneous groups (Allen, 2011). Some small groups are more homogenous, meaning the members are more similar, and some are more heterogeneous, meaning the members are more different. Diversity and difference within groups has advantages and disadvantages. In terms of advantages, research finds that, in general, groups that are culturally heterogeneous have better overall performance than more homogenous groups (Haslett & Ruebush, 1999). Additionally, when group members have time to get to know each other and competently communicate across their differences, the advantages of diversity include better decision making due to different perspectives (Thomas, 1999). Unfortunately, groups often operate under time constraints and other pressures that make the possibility for intercultural dialogue and understanding difficult. The main disadvantage of heterogeneous groups is the possibility for conflict, but given that all groups experience conflict, this isn't solely due to the presence of diversity. We will now look more specifically at how some of the cultural value orientations we've learned about already in this book can play out in groups with international diversity and how domestic diversity in terms of demographics can also influence group decision making.

International Diversity in Group Interactions

Cultural value orientations such as individualism/collectivism, power distance, and high-/low-context communication styles all manifest on a continuum of communication behaviors and can influence group decision making. Group members from individualistic cultures are more likely to value task-oriented, efficient, and direct communication. This could manifest in behaviors such as dividing up tasks into individual projects before collaboration begins and then openly debating ideas during discussion and decision making. Additionally, people from cultures that value individualism are more likely to openly express dissent from a decision, essentially expressing their disagreement with the group. Group members from collectivistic cultures are more likely to value relationships over the task at hand. Because of this, they also tend to value conformity and face-saving (often indirect) communication. This could manifest in behaviors such as establishing norms that include periods of socializing to build relationships before task-oriented communication like negotiations begin or norms that limit public disagreement in favor of more indirect communication that doesn't challenge the face of other group members or the group's leader. In a group composed of people from a collectivistic culture, each member would likely play harmonizing roles, looking for signs of conflict and resolving them before they become public.

Power distance can also affect group interactions. Some cultures rank higher on power-distance scales, meaning they value hierarchy, make decisions based on status, and believe that people have a set place in society that is fairly unchangeable. Group members from high-power-distance cultures would likely appreciate a strong designated leader who exhibits a more directive leadership style and prefer groups in which members have clear and assigned roles. In a group that is homogenous in terms of having a high-power-distance orientation, members with higher status would be able to openly provide information, and those with lower status may not provide information unless a higher status member explicitly seeks it from them. Low-power-distance cultures do not place as much value and meaning on status and believe that all group members can participate in decision making. Group members from low-power-distance cultures would likely freely speak their mind during a group meeting and prefer a participative leadership style.

How much meaning is conveyed through the context surrounding verbal communication can also affect group communication. Some cultures have a high-context communication style in which much of the meaning in an interaction is conveyed through context such as nonverbal cues and silence. Group members from high-context cultures may avoid saying something directly, assuming that other group members will understand the intended meaning even if the message is indirect. So if someone disagrees with a proposed course of action, he or she may say, "Let's discuss this tomorrow," and mean, "I don't think we should do this." Such indirect communication is also a face-saving strategy that is common in collectivistic cultures. Other cultures have a low-context communication style that places more importance on the meaning conveyed through words than through context or nonverbal cues. Group members from low-context cultures often say what they mean and mean what they say. For example, if someone doesn't like an idea, they might say, "I think we should consider more options. This one doesn't seem like the best we can do."

In any of these cases, an individual from one culture operating in a group with people of a different cultural orientation could adapt to the expectations of the host culture, especially if that person possesses a high degree of intercultural communication competence (ICC). Additionally, people with high ICC can also adapt to a group member with a different cultural orientation than the host culture. Even though these cultural orientations connect to values that affect our communication in fairly consistent ways, individuals may exhibit different communication behaviors depending on their own individual communication style and the situation.

Domestic Diversity and Group Communication

While it is becoming more likely that we will interact in small groups with international diversity, we are guaranteed to interact in groups that are diverse in terms of the cultural identities found within a single country or the subcultures found within a larger cultural group.

Gender stereotypes sometimes influence the roles that people play within a group. For example, the stereotype that women are more nurturing than men may lead group members (both male and female) to expect that women will play the role of supporters or harmonizers within the group. Since women have primarily performed secretarial work since the 1900s, it may also be expected that women will play the role of recorder. In both of these cases, stereotypical notions of gender place women in roles that are typically not as valued in group communication. The opposite is true for men. In terms of leadership, despite notable exceptions, research shows that men fill an overwhelmingly disproportionate amount of leadership positions. We are socialized to see certain behaviors by men as indicative of leadership abilities, even though they may not be. For example, men are often perceived to contribute more to a group because they tend to speak first when asked a question or to fill a silence and are perceived to talk more about task-related matters than relationally oriented matters. Both of these tendencies create a perception that men are more engaged with the task. Men are also socialized to be more competitive and self-congratulatory, meaning that their communication may be seen as dedicated and their behaviors seen as powerful, and that when their work isn't noticed they will be more likely to make it known to the group rather than take silent credit. Even though we know that the relational elements of a group are crucial for success, even in high-performance teams, that work is not as valued in our society as the task-related work.

Despite the fact that some communication patterns and behaviors related to our typical (and stereotypical) gender socialization affect how we interact in and form perceptions of others in groups, the differences in group communication that used to be attributed to gender in early group communication research seem to be diminishing. This is likely due to the changing organizational cultures from which much group work emerges, which have now had more than sixty years to adjust to women in the workplace. It is also due to a more nuanced understanding of gender-based research, which doesn't take a stereotypical view from the beginning as many of the early male researchers did. Now, instead of biological sex being assumed as a factor that creates inherent communication differences, group communication scholars see that men and women both exhibit a range of behaviors that are more or less feminine or masculine. It is these gendered behaviors, and not a person's gender, that seem to have more of an influence on perceptions of group communication. Interestingly, group interactions are still masculinist in that male and female group members prefer a more masculine communication style for task leaders and that both males and females in this role are more likely to adapt to a more masculine communication style. Conversely, men who take on social-emotional leadership behaviors adopt a more feminine communication style. In short, it seems that although masculine communication traits are more often associated with high status positions in groups, both men and women adapt to this expectation and are evaluated similarly (Haslett & Ruebush, 1999).

Other demographic categories are also influential in group communication and decision making. In general, group members have an easier time communicating when they are more similar than different in terms of race and age. This ease of communication can make group work more efficient, but the homogeneity may sacrifice some creativity. As we learned earlier, groups that are diverse (e.g., they have members of different races and generations) benefit from the diversity of perspectives in terms of the quality of decision making and creativity of output.

In terms of age, for the first time since industrialization began, it is common to have three generations of people (and sometimes four) working side by side in an organizational setting. Although four generations often worked together in early factories, they were segregated based on their age group, and a hierarchy existed with older workers at the top and younger workers at the bottom. Today, however, generations interact regularly, and it is not uncommon for an older person to have a leader or supervisor who is younger than him or her (Allen, 2011). The current generations in the US workplace and consequently in work-based groups include the following:

- **The Silent Generation.** Born between 1925 and 1942, currently in their mid-sixties to mid-eighties, this is the smallest generation in the workforce right now, as many have retired or left for other reasons. This generation includes people who were born during the Great Depression or the early part of World War II, many of whom later fought in the Korean War (Clarke, 1970).
- **The Baby Boomers.** Born between 1946 and 1964, currently in their late forties to mid-sixties, this is the largest generation in the workforce right now. Baby boomers are the most populous generation born in US history, and they are working longer than previous generations, which means they will remain the predominant force in organizations for ten to twenty more years.
- **Generation X.** Born between 1965 and 1981, currently in their early thirties to mid-forties, this generation was the first to see technology like cell phones and the Internet make its way into classrooms and our daily lives. Compared to previous generations, "Gen-Xers" are more diverse in terms of race, religious beliefs, and sexual orientation and also have a greater appreciation for and understanding of diversity.
- **Generation Y.** Born between 1982 and 2000, "Millennials" as they are also called are currently in their late teens up to about thirty years old. This generation is not as likely to remember a time without technology such as computers and cell phones. They are just starting to enter into the workforce and have been greatly affected by the economic crisis of the late 2000s,

experiencing significantly high unemployment rates.

The benefits and challenges that come with diversity of group members are important to consider. Since we will all work in diverse groups, we should be prepared to address potential challenges in order to reap the benefits. Diverse groups may be wise to coordinate social interactions outside of group time in order to find common ground that can help facilitate interaction and increase group cohesion. We should be sensitive but not let sensitivity create fear of "doing something wrong" that then prevents us from having meaningful interactions.

References

Adams, K., and Gloria G. Galanes, *Communicating in Groups: Applications and Skills*, 7th ed. (Boston, MA: McGraw-Hill, 2009), 220–21.

Allen, B. J., *Difference Matters: Communicating Social Identity*, 2nd ed. (Long Grove, IL: Waveland, 2011), 5.

Bormann, E. G., and Nancy C. Bormann, *Effective Small Group Communication*, 4th ed. (Santa Rosa, CA: Burgess CA, 1988), 112–13.

Clarke, G., "The Silent Generation Revisited," *Time*, June 29, 1970, 46.

Cragan, J. F., and David W. Wright, *Communication in Small Group Discussions: An Integrated Approach*, 3rd ed. (St. Paul, MN: West Publishing, 1991), 77–78.

de Bono, E., *Six Thinking Hats* (Boston, MA: Little, Brown, 1985).

Delbecq, A. L., and Andrew H. Ven de Ven, "A Group Process Model for Problem Identification and Program Planning," *The Journal of Applied Behavioral Science* 7, no. 4 (1971): 466–92.

Haslett, B. B., and Jenn Ruebush, "What Differences Do Individual Differences in Groups Make?: The Effects of Individuals, Culture, and Group Composition," in *The Handbook of Group Communication Theory and Research*, ed. Lawrence R. Frey (Thousand Oaks, CA: Sage, 1999), 133.

Napier, R. W., and Matti K. Gershenfeld, *Groups: Theory and Experience*, 7th ed. (Boston, MA: Houghton Mifflin, 2004), 292.

Osborn, A. F., *Applied Imagination* (New York: Charles Scribner's Sons, 1959).

Spranger, E., *Types of Men* (New York: Steckert, 1928).

Stanton, C., "How to Deliver Group Presentations: The Unified Team Approach," *Six Minutes Speaking and Presentation Skills*, November 3, 2009, accessed August 28, 2012, http://sixminutes.dlugan.com/group-presentations-unified-team-approach.

Thomas, D. C., "Cultural Diversity and Work Group Effectiveness: An Experimental Study," *Journal of Cross-Cultural Psychology* 30, no. 2 (1999): 242–63.

16.5 ENRICHMENT

Discussion Questions

1. What do you believe to be the major drawbacks and benefits to working with groups?
2. What advice would you give to a friend who was placed in an in-class group that was extremely adversarial and full of conflict?
3. In what situations would a designated leader be better than an emergent leader, and vice versa? Why?
4. Think of a leader that you currently work with or have worked with who made a strong (positive or negative) impression on you. Which leadership style did he or she use most frequently? Cite specific communication behaviors to back up your analysis.
5. Which of the task-related roles do you think has the greatest potential of going wrong and causing conflict within the group and why?
6. Which maintenance role do think you've performed the best in previous group experiences? How did your communication and behaviors help you perform the role's functions? Which maintenance role have you had the most difficulty or least interest in performing? Why?
7. Describe a situation in which you have witnessed a person playing one of the self-centered roles in a group. How did the person communicate? What were the effects? Now describe a situation in which you have witnessed a person playing one of the unproductive roles in a group. How did the person communicate? What were the effects?
8. Group communication researchers have found that heterogeneous groups (composed of diverse members) have advantages over homogenous (more similar) groups. Discuss a group situation you have been in where diversity enhanced your and/or the group's experience.
9. Why do you think people tasked with a group presentation (especially students) prefer to divide the parts up and have members work on them independently before coming back together and integrating each part? What problems emerge from this method? In what ways might developing a main presentation and then assigning parts to different speakers be better than the more divided method? What are the drawbacks to the main presentation method?

Activities

1. With your assigned small group members, use the small group problem-solving sequence to prepare a three to four minute speech to solve what the group perceives as a current problem at OSU. Begin by identifying a problem from your perspective, specifically focusing on how OSU could improve. As a group, (1) define the problem, (2) analyze the problem and define criteria, (3) generate possible solutions, (4) select what the group considers the best solution using the established criteria, and (5) provide information on how your group suggests implementing and assessing the solution. Explain why the group felt that the selected solution is better than the other possible solutions. Groups will have the opportunity to present their speech to the class.
2. In class, move to your problem-solving groups. Using the Nominal Group Technique described in section 16.4, come up with solutions to the problem of "roommate conflict." Your group can specify if it's over cleanliness, boundaries, communication difficulties, shared tasks, etc.
3. Write a few paragraphs summarizing your responses to the following questions and submit it to your instructor:

    - What communication competencies do you think are most important for a leader to have and why? How are men and women judged differently in regard to competencies? How do YOU rate in terms of the competencies you ranked as most important?

    - Who do you know who would be able to give you constructive feedback on your leadership skills? What do you think this person would say? You may want to consider actually asking the person for feedback.

4. With your assigned small group, identify the decision-making technique that would be best for each of the following scenarios. Explain your reasoning as well.

    - A professor asks her class to decide whether the final exam should be a notable presentation given in class or a comprehensive exam taken online.

    - A family needs to decide who will care for their aging father who is battling dementia or how they will pay for a nursing home with memory care.

- A group of co-workers must decide which person in their department should be nominated for Employee of the Year award, which includes an extra week of paid vacation as well as an all-expenses paid trip to Hawaii.

17 PERSUASIVE SPEAKING

Learning Objectives

- Define persuasion.
- Define ethos, logos, and pathos.
- Explain the barriers to persuading an audience.
- Construct a clear, reasonable proposition for a short classroom speech.
- Compose an outline for a well-supported persuasive speech using an appropriate organizational pattern such as Monroe's Motivated Sequence.
- Analyze the audience to determine appropriate emotional and personal appeals.

Key Terms

- **Cognitive Dissonance**
- **Ethos**
- **Logos**
- **Mental Dialogue**
- **Monroe's Motivated Sequence**
- **Pathos**

- **Persuasion**
- **Proposition**
- **Selective Exposure**
- **Target Audience**
- **Two-Tailed Arguments**

17.1 WHY PERSUADE?

"Speech is power. Speech is to persuade, to convert, to compel. It is to bring another out of his bad sense into your good sense." -Ralph Waldo Emerson

When your instructor announced on the syllabus or in class that you would be required to give a persuasive speech for this class, what was your reaction? "Oh, good, I've got a great idea," or, "Oh, no!"? For many people, there is something a little uncomfortable about the word "persuasion." It often gets paired with ideas of seduction, manipulation, force, lack of choice, or inducement as well as more positive concepts such as encouragement, influence, urging, or logical arguments. You might get suspicious if you think someone is trying to persuade you. You might not appreciate someone telling you to change your viewpoints. On the other hand, you might not think you have any beliefs, attitudes, values, or positions that are worth advocating for in front of an audience.

However, if you think of persuasion simply as a formal speech with a purpose of getting people to do something they do not want to do, then you will miss the value of learning persuasion and its accompanying skills of appeal, argument, and logic. Persuasion is something you do every day, in various forms. Convincing a friend to go see the latest movie instead of staying in to watch TV; giving your instructor a reason to give you an extension on an assignment (do not try that for this speech, though!); writing a cover letter and resume and going through an interview for a job—all of these and so many more are examples of persuasion. In fact, it is hard to think of life without the everyday give-and-take of persuasion.

You may also be thinking, "I've given an informative speech. What's the difference?" While this chapter will refer to all of the content of the preceding chapters as it walks you through the steps of composing your persuasive speech, there is a difference. Although your persuasive speech will involve information—probably even as much as in your informative speech—the key difference is the word "change." Think of it like this:

INFORMATION + CHANGE = PERSUASION

You will be using the information for the purpose of changing something. First, we try to change the audience's beliefs, attitudes, and actions, and second, possibly the context they act upon. In the next section we will investigate the persuasive act and then move on to the barriers to persuasion.

Pete's Persuasion Plans

As Pistol Pete sat at his desk, he began to contemplate the rhetorical techniques he could use to make his upcoming speech on strengthening the OSU community more persuasive. He understood the power of well-placed rhetoric in swaying an audience, and he was determined to use this to his advantage.

First, he thought about ethos, or establishing credibility and trust. He planned to draw on his role as the university's mascot to establish common ground with his audience. He would remind them of the times they've celebrated together, the victories they've shared, and the challenges they've faced, reinforcing his investment and dedication to the OSU community.

Next, he pondered on logos, the appeal to logic and reason. Here, he would include facts and statistics about the impact of a strong community on individuals and the university as a whole. He would cite studies showing the correlation between a sense of community and student success, both academically and personally.

Then, he considered pathos, which involves invoking emotions. Pistol Pete decided to share heartfelt stories of times when the OSU community came together in the face of adversity. He would speak of the resilience and unity he had witnessed, hoping to stir feelings of pride and a sense of belonging among his audience.

He also thought about employing the rhetorical technique of repetition for emphasis. He would repeatedly refer back to the idea of the "Cowboy spirit," reinforcing this central theme throughout his speech. He hoped this would underscore his message and make it more memorable.

Finally, Pete decided he would use a call to action as his conclusion. He wanted to empower his audience to contribute to strengthening the community. By giving them concrete steps they could take—like participating in university events, volunteering, or even simply checking in on their peers—he aimed to inspire active participation.

As he considered these rhetorical techniques, Pistol Pete felt more confident about crafting his speech. He understood that effective persuasion involves more than just presenting an argument; it requires building trust, appealing to both logic and emotion, emphasizing key points, and inspiring action. Armed with these techniques, he was ready to make a compelling case for the importance of a strong OSU community. What do you think of Pete's persuasion plans?

17.2 A DEFINITION OF PERSUASION

Persuasion can be defined in two ways, for two purposes. The first (Lucas, 2015) is "the process of creating, reinforcing, or changing people's beliefs or actions" (p. 306). This is a good, simple straightforward definition to start with, although it does not encompass the complexity of persuasion. This definition does introduce us to what could be called a "scaled" way of thinking about persuasion and change.

Think of persuasion as a continuum or line going both directions (see Figure 13.1). Your audience members, either as a group or individually, are sitting somewhere on that line in reference to your central idea statement, or what we are going to call a proposition in this chapter. In your speech you are proposing the truth or validity of an idea, one which the audience may not find true or acceptable. Sometimes the word "claim" is used for proposition or central idea statement in a persuasive speech, because you are claiming an idea is true or an action is valuable.

For example, your proposition might be, "The main cause of climate change is human activity." In this case you are not denying that natural forces, such as volcanoes, can affect the climate, but you are claiming that climate change is mainly due to pollution and other harmful things humans have done to the environment. To be an effective persuasive speaker, one of your first jobs after coming up with this topic would be to determine where your audience "sits" on the continuum described below.

+3 means strongly agree to the point of making lifestyle choices to lessen climate change (such as riding a bike instead of driving a car, recycling, eating certain kinds of foods, and advocating for government policy changes).

+2 means agree but not to the point of acting upon it or only acting on it in small ways.

+1 as mildly in favor of your proposition; that is, they think it's probably true but the issue doesn't affect them personally.

0 means neutral, no opinion, or feeling too uninformed to make a decision.

-1 means mildly opposed to the proposition but willing to listen to those with whom they disagree.

-2 means disagreement to the point of dismissing the idea pretty quickly.

-3 means strong opposition to the point that the concept of climate change itself is not even listened to or acknowledged as a valid subject .

Since everyone in the audience is somewhere on this line or continuum, persuasion in this case means moving them to the right, somewhere closer to +3. Thinking about persuasion this way has three values:

- You can visualize and quantify where your audience "sits."
- You can accept the fact that any movement toward +3 or to the right is a win.
- You can see that trying to change an audience from -3 to +3 in one speech is just about impossible. Therefore, you will be able to take a reasonable approach. In this case, if you knew most of the audience was at -2 or -3, your speech would be about the science behind climate change in order to open their minds to its possible existence. However, that audience is not ready to hear about its being caused mainly by humans or what action should be taken to reverse it.

Your instructor may have the class engage in some activity about your proposed topics in order for you to write your proposition in a way that it is more applicable to your audience. For example, you might have a group discussion on the topics or administer surveys to your fellow students. Some topics are so controversial and divisive that trying to persuade about them in class is inappropriate. Your instructor may forbid some topics or steer you in the direction of others.

You might also ask if it is possible to persuade to the negative, for example, to argue against something or try to move the audience to be opposed to something. In this case you would be trying to move your audience to the left on the continuum rather than to the right. Yes, it is possible to do so, but it might confuse the audience. Also, you might want to think in terms of phrasing your proposition so that it is favorable as well as reasonable. For example, "Elderly people should not be licensed to drive" could be replaced with "Drivers over the age of 75 in our state of should be required to pass a vision and health test every two years to renew their drivers' licenses." The first one is not clear (what is "elderly?"), reasonable (no license at all?), or positive (based on restriction) in approach. The second is specific, reasonable, doable, and positive.

It should also be added that the proposition is assumed to be controversial. By that is meant that some people in the audience disagree with your proposition or at least have no opinion; they are not "on your side." It would be foolish to give a speech when everyone in the audience totally agrees with you at the beginning of the speech. For example, trying to convince your classroom audience that attending college is a good idea is a waste of everyone's time since, for one reason or another, everyone in your audience has already made that decision. That is not persuasive.

Those who disagree with your proposition but are willing to listen could be called the **target audience**. These are the members of your audience on whom you are truly focusing your persuasion. At the same time, another cluster of your audience that is not part of your target audience are those who are extremely opposed to your position to the point that they probably will not give you a fair hearing. Finally, some members of your audience may already agree with you, although they don't know why.

To go back to our original definition, "the process of creating, reinforcing, or changing people's beliefs or actions," and each of these purposes implies a different approach. You can think of *creating* as moving an audience from 0 to +1, +2, or +3. You only really "create" something when it does not already exist, meaning the audience's attitude will be a 0 since they have no opinion. In creating, you have to first engage the audience that there is a vital issue at stake. Then you must provide arguments in favor of your claim to give the audience a basis for belief.

Reinforcing is moving the audience from +1 toward +3 in the hope that they take action (since the real test of belief is whether people act on it). In reinforcing, the audience already agrees with you but need steps and pushes (nudges) to make it action. *Changing* is moving from -1 or -2 to +1 or higher. In changing, you must first be credible, provide evidence for your side but also show why the audience's current beliefs are mistaken or wrong in some way.

However, this simple definition from Lucas, while it gets to the core of "change" that is inherent in persuasion, could be improved with some attention to the ethical component and the "how" of persuasion. For that purpose, let's look at Perloff's (2003) definition of persuasion:

> A symbolic process in which communicators try to convince other people to change their attitudes or behavior regarding an issue through the transmission of a message, in an atmosphere of free choice. (p. 8)

There are several important factors about this definition. First, notice that persuasion is symbolic, that is, uses language or other symbols (even graphics can be symbols), rather than force or other means. Second, notice that it is an attempt, not always fully successful. Third, there is an "atmosphere of free choice," in that the persons being persuaded can choose not to believe or act. And fourth, notice that the persuader is "trying to convince others to change." Modern psychological research has confirmed that the persuader does not change the audience directly. The processes that the human mind goes through while it listens to a persuasive message is like a silent, **mental dialogue** the audience is having with the speaker's ideas. The audience members as individuals eventually convince themselves to change based on the "symbols" used by the speaker.

Some of this may sound like splitting hairs, but these are important points. The fact that an audience has free choice means that they are active participants in their own persuasion and that they can choose whether the speaker is successful. This factor calls on the student speaker to be ethical and truthful. Sometimes students will say, "It is just a class assignment, I can lie in this speech," but that is not a fair or respectful way to treat your classmates.

Further, the basis of your persuasion is language; even though "a picture is worth a thousand words" and can help add emotional appeal to your speech, you want to focus on communicating through words. Also, Perloff's definition distinguishes between "attitude" and "behavior," meaning that an audience may be persuaded to think, to feel, or to act. Finally, persuasion is a process. Successful persuasion actually takes a while. One speech can be effective, but usually other messages influence the listener in the long run.

17.3 WHY IS PERSUASION HARD?

Persuasion is hard mainly because we have a bias against change. As much as we hear statements like "The only constant is change" or "Variety is the spice of life," the evidence from research and from our personal experience shows that, in reality, we do not like change. Recent research, for example, in risk aversion, points to how we are more concerned about keeping from losing something than with gaining something. Change is often seen as a loss of something rather than a gain of something else. Change is a step into the unknown, a gamble (Vedantam & Greene, 2013).

In the 1960s psychiatrists Thomas Holmes and Richard Rahe wanted to investigate the effect of stress on life and health. As explained on the Mindtools website:

> They surveyed more than 5,000 medical patients and asked them to say whether they had experience any of a series of 43 life events in the previous two years. Each event, called a Life Change Unit (LCU), had a different "weight" for stress. The more events the patient added up, the higher the score. The higher the score, and the larger the weight of each event, the more likely the patient was to become ill. (The Holmes and Rahe Stress Scale, 2015)

You can find the Holmes-Rahe stress scale on many websites. What you will find is that the stressful events almost all have to do with change in some life situations—death of a close family member (which might rate 100 LCUs), loss of a job, even some good changes like the Christmas holidays(12 LCUs). Change is stressful. We do not generally embrace things that bring us stress.

Additionally, psychologists have pointed to how we go out of our way to protect our beliefs, attitudes, and values. First, we selectively expose ourselves to messages that we already agree with, rather than those that confront or challenge us. This **selective exposure** is especially seen in choices of mass media that individuals listen to and read, whether TV, radio, or Internet sites. Not only do we selectively expose ourselves to information, we selectively attend to, perceive, and recall information that supports our existing viewpoints (referred to as selective attention, selective perception, and selective recall).

This principle led Leon Festinger (1957) to form the theory of **cognitive dissonance**, which states, among other ideas, that when we are confronted with conflicting information or viewpoints, we reach a state of dissonance. This state can be very uncomfortable, and we will do things to get rid of the dissonance and maintain "consonance." Ideally, at least for a public speaker, the dissonance is relieved or resolved by being persuaded (changed) to a new belief, attitude, or behavior. However, the easiest way to avoid dissonance is to not expose oneself to conflicting messages in the first place.

Additionally, as mentioned before, during a persuasive speech the audience members are holding a mental dialogue with the speaker or at least the speaker's content. They are putting up rebuttals or counter-arguments. These have been called *reservations* (as in the audience member would like to believe the speaker but has reservations about doing so). They could be called the "yeah-buts"—the audience members are saying in their minds, "Yeah, I see what you are arguing, but—". Reservations can be very strong, since, again, the bias is to be loss averse and not to change our actions or beliefs.

In a sense, the reasons *not* to change can be stronger than even very logical reasons to change. For example, you probably know a friend who will not wear a seatbelt in a car. You can say to your friend, "Don't you know that the National Highway Traffic Safety Administration (2009) says, and I quote, '1,652 lives could be saved and 22,372 serious injuries avoided each year on America's roadways if seat belt use rates rose to 90 percent in every state'?" What will your friend probably say, even though you have cited a credible source?

They will come up with some reason for not wearing it, even something as dramatic as "I knew a guy who had a cousin who was in an accident and the cop said he died because he was wearing his seatbelt." You may have had this conversation, or one like it. Their arguments may be less dramatic, such as "I don't like how it feels" or "I don't like the government telling me what to do in my car." For your friend, the argument for wearing a seat belt is not as strong as the argument against it, at least at this moment. If they are open-minded and can listen to evidence, they might experience cognitive dissonance and then be persuaded.

Solutions to the Difficulty of Persuasion

With these reasons for the resistance audience members would have to persuasion, what is a speaker to do? Here are some strategies.

Since change is resisted, we do not make many large or major changes in our lives. We do, however, make smaller, concrete, step-by-step or incremental changes in our lives every day. Going back to our scale in Figure 13.1, trying to move an audience from -3 to +2 or +3 is too big a move. Having reasonable persuasive goals is the first way to meet resistance. Even moving someone from -3 to -2 is progress, and over time these small shifts can eventually result in a significant amount of persuasion.

Secondly, a speaker must "deal with the reservations." First, the speaker must acknowledge they exist, which shows audience awareness, but then the speaker must attempt to rebut or refute them. In reality, since persuasion involves a mental dialogue, your audience is more than likely thinking of counter-arguments in their minds. Therefore, including a refutation section in your speech, usually after your presentation of arguments in favor of your proposition, is a required and important strategy.

However, there are some techniques for rebuttal or refutation that work better than others. You would not want to say, "One argument against my proposition is . . . , and that is wrong" or "If you are one of the people who believe this about my proposition, you are wrong." On the other hand, you could say that the reservations are "misconceptions," "myths," or "mistaken ideas" that are commonly held about the proposition.

Generally, strong persuasive speeches offer the audience what are called **two-tailed arguments**, which bring up a valid issue against your argument which you, as the speaker, must then refute. After acknowledging them and seeking to refute or rebut the reservations, you must also provide evidence for your refutation. Ultimately, this will show your audience that you are aware of both sides of the issue you are presenting and make you a more credible speaker. However, you cannot just say something like this:

> One common misconception about wearing seatbelts is that if the car goes off a bridge and is sinking in water, you would not be able to release the belt and get out. First, that rarely happens. Second, if it did, getting the seat belt unbuckled would be the least of your worries. You would have to know how to get out of the car, not just the seat belt. Third, the seat belt would have protected you from any head injuries in such a crash, therefore keeping you conscious and able to help anyone else in the car.

This is a good start, but there are some assertions in here that would need support from a reliable source, such as the argument that the "submerging in water" scenario is rare. If it has happened to someone you know, you probably would not think it is rare.

The third strategy is to keep in mind that since you are asking the audience to change something, they must view the benefits of the change as worth the stress of the change. If you do good audience analysis, you know they are asking, "What's in it for me?" What benefit or advantage or improvement would happen for the audience members?

If the audience is being persuaded to sign an organ donor card, which is an altruistic action that cannot benefit them in any way because they will be dead, what would be the benefit? Knowing others would have better lives, feeling a sense of contribution to the good of humanity, and helping medical science might be examples. The point is that a speaker should be able to engage the audience at the level of needs, wants, and values as well as logic and evidence.

17.4 TRADITIONAL VIEWS OF PERSUASION

In the fourth century BCE, Aristotle took up the study of the public speaking practices of the ruling class in Athenian society. For two years he observed the rhetoric of the men who spoke in the assembly and the courts. In the end, he wrote

Rhetoric to explain his theories about what he saw. Among his many conclusions, which have formed the basis of communication study for centuries, was the classification of persuasive appeals into ethos, logos, and pathos. Over the years, Aristotle's original understanding and definition of these terms have been refined as more research has been done.

Ethos

Ethos has come to mean the influence of speaker credentials and character in a speech. Ethos is one of the more studied aspects of public speaking. During the speech, a speaker should seek to utilize their existing credibility, based on the favorable things an audience already knows or believes about the speaker, such as education, expertise, background, and good character. The speaker should also improve or enhance credibility through citing reliable, authoritative sources, strong arguments, showing awareness of the audience, and effective delivery.

The word "ethos" looks very much like the word "ethics," and there are many close parallels to the trust an audience has in a speaker and their honesty and ethical stance. In terms of ethics, it goes without saying that your speech will be truthful. Another matter to consider is your own personal involvement in the topic. Ideally you have chosen the topic because it means something to you personally.

For example, perhaps your speech is designed to motivate audience members to take action against bullying in schools, and it is important to you because you work with the Boys and Girls Club organization and have seen how anti-bullying programs can have positive results. Sharing your own involvement and commitment is key to the credibility and emotional appeal (ethos and pathos) of the speech, added to the logos (evidence showing the success of the programs and the damage caused by bullying that goes unchecked). However, it would be wrong to manufacture stories of personal involvement that are untrue, even if the proposition is a socially valuable one.

Logos

Aristotle's original meaning for **logos** had philosophical meanings tied to the Greek worldview that the universe is a place ruled by logic and reason. Logos in a speech was related to standard forms of arguments that the audience would find acceptable. Today we think of logos as both logical and organized arguments and the credible evidence to support the arguments.

Pathos

In words like "empathy," "sympathy," and "compassion" we see the root word behind pathos. **Pathos**, to Aristotle, was using the emotions such as anger, joy, hate, desire for community, and love to persuade the audience of the rightness of a proposition. One example of emotional appeals is using strong visual aids and engaging stories to get the attention of the audience. Someone's just asking you to donate money to help homeless pets may not have a strong effect, but seeing the ASPCA's commercials that feature emaciated and mistreated animals is probably much more likely to persuade you to donate (add the music for full emotional effect).

Emotions are also engaged by showing the audience that the proposition relates to their needs. However, we recognize that emotions are complex and that they also can be used to create a smokescreen to logic. Emotional appeals that use inflammatory language—name-calling—are often unethical or at least counterproductive. Some emotions are more appropriate for persuasive speeches than others. Anger and guilt, for example, do have effectiveness but they can backfire. Positive emotions such as pride, sympathy, and contentment are usually more productive.

One negative emotion that is useful and that can be used ethically is fear. When you think about it, we do a number of things in life to avoid negative consequences, and thus, out of fear. Why don't we drive 100 miles an hour on the interstate? Fear of getting a ticket, fear of paying more for insurance, fear of a crash, fear of hurting ourselves or others. Fear is not always applicable to a specific topic, but research shows that mild fear appeals, under certain circumstances, are very useful. When using fear appeals, the speaker must:

- Prove the fear appeal is valid.
- Prove that it applies to the audience
- Prove that the solution can work
- Prove the solution is available to the audience

Without these "proofs," the audience may dismiss the fear appeal as not being real or not applying to them (O'Keefe, 2002). Mild and reasonable are the keys here. Intense, over-the-top fear appeals, especially showing gory photos, are often dismissed by the audience.

For example, a student gave a speech in one of our classes about flossing teeth. This may seem like an overdone subject, but in this case it wasn't. He used dramatic and disturbing photos of dental and gum problems but also proved that these photos of gum disease really did come from lack of flossing. He also showed the link between lack of flossing and heart disease. The solution to avoid the gum disease and other effects was readily available, and the student proved through his evidence that the solution of flossing regularly did work to avoid the disease. Fear appeals can be overdone, but mild ones supported by evidence are very useful.

Because we feel positive emotions when our needs are met and negative ones when our needs are not met, aligning your proposition with strong audience needs is part of pathos. One way to better understand human needs is by examining Maslow's hierarchy of needs. Students are often so familiar with it that they do not see its connection to real-life experiences. For example, safety and security needs, the second level on the hierarchy, is much broader than what many of us initially think. It includes:

- supporting the military and homeland security;
- buying insurance for oneself and one's family;
- having investments and a will;
- personal protection such as taking self-defense classes;
- policies on crime and criminal justice in our communities;
- buying a security system for your car or home; seat belts and automotive safety; or even
- having the right kind of tires on one's car (which is actually a viable topic for a speech).

The third level up in Maslow's hierarchy of needs, love and belongingness, deals with a whole range of human experiences, such as connection with others and friendship; involvement in communities, groups, and clubs; prioritizing family time; worship and connection to a faith community; being involved in children's lives; patriotism; loyalty; and fulfilling personal commitments.

In the speech outline at the end of the chapter about eliminating Facebook time, the speaker appeals to the three central levels of the hierarchy in her three points: safety and security from online threats, spending more time with family and friends in real time rather than online (love and belonging), and having more time to devote to schoolwork rather than on Facebook (esteem and achievement). Therefore, utilizing Maslow's hierarchy of needs works as a guide for finding those key needs that relate to your proposition, and by doing so, allows you to incorporate emotional appeals based on needs.

Up to this point in the chapter, we have looked at the goals of persuasion, why it is hard, and how to think about the traditional modes of persuasion based on Aristotle's theories. In the last section of this chapter, we will look at generating an overall organizational approach to your speech based on your persuasive goals.

17.5 THEORIES OF PERSUASIVE COMMUNICATION

There are many theories of persuasion in communication studies. Three of the main theories that are often associated with persuasion are the social judgment theory, cognitive dissonance theory, and the elaboration likelihood model.

Social Judgment Theory

Muzafer Sherif and Carl Hovland created social judgment theory in an attempt to determine what types of communicative messages and under what conditions communicated messages will lead to a change in someone's behavior (Sherif & Hovland, 1961). In essence, Sherif and Hovland found that people's perceptions of attitudes, values, beliefs, and behaviors exist on a continuum including latitude of rejection, latitude of noncommitment, and latitude of acceptance.

Latitudes of Judgments

Imagine that you are planning to persuade your peers to major in a foreign language in college. Some of the students in your class may disagree with you right off the bat, representing the latitude of rejection. Other students may think majoring in a foreign language is a great idea, representing the latitude of acceptance. Still others are really going to have no opinion either way, representing the latitude of noncommitment. Within each of these different latitudes there is a range of possibilities. For example, one of your listeners may be perfectly willing to accept the idea of minoring in a foreign language, but when asked to major or even double major in a foreign language, he or she may end up in the latitude of noncommitment or even rejection.

Not surprisingly, Sherif and Hovland found that persuasive messages are the most likely to succeed when they fall into an individual's latitude of acceptance. For example, if you are giving your speech on majoring in a foreign language, people who are in favor of majoring in a foreign language are more likely to positively evaluate your message, assimilate your advice into their own ideas, and engage in desired behavior. On the other hand, people who reject your message are more likely to negatively evaluate your message, not assimilate your advice, and not engage in desired behavior.

In an ideal world, we would always be persuading people who agree with our opinions, but that is not reality. Instead, we often find ourselves in situations where we are trying to persuade others to accept attitudes, values, beliefs, and behaviors with which they may not agree. To help us persuade others, what we need to think about is the range of possible attitudes, values, beliefs, and behaviors that exist. For example, in our foreign language case, we may see the following possible opinions from our audience members:

1. Complete agreement. All of us should major in foreign languages.
2. Strong agreement. I will not major in a foreign language, but I will double major in a foreign language.
3. Agreement in part. I will not major in a foreign language, but I will minor in a foreign language.
4. Neutral. While I think studying a foreign language can be worthwhile, I also think a college education can be complete without it. I really do not feel strongly one way or the other.
5. Disagreement in part. I will only take the foreign language classes required by my major.
6. Strong disagreement. I do not think I should have to take any foreign language classes.
7. Complete disagreement. Majoring in a foreign language is a complete waste of

a college education.

These seven possible opinions on the subject do not represent the full spectrum of choices, but give us various degrees of agreement with the general topic. Sherif and Hovland theorized that persuasion is a matter of knowing how great the discrepancy or difference is between the speaker's viewpoint and that of the audience. If the speaker's point of view is similar to that of audience members, then persuasion is more likely. If the discrepancy between the idea proposed by the speaker and the audience's viewpoint is too great, then the likelihood of persuasion decreases dramatically.

Discrepancy and Attitude Change

Furthermore, Sherif and Hovland (1961) predicted that there was a threshold for most people where attitude change was not possible and people slipped from the latitude of acceptance into the latitude of noncommitment or rejection. Figure 17.2 "Discrepancy and Attitude Change" represents this process. All the area covered by the left side of the curve represents options a person would agree with, even if there is an initial discrepancy between the speaker and audience member at the start of the speech. However, there comes a point where the discrepancy between the speaker and audience member becomes too large, which moves into the options that will be automatically rejected by the audience member. In essence, it becomes essential for you to know which options you can realistically persuade your audience to and which options will never happen. Maybe there is no way for you to persuade your audience to major or double major in a foreign language, but perhaps you can get them to minor in a foreign language.

Cognitive Dissonance Theory

In 1957, Leon Festinger proposed another theory for understanding how persuasion functions: cognitive dissonance theory (Festinger, 1957). Cognitive dissonance is an aversive motivational state that occurs when an individual entertains two or more contradictory attitudes, values, beliefs, or behaviors simultaneously. For example, maybe you know you should be working on your speech, but you really want to go to a movie with a friend. In this case, practicing your speech and going to the movie are two cognitions that are inconsistent with one another. The goal of persuasion is to induce enough dissonance in listeners that they will change their attitudes, values, beliefs, or behaviors.

Frymier and Nadler (2007) noted that for cognitive dissonance to work effectively there are three necessary conditions: aversive consequences, freedom of choice, and insufficient external justification. First, for cognitive dissonance to work, there needs to be a strong enough aversive consequence, or punishment, for not changing one's attitudes, values, beliefs, or behaviors. For example, maybe you are giving a speech on why people need to eat more apples. If your aversive consequence for not eating apples is that your audience will not get enough fiber, most people will simply not be persuaded, because the punishment is not severe enough. Instead, for cognitive dissonance to work, the punishment associated with not eating apples needs to be significant enough to change behaviors. If you convince your audience that without enough fiber in their diets they are at higher risk for heart disease or colon cancer, they might fear the aversive consequences enough to change their behavior.

The second condition necessary for cognitive dissonance to work is that people must have a freedom of choice. If listeners feel they are being coerced into doing something, then dissonance will not be aroused. They may alter their behavior in the short term, but as soon as the coercion is gone, the original behavior will reemerge. It is like the person who drives more slowly when a police officer is nearby but ignores speed limits once officers are no longer present. As a speaker, if you want to increase cognitive dissonance, you need to make sure that your audience does not feel coerced or manipulated, but rather that they can clearly see that they have a choice of whether to be persuaded.

The final condition necessary for cognitive dissonance to work has to do with external and internal justifications. External justification refers to the process of identifying reasons outside of one's own control to support one's behaviors, beliefs, and attitudes. Internal justification occurs when someone voluntarily changes a behavior, belief, or attitude to reduce cognitive dissonance. When it comes to creating change through persuasion, external justifications are less likely to result in change than internal justifications (Festinger & Carlsmith, 1959).

Elaboration Likelihood Model

The elaboration likelihood model created by Petty and Cacioppo (1986) has a continuum from high elaboration or thought to low elaboration or thought. For the purposes of Petty and Cacioppo's model, the term elaboration refers to the amount of thought or cognitive energy someone uses for analyzing the content of a message. High elaboration uses the central route and is designed for analyzing the content of a message. As such, when people truly analyze a message, they use cognitive energy to examine the arguments set forth within the message. In an ideal world, everyone would process information through this central route and actually analyze arguments presented to them. Unfortunately, many people often use the peripheral route for attending to persuasive messages, which results in low elaboration or thought. Low elaboration occurs when people attend to messages but do not analyze the message or use cognitive energy to ascertain the arguments set forth in a message.

For researchers of persuasion, the question then becomes: how do people select one route or the other when attending to persuasive messages? Petty and Cacioppo noted that there are two basic factors for determining whether someone centrally processes a persuasive message: ability and motivation. First, audience members must be able to process the persuasive message. If the language or message is too complicated, then people will not highly elaborate on it because they will not understand the persuasive message. Motivation, on the other hand, refers to whether the audience member chooses to elaborate on the message. Frymier and Nadler discussed five basic factors that can lead to high elaboration: personal relevance and personal involvement, accountability, personal responsibility, incongruent information, and need for cognition (Frymier & Nadler, 2007).

Personal Relevance and Personal Involvement

The first reason people are motivated to take the central route or use high elaboration when listening to a persuasive message involves personal relevance and involvement. Personal relevance refers to whether the audience member feels that he or she is actually directly affected by the speech topic. For example, if someone is listening to a speech on why cigarette smoking is harmful, and that listener has never smoked cigarettes, he or she may think the speech topic simply is not relevant. Obviously, as a speaker you should always think about how your topic is relevant to your listeners and make sure to drive this home throughout your speech. Personal involvement, on the other hand, asks whether the individual is actively engaged with the issue at hand: sends letters of support, gives speeches on the topic, has a bumper sticker, and so forth. If an audience member is an advocate who is constantly denouncing tobacco companies for the harm they do to society, then he or she would be highly involved (i.e., would engage in high elaboration) in a speech that attempts to persuade listeners that smoking is harmful.

Accountability

The second condition under which people are likely to process information using the central route is when they feel that they will be held accountable for the information after the fact. With accountability, there is the perception that someone, or a group of people, will be watching to see if the receiver remembers the information later on. We have all witnessed this phenomenon when one student asks the question "will this be on the test?" If the teacher says "no," you can almost immediately see the glazed eyes in the classroom as students tune out the information. As a speaker, it is often hard to hold your audience accountable for the information given within a speech.

Personal Responsibility

When people feel that they are going to be held responsible, without a clear external accounting, for the evaluation of a message or the outcome of a message, they are more likely to critically think through the message using the central route. For example, maybe you are asked to evaluate fellow students in your public speaking class. Research has shown that if only one or two students are asked to evaluate any one speaker at a time, the quality of the evaluations for that speaker will be better than if everyone in the class is asked to evaluate every speaker. When people feel that their evaluation is important, they take more responsibility and, therefore, are more critical of the message delivered.

Incongruent Information

Some people are motivated to centrally process information when it does not adhere to their own ideas. Maybe you are a highly progressive liberal, and one of your peers delivers a speech on the importance of the Tea Party movement in American politics. The information presented during the speech will most likely be in direct contrast to your personal ideology, which causes incongruence because the Tea Party ideology is opposed to a progressive liberal ideology. As such, you are more likely to pay attention to the speech, specifically looking for flaws in the speaker's argument.

Need for Cognition

The final reason some people centrally process information is because they have a personality characteristic called need for cognition. Need for cognition refers to a personality trait characterized by an internal drive or need to engage in critical thinking and information processing. People who are high in need for cognition simply enjoy thinking about complex ideas and issues. Even if the idea or issue being presented has no personal relevance, high need for cognition people are more likely to process information using the central route.

References

Festinger, L. (1957). *A theory of cognitive dissonance.* Row, Peterson, & Company.

Festinger, L., & Carlsmith, J. M. (1959). Cognitive consequences of forced compliance. *Journal of Abnormal and Social Psychology, 58,* 203–210.

Frymier, A. B., & Nadler, M. K. (2007). *Persuasion: Integrating theory, research, and practice.* Kendall/Hunt.

Petty, R. E., & Cacioppo, J. T. (1986). The elaboration likelihood model of persuasion. *Advances in Experimental Social Psychology, 19,* 123–205.

Sherif, M., & Hovland, C. I. (1961). *Social judgment: Assimilation and contrast effects in communication and attitude change.* Yale University Press.

17.6 CONSTRUCTING A PERSUASIVE SPEECH

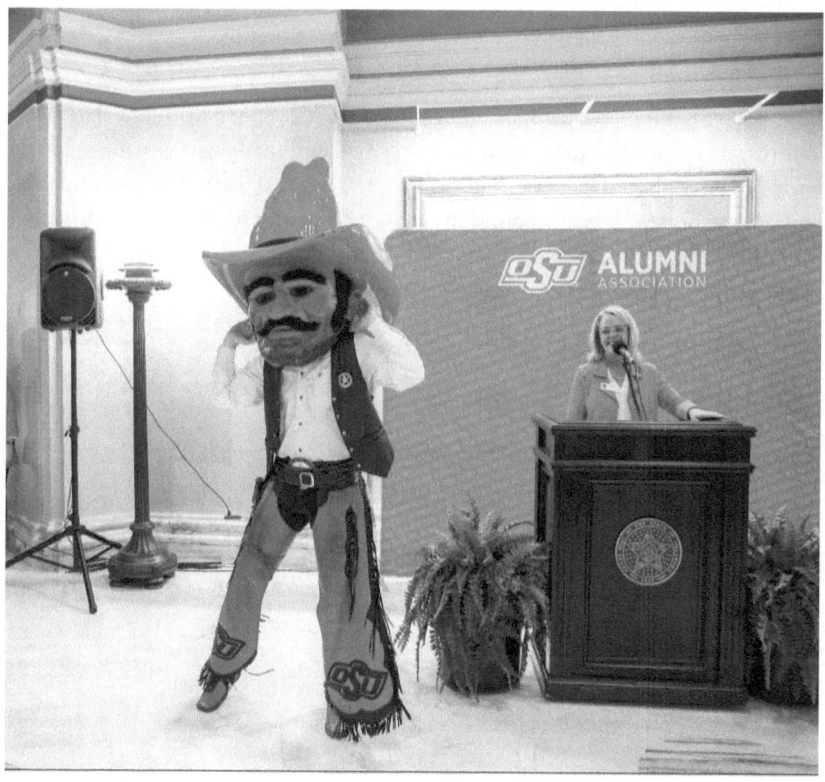

In a sense, constructing your persuasive speech is the culmination of the skills you have learned already. In another sense, you are challenged to think somewhat differently. While the steps of analyzing your audience, formulating your purpose and central idea, applying evidence, considering ethics, framing the ideas in appropriate language, and then practicing delivery will of course apply, you will need to consider some expanded options about each of these steps.

Formulating a Proposition

As mentioned before, when thinking about a central idea statement in a persuasive speech, we use the terms "proposition" or claim. Persuasive speeches have one of four types of propositions or claims, which determine your overall approach. Before you move on, you need to determine what type of proposition you should have (based on the audience, context, issues involved in the topic, and assignment for the class).

Proposition of Fact

Speeches with this type of proposition attempt to establish the truth of a statement. The core of the proposition (or claim) is not whether something is morally right and wrong or what should be done about the topic, only that a statement is supported by evidence or not. These propositions are not facts such as "the chemical symbol for water is H20" or "Barack Obama won the presidency in 2008 with 53% of the vote." Propositions or claims of fact are statements over which persons disagree and there is evidence on both sides, although probably more on one than the other. Some examples of propositions of fact are:

> Converting to solar energy can save homeowners money.
> John F. Kennedy was assassinated by Lee Harvey Oswald working alone.
> Experiments using animals are essential to the development of many life-saving medical procedures.
> Climate change has been caused by human activity.
> Granting tuition tax credits to the parents of children who attend private schools will perpetuate educational inequality.
> Watching violence on television causes violent behavior in children.
> William Shakespeare did not write most of the plays attributed to him.
> John Doe committed the crime of which he is accused.

Notice that in none of these are any values—good or bad—mentioned. Perpetuating segregation is not portrayed as good or bad, only as an effect of a policy. Of course, most people view educational inequality negatively, just as they view life-saving medical procedures positively. But the point of these propositions is to prove with evidence the truth of a statement, not its inherent value or what the audience should do about it. In fact, in some propositions of fact no action response would even be possible, such as the proposition listed above that Lee Harvey Oswald acted alone in the assassination of President Kennedy.

Propositions of Definition

This is probably not one that you will use in your class, but it bears mentioning here because it is used in legal and scholarly arguments. Propositions of definitions argue that a word, phrase, or concept has a particular meaning. There are various ways to define words, such as by negation, operationalizing, and classification and division. It may be important for you to define your terms, especially if you have a value proposition. Lawyers, legislators, and scholars often write briefs, present speeches, or compose articles to define terms that are vital to defendants, citizens, or disciplines. We saw a proposition of definition defended in the Supreme Court's 2015 decision to redefine marriage laws as applying to same-sex couples, based on arguments presented in court. Other examples might be:

> The Second Amendment to the Constitution does not include possession of automatic weapons for private use.
> Alcoholism should be considered a disease because…
> The action committed by Mary Smith did not meet the standard for first-degree murder.
> Thomas Jefferson's definition of inalienable rights did not include a right to privacy.

In each of these examples, the proposition is that the definition of these things (the Second Amendment, alcoholism, crime, and inalienable rights) needs to be changed or viewed differently, but the audience is not asked to change an attitude or action.

Propositions of Value

It is likely that you or some of your classmates will give speeches with propositions of value. When the proposition has a word such as "good," "bad," "best," "worst," "just," "unjust," "ethical," "unethical," "moral," "immoral," "beneficial," "harmful," "advantageous," or "disadvantageous," it is a proposition of value. Some examples include:

> Hybrid cars are the best form of automobile transportation available today.
> Homeschooling is more beneficial for children than traditional schooling.
> The War in Iraq was not justified.
> Capital punishment is morally wrong.
> Mascots that involve Native American names, characters, and symbols are demeaning.
> A vegan diet is the healthiest one for adults.

Propositions of value require a first step: defining the "value" word. If a war is unjustified, what makes a war "just" or "justified" in the first place? That is a fairly philosophical question. What makes a form of transportation "best" or "better" than another? Isn't that a matter of personal approach? For different people, "best" might mean "safest," "least expensive," "most environmentally responsible," "stylish," "powerful," or "prestigious." Obviously, in the case of the first proposition above, it means "environmentally responsible." It would be the first job of the speaker, after introducing the speech and stating the proposition, to explain what "best form of automobile transportation" means. Then the proposition would be defended with separate arguments.

Propositions of Policy

These propositions are easy to identify because they almost always have the word "should" in them. These propositions call for a change in policy or practice (including those in a government, community, or school), or they can call for the audience to adopt a certain behavior. Speeches with propositions of policy can be those that call for passive acceptance and agreement from the audience and those that try to instigate the audience to action, to actually do something immediately or in the long-term.

> Our state should require mandatory recertification of lawyers every ten years.
> The federal government should act to ensure clean water standards for all citizens.
> The federal government should not allow the use of technology to choose the sex of an unborn child.
> The state of Georgia should require drivers over the age of 75 to take a vision test and present a certificate of good health from a doctor before renewing their licenses.
> Wyeth Daniels should be the next governor of the state.
> Young people should monitor their blood pressure regularly to avoid health problems later in life.

As mentioned before, the proposition determines the approach to the speech, especially the organization. Also as mentioned earlier in this chapter, the exact phrasing of the proposition should be carefully done to be reasonable, positive, and appropriate for the context and audience. In the next section we will examine organizational factors for speeches with propositions of fact, value, and policy.

Organization Based on Type of Proposition

Organization for a Proposition of Fact

If your proposition is one of fact, you will do best to use a topical organization.

Essentially that means that you will have two to four discrete, separate arguments in support of the proposition. For example:

Proposition: Converting to solar energy can save homeowners money
I. Solar energy can be economical to install.
    A. The government awards grants.
    B. The government gives tax credits.
II. Solar energy reduces power bills.
III. Solar energy requires less money for maintenance.
IV. Solar energy works when the power grid goes down.

Here is a first draft of another outline for a proposition of fact:
Proposition: Experiments using animals are essential to the development of many life-saving medical procedures.

1. Research of the past shows many successes from animal experimentation.
2. Research on humans is limited for ethical and legal reasons.
3. Computer models for research have limitations.

However, these outlines are just preliminary drafts because preparing a speech of fact requires a great deal of research and understanding of the issues. A speech with a proposition of fact will almost always need an argument or section related to the "reservations," refuting the arguments that the audience may be preparing in their minds, their mental dialogue. So the second example needs revision, such as:

I. The first argument in favor of animal experimentation is the record of successful discoveries from animal research.
II. A second reason to support animal experimentation is that research on humans is limited for ethical and legal reasons.
III. Animal experimentation is needed because computer models for research have limitations.
IV. Many people today have concerns about animal experimentation.
    A. Some believe that all experimentation is equal.
        1. There is experimentation for legitimate medical research.
        2. There is experimentation for cosmetics or shampoos.
    B. Others argue that the animals are mistreated.
        1. There are protocols for the treatment of animals in experimentation.
        2. Legitimate medical experimentation follows the protocols.
    C. Some believe the persuasion of certain advocacy groups like PETA.
        1. Many of the groups that protest animal experimentation have extreme views.
        2. Some give untrue representations.

To complete this outline, along with introduction and conclusion, there would need to be quotations, statistics, and facts with sources provided to support both the pro-arguments in Main Points I-III and the refutation to the misconceptions about animal experimentation in Subpoints A-C under Point IV.

Organization for a Proposition of Value

A persuasive speech that incorporates a proposition of value will have a slightly different structure. As mentioned earlier, a proposition of value must first define the "value" word for clarity and provide a basis for the other arguments of the speech. The second or middle section would present the defense or "pro" arguments for the proposition based on the definition. The third section would include refutation of the counter arguments or "reservations." The following outline draft shows a student trying to structure a speech with a value proposition. Keep in mind it is abbreviated for illustrative purposes, and thus incomplete as an example of what you would submit to your instructor, who will expect more detailed outlines for your speeches.

 Proposition: Hybrid cars are the best form of automotive transportation available today.

I. Automotive transportation that is best meets three standards. (Definition)
 A. It is reliable and durable.
 B. It is fuel efficient and thus cost efficient.
 C. It is therefore environmentally responsible.

II. Studies show that hybrid cars are durable and reliable. (Pro-Argument 1)
 A. Hybrid cars have 99 problems per 100 cars versus 133 problem per 100 conventional cars, according to TrueDelta, a car analysis website much like Consumer Reports.
 B. J.D. Powers reports hybrids also experience 11 fewer engine and transmission issues than gas-powered vehicles, per 100 vehicles.

III. Hybrid cars are fuel-efficient. (Pro-Argument 2)
 A. The Toyota Prius gets 48 mpg on the highway and 51 mpg in the city.
 B. The Ford Fusion hybrid gets 47 mpg in the city and in the country.

IV. Hybrid cars are environmentally responsible. (Pro-Argument 3)
 A. They only emit 51.6 gallons of carbon dioxide every 100 miles.
 B. Conventional cars emit 74.9 gallons of carbon dioxide every 100 miles.
 C. The hybrid produces 69% of the harmful gas exhaust that a conventional car does.

V. Of course, hybrid cars are relatively new to the market and some have questions about them. (Reservations)
 A. Don't the batteries wear out and aren't they expensive to replace?

        1. Evidence to address this misconception.
        2. Evidence to address this misconception.
    B. Aren't hybrid cars only good for certain types of driving and drivers?
        1. Evidence to address this misconception.
        2. Evidence to address this misconception.
    C. Aren't electric cars better?
        1. Evidence to address this misconception.
        2. Evidence to address this misconception.

Organization for a Proposition of Policy

The most common type of outline organizations for speeches with propositions of policy is problem-solution or problem-cause-solution. Typically we do not feel any motivation to change unless we are convinced that some harm, problem, need, or deficiency exists, and even more, that it affects us personally. As the saying goes, "If it ain't broke, why fix it?" As mentioned before, some policy speeches look for passive agreement or acceptance of the proposition. Some instructors call this type of policy speech a "think" speech since the persuasion is just about changing the way your audience thinks about a policy.

On the other hand, other policy speeches seek to move the audience to do something to change a situation or to get involved in a cause, and these are sometimes called a "do" speech since the audience is asked to do something. This second type of policy speech (the "do" speech) is sometimes called a "speech to actuate." Although a simple problem-solution organization with only two main points is permissible for a speech of actuation, you will probably do well to utilize the more detailed format called Monroe's Motivated Sequence.

This format, designed by Alan Monroe (1951), who wrote a popular speaking textbook for many years, is based on John Dewey's reflective thinking process. It seeks to go in-depth with the many questions an audience would have in the process of listening to a persuasive speech. **Monroe's Motivated Sequence** involves five steps, which should not be confused with the main points of the outline. Some steps in Monroe's Motivated Sequence may take two points.

Monroe's Motivated Sequence

1. **Attention**. This is the introduction, where the speaker brings attention to the importance of the topic as well as his or her own credibility and connection to the topic. This step will include the thesis and preview. More specifically, sub steps under "Attention" are: the attention getter, the orientation (which

includes background information, self introduction, and thesis), the establishment of credibility, and the preview statement. The attention getter should be just that, a statement that pulls the audience into the presentation and makes them want to listen. The orientation serves to establish the topic and tone of the presentation. It includes any relevant background information, a self introduction, and a thesis statement. Establishing credibility can be done verbally or nonverbally. If the speaker has specific credentials or experience with the topic, they should tell the audience about it in the introduction. If they do not have specific credentials, speakers may establish credibility by dressing nice, making good eye contact, properly citing sources, and demonstrating confidence. The preview statement is the roadmap for the presentation. The preview will indicate the problem, that it has negative impacts, and the speaker has a solution. It is not recommended for speakers to give away the solution in most cases in the preview statement. Usually it's best to let the curiosity build in the audience and introduce it for the first time in the Satisfaction step.

2. **Need**. Here, the problem is defined and established with evidence. It is important to make the audience see the severity of the problem, and how it affects them, their family, or their community. The harm or need can be physical, financial, psychological, legal, emotional, educational, social, or a combination. Specific sub steps for "Need" are: problem statement, illustration, ramifications (side effects), pointing, and establishing clear criteria (features that should be in an acceptable solution). The problem statement should be a direct statement that focuses on a specific concern or problem that exists. The illustration is a real life instance of the problem's existence. Ramifications are the side effects and harms of the problem. Ramifications may be a variety of supporting materials that underscore the significance of the problem and its effects. Pointing is a clear, direct statement that draws a clear connection between the audience and the topic. As obvious as it may be, speakers need to explicitly tell the audience why they should care about this problem. Establishing criteria is a persuasive tactic. Speakers outline a few vital features that must be in a solution in order for it to be effective. The speaker does not give away the solution yet, but outlines criteria that a good solution should meet.

3. **Satisfaction**. A need calls for satisfaction in the same way a problem requires a solution. Not only does the speaker present the solution and describe it, but they must also defend that it works and will address the causes of the problem as well as the symptoms. Sub steps required for "Satisfaction" are: solution statement, explanation, theoretical demonstration, practical experience, and meeting objections. The solution statement is when the solution or advocated behavior is introduced. The explanation will detail the solution and how it will

work. The theoretical demonstration shows or explains how the solution meets the criteria from the Need step or has the necessary features. Practical experience presents an opportunity to show where the solution has proven successful. This may be in the form of a success story or specific instance where the solution made a difference. Meeting objections gives speakers an opportunity to respond to the potential reservations the audience may ben thinking while listening. It gives the speaker an opportunity to acknowledge what critics might be thinking and refute those concerns.

4. **Visualization.** This step looks to the future either positively or negatively. The speaker creates a hypothetical scenario that places each audience member in their own future. If positive, the benefits from enacting or choosing the solution are shown. If negative, the disadvantages of not doing anything to solve the problem are shown. There may be times when it is acceptable to skip this step, especially if time is limited. If a speaker wishes to use both positive and negative scenarios, it is known as the method of contrast. The purpose of visualization is to motivate the audience by revealing future benefits or through fear appeals by showing future harms. The conditions in this situation should be probable and must be a personalized scenario for the audience members. This step requires imagery and vivid language.

5. **Action.** The action step serves as the conclusion. In the action step, the goal is to give specific steps for the audience to take as soon as possible to move toward solving the problem. Whereas the satisfaction step explains the solution overall, the action step gives concrete, individual ways to begin making the solution happen. The sub steps of the "Action" step are: brakelight, summary, challenge/appeal, and note of finality. The brake light is the indication that a speaker is nearing the end. It is usually demonstrated by phrases like, "In conclusion,..." or "In summary,..." The summary statement should be a restatement of the preview statement, but in past tense. Instead of being vague about the solution, it is emphasized in the summary statement. The challenge or appeal is why this step is called Action. Speakers tell the audience what they should do individually as a result of hearing the speech. The note of finality serves as a strong closing statement. It leaves the audience reflecting on the presentation.

The more concrete you can make the action step, the better. Research shows that people are more likely to act if they know how accessible the action can be. For example, if you want students to be vaccinated against the chicken pox virus (which can cause a serious disease called shingles in adults), you can give them directions to and hours for a clinic or health center where vaccinations at a free or discounted price can be obtained.

In some cases for speeches of policy, no huge problem needs solving. Or, there is a problem, but the audience already knows about it and is convinced that the problem exists and is important. In those cases, a format called "comparative advantages" is used, which focuses on how one possible solution is better than other possible ones. The organizational pattern for this kind of proposition might be topical:

I. This policy is better because...
II. This policy is better because...
III. This policy is better because...

If this sounds a little like a commercial that is because advertisements often use comparative advantages to show that one product is better than another. Here is an example:

Proposition: Owning the Barnes and Noble Nook is more advantageous than owning the Amazon Kindle.
I. The Nook allows owners to trade and loan books to other owners or people who have downloaded the Nook software, while the Kindle does not.
II. The Nook has a color-touch screen, while the Kindle's screen is black and grey and non-interactive.
III. The Nook's memory can be expanded through microSD, while the Kindle's memory cannot be upgraded.

Building Upon Your Persuasive Speech's

Arguments

Once you have constructed the key arguments and order of points (remembering that if you use topical order, to put your strongest or most persuasive point last), it is time to be sure your points are well supported. In a persuasive speech, there are some things to consider about evidence.

First, your evidence should be from sources that the audience will find credible. If you can find the same essential information from two sources but know that the audience will find the information more credible from one source than another, use and cite the information from the more credible one. For example, if you find the same statistical data on Wikipedia and the U.S. Department of Labor's website, cite the U.S. Department of Labor (your instructor will probably not accept the Wikipedia site anyway). Audiences also accept information from sources they consider unbiased or indifferent. Gallup polls, for example, have been considered reliable sources of survey data because unlike some organizations, Gallup does not have a cause (political or otherwise) it is supporting.

Secondly, your evidence should be new to the audience. In other words, the best evidence is that which is from credible sources and the audience has not heard before (Reinard, 1988; McCroskey, 1969). If they have heard it before and discounted it, they will not consider your argument well supported. An example is telling people who smoke that smoking will cause lung cancer. Everyone in the U.S. has heard that thousands of times, but 14% of the population still smokes, which is about one in seven (Centers for Disease Control and Prevention, 2017)). Many of those who smoke have not heard the information that really motivates them to quit yet, and of course quitting is very difficult. Additionally, new evidence is more attention-getting, and you will appear more credible if you tell the audience something new (as long as you cite it well) than if you use the "same old, same old" evidence they have heard before.

Third, in order to be effective and ethical, your supporting evidence should be relevant and not used out of context, and fourth, it should be timely and not out of date.

After choosing the evidence and apportioning it to the correct parts of the speech, you will want to consider use of metaphors, quotations, rhetorical devices, and narratives that will enhance the language and "listenability" of your speech. Narratives are especially good for introduction and conclusions, to get attention and to leave the audience with something dramatic. You might refer to the narrative in the introduction again in the conclusion to give the speech a sense of finality.

Next you will want to decide if you should use any type of presentation aid for the speech. The decision to use visuals such as PowerPoint slides or a video clip in a persuasive speech should take into consideration the effect of the visuals on the audience and the time allotted for the speech (as well as your instructor's specifications). The charts, graphs, or photographs you use should be focused and credibly done.

One of your authors remembers a speech by a student about using seat belts (which is, by the way, an overdone topic). What made the speech effective in this case were photographs of two totaled cars, both of which the student had been driving when they crashed. The devastation of the wrecks and his ability to stand before us and give the speech because he had worn his seat belt was effective (although it didn't say much for his driving ability). If you wanted an audience to donate to disaster relief after an earthquake in a foreign country, a few photographs of the destruction would be effective, and perhaps a map of the area would be helpful. But in this case, less is more. Too many visual aids will likely distract from your overall speech claim.

Finally, since you've already had experience in class giving at least one major speech prior to this one, your delivery for the persuasive speech should be especially strong. Since delivery does affect credibility (Burgoon, Birk, & Pfau, 1990), you want to be able to connect visually as you make your appeals. You want to be physically involved and have vocal variety when you tell dramatic narratives that emphasize the human angle on your topic. If you do use presentation slides, you want them to work in seamlessly, using black screens when the visuals are not necessary.

Conclusion

Your persuasive speech in class, as well as in real life, is an opportunity to share a passion or cause that you believe will matter to society and help the audience live a better life. Even if you are initially uncomfortable with the idea of persuasion, we use it all the time in different ways. Choose your topic based on your own commitment and experience, look for quality evidence, craft your proposition so that it will be clear and audience appropriate, and put the finishing touches on it with an eye toward enhancing your logos, ethos, and pathos.

17.8 ENRICHMENT

Discussion Questions

1. How might your audience respond to your upcoming persuasive presentation? How will you adapt to their response?
2. What kind of misinformation exists about your persuasive topic? How will you clarify the truth in your presentation?
3. What does it mean to have strong ethos with your audience? What are some of the characteristics of ethos? How can you ensure the audience views you as someone with good character?
4. What did Aristotle mean by logos? What happens when there are logical missteps or fallacies in a speaker's message? Why might a speaker rely on faulty reasoning?
5. We know that pathos, according to Aristotle, is utilizing emotion to persuade the audience. While we know that emotions are involved in every decision we make, can you think of examples of speakers who are over-reliant on emotional appeals? How are their messages helped or hindered by the emotional appeals they choose?

Activities

1. With a group, decide on an app that is beneficial. As a group, create and present a persuasive sales pitch as to why your classmates should buy/download this app. After all the presentations, survey the class to see which apps they are most likely to download.
2. Choose a current TED Talk to watch and to analyze. Which rhetorical devices (ethos, logos, and pathos) did the speaker use to persuade the audience? Which one(s) seemed the most effectively used? In what ways could the speaker have improved their use of ethos, logos, and/or pathos?
3. In groups, your instructor will pass out a couple of different newspapers (*O'Colly, Stillwater News Press,* etc.). Each member should thumb through the newspaper and pay attention to articles they would be most likely to read outside of class. Have each group member share which articles stuck out and why. Each group should create a list of the article titles/subject matter. After the discussion, the group should go back to the newspaper and note which articles no one mentioned and which topics were most often stated by group members. Group members should then discuss how this may impact their

viewing selections, news gathering, social media feeds, etc. Each member should think about how selective exposure affects them personally.

18 SPECIAL OCCASION SPEAKING

Learning Objectives

- Recognize the differences between research-based speeches (informative and persuasive) and special occasion speeches.
- Identify the types of special occasion speeches.
- Use language to create emotional and evocative phrases.
- Describe the proper techniques for delivering a special occasion speech.

Key Terms

- **After Dinner Speeches**
- **Console**
- **Eulogy**
- **Hero Speech**
- **Lament**
- **Motivational Speech**
- **Religious Speech**
- **Roast**
- **Special Occasion Speech**
- **Speech of Acceptance**

- **Speech of Commencement**
- **Speech of Dedication**
- **Speech of Farewell**
- **Speech of Introduction**
- **Speech of Presentation**
- **Success Speech**
- **Survivor Speech**
- **Toast**

18.1 UNDERSTANDING SPECIAL OCCASION SPEAKING

"That's the second best introduction I ever received. The best was when the emcee didn't arrive and I had to do it myself." -Westside Toastmasters

Often the speaking opportunities life brings our way have nothing to do with specifically informing or persuading an audience; instead, we are commonly asked to speak during special occasions in our lives. Whether you are standing up to give a speech at an awards ceremony or a toast at a wedding, knowing how to deliver speeches in a variety of different contexts is the nature of special occasion speaking. In this chapter, we are going to explore what special occasion speeches are as well as a number of types of special occasion speeches ranging from humorous to somber.

In broad terms, a **special occasion speech** is a speech designed to designed to address and engage the context and audience's emotions on a specific occasion. Like informative or persuasive speeches, special occasion speeches should communicate a clear message, but the manner of speaking used is typically different. The word "special" in the term "special occasion speeches" is somewhat subjective in that while some speaking occasions truly are special occasions (e.g., a toast at a wedding, an acceptance speech at an awards banquet, a eulogy for a loved one), they can also be given at more mundane events, such as the hundreds of public relations speeches that big companies give every day. The goal of a special occasion speech is ultimately to stir an audience's emotions and make them feel a certain way in response to the situation or occasion.

Of all the types of speeches we are most likely to have to give during our lives, many of them will fall into the special occasion category. These often include speeches that are designed to inspire or motivate an audience to do something. These are, however, different from a traditional persuasive speech. Let's say you're the coach of your child's Little League team or a project leader at your work. In both cases you might find yourself delivering a speech to motivate and inspire your teams to do their best. You can imagine how giving a motivational speech like that would be different from a traditional persuasive speech, focusing on why a group of 50-somethings should change their investment strategy or a group of your peers to vote for a certain candidate for Student Senate.

To help us think through how to be effective in delivering special occasion speeches, let's look at four key ingredients: preparation, adaptation to the occasion, adaptation to the audience, and mindfulness about the time.

Be Prepared

First, and foremost, the biggest mistake you can make when standing to deliver a special occasion speech is to underprepare or simply not prepare at all. We've stressed the need for preparation throughout this text, so just because you're giving a wedding toast or a eulogy doesn't mean you shouldn't think through the speech before you stand up and speak out. If the situation is impromptu, even jotting some basic notes on a napkin is better than not having any plan for what you are going to say.

Adapt to the Occasion

Not all content is appropriate for all occasions. If you are asked to deliver a speech commemorating the first anniversary of a school shooting, then obviously using humor and telling jokes wouldn't be appropriate. But some decisions about adapting to the occasion are less obvious. Consider the following examples:

- You are the maid of honor giving a toast at the wedding of your younger sister.
- You are receiving a Most Valuable Player award in your favorite sport.
- You are a sales representative speaking to a group of clients after a mistake has been discovered.
- You are a cancer survivor speaking at a high school student assembly.

- You are giving an after-dinner speech to the members of your fraternity.

How might you adapt your message and speaking style to successfully convey your message to these various audiences?

Remember that being a competent speaker is about being both personally effective and socially appropriate. Different occasions will call for different levels of social appropriateness. One of the biggest mistakes entertaining speakers can make is to deliver one generic speech to different groups without adapting the speech to the specific occasion. In fact, professional speakers always make sure that their speeches are tailored for different occasions by getting information about the occasion from their hosts. When we tailor speeches for special occasions, people are more likely to remember those speeches than if we give a generic speech.

Adapt to Your Audience

Once again, we cannot stress the importance of audience adaptation enough in this text. Different audiences will respond differently to speech material, so the more you know about your audience, the more likely you'll succeed in your speech. One of our coauthors was once at a conference for teachers of public speaking. The keynote speaker stood and delivered a speech on the importance of public speaking. While the speaker was good and funny, the speech really fell flat. The keynote speaker basically told the public speaking teachers that they should take public speaking courses because public speaking is important. Right speech, wrong audience!

Be Mindful of the Time

The last major consideration for delivering special occasion speeches successfully is to be mindful of your time. Different speech situations have their own conventions and rules with regard to time. Acceptance speeches and toasts, for example, should be relatively short (typically under two minutes). A speech of introduction should be extremely brief—just long enough to tell the audience what they need to know about the person being introduced in a style that prepares them to appreciate that person's remarks. In contrast, commencement speeches, eulogies, and speeches to commemorate events can run ten to twenty minutes in length, depending on the context.

It's also important to recognize that audiences on different occasions will expect speeches of various lengths. For example, although it's true that graduation commencement speakers generally speak for ten to twenty minutes, the closer that speaker heads toward twenty minutes the more fidgety the audience becomes. To hold the audience's attention, a commencement speaker would do well to make the closing minutes of the speech the most engaging and inspiring portion of the speech. If you're not sure about the expected time frame for a speech, ask the person who has invited you to speak.

Pete's Wedding Toast

The text message came in as a complete surprise to Pistol Pete: "Hey Pete, our best man has lost his voice! We'd be honored if you could step in and give a toast at our wedding tonight."

Pete stared at his phone in disbelief. It was his good friend's wedding day, a momentous occasion, and he was being asked to give an impromptu speech with no preparation. The initial wave of panic washed over him, but as he took a deep breath, he realized that he needed to harness that cowboy spirit and take on the challenge.

Firstly, Pete focused on calming his nerves. He reminded himself that he wasn't there to impress anyone but to honor his friend's special day. This realization helped put things into perspective, allowing him to approach the task with a sense of calm.

Next, he brainstormed some key points he wanted to include in his toast. He thought about his friend, their shared memories, the friend's qualities, and the love between the couple. He noted these points down, making sure to include anecdotes and moments that reflected these aspects.

Understanding the importance of brevity in toasts, he decided to structure his speech simply: an introduction where he would express his honor at being asked to toast, a body where he'd share a short anecdote about his friend and the couple, and a conclusion that would contain his well-wishes and a toast to their future.

While content was key, Pete also knew that delivery mattered. He practiced his speech a few times, focusing on speaking clearly, maintaining a steady pace, and ensuring his voice conveyed the warmth and sincerity of his words. He made mental notes to make eye contact with his friend and the spouse, making the speech more personal and engaging.

Even though he was stepping in at the last minute, Pete was determined to add a touch of personalization to his toast. He decided to weave in a few friendly jokes and a quote about love that he knew would resonate with the couple.

As the wedding hour approached, Pete reminded himself that the most important thing was to speak from the heart. After all, he wasn't just Pistol Pete, the OSU mascot, but also a friend who was truly happy for the couple.

As he rose to his feet when the moment came, he took one last deep breath, reminded himself of the cowboy spirit within him, and delivered a heartfelt, charming toast that not only honored his friend's most important day but also brought smiles, laughter, and even a few joyful tears to the wedding party.

How would you respond if you were asked at the last minute to give a wedding toast?

18.2 TYPES OF SPECIAL OCCASION SPEECHES

Unlike the informative and persuasive speeches you were required to give, special occasion speeches are much broader and allow for a wider range of topics, events, and approaches to be employed. However, while the following list of special occasion speeches is long, your instructor will have specific types of special occasion speeches that you will be allowed (or required) to do for class. Since you are like to give many special occasion speeches in your life, we want to cover everything you might need to know to give a good one.

Speeches of Introduction

The first type of special occasion speech is the **speech of introduction**, which is a mini-speech given by the host of a ceremony that introduces another speaker and their speech. Few things are worse than when the introducer of a speaker stands up and says, "This is Wyatt Ford. He's going to talk about stress." While we did learn the speaker's name and the topic, the introduction falls flat. Audiences won't be the least bit excited about listening to Wyatt's speech.

Just like any other speech, a speech of introduction should be a complete speech and have a clear introduction, body, and conclusion—and you should try to do it all in under two minutes. This brings up another "few things are worse" scenario: an introductory speaker who rambles on for too long or who talks about himself or herself instead of focusing on the person being introduced.

For an introduction, think of a hook that will make your audience interested in the upcoming speaker. Did you read a news article related to the speaker's topic? Have you been impressed by a presentation you've heard the speaker give in the past? You need to find something that can grab the audience's attention and make them excited about hearing the main speaker.

The body of your speech of introduction should be devoted to telling the audience about the speaker's topic, why the speaker is qualified, and why the audience should listen (notice we now have our three main points). First, tell your audience in general terms about the overarching topic of the speech. Most of the time as an introducer, you'll only have a speech title and maybe a paragraph of information to help guide this part of your speech. That's all right. You don't need to know all the ins and outs of the main speaker's speech; you just need to know enough to whet the audience's appetite. Next, you need to tell the audience why the speaker is a credible presenter on the topic. Has the speaker written books or articles on the subject? Has the speaker had special life events that make him or her qualified? Lastly, you need to briefly explain to the audience why they should care about the upcoming speech. The outline can be adjusted; for example, you can give the biographical information first, but these three areas should be covered.

The final part of a good introduction is the conclusion, which is generally designed to welcome the speaker to the platform. Many introducers will conclude by saying something like, "I am looking forward to hearing how Wyatt Ford's advice and wisdom can help all of us today, so please join me in welcoming Dr. Wyatt Ford." At this point, you as the person introducing the speaker are "handing off" the speaking duties to someone else, so it is not uncommon to end your speech of introduction by clapping as the speaker comes on stage or shaking the speaker's hand.

Speeches of Presentation

The second type of special occasion speech is the **speech of presentation**. A speech of presentation is a brief speech given to accompany a prize or honor. Speeches of presentation can be as simple as saying, "This year's recipient of the Lavache Public Speaking prize is Ryann Curley," or could last up to five minutes as the speaker explains why the honoree was chosen for the award. An interesting example of a speech presenting an award is this one by Zoe Saldana for J.J. Abrams (https://www.youtube.com/watch?v=x03cGSszr8Q).

When preparing a speech of presentation, it's always important to ask how long the speech should be. Once you know the time limit, then you can set out to create the speech itself. First, you should explain what the award or honor is and why the presentation is important. Second, you can explain what the recipient has accomplished in order for the award to be bestowed. Did the person win a race? Did the person write an important piece of literature? Did the person mediate conflict? Whatever the recipient has done, you need to clearly highlight his or her work. Lastly, if the race or competition was conducted in a public forum and numerous people didn't win, you may want to recognize those people for their efforts as well. While you don't want to steal the show away from winner, you may want to highlight the work of the other competitors or nominees.

Speeches of Acceptance

The complement to a speech of presentation is the **speech of acceptance**. The speech of acceptance is a speech given by the recipient of a prize or honor. There are three typical components of a speech of acceptance: 1) thank the givers of the award or honor, 2) thank those who helped you achieve your goal, and 3) put the award or honor into perspective. First, you want to thank the people who have given you the award or honor and possibly those who voted for you. We see this done every year during the Oscars, "First, I'd like to thank the Academy and all the Academy voters."

Second, you want to give credit to those who helped you achieve the award or honor. No person accomplishes things in life on his or her own. We all have family members, friends, and colleagues who support us and help us achieve what we do in life, and a speech of acceptance is a great time to graciously recognize those individuals. Lastly, put the award in perspective. Tell the people listening to your speech why the award is meaningful to you. If you know you are up for an award, the odds of your winning are high. In order to avoid blubbering through an acceptance speech, have one ready. A good rule to remember is: Be thankful, be gracious, be short.

Speeches of Dedication

A fourth special occasion speech is the **speech of dedication**. A speech of dedication is delivered when a new store opens, a building is named after someone, a plaque is placed on a wall, a new library is completed, and so on. These speeches are designed to highlight the importance of the project and possibly those to whom the project has been dedicated.

When preparing a speech of dedication, start by explaining how you are involved in the dedication. If the person to whom the dedication is being made is a relative, tell the audience about your relationship and your relative's accomplishments. Second, you want to explain what is being dedicated. If the dedication is a new building or a pre-existing building, you want to explain the importance of the structure. You should then explain who was involved in the project.

If the project is a new structure, talk about the people who built the structure or designed it. If the project is a pre-existing structure, talk about the people who put together and decided on the dedication. Lastly, explain why the structure is important for the community in which it is located. If the dedication is for a new store, talk about how the store will bring in new jobs and new shopping opportunities. If the dedication is for a new wing of a hospital, talk about how patients will be served and the advances in medicine the new wing will provide the community.

Toasts

At one time or another, almost everyone is going to be asked to deliver a **toast**. A toast is a speech designed to congratulate, appreciate, or remember. First, toasts can be delivered for the purpose of congratulating someone for an honor, a new job, or getting married. You can also toast someone to show your appreciation for something he or she has done. Lastly, we toast people to remember them and what they have accomplished.

When preparing a toast, the first goal is always to keep your remarks brief. Toasts are generally given during the middle of some kind of festivities (e.g., wedding, retirement party, farewell party), and you don't want your toast to take away from those festivities for too long. Second, the goal of a toast is to focus attention on the person or persons being toasted—not on the speaker.

As such, while you are speaking, you need to focus your attention toward the people being toasted, both by physically looking at them and by keeping your message about them. You should also avoid any inside jokes between you and the people being toasted because toasts are public and should be accessible for everyone who hears them. To conclude a toast, simply say something like, "Please join me in recognizing Gina for her achievement" and lift your glass. When you lift your glass, this will signal to others to do the same and then you can all take a drink, which is the end of your speech.

Roasts

A **roast** is a very interesting and peculiar speech because it is designed to both praise and good-naturedly insult a person being honored. Because of this combination of purposes, it is not hard to argue that the roast is probably a challenging type of speeches to write given the difficult task of simultaneously praising and insulting the person. Generally, roasts are given at the conclusion of a banquet in honor of someone's life achievements. The television station Comedy Central has been conducting roasts of various celebrities for a few years, and if you've ever watched one, you know that the "roasters" say some harsh things about the "roastees" even though they are friends.

During a roast, the roaster will stand behind a lectern while the roastee is seated somewhere where he or she is clearly on display for the audience to see, thus allowing the audience to take in his or her reactions. Since half the fun of a good roast is watching the roastee's reactions during the roast, it's important to have the roastee clearly visible to the audience.

How does one prepare for a roast? First, you want to really think about the person who is being roasted. Does he or she have any strange habits or amusing stories in their past that you can discuss? When you think through these questions, you want to make sure that you cross anything off your list that is truly private information or will really hurt the person. The goal of a roast is to poke at him, not massacre him.

Second, when selecting which aspects to poke fun at, you need to make sure that the items you choose are widely known by your audience. Roasts work when the majority of people in the audience can relate to the jokes being made. If you have an inside joke with the roastee, bringing it up during roast may be great fun for the two of you, but it will leave your audience unimpressed. Lastly, end on a positive note. While the jokes are definitely the fun part of a roast, you should leave the roastee and the audience knowing that you truly do care about and appreciate the person.

Eulogies

A **eulogy** is a speech given in honor of someone who has died (Don't confuse "eulogy" with "elegy," a poem or song of mourning). Not to sound depressing, but since everyone who is alive will someday die, the chance of your being asked to give a eulogy someday for a friend or family member is significant. However, when the time comes to deliver a eulogy, it's good to know what you're doing and to adequately prepare your remarks.

When preparing a eulogy, first you need to know as much information about the deceased as possible. The more information you have about the person, the more personal you can make the eulogy. While you can rely on your own information if you were close to the deceased, it is always a good idea to ask friends and relatives of the deceased for their memories, as these may add important facets that may not have occurred to you. Of course, if you were not very close to the deceased, you will need to ask friends and family for information. Second, although eulogies are delivered on the serious and sad occasion of a funeral or memorial service for the deceased, it is very helpful to look for at least one point to be lighter or humorous. In some cultures, in fact, the friends and family attending the funeral expect the eulogy to be highly entertaining and amusing.

Take, for example, Tom Arnold's eulogy of *Saturday Night Live* actor Chris Farley. During his speech at Farley's funeral, Arnold noted, "Chris was concerned about his size, and so he made sure that all of us who knew him well saw him naked at least once" (Glionna, 1998). Picturing the heavy-set comedian naked surely brought some humor to the somber proceedings, but Arnold knew Farley (and his audience) well enough to know that the story would be appropriate.

Knowing the deceased and the audience is vital when deciding on the type and amount of humor to use in a eulogy. It's doubtful statements like Tom Arnold's would fit many eulogies. But it would be appropriate to tell a funny story about Uncle Joe's love for his rattletrap car or Aunt Mary's love of tacky Christmas sweaters. Ultimately, the goal of the humor or lighter aspects of a eulogy is to relieve the tension that is created by the serious nature of the occasion.

If you are ever asked to give a eulogy, that means you were probably close to the deceased and are experiencing shock, sadness, and disbelief at your loved one's passing. The last thing that you will want to do (or be in a mental state to do) is figure out how to structure your eulogy. To that end, here are three parts of a eulogy (i.e. main points) you can use to write one without worrying about being original with structure or organizational patterns: praise, lament, and consolation.

Praise

The first thing you want to do when remembering someone who has passed away is remind the audience what made that person so special. So you will want to praise them and their accomplishments. This can include notable achievements (being an award winner; helping with charities), personal qualities ("she was always willing to listen to your problems and help in any way she could"), or anecdotes and stories (being a great mother; how she drove to college to visit you when you were homesick).

Lament

The second thing you want to do in a eulogy is to **lament** the loss. To lament means to express grief or sorrow, which is what everyone at a funeral has gathered to do. You will want to acknowledge that everyone is sad and that the deceased's passing will be difficult to get through. Here you might mention all the things that will no longer happen as a result of the death. "Now that Grandpa is gone, there won't be any more Sunday dinners where he cooks chicken on the grill or bakes his famous macaroni and cheese."

Console

The final step (or main point) in a eulogy is to console the audience, or to offer comfort in a time of grief. What you must remember (and many people often forget) is that a eulogy is not a speech for the person who has died; it is a speech for the people who are still living to try to help them deal with the loss. You will want to end your eulogy on a positive note. Offer some hope that someday, things will get better. If the deceased was a religious person, this is where you might want to incorporate elements of that belief system. Some examples would include ideas like:

> "Jim has gone home to be with the Lord and is looking down on us fondly today."
> "We may miss Aunt Linda deeply, but our memories of her will live on forever, and her impact on this world will not soon be forgotten."

Using the Praise-Lament-Console format for eulogies gives you a simple system where you can fill in the sections with 1) why was the person good, 2) why you will miss him or her, and 3) how you and the audience will get through this loss. It sometimes also helps to think of the three points in terms of Past-Present-Future: you will praise the deceased for what he did when he was alive (the past), lament the loss you are feeling now (the present), and console your audience by letting them know that things will be all right (the future).

With regard to a eulogy you might give in class, you generally have two options for how to proceed: you can eulogize a real person who has passed away, or you can eulogize a fictional character (if your instructor permits that). If you give a eulogy in class on someone in your life who has actually passed away, be aware that it is very common for students to become emotional and have difficulty giving their speech. Even though you may have been fine practicing at home and feel good about giving it, the emotional impact of speaking about a deceased loved one in front of others can be surprisingly powerful. Conversely, if you give a eulogy on a fictional character, you must treat your classroom assignment eulogy as you would a real eulogy. You wouldn't make fun of or trivialize someone's life at an actual funeral, so don't do that in your eulogy for a serious speech assignment either.

Speeches of Farewell

A **speech of farewell** allows someone to say good-bye to one part of his or her life as he or she is moving on to the next part of life. Maybe you've accepted a new job and are leaving your current job, or you're graduating from college and entering the work force. Periods of transition are often marked by speeches of farewell. When preparing a speech of farewell, the goal should be to thank the people in your current position and let them know how much you appreciate them as you make the move to your next position in life. Second, you want to express to your audience how much the experience has meant to you. A farewell speech is a time to commemorate and think about the good times you've had. As such, you should avoid negativity during this speech. Lastly, you want to make sure that you end on a high note.

Speeches for Commencements

A **speech of commencement** (or, as it is more commonly known, a "commencement speech") is designed to recognize and celebrate the achievements of a graduating class or other group of people. These typically take place at graduation ceremonies. Nearly every one of us has sat through commencement speeches at some point in our lives. And if you're like us, you've heard good ones and bad ones. Numerous celebrities and politicians have been asked to deliver commencement speeches at colleges and universities. A famous and well-thought-out commencement speech was given by famed Harry Potter author J. K. Rowling at Harvard University in 2008 (found at http://www.youtube.com/watch?v=nkREt4ZB-ck). Rowling's speech has the perfect balance of humor and inspiration, which are two of the main ingredients of a great commencement speech.

If you're ever asked to deliver a commencement speech, there are some key points to think through when deciding on your speech's content.

- If there is a specific theme for the graduation, make sure that your commencement speech addresses that theme. If there is no specific theme, come up with one for your speech. Some common commencement speech themes are commitment, competitiveness, competence, confidence, decision making, discipline, ethics, failure (and overcoming failure), faith, generosity, integrity, involvement, leadership, learning, persistence, personal

improvement, professionalism, reality, responsibility, and self-respect.
- Talk about your life and how graduates can learn from your experiences to avoid pitfalls or take advantages of life. How can your life inspire the graduates in their future endeavors?
- Make the speech humorous. Commencement speeches should be entertaining and make an audience laugh.
- Be brief! Nothing is more painful than a commencement speaker who drones on and on. Remember, the graduates are there to get their diplomas; their families are there to watch the graduates walk across the stage.
- Remember, while you may be the speaker, you've been asked to impart wisdom and advice for the people graduating and moving on with their lives, so keep it focused on them.
- Place the commencement speech into the broader context of the graduates' lives. Show the graduates how the advice and wisdom you are offering can be utilized to make their own lives better.

Overall, it's important to make sure that you have fun when delivering a commencement speech. Remember, it's a huge honor and responsibility to be asked to deliver a commencement speech, so take the time to really think through and prepare your speech.

After-Dinner Speeches

After-dinner speeches are humorous speeches that make a serious point. These speeches get their name from the fact that they historically follow a meal of some kind. After-dinner speakers are generally asked to speak (or hired to speak) because they have the ability both to speak effectively and to make people laugh. First and foremost, after-dinner speeches are speeches and not stand-up comedy routines. All the basic conventions of public speaking previously discussed in this text apply to after-dinner speeches, but the overarching goal of these speeches is to be entertaining and to create an atmosphere of amusement.

After-dinner speaking is an extremely difficult type of speaking to do well because it is an entertaining speech that depends on the successful delivery of humor. People train for years to develop comic timing, or the verbal and nonverbal delivery used to enhance the comedic value of a message. But after-dinner speaking is difficult, not impossible. What follows is the method we recommend for developing a successful after-dinner speech.

First, use all that you have learned about informative or persuasive speeches to prepare a real informative or persuasive speech roughly two-thirds the length of what the final speech will become. That is, if you're going to be giving a ten-minute speech, then your "real" informative or persuasive speech should be six or seven minutes in length. This is the "serious message" portion of the speech where you will try to make a point of educating your audience.

Next, go back through the speech and look for opportunities to insert humorous remarks. Once you've looked through your speech and examined places for verbal humor, think about any physical humor or props that would enhance your speech. Physical humor is great if you can pull it off without being self-conscious. One of the biggest mistakes any humorist makes is to become too aware of what his or her body is doing because it's then harder to be free and funny. As for props, after-dinner speakers have been known to use everything from oversized inflatable baseball bats to rubber clown noses. The goal for a funny prop is that it adds to the humor of the speech without distracting from its message.

Last, and probably most important, try the humor out on real, live people. This is important for three reasons. First, the success of humor depends heavily on delivery, and especially timing in delivery. You will need practice to polish your delivery so that your humor comes across. If you can't make it through one of your jokes without cracking up, you will need to either incorporate the self-crackup into your delivery or forgo using that joke.

Just because you find something unbelievably funny in your head doesn't mean that it will make anyone else laugh. Often, humor that we have written down on paper just doesn't translate when orally presented. You may have a humorous story that you love reading on paper, but find that it just seems to drone on once you start telling it out loud. Furthermore, remember there is a difference between written and verbal language, and this also translates to how humor is interpreted. Third, you need to make sure the humor you choose will be appropriate for a specific audience. What one audience finds funny another may find offensive. Humor is the double-edged sword of public speaking. On one side, it is an amazing and powerful speaking tool, but on the other side, few things will alienate an audience more than offensive humor. If you're ever uncertain about whether a piece of humor will offend your audience, don't use it.

So you may now be asking, "What kind of topics are serious that I can joke about?" The answer to that, like the answer to most everything else in the book, is dependent on your audience and the speaking situation, which is to say any topic will work, while at the same time you need to be very careful about how you choose your topic.

Take, for example, the experience one of your authors had while he was attending a large university. One of the major problems that any large university faces is parking: the ratio of parking spaces to students at some of these schools can be 1:7 (one parking space for every seven students). In addressing this topic at a banquet, a student gave an after-dinner speech that addressed the problem of the lack of student parking. To do so, he camouflaged his speech as a faux-eulogy (fake eulogy) for the yellow and black board on the parking lot gates (see Image 15.1) that was constantly and consistently driven through by students wanting to access restricted parking. The student personified the board by noting how well it had done its job and lamented that it would never get to see its little toothpick children grow up to guard the White House. But underneath the humor incorporated into the speech was a serious message: this wouldn't keep happening if adequate parking was provided for students on campus.

Motivational Speeches

A **motivational speech** is designed not only to make an audience experience emotional arousal (fear, sadness, joy, excitement) but also to motivate the audience to do something with that emotional arousal. Whereas a traditional persuasive speech may want listeners to purchase product X or agree with idea Y, a motivational speech helps to inspire people in a broader fashion, often without a clearly articulated end result in mind. As such, motivational speaking is a highly specialized form of persuasive speaking commonly delivered in schools, businesses, religious houses of worship, and club or group contexts. The Toastmasters International Guide to Successful Speaking (Slutsky & Aun, 1997) lists four types of motivational speeches: hero, survivor, religious, and success.

The **hero speech** is a motivational speech given by someone who is considered a hero in society (e.g., military speakers, political figures, and professional athletes). Just type "motivational speech" into YouTube and you'll find many motivational speeches given by individuals who can be considered heroes or role models.

The **survivor speech** is a speech given by someone who has survived a personal tragedy or who has faced and overcome serious adversity. In the following clip, cancer survivor Becky M. Olsen discusses being a cancer survivor (http://www.youtube.com/watch?v=zuo1u_C9_3g). Becky Olsen goes all over the country talking with and motivating cancer survivors to beat the odds.

The **religious speech** is fairly self-explanatory; it is designed to incorporate religious ideals into a motivational package to inspire an audience into thinking about or changing aspects of their religious lives. The final type of motivational speech is the success speech, which is given by someone who has succeeded in some aspect of life and is giving back by telling others how they too can be successful.

Summary

As stated at the beginning of this section, you will almost certainly be limited by your professor with regards to which of these types of speeches you can give for your special occasion speech in class, but it is not unrealistic to think that you will be called upon at various points in your life to give one or more of these speeches. Knowing the types and basic structures will help when those moments arise.

18.3 SPECIAL OCCASION LANGUAGE

Special occasion speaking is so firmly rooted in the use of good language that it makes sense to address it here. More than any other category of speech, the special occasion speech is arguably one where the majority of your preparation time will be specifically allocated towards the words you choose. This isn't to say you shouldn't have used good language in your informative and persuasive speeches, but that the emphasis shifts slightly in a special occasion speech.

For example, for your informative and persuasive speeches you were required to conduct research and cite your sources in a bibliography or references/works cited page, which took you some time to look up and format. In most cases, that will not be necessary in a special occasion speech, although there may be reasons to consult sources or other persons for information in crafting your speech. So for special occasion speeches, there is a trade-off. The time you *don't* spend doing research is now going to be reallocated towards crafting emotional and evocative phrases that convey the sentiment your speech is meant to impart.

The important thing to remember about using language effectively is that we are not talking about using big words just to sound smart. Do not touch a thesaurus! Good language isn't about trying to impress us with fancy words. It's about taking the words you are already comfortable and familiar with and putting them in the best possible order. Consider the following example from the then-president of the Ohio State University, Gordon Gee, giving a commencement address at Florida State University in 1997:

> As you look back on your years at Florida State I hope you remember many good

things that have happened. These experiences are, for the most part, events of the mind. The memories, ladies and gentlemen, however, are treasures of the heart.

Notice three things about his use of language: first, he doesn't try to use any fancy words, which he certainly could if he wanted to. Every word in this portion of his speech is one that all of us knew by the time we left elementary school, so again, don't mistake good language for big words. Using a five-syllable word when a two-syllable word will work just as well often means a speaker is trying too hard to sound smart. And given that the use of those big words often comes off sounding awkward or inappropriate, you're better off just sticking with what you know.

Second, notice how he uses those basic words to evoke emotion and wonderment. Putting the words you know into the best possible order, when done well, will make your speech sound extremely eloquent and emotional. Third, he uses parallelism in this brief snippet. The use of "events of the mind" and "treasures of the heart" to compare what is truly important about the college experience is powerful. Indeed, Gee's commencement address is full of various rhetorical devices, with the twelve-minute speech also containing alliteration, assonance, and antithesis.

18.4 SPECIAL OCCASION DELIVERY

Just as the language for special occasion speaking is slightly different, so too are the ways in which you will want to deliver your speech. First and foremost, since you will be spending so much time crafting the perfect language to use and putting your words in the right order, it is imperative that you say exactly what you have written; otherwise, what was the point? To that end, your delivery for a special occasion speech will skew slightly more in favor of manuscript speaking. While it is still vital to establish eye contact with your audience and to not sound like you are reading, it is also important to get the words exactly right.

You will need to practice your special occasion speech as much as or even more than you did for your informative or persuasive speeches. You need to know what you are going to say and feel comfortable knowing what is coming next. This is not to say you should have your speech memorized, but you need to be able to take your eyes off the page in order to establish and maintain a rapport with your audience, a vital element in special occasion speaking because of the emotional component at the core of these speeches. Knowing your speech will also allow you to counteract the flow of adrenaline into your system, something particularly important given that special occasion speeches tend to be very emotional, not just for the audience, but for you as well.

Basically, knowing your speech well allows you to incorporate the emotion that a special occasion speech is meant to convey, something that is hard to do when you read the entirety of your speech. In this way your audience will sense the pride you feel for a graduating class during a commencement speech, the sorrow you feel for the deceased during a eulogy, or the gratitude you have when accepting an award.

Conclusion

Special occasion speaking is the most varied type of speaking to cover; however, there are some general rules to keep in mind regardless of what type you are engaged in. Remember that using good, evocative language is key, and that it is important that you deliver your speech in a way that both conveys the proper emotion for the occasion as well as allows you to give the speech exactly as you wrote it.

18.6 ENRICHMENT

Discussion Questions

1. Which special occasion speech do you think will be one you will most likely give in the next 10-15 years? Why?
2. How would you give a speech if you were giving an award versus receiving an award?
3. Why should a special occasion speech be kept short?
4. Imagine that you have been instructed to deliver a speech of introduction for a controversial figure (such as Lance Armstrong, Eminem, Bill Maher, or Ann Coulter). How might you introduce someone whom the audience may view unfavorably? How would you introduce someone whom you either do not like or do not respect?

Activities

1. With a classmate write a speech of acceptance for a real or hypothetical award for each other. Present the speech to the class.
2. In a group, think of a guest speaker you would like to see visit the university, and write a two-minute speech of introduction for them.
3. Watch this video of a touching toast given by John Travolta to Oprah Winfrey on her birthday. As you're watching, keep the following advice from Section 18.2: Types of Special Occasion Speeches in mind. Keep toasts brief and focus the attention on the person being toasted, not the speaker.

    - What do you think about the length of Travolta's toast? Too fast? Too slow? Why?
    - How did Travolta make sure to keep the focus on Oprah?
    - How do you think Travolta did with his delivery of this toast? What are some suggestions for improvements?

4. In class, students write a toast they could give while out to eat with friends to celebrate their friendships and college experiences. Ask for a volunteer to share with the class.

www.ingramcontent.com/pod-product-compliance
Lightning Source LLC
Chambersburg PA
CBHW031842220426
43663CB00006B/464